Wal-Mart

Wal-Mart

The Face of Twenty-First-Century Capitalism

Edited by Nelson Lichtenstein

THE NEW PRESS

NEW YORK
LONDON

Requests for permission to reproduce selections from this book should be mailed to:
Permissions Department, The New Press, 38 Greene Street, New York, NY 10013.

Published in the United States by The New Press, New York, 2006
Distributed by W. W. Norton & Company, Inc., New York

LIBRARY OF CONGRESS CATALOGING-IN-PUBLICATION DATA
   Wal-Mart: The face of twenty-first-century capitalism / edited by Nelson Lichtenstein.
     p. cm.
   Includes bibliographical references and index.
   ISBN 1-59558-035-2 (hc.)—ISBN 1-59558-021-2 (pbk.)
1. Wal-Mart (Firm)—Management. 2. Discount houses (Retail trade)—United States—Management.
3. Wages—United States. 4. Labor unions—United States. 5. Employee fringe benefits—United
States. I. Lichtenstein, Nelson.

   HF5429.215.U6W35 2005
   381'.14906573—dc22   2005049147

The New Press was established in 1990 as a not-for-profit alternative to the large, commercial
publishing houses currently dominating the book publishing industry. The New Press operates in the
public interest rather than for private gain, and is committed to publishing, in innovative ways, works of
educational, cultural, and community value that are often deemed insufficiently profitable.

www.thenewpress.com

COMPOSITION BY DIX!
THIS BOOK WAS SET IN FAIRFIELD LH LIGHT

Printed in Canada

10   9   8   7   6   5   4   3   2   1

Contents

A Global Corporation

Working at Wal-Mart

Acknowledgments

Dick Hebdige, Director of the Interdisciplinary Humanities Center at the University of California, Santa Barbara, deserves the greatest thanks because he was the first to ask me, "Hey Nelson, why don't we have a conference about Wal-Mart?" So we did, with much moral and financial support from his Humanities Center, where Theo Alexopoulous, Carly Andrews, and Tom Bennett pitched in to make the conference a success. Along the way, Richard Appelbaum, Eileen Boris, Richard Flacks, Dana Frank, Meg Jacobs, Jennifer Klein, Julio Moreno, Erica Rappaport, Amy Stanley, and most of the contributors to this collection offered good advice and much encouragement.

Our April 2004 conference, "Wal-Mart: Template for Twenty-First-Century Capitalism?" was supported by the Center for Work, Labor, and Democracy at the University of California, Santa Barbara; by the Hull Center for Research on Women and Social Justice; by the UC Institute on Global Conflict and Cooperation; by UC MEXUS, the UCSB College of Letters and Science, and the Divisions of Humanities and Fine Arts, and Social Sciences. After it was over dozens of journalists rang me up, and they deserve a word of thanks as well because their questions, whether pointed or superficial, convinced me that the historical and sociological research we were undertaking was an important way that we could fulfill our responsibility as citizens.

As the conference papers were turned into book chapters, Marc Favreau at the New Press proved himself a supportive and creative editor. Sarah Fan and Melissa Richards were most professional. Copy editor Adam Goldberger was wonderfully thorough, and in Santa Barbara undergraduate assistant Taylor Ernst helped put together many of the pictures, graphs, and tables in the collection. And finally, Eileen Boris has once again proven herself my most thoughtful critic, the staunchest supporter, and the loving presence that makes life, academic and otherwise, all so much richer.

Preface

Nelson Lichtenstein

This book had its origins in a strike. On October 11, 2003, fifty-nine thousand grocery workers struck, or were locked out of, more than 850 Southern California supermarkets. They were fighting to maintain the wages and health care insurance that the United Food and Commercial Workers had negotiated with their employers over nearly half a century of relatively peaceful labor-management relations. But this strike was different. It was bitter, it was long, and it ended in a decisive defeat for the union when workers finally filtered back to their cash registers, produce stands, and deli counters in February and March 2004. Safeway, Albertsons, and other national chains forced the union to accept a new contract that slashed starting wages, capped health insurance payouts, and reduced overall labor costs.

The strike was convulsive because the most important player was not at the negotiating table. Supermarket executives, in Southern California and elsewhere, were taking a hard line against their employees because Wal-Mart was ready, willing, and anxious to eat their lunch. By 2003 Wal-Mart was the largest company in the world, and it was moving rapidly into the grocery business by building hundreds of "supercenters," mammoth big box stores of two hundred thousand square feet that combined under one roof a full-sized grocery supermarket with a sprawling general merchandise outlet. And Wal-Mart was notorious for the low wages it paid its million-plus nonunion workers. When the strike began, Wal-Mart had but 1 percent of the retail market in California, but the

Bentonville, Arkansas, retailer made clear that it intended to build at least forty super-centers in the Golden State during the next few years, perhaps two or three hundred in a decade.[1]

With the strike on, and no end in sight, reporters from across the country started to look at the story from a different angle. They sought out historians, like myself, familiar with the relationships between labor, business, and politics during the last century. What's at stake in this endless strike? they asked. Why is everyone so afraid of Wal-Mart? And what makes that company such a fierce competitor? How did this Arkansas-based retailer become such a giant presence, with more than 3,500 stores in the United States and a workforce that was now the largest of any nongovernmental institution in North America?

Well, I'm an academic, and when confronted with a puzzle, academics do what comes naturally: hold a conference, which we did in April 2004. There is no such field as "Wal-Mart Studies," at the University of California or elsewhere, but the gravitational force exerted by this global phenomenon has made itself felt throughout numerous academic disciplines. It was therefore not difficult to identify key scholars who were delighted to share their expertise. Indeed, they leaped at the chance to compare notes and perspectives, both on Wal-Mart and on the global manufacturing-transport-distribution chain in which that corporation is the largest and most significant link.

The theme of this book, and of the conference from which it arose, is "Wal-Mart: Template for Twenty-First-Century Century Capitalism?" There's a question mark after the last word because we are still exploring the degree to which the company will in fact establish the frame for an entirely new era in the history of world capitalism. That is a rather large issue, which is why we think the study of this corporation—or of any large business enterprise—is too important to be left to Wall Street, to the business schools, or to the economists alone. By "template," we mean not just the internal organization of a business, or the character of the market it taps or creates, but the entire range of economic, social, cultural, and political transmutations generated by a particularly successful form of business enterprise.

Great corporations are the "representative social actuality," wrote Peter Drucker, the founder of modern management science, in *The Concept of the Corporation,* a pioneering study that illuminated the world engendered by General Motors in its mid-twentieth-century heyday. The "emergence of big business is the most important event in the recent social history of the Western world," declared Drucker.[2] He wrote that in 1946, but his understanding is just as true today, if on a scale that includes not only the West, but the East and global South as well. Thus it was entirely appropriate that the Interdisciplinary Humanities Center at the University of California, Santa Barbara, served as the official sponsor for the conference, along with the Center for Work, Labor and Democracy at that university.

No one from Wal-Mart accepted our invitation, but executives did take note of the scholarly effort to link their company to a new and problematic stage of American capitalism. And they were not long in responding. When Wal-Mart CEO H. Lee Scott delivered a defense of his company before a Los Angeles town hall meeting early in 2005, he entitled it "Wal-Mart and California: A Key Moment in Time for American Capitalism." Business executives do not normally cast the fate of their company in such sweeping terms, but Scott seemed anxious to take up some of the issues we had posed at our conference, which had been publicized in the national press and in a couple of television documentaries.[3] "Let me be direct," he told an audience of influential Californians. "I believe we meet at an auspicious moment, when large questions about the future of American capitalism are being confused in the public mind." Scott then went on to defend the wages and working conditions of those who worked at his company, and the multibillion-dollar rise in the purchasing power enjoyed by tens of millions of Wal-Mart shoppers. But he also took pains to refute the notion, discussed at the conference and in this collection, that low-wage Wal-Mart had replaced a high-wage, high-benefit General Motors as the template corporation setting the work, wage, and benefit standards for so many American workers and the enterprises for which they labored.[4]

This collection continues that dialogue, with contributions from social and cultural historians, sociologists, economists, anthropologists, students of American management, and union advocates participating in the conversation. In my introductory essay, I frame some of the questions posed by the emergence of discount retailers, who have become the template businesses of our era. Led by Wal-Mart, they are legislating de facto wage and benefit standards, reshaping and subordinating the once-powerful manufacturing sector, and generating the most profound transformation in the spacial and demographic landscape since the emergence of suburbia in the immediate post–World War II years. In the second contribution to the volume Susan Strasser, a noted historian of consumer culture, explains that many of the phenomena we identify with Wal-Mart, including high turnover for low-paid female clerks, the squeeze on suppliers, sophisticated technology, and the eager search for public subsidies, were pioneered by the great retailers of the past. Woolworth, Sears, and A & P helped construct the nation's consumer culture. Wal-Mart is but the latest enterprise to figure out the best way to make a profit on it.

But Wal-Mart is more than just an enlarged version of those early twentieth-century retailers. Social historian Bethany Moreton explores the southern, neopopulist roots of Wal-Mart's distinctively cohesive managerial culture. Sam Walton founded his company in northwest Arkansas when it was almost entirely white, rural, nonunion, and desperately poor. But the managerial ethos that proved so effective in that "backward" region has proven adaptable, profitable, and competitive in the far more densely populated and ethnically cosmopolitan America of the early twenty-first century. Likewise, the management historian James Hoopes demonstrates that Wal-Mart is successfully breaking another set of business expectations. Although many business icons like Lucent Technology, General Electric, and Verizon have deployed new telecommunications and data-control technology to outsource and downsize themselves, Wal-Mart has moved in just the opposite direction. Wal-Mart does more insourcing than outsourcing because it uses a variety of technological and organizational innovations to make it a far more efficient and more centralized firm than its competitors. From Bentonville outward, the visible hand of management has replaced the invisible hand of the market. This is nowhere clearer than in the realm of labor management and employment cost control. As the labor historian Thomas Adams makes clear, the post–World War II emergence of discount retailing could flourish only if management slashed labor costs and instituted the kind of tightly controlled labor-relations regime that was once exemplified by the auto assembly line or the garment-industry sweatshop. Wal-Mart did not invent this "new shop floor" in the 1960s and 1970s, but it did perfect and enlarge it more than any other retailer.

Wal-Mart is a global corporation, but it is more than a company that buys and sells products in several nations. Wal-Mart's relentless search for new markets, more customers, and cheaper goods has begun to establish the template for a new structure in which manufacturers, transport companies, and the retailers themselves must now function. The Wal-Mart supply chain, increasingly focused on the movement of vast quantities of merchandise from East Asia to North America, has become the axis around which the economies of more than a score of countries revolve. Sociologists Misha Petrovic and Gary Hamilton explain how Wal-Mart has constructed a market in which the retailer, not the manufacturer, holds the pricing and contracting power; finds, retrains, and disciplines commercial partners; and establishes the framework by which products are moved through the global trading system. In their contribution, sociologists Edna Bonacich and Khaleelah Hardie illuminate the fascinating complexity and strategic importance of that portion of the Wal-Mart supply chain which moves thousands of giant container ships through the port of Los Angeles, the nodal center of global commerce today. Containerization, which began in the 1960s, has played a critical role in making transnational production chains possible, because the intermodal transport of all those forty-foot-long containers—from ships to port to rail and truck—has been essential to Wal-Mart's cheap and timely import strategy.

Although Wal-Mart is the dominant retailer in the United States and Canada, and the second largest in the United Kingdom, it is not merely an Anglo phenomenon. During the 1990s, as economist Chris Tilly reminds us, Wal-Mart became the largest retailer in Mexico. Wal-Mart prospered there in part because of the free trade pact with the United States and the rise of a middle class. But the increasingly radical stratification of the Mexican economy, and the polarization of the consumer market, may well put a ceiling on Wal-Mart's growth in Mexico despite the company's efficient supply links to the United States. Not all of Latin America has proven as conductive to Wal-Mart's expansion as Mexico. In Brazil, Carrefour arrived first, and in Argentina a currency crisis, a radical drop in the standard of living, and a failure to find adequate suppliers have thwarted Wal-Mart growth.[5]

Wal-Mart's employment practices and its aggressive expansion plans have become extraordinarily controversial within the United States. In her study of retail sales "production" sociologist Ellen Rosen demonstrates that each store manager has an extremely tight labor budget that forces him (and sometimes her) to speed up the work, avoid overtime pay, and constantly struggle to "put out fires." Despite repeated assertions from Wal-Mart's top executives that the company obeys all labor and safety laws, store managers find it very difficult to meet cost-containment goals or increase sales without illegally exploiting themselves and the two hundred–plus "associates" who are employed in each Wal-Mart store. Gender discrimination is rife in such an authoritarian management hierarchy, a contention that attorney Brad Seligman is moving through the courts in the largest sex-discrimination case in U.S. history. His findings in *Dukes v. Wal-Mart* confirm that the pattern of patriarchal management described by Bethany Moreton has been institutionalized at Wal-Mart to a far greater degree than at competitors like Kmart, Home Depot, and Target.

Wal-Mart's impact on the urban environment is just as controversial as its employment practices, which is why anthropologist David Karjanen frames the company's effort to site stores in urban America in the widest possible terms. During the era of nineteenth-century commercial urbanism and twentieth-century industrial development, the growth of corporations coincided with the rise of those cities and towns that were their manufacturing host or sales outlet. But with the rise of globalized markets, capital liquidity, and exurban production, many firms, above all Wal-Mart, have become detached from specific communities and specific labor pools. Indeed, Wal-Mart is the quintessential example of the spatial dislocation of production from consumption. In a close study of Wal-Mart's entry into exurban San Diego, Karjanen demonstrates that the opening of a new generation of supercenter stores has had little net impact on overall employment, but these new stores have had a highly negative impact on traffic, municipal finances, small business competition, and freeway sprawl. Wal-Mart is therefore one of the great engines driving the growth of American inequality: economic, social, and spatial.

In the concluding essay, unionist Wade Rathke considers the question "What is to be done?" He argues that Wal-Mart is too powerful, labor laws are too weak, and U.S. trade unions are too small to actually "organize" the company at any point in the foreseeable future. But this does not mean that those who seek reform at Wal-Mart are without leverage. Drawing upon a wealth of recent experiments and experiences, Rathke advocates the formation of a "Wal-Mart Workers Association" that does not seek to bargain formally with the company but instead provides a voice and a vision for current and former Wal-Mart workers. In alliance not only with the unions, but also with local government officials, environmental and land-use activists, and living-wage advocates, such an association might well provide the long-term pressure necessary to gradually modify the Wal-Mart business model so that this template enterprise eventually generates a far better level of wages, jobs, health benefits, and supply-chain relationships.

For the writers in this book, as well as for millions of others, Wal-Mart has become an object of fascination, admiration, denunciation, and wonder. Like the railroads and steel mills of the nineteenth century and the great automotive factories of the twentieth, it has become the enterprise that embodies so much of what we fear about a system of production and distribution that has an utterly pervasive impact, but whose control lies so far beyond our grasp. But knowledge is power, so if we understand the nature of this retail phenomenon, perhaps we can learn to master it.

History, Culture, Capitalism

ONE

Wal-Mart: A Template for Twenty-First-Century Capitalism

Nelson Lichtenstein

Wal-Mart, the largest corporation in the world, provides the template for a global economic order that mirrors the right-wing politics and imperial ambitions of those who now command so many strategic posts in American government and society. Like the conservatism at the heart of the Reagan-Bush ascendancy, Wal-Mart emerged out of a rural South that barely tolerated New Deal social regulation, the civil rights revolution, or the feminist impulse. In their place the corporation has projected an ideology of family, faith, and small-town sentimentality that coexists in strange harmony with a world of transnational commerce, stagnant living standards, and a stressful work life.[1]

Founded less than fifty years ago by Sam Walton and his brother Bud, this Bentonville, Arkansas, company is today the largest profit-making enterprise in the world. With sales over $300 billion a year, Wal-Mart has revenues larger than those of Switzerland. It operates more than five thousand huge stores worldwide, 80 percent in the United States. In selling general merchandise, Wal-Mart has no true rival, and in 2003 *Fortune* magazine ranked Wal-Mart as the nation's most admired company.[2] It does more business than Target, Home Depot, Sears, Kmart, Safeway, and Kroger combined. It employs more than 1.5 million workers around the globe, making Wal-Mart the largest private employer in Mexico, Canada, and the United States. It imports more goods from China than either the United Kingdom or Russia. Its sales will probably top $1 trillion per year within a decade.[3] Sam Walton was crowned the richest man in

America in 1985; today his heirs, who own 39 percent of the company, are twice as wealthy as the family of Bill Gates.[4]

The competitive success and political influence of this giant corporation enable Wal-Mart to rezone our cities, determine the real minimum wage, break trade unions, set the boundaries for popular culture, channel capital throughout the world, and conduct a kind of international diplomacy with a dozen nations. In an era of waning governmental regulation, Wal-Mart management may well have more power than any other entity to legislate key components of American social and industrial policy. The Arkansas-based giant is well aware of this leverage, which is why it is spending millions of dollars on TV advertisements that tout, not its "always low prices," but the community revitalization, happy workers, and philanthropic good works it believes come when it opens another store.[5]

Wal-Mart is thus the template business setting the standards for a new stage in the history of world capitalism. In each epoch a huge, successful, rapidly emulated enterprise embodies a new and innovative set of technological advances, organizational structures, and social relationships. It becomes the template economic institution of its age. At the end of the nineteenth century the Pennsylvania Railroad declared itself "the standard of the world." U.S. Steel defined the meaning of corporate power and efficiency for decades after J. P. Morgan created the first billion-dollar company in 1901. In the mid-twentieth century General Motors symbolized bureaucratic management, mass production, and the social, political enfranchisement of a unionized, blue-collar workforce. When Peter Drucker wrote the pioneering management study *The Concept of the Corporation* in 1946 it was the General Motors organization, from the Flint assembly lines to the executive offices in Detroit and New York, that exemplified corporate modernity in all its variegated aspects. And in more recent years, first IBM and then Microsoft have seemed the template for an information economy that has transformed the diffusion and production of knowledge around the globe.

Wal-Mart is now the template business for world capitalism because it takes the most potent technological and logistic innovations of the twenty-first century and puts them at the service of an organization whose competitive success depends upon the destruction of all that remains of New Deal–style social regulation and replaces it, in the U.S. and abroad, with a global system that relentlessly squeezes labor costs from South Carolina to south China, from Indianapolis to Indonesia. For the first time in the history of modern capitalism the Wal-Mart template has made the retailer king and the manu-facturer his vassal. So the company has transformed thousands of its supplier firms into quaking supplicants who scramble to cut their costs and squeeze the last drop of sweated productivity from millions of workers and thousands of subcontractors.

The Wal-Mart Phenomenon

Snapshots from the lives of four women help us understand the impact of the Wal-Mart phenomenon upon the lives of tens of millions of ordinary people.

Chastity Ferguson kept watch over a sleepy three-year-old late one Friday as she flipped a pack of corn dogs into a cart at her new favorite grocery store: Wal-Mart. At this Las Vegas supercenter, pink stucco on the outside, a wide-isled, well-lighted empo-rium within, a full-scale supermarket is combined with a discount megastore to offer

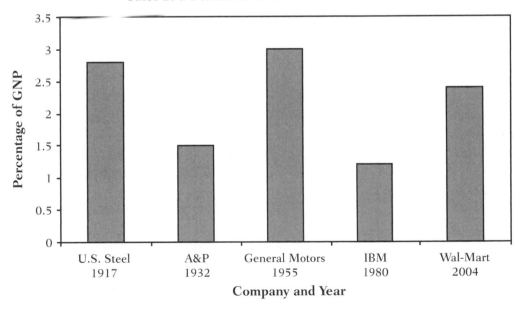

Template Corporations
Sales as a Portion of U.S. Gross National Product

Source: Jerry Useem, "One Nation Under Wal-Mart," *Fortune*, March 3, 2003.

shoppers everything they might need in their daily life. For Ferguson, a harried twenty-six-year-old mother, the draw is obvious. "You can't beat the prices," said the hotel cashier, who makes $400 a week. "I come here because it's cheap."

Across town, another mother also is familiar with the supercenter's low prices. Kelly Gray, the chief breadwinner for five children, lost her job as a Raley's grocery clerk late in 2002 after Wal-Mart expanded into the supermarket business in Las Vegas. California-based Raley's closed all eighteen of its southern Nevada stores, laying off 1,400 workers. Gray earned $14.98 an hour with a pension and family health insurance. Wal-Mart grocery workers typically make less than $10 an hour, with inferior benefits. "It's like somebody came and broke into your home and took something huge and important away from you," said the thirty-six-year-old. "I was scared. I cried. I shook."[6]

Halfway around the world, twenty-year-old Li Xiao Hong labors in a Guangzhou factory that turns out millions of the Mattel toys that Wal-Mart sells across America. She is part of an army of 40 million newly proletarianzed peasants who are turning south China into the workshop of the world. The plant's work areas are so poorly lighted that they seem permanently shrouded in gray. A smell of solvent wafts across the facility as rows of workers hunch over pedal-operated sewing machines and gluepots.

Li is the fastest worker on a long, U-shaped assembly line of about 130 women. They put together animated Disney-themed dolls that can be activated by the nudge of a small child. Li's hands move with lightning speed, gluing the pink bottom, screwing it into place, getting the rest of the casing to adhere, tamping it down with a special hammer, pulling the battery cover through its slats, soldering where she glued, then sending it down the line. The entire process takes twenty-one seconds.

Li generally works five and one-half days a week, up to ten hours at a time. Her monthly wage—about $65—is typical for this part of China, enough for Li to send money back home to her rural family. But Li pays a heavy price. Her hands ache terribly, and she is always exhausted, but she seems resigned more than angry. "People at my age should expect some hardship. I should taste some hardship while I'm young."[7]

And finally there is Crystal, the wife of a Wal-Mart assistant store manager, who brings home about $40,000 a year after a decade of hard, devoted work. Crystal took umbrage at the invective posted on one of the many anti–Wal-Mart Web sites that current and former employees have created in recent years. So she fired back.

"Wal-Mart has been very good to us. The people at the store work not only as a team but as a family unit. When families in our community have trouble Wal-Mart is there to help. Wal-Mart helps with tuition for college, they give out scholarships. Every company has its faults, no job site or company is perfect. You are only upset because Wal-Mart is Pro-Associate and Anti-Union. And I pray to GOD as a Christian woman that it stays the way it is. Wal-Mart is a good place to work, they do care about their Associates. I think that Sam Walton would be proud of the store that my husband works at."[8]

The experience of these four women provides a set of markers for understanding this giant firm. Hundreds of millions of shoppers agree with Chastity Ferguson: Wal-Mart prices are low, cheap enough to enable hard-pressed working-class families to stretch their dollars and survive until the next paycheck. But the experience of Kelly Gray has also made Wal-Mart a touchstone for political and economic controversy. The famed economist Joseph Schumpeter might well have been thinking of a dynamically successful firm like Wal-Mart when he coined the phrase "creative destruction," the process by which one mode of capitalist production and distribution replaces another. As Schumpeter made clear early in the last century, such transformations are not inevitable, nor do they come without an immense social cost, which is why Wal-Mart's growth has generated one high-profile conflict after another.[9]

In California, where Wal-Mart's actual footprint has been modest, the expectation that this corporation will build scores of supercenters, staffed by low-wage workers, helped ignite a four-month strike by unionists in the old-line supermarkets, who wanted to preserve their wage and benefit standards. Their strike ended in a bitter defeat in February 2004, but barely a month later Inglewood residents created a stir when that majority black and Latino city voted down a Wal-Mart–sponsored referendum designed to pave the way for construction of one of the first supercenters in Southern California. Energized by this anti–Wal-Mart show of strength, the Los Angeles city council enacted an ordinance requiring big-box stores like Wal-Mart to fund an "economic impact" analysis to determine their effect on community wages, existing businesses, and traffic patterns.[10] But Wal-Mart struck back in the November 2004 elections, helping fund a referendum that overturned a recently enacted California law requiring large, labor-intensive firms to pay substantially more of the health insurance costs of their employees.[11] And while all this was going on, a San Francisco judge gave the Berkeley-based Impact Fund permission to seek higher pay and back pay for more than a million women workers at Wal-Mart, in the largest class-action employment-discrimination suit ever certified by a federal court.

Li Xiao Hong does not work directly for Wal-Mart, but the conditions of her life are inexorably bound to the capitalist template the corporation is now putting in place around the globe. She is a participant in the most sweeping process of proletarian industrialization since the dawn of the factory revolution nearly two centuries ago. Li is a cousin to the mill girls of Lowell, the immigrant needle workers of the Lower East Side, and the Mexican women who poured into the border region maquiladoras just one generation ago. Now she stands on the lowest rung of a supply chain that feeds the enormous buying power assembled by the big-box stores that are becoming dominant throughout the global North. Although Wal-Mart deploys the most sophisticated telecommunications system to efficiently channel her labor power, Li's sweated work life, and that of her tens of millions of workmates, demonstrates that we still live in an industrial world. More people labor on an assembly line today, making actual things, than at any other time in human history. Still more sell, talk, or manipulate a keyboard under assembly-line conditions. The postindustrial age, heralded by so many pundits and academics, has not yet arrived.[12]

And finally there is Crystal, a product of the Wal-Mart "family" itself. Her husband, who worked his way up from maintenance, has the toughest job in the company. He is in the hot seat because he has to accommodate the insistent demands that flow down from the store and district manager, while at the same time keeping the shelves stocked, the cash registers staffed, and the store profits growing. Bentonville's computers assign Crystal's husband a labor budget that is as tight as a drum and a sales target that moves upward with inexorable momentum. He is in a constant squeeze, and when workers quit—Wal-Mart's annual turnover is above 40 percent a year, not far below that of McDonald's—Crystal's spouse has to fill in the gaps, which accounts for a managerial workweek of sixty hours and more. But none of this seems to have diminished the loyalty of people like Crystal and her spouse to Wal-Mart as an institution and an idea. Promotion from within, frequent contact with upper management, a measure of paternalism, and a loosely cloaked Christian identity have helped generate a remarkably cohesive corporate culture in which a substantial proportion of those who pursue careers at Wal-Mart participate. "Ordinary people doing extraordinary things": there is a measure of truth in this Wal-Mart slogan.

Why Is Wal-Mart So Big?

What makes for giantism in big business? Why was General Motors so big during the middle decades of the twentieth century and why is Wal-Mart so huge today? In his contribution to this collection, historian James Hoopes recalls the work of the Nobel Prize–winning economist Ronald Coase, who described the corporation as an "island of conscious power" in an "ocean of unconscious cooperation, like lumps of butter coagulating in a pail of buttermilk." Every firm has an optimal size beyond which the risk of loss from mismanagement more than offsets the chance of gain from the economies of scale it can realize. In the first half of the twentieth century GM became a vertically integrated conglomerate because Teletype, telephones, and good roads enabled the corporation to deploy its famous system of centralized control and decentralized operations across dozens of states and scores of factories. But such highly integrated production and distribution within a single firm may not always be the most cost-efficient way to make the most money. If new inventions and sociopolitical mores make

Source: Wal-Mart annual reports.

it cheaper and faster to purchase rather than make the same goods and services, then executives will begin to dismantle the huge enterprise. According to the most savvy, technologically hip business writers, the contemporary corporation is doomed to fragment within a world of cheap, rapid communications and increasingly efficient markets. The "virtual" corporation of the twenty-first century should consist of a few thousand highly skilled managers and professionals who contract out nonessential services to cheaper specialist firms.

Thus we have the outsourcing of both call-center work and janitorial services to an ever shifting coterie of independent firms, while "branded" companies like Nike and Dell farm out virtually all the manufacturing work that goes into their core products. This has been the path followed by General Motors, which has spun off Delco, once a vertically integrated parts division. Except for final assembly and the manufacture of key components, GM and the other big car companies seek to outsource as much work as possible, even sharing space with suppliers under the same roof and on the same shop floor. So the GM payroll, white collar and blue, is about half the size it was in 1970. Giving all this a metahistorical punch, *Forbes* columnist Peter Huber declared that it was "market forces and the information age" that had beaten the Soviets and would soon force the dissolution of America's largest corporations. "If you have grown accustomed to a sheltered life inside a really large corporation," he advised, take care. "The next Kremlin to fall may be your own."[13]

But Wal-Mart has found giantism efficient and highly profitable. This is because the price of goods and services it purchases on the open market has not fallen as rapidly as has the cost of "managing," within a single organization, the production or deployment of those same economic inputs. For Wal-Mart it is still cheaper to build than to buy, and to employ workers rather than subcontract them. As Linda Dillman, the chief information officer at Wal-Mart, put it in 2004: "We'd be nuts to outsource." And the reason for her disdain? "We can implement things faster than any third party," Dillman says. "We run the entire world out of the facilities in this area [Bentonville] at a cost that no one can touch."[14] Thus the same technologies and cost imperatives that have led to the decomposition and decentralization of so many other institutions, including government, health care, entertainment, and domestic manufacturing, have enabled Wal-Mart and other retail distribution companies to vastly enhance their own managerial "span of control."

By 1988 Wal-Mart had the largest privately owned satellite communications network in the country, a system with six channels that not only let Sam Walton give pep talks to hundreds of thousands of employees, but on which a buyer could demonstrate for department heads in every store the precise way to display new products. As Walton biographer Bob Ortega summarized these pioneering innovations, "Wal-Mart was building a system that would give its executives a complete picture, at any point in time, of where goods were and how fast they were moving, all the way from the factory to the checkout counter." And they knew precisely the labor costs involved, from the truck driver, to the warehouse, to the wages, hours, break time, and benefits of each sales clerk in each store. Indeed, when it became clear that Wal-Mart store managers were routinely failing to give checkout clerks their breaks, a violation of the wage and hour law, Wal-Mart announced that the computers in Bentonville would henceforth shut off the cash registers at the prescribed interval, overriding, if necessary, the local manager's wishes. Here was the kind of centralized control never quite achieved in even the most authoritarian manufacturing enterprises. Ortega reported that at individual Wal-Mart stores, thermostats were manipulated from Bentonville.[15]

Wal-Mart's Asian Empire

One of the most important innovations enhancing Wal-Mart's span of control has been a worldwide "logistics revolution." Its icon is the intermodal container, a forty-foot-long metal box that has become pervasive at every port, warehouse, and rail yard. There are more than a million of them sailing to and fro on a never ending maritime highway that stretches from Hong Kong and Singapore to Long Beach and Los Angeles, now the largest ports in the United States. This bridge of giant container ships is filled with products destined for the big-box stores of the United States. Of the top twenty importers, eight are retailers. Wal-Mart, Home Depot, and Target alone account for 45 percent of the merchandise imported by these big companies. Wal-Mart's insatiable sales engine pulls more than 230,000 containers across the Pacific each year. That is the equivalent of about one hundred mammoth containerships, hauling about 20 percent of everything trans-shipped through Southern California ports.

As Edna Bonacich points out in her contribution to this volume, these containers are "pulled" across the Pacific, not "pushed." In a push system, characteristic of consumer manufacturing in the last century, long production runs generate efficiencies of scale, which lead to inventory surpluses. These are pushed out to retailers, which is why so many car dealers were in a chronic war with Detroit, or why garment makers have often dumped cut-rate product on the retailer. But under the pull system, the retailer tracks consumer behavior with meticulous care and then transmits consumer preferences down the supply chain. Replenishment is put in motion almost immediately, with the suppler required to make more frequent deliveries of smaller lots. This is just-in-time for retailers, or "lean retailing." To make it all work, the supply firms and the discount retailers have to be functionally linked, even if they retain a separate legal and administrative existence. Wal-Mart is therefore not simply a huge retailer, but increasingly a manufacturing giant in all but name.

Wal-Mart has installed its Asian proconsul in Shenzhen, the epicenter of Chinese export manufacturing. There a staff of four hundred coordinates the purchase of some $20 billion worth of South Asian products. Because the company itself has an intimate understanding of the manufacturing process and because its purchasing power is so immense, Wal-Mart has transformed its three thousand Chinese suppliers into powerless price takers, rather than partners, deal makers, or oligopolistic price administrators. While many of these suppliers are small and undercapitalized, a growing number of East Asian contractors manage factories that are of stupendous size. For example, Tue Yen Industrial, a Hong Kong–listed shoe manufacturer, employs more than 150,000 workers worldwide, most in low-cost factories throughout southern China. A factory complex in Dongguan employs more than 40,000 workers, and its Huyen Binh Chanh megafactory in Vietnam will soon be the largest workplace on the planet, employing 65,000.[16] To remember the last time so many workers were assembled in a similarly gigantic manufacturing complex you have to reach back to the armament factories of World War II—to the River Rouge, Willow Run, Boeing-Seattle, and Douglas–El Segundo in the United States, to Gorki and Magnitogorsk in the Soviet Union, and to Dagenham outside London—to find such proletarian concentrations.

The Wal-Mart supply chain is just as tightly monitored within the United States as without. Here, those manufacturers that manage to survive do so only by bending the knee to their retail overlord.[17] Take Procter and Gamble, for example. The venerable Ohio home product manufacturer long used its market power and sophisticated research on consumer buying habits to secure an outsized share of shelf space from traditional retailers. Although many drug and grocery chains considered P&G a self-aggrandizing bully, Wal-Mart turned this power relationship on its head. The retailer's superior point-of-sale data-collection system enabled Wal-Mart to more accurately and profitably source its home care products. Wal-Mart came to know more about the consumers of P&G products than did the manufacturer, so in the late 1980s P&G moved an entire sales office to northwest Arkansas. P&G received continuous data via satellite on sales, inventory, and prices, enabling it to replenish goods rapidly, accurately, and often directly from the factory to individual stores. By the mid 1990s, Wal-Mart was P&G's largest customer, generating more than $3 billion in revenues, or about 20 percent of P&G's total sales. But executives at the Cincinnati soap maker were well aware that their good fortune turned on Wal-Mart's sufferance, which explains why they bought Gillette in 2005. The $57 billion deal was designed to transform P&G into an even larger supply firm that could challenge Wal-Mart's pricing power and its private label brands. But even this megamerger may not be enough. "If you want to service Wal-Mart you have got to be more efficient," asserted the retail consultant Howard Davidowitz. "The power will stay with Wal-Mart."[18]

Wal-Mart vs. New Deal America

Wal-Mart's mastery of information technology and the logistics revolution explains but a slice of the company's success. Equally important, Wal-Mart has been the beneficiary and a driving force behind the transformation in the politics and culture of a business system that has arisen in a southernized, deunionized post–New Deal America. The controversies sparked by Wal-Mart's entry into metropolitan markets—Chicago, Los Angeles, the Bay Area—embody the larger conflict between what remains of New Deal America and the aggressive, successful effort waged by Sunbelt politicians and entrepreneurs to eviscerate it.

Discount retailing depends on continual, near-obsessive attention to wages and labor costs. Discounters must have two or three times the turnover of traditional department stores, like Sears and Macy's, in order to make the same profit. Stock movement of this velocity depends on a low markup, which in turn demands that labor costs remain below 15 percent of total sales, about half that of traditional department stores. And Wal-Mart is clearly at the head of this discount class, with selling and general administration costs—wages mainly—coming in at about 25 percent less than those of Kmart, Target, Home Depot, and other contemporary big-box retailers. In 1958, when manufacturing jobs outnumbered those in retail by three to one, the impact of this downward wage pressure might have been limited. Today, when nonsupervisory retail workers compose a larger proportion of the workforce than those in the production of durable goods, we get a downward ratcheting of the pay scale for tens of millions.

Of course, Wal-Mart's success in establishing a pervasive low-wage standard in big-box retailing is not just a product of retail economics, Sam Walton's thrifty ways, or technologically advanced control mechanisms. The company had its origins and began its stupendous growth at a particularly fortuitous place and time. Neither the New Deal nor the civil rights revolution had really come to northwest Arkansas when Walton began to assemble his small-town retailing empire. But the agricultural revolution of the early postwar era was in full swing, depopulating Arkansas farms, and putting tens

Wal-Mart Locations in 1980

Source: Wal-Mart annual reports.

of thousands of white women and men in search of their first real paycheck. In the 1950s and 1960s a road-building frenzy in the rural South doomed thousands of hamlet stores sited at the confluence of a couple of dirt tracks. But the new highways and interstates brought a far larger group of potential consumers within reach of the small, but growing, commercial centers, towns like Rogers, Harrison, Springdale, and Fayetteville. And these same highways enabled nonmetropolitan retailers to build and service the large, efficient warehouses necessary for discount operations.[19]

Walton took full advantage of these circumstances. His folksy paternalism was not a new management style, but he carried it off with brio. Meanwhile, like so many southern employers, Walton frequently played fast and loose with minimum-wage laws and overtime standards. And Walton was an early client of the antiunion law firms that were beginning to flourish in the border South. Wal-Mart stanched Teamster and Retail Clerks International Union organizing drives in the early 1970s by securing the services of one John E. Tate, an Omaha lawyer whose militant antiunionism had its origins in the racially charged warfare that convulsed the North Carolina tobacco industry in the late Depression era. It was Tate who convinced Walton that a profit-sharing scheme for hourly employees would help the company generate good PR and avoid new union threats, while keeping wage pressures at a minimum.[20] Indeed, profit sharing and low wages are Siamese twins. Low pay generated high turnover, and high turnover ensured that few employees could take advantage of the profit-sharing plan, which required two years to qualify.

Wal-Mart growth after the mid-1970s, when the chain had about a hundred stores, was nurtured by the Reaganite transformation of the business environment that relieved labor-intensive employers of hundreds of billions of dollars in annual labor costs. In the immediate post–World War II era, when Sears and Montgomery Ward expanded into the suburbs and exurbs, the threat of unionism forced these companies to pay relatively high wages, especially to the male salesmen who sold the stoves and refrigerators. But the failure of labor law reform in 1978, followed by the PATCO debacle in 1981, meant that unionism would not be much of a threat in discount retailing. Indeed, real wages at Wal-Mart actually declined in the years after 1970, tracking the 35 percent decline in the real value of the minimum wage during the next three decades. The failure of the Clinton health insurance scheme in 1994 made it possible for Wal-Mart to continue to externalize these labor costs, giving the company a $2,000 per employee cost advantage in the grocery sector that Wal-Mart was just then entering. And the passage of free trade legislation, including China's entry into the World Trade Organization, meant that Wal-Mart could easily take advantage of the global market in sweatshop labor.

One way to recognize the reactionary particularities of the Wal-Mart business model is to briefly contrast it with that of Costco, a Washington-headquartered warehouse-retailer whose Fed-Mart and Price Club predecessors Walton frequently acknowledged as the model that provided many of the ideas that he incorporated into his own retail operations. But there was one big exception: Wal-Mart would have no truck with the Fed-Mart–Price Club–Costco personnel program. Costco owes its character to Sol Price, the Jewish, New Deal Democrat whose social and cultural values were those of Depression-era New York. Price became a multimillionaire, but even in the era of Ronald Reagan, he favored increased taxes on high incomes, enhanced social welfare spending, and a confiscatory tax on wealth. He once remarked that in his entrepreneurial youth he still read the *Daily Worker* more than the *Wall Street Journal*.[21]

Price instituted a high-wage, high-benefit personnel policy that kept Costco turnover at less than a third that of Wal-Mart. And he visualized his shoppers in a very different fashion from those of Wal-Mart. They were neither ex-farmers nor small-town service workers, but derived their identity and income from that thick middle stratum who had been organized and enriched by the institutions of the New Deal and the warfare-welfare state that followed. In his early years Price sold only to those with steady jobs and good credit: aside from licensed businessmen, he sold club "memberships" exclusively to unionists, federal employees, schoolteachers, hospital and utility workers, and people who had joined credit unions. The company soon generated a bicoastal reputation for low-cost, high-volume quality, so customers spent about 50 percent more on each shopping visit than the clientele of other big-box retailers. Indeed, with few stores in the Midwest and none in the Deep South, Costco is definitely a blue-state phenomenon. Its executives donate to the Democrats and have taken a comparatively hands-off attitude toward Teamster efforts to organize their employees.[22]

Culture and Ideology

Wal-Mart, of course, is red state to the core. It is a Republican firm, certainly among the top managerial ranks, whose political contributions in 2000 and 2004 flowed almost exclusively to George Bush and his party.[23] But the red state character of Wal-Mart is about a lot more than electoral politics, just as modern conservatism represents far more than allegiance to any single political party. Wal-Mart has proven remarkably successful in propagating a distinctive brand of Christian entrepreneurialism and faux egalitarianism well beyond its Arkansas-Missouri-Oklahoma roots. The company prides itself on its corporate culture, but the resonance of that ideology arises not from its uniqueness but from the way that Wal-Mart executives have played a systematic role in translating a Reagan-era conservative populism into a set of ideological tropes that work effectively to legitimize Wal-Mart's hierarchical structure and insulate most employees from other calls upon their loyalty.

The ideological culture projected by Wal-Mart has several interwoven components, some not all that different from the welfare capitalism pioneered by paternalistic firms, including Pullman, Heinz, and National Cash Register, in the years before World War I. The first theme is that of family, community, and a corporate egalitarianism that unites $9-an-hour sales clerks with the millionaires who work out of the Bentonville corporate headquarters. Wal-Mart's small-town communitarianism is usually identified with the persona of Sam Walton, famous for his Ozark twang, shirtsleeve dress, and the aging pickup trucks he drove around Bentonville. In her contribution to this volume, Bethany Moreton explores the contemporary efficacy of such neo-populist symbolism with wit and brilliance. Indeed, Walton strove mightily, and often successfully, to project Wal-Mart as the embodiment of a more virtuous and earthy enterprise. Despite the technological sophistication of the Wal-mart infrastructure, Walton derided computer-age expertise and instead celebrated hard work, steadfast loyalty, and the mythos of small-town America as the key that has unlocked success both for the corporation and the individuals who labor within it. "We are no tech, not high tech or low tech," Walton told thousands of admirers who attended his last shareholder meeting in 1991.[24]

Walton and other executives institutionalized this imaginary social projection through an adroit shift in the linguistic landscape. They labeled all employees "associates," routinely used first names in conversation and on identification badges, and renamed the personnel department the Wal-Mart "people division." Associates who perform below par are not disciplined, but rather "coached" to achieve their potential.[25] Symbolic leveling of this sort often takes on a carnivalesque flavor at the corporation's stadium-size annual meeting, where top executives are put through skits, songs, and vaudeville-like routines that embarrass them before thousands of raucous associates.[26]

Even more important than this faux classlessness is the Wal-Mart culture of country, faith, and entrepreneurial achievement. Large U.S. firms have always linked themselves to a patriotic impulse and not only in times of war or crisis. In the 1950s General Motors sought to sell its lowest priced car with a jingle that told working-class consumers to "See the USA, in your Chevrolet. America's the greatest land of all!" Wal-Mart has been even more intent on such a linkage, beginning with its abortive "Made in the USA" advertising and purchasing campaign of the late 1980s to its contemporary efforts celebrating the guardsmen and troops—many former Wal-Mart employees—who are serving in the Middle East.[27] But overt U.S. nationalism has its limits in a firm dedicated to international expansion, which is why Wal-Mart annual meetings have taken on a decidedly multinational flavor during the last decade. As Don Soderquist, Wal-Mart's chief operating officer during most of the 1990s, told associates, "We have pride in our country, and they have the same pride in theirs. What's transferable is the culture of Wal-Mart, making people feel good, treating them right."[28]

Soderquist, who has taken it upon himself to be the foremost articulator of the Wal-Mart culture, wrote in his 2005 memoir, *The Wal-Mart Way,* "I'm not saying that Wal-Mart is a Christian company, but I can unequivocally say that Sam founded the company on the Judeo-Christian principles found in the Bible."[29] Actually, Walton took his Presbyterian identity rather lightly, and unlike Soderquist, who has contributed heavily to Arkansas evangelical churches, the company founder thought profit sharing schemes and Ozark high jinks more central to the Wal-Mart ethos than do contemporary executives.[30] But Soderquist is right in emphasizing the extent to which Wal-Mart exists within a cultural universe that is Protestant—Christian in contemporary parlance—even if corporate officers refrain from declaring this evangelical sensibility an overt component of the Wal-Mart culture.

But it is there. Like the mega-churches, the TV evangelists, and the Zig Ziglar motivational seminars, Wal-Mart is immersed in a Christian ethos that links personal salvation to entrepreneurial success and social service to free enterprise.[31] Wal-Mart publications are full of stories of hard-pressed associates, once down on their luck, who find redemption, economic and spiritual, through dedication to the company. Selfless service to the customer, the community, and Wal-Mart will soon reap its own reward.

The telephone company—the old AT&T—also once declared itself devoted to "universal service," to projecting the "voice with a smile," but Wal-Mart's invocation of this imperative has a decidedly less secular flavor. Thus the 1991 *Sam's Associate Handbook* declared that Wal-Mart "believes management's responsibly is to provide leadership that serves the associate. Managers must support, encourage and provide opportunities for associates to be successful. Mr. Sam calls this 'Servant Leadership.'"[32] That phrase, with its subtle Christian connotation, has appeared with increasing frequency in Wal-Mart publications and also among a growing number of company vendors.[33] In 1999, when H. Lee Scott was being groomed to take over the company, Joe Hardin, a former Sam's Club executive, then CEO of Kinko's, told *Discount Store News,* "Lee is a great Wal-Mart person. He is someone who has grown up in the culture, and he openly com-

Sam Walton in 1986. Photograph by Steve McHenry.
AP/WIDE WORLD PHOTOS

municates and listens to other people's ideas. He is a true servant leader who knows how to build a team and get them to work together."[34]

It is one thing to formulate a distinctive corporate culture, but it is quite another to preserve and reproduce that set of ideological and organizational structures when Wal-Mart builds stores and distribution centers outside its home territory. But Wal-Mart has succeeded. In the 1970s and 1980s the company did not leapfrog into the rich but culturally alien suburban markets but expanded like molasses, spreading through tier after tier of rural and exurban counties. Although Wal-Mart was opening or acquiring hundreds of stores in the late 1970s, the average distance of a new store from Bentonville was just 273 miles then. Moreover, Wal-Mart recruited executive talent almost exclusively from the South Central states—the company's two most recent CEOs are graduates of Southwest Missouri State University and Pittsburg State University in Kansas—and when Wal-Mart did put its stores beyond a hard drive from Northwest Arkansas, its high degree of centralization insured that the Bentonville ethos would not be diluted.[35] Wal-Mart's large fleet of corporate jets enables many regional managers to live in Bentonville, even as they administer a far-flung retail territory. Like the yearly extravaganza in Fayetteville, the weekly Saturday morning show-and-tell puts the top brass, scores of middle managers, and a selected group of lesser folk together in a ritualized setting that may be "quaint and hokey" but which a visiting *Fortune* reporter avers "makes the world's largest enterprise continue to feel as small and folksy as Bentonville. And whatever makes Wal-Mart feel smaller and folksier only makes it stronger. Or scarier."[36]

But Wal-Mart's real business takes place not in Bentonville but in thousands of discount stores and supercenters. Here the essential corporate cadre consists of the managers and assistant managers. They are responsible for meeting the sales targets and expense ratios that Bentonville's computers relentlessly put before them each week. The Wal-Mart corporate culture may smooth their way, but the job of the manager and his assistants, among the handful of salaried people in each store, is essentially one of labor management, conducted with more sticks than carrots, more actual sweat than inspirational speeches. The job is difficult, the hours long, and the career prospects not always golden.

In the early 1980s Wal-Mart faced a recruitment crisis. With more than a hundred new stores opening each year, Wal-Mart had to hire or promote upwards of a thousand managers or management trainees during the same time frame. The company faltered. Recruitment from within meant the promotion of a lot of women, and that ran headlong into those Wal-Mart family values that tilted toward small-town patriarchy. Of course, the company's sexism had its own logic. The feminist revolution had barely reached middle America, which meant that the kind of women who worked for Wal-Mart were still largely responsible for rearing the children, putting dinner on the table, and taking care of Grandma. Most were not about to pick up stakes and move to a distant town in order to move up Wal-Mart's short and unpredictable managerial ladder. But if Wal-Mart promoted them into management in their hometown store, then they were likely to be poor disciplinarians. How were they to "coach" old friends and relatives who had once shared gossip in the break room?[37]

So Wal-Mart looked to the universities to recruit a new generation of managers. But here they faced another problem. Few freshly minted MBAs were going take an arduous $25,000-per-year assistant manager job, and even the undergraduate business majors at the big schools became frustrated when they found that Wal-Mart had little use for their accounting and marketing skills. The solution was to search for a fresh cohort of management trainees in the denominational colleges and the branch campuses of the state universities, where diligence, Christian culture, and modest career expectations were already the norm. Wal-Mart wanted the B and C students, the organization men, the undergraduates who were the first in their family to take college courses. They wanted young men, and a few women, who could fully commit to the Wal-Mart ethos and the corporate culture.

Wal-Mart sent recruiters to small middle South colleges, worked with established organizations like the Distributive Education Clubs of America, and advertised on cable, at local military bases, and in area churches. However, Wal-Mart would soon recruit as many as a third of its management trainees from the ranks of a dynamic new group, Students in Free Enterprise (SIFE), which claimed a presence on more than seven hundred U.S. campuses by the end of the century.[38]

SIFE was and remains an ideological formation that propagandizes on behalf of free-market capitalism within the conservative Christian world nurtured at places like College of the Ozarks; John Brown University in Siloam Spring, Arkansas; Southwest Baptist University in Bolivar, Missouri; Drury University in nearby Springfield; and La Sierra University in Riverside, California. But, like Wal-Mart, which put several of its top executives on the SIFE board and funded hundreds of faculty as Sam Walton Free Enterprise Fellows, SIFE did not celebrate a neoliberal world of naked self-interest and Darwinian struggle. Unlike *Wall Street*'s Gordon Gekko, SIFE does not preach that greed is good. Instead the organization, which was revitalized by Wal-Mart in the early 1980s, has prepared students for entry-level management posts by linking the collegiate quest for self-esteem and humanitarian good works to an ideology of market capitalism and career advancement. Thus the SIFE statement of principles declares: "We believe that the best way to improve the lives of others is through Free Enterprise practiced morally." Propagated successfully, this was just the kind of philosophy needed to generate the devoted, youthful cadre Wal-Mart wanted to staff its ever-expanding retail empire. And it was enough to earn this "student" group a coveted place on the official Wal-Mart Web site.[39]

Like Wal-Mart, SIFE is highly centralized and hugely ambitious. It is a "missionary organization," observed one Sam Walton Fellow, whose annual convention taps into some of the same enthusiasms that energize the larger Wal-Mart conclaves. The SIFE board largely replicates the set of firms with the largest stake in the Wal-Mart supply network, plus a few specialty retailers like Walgreens and Radio Shack that do not compete directly with the Bentonville monarch. As Wal-Mart expands abroad, so too does SIFE, which now claims campus "teams" at more than six hundred foreign schools. Sam Walton Fellows are now mentoring young people in free enterprise education in the republics of the former Soviet Union, in South Africa, throughout Britain and Western Europe—where Wal-Mart is trying to establish a bigger footprint—and above all in East Asia, which is truly capitalism's most dynamic frontier. SIFE claims to be growing rapidly in the Philippines, Malaysia, and South Korea, and it has established itself in China where some twenty-nine universities host Sam Walton Free Enterprise Fellows.[40]

A Tale of Two Countries

Wal-Mart expansion outside of North America has not always gone smoothly. Despite the strength of its corporate culture, the success of the company's business model is largely dependent upon the strength or weakness of the regulatory employment regime that it encounters. This is especially true across the Atlantic, where Wal-Mart has announced that it wants "stores in every country in Europe." To this end it has either acquired or opened negotiations with existing retail and grocery firms in France, Germany, Holland, Ireland, and the UK. With at least 200 million reasonably affluent consumers, Europe has far more purchasing power than any region outside of North America.

Wal-Mart purchased Asda, the UK's second biggest supermarket chain, in 1999. Given the ascendancy of Thatcherism in the United Kingdom, Asda, which operated almost three hundred stores, had little difficulty in following Wal-Mart's low-wage, part-time business practices all through the 1990s. "When we were acquired," asserted Asda CEO Tony Denunzio, "it was like acquiring a clone."[41]

Britain is not the United States of course, so Asda expansion has encountered considerable resistance: from those who enforce the tough zoning and green belt laws, from farmers and other domestic producers who have been hurt by Wal-Mart's notorious squeeze on its supply chain, by the strong network of UK-based nongovernmental organizations like Oxfam and the Fairtrade Foundation, and by the unions, which still retain a foothold in the retail sector. But none of this has stopped the rise of Asda, which took over Sainbury's in 2003 and which had the ear of Tony Blair's New Labour. The prime minister has asserted that UK citizens like to shop at the edge-of-city big boxes, much to the annoyance of his government's own planners, who see such construction as the death knell of an efficient urban-suburban rail transport plan.[42]

In Germany, by way of contrast, Wal-Mart's effort to import American-style retailing has been a failure, bleeding Bentonville red ink from Berlin to Bonn. It has been "a fiasco" reports Andreas Knorr, a leading German student of the retail industry. Wal-Mart acquired Wertkauf, a twenty-one-store German hypermarket chain, in 1997 and then bought seventy-four more German stores from Interspar the next year. But Wal-Mart has probably lost about $250 million a year, and it has not increased its tiny share of the German retail market. The reasons are both political and cultural.

Despite neoliberal efforts to erode the German social market regime, the regulatory environment there is quite different from that of Anglo-America. In Germany Wal-Mart has failed to achieve a competitive advantage because stringent planning and zoning regulations have hindered green field expansion or urban remolding of existing stores. Restrictive shopping-hour regulations have limited the extent to which Wal-Mart can take advantage of multiple shifts and high product turnover. At eighty hours per week, these store hours are the shortest in all of Europe. And antitrust regulations in Germany have restricted price competition and eviscerated Wal-Mart efforts to squeeze German suppliers and introduce its trademark "always low prices." A remarkably large proportion of all German retail stores are family-owned, thus downgrading the maximization of shareholder value as the supreme object of the enterprise.

Culturally, it seems as if German citizens are not quite as enchanted by consumerism as those in North America or the United Kingdom. They seem to have an allergy to the faux cheerfulness that Wal-Mart projects throughout its stores, and of late they have not been spending all that much. German consumers spend 30 percent of their available income with retailers, down from 40 percent only ten years ago. And Wal-Mart's German management has been described as arrogant, inept, and characterized by a "clash of cultures," even "hubris." The Bentonville-based multinational appointed four CEOs during the first four years after acquiring its first group of German stores. Some did not speak German, and when Wal-Mart did acquire native managers, many found Wal-Mart's distinctive managerial culture quite alien. To Andreas Knorr, "Wal-Mart's failure on the German market" has been the inevitable result of its inability to manage an intercultural relationship. "In Germany the company seems to be the prey rather than the hunter."[43]

Working at Wal-Mart

Wal-Mart is a largely Protestant firm, but it has a lot of chutzpah. The company defends its low-wage, low-benefit personnel policy by arguing that it employs workers who are marginal to the income stream required by most American families. Only 7 percent of the company's hourly employees try to support a family with children on a single Wal-Mart income. The company therefore seeks out school-age youth, retirees, people with two jobs, and those willing or forced to work part-time.[44] The managerial culture at Wal-Mart, if not the formal company personnel policy, justifies its discrimination against women workers, who now compose two-thirds of the workforce, on the grounds that they are not the main family breadwinner. Not since the rise of the textile industry early in the nineteenth century, when women and children composed a majority of the labor force, has the leadership of an industry central to American economic development sought a workforce that it defined as marginal to the family economy.[45]

All this stands in stark contrast to the personnel policies of another powerful corporation that once stood at the epicenter of the American economy. Half a century ago General Motors was the largest and most profitable American corporation, with sales that amounted to about 3 percent of the gross national product, which made the car maker an even larger economic presence than Wal-Mart is today.[46] In its heyday, from the late 1920s through the 1970s, General Motors produced almost half the cars manufactured each year in the United States. And it was not just a builder of automobiles, but also of heavy trucks, locomotives, and military equipment. It was a major player in aircraft production and household appliances, and the GM Acceptance Corporation was by far the largest retail credit institution in the United States.[47] Like Wal-Mart today, it had no competition that could threaten its market supremacy. And also like Wal-Mart, whose ever present TV spots claim a beneficial link between the corporation's fortune and that of workers, customers, and community, one might scoff at the claim, but no one could ignore it.

Of course, GM was not a charitable institution; it was a hard nosed corporation that sought to ensure a 20 percent return on shareholder investment, year in and year out. It even made a profit in 1932 when tens of thousands of its employees were on the street. But after 1937 GM was a unionized firm, strikes were frequent, and the organized pressure of its workers, seeking a larger share of the GM productivity dividend, was incessant. Right after World War II the United Automobile Workers actually struck on behalf of the low-price policy that Wal-Mart would make famous thirty-five years later: labor wanted GM to freeze car prices, but still raise wages, so as to share with the public the cost savings made possible by the World War II investment surge. To GM executives this seemed a union assault on cherished managerial prerogatives, and they battled the UAW all through the winter of 1946, successfully sidelining this idea.

Instead General Motors agreed, in the landmark collective-bargaining negotiations of 1948 and 1950, that the corporation would guarantee an annual increase in the real income of its three hundred thousand blue-collar workers regardless of inflation, recession, or corporate profitability. *Fortune* magazine called this "the Treaty of Detroit." Thus between 1947 and 1973 the real income of auto workers doubled, and because GM was the template firm of the mid-twentieth century, the auto industry wage pattern was quickly adopted by a large slice of all the big manufacturing firms, unionized or not. For the first and only time during the twentieth century, the real income of those in the bottom half of the income distribution rose as rapidly as those in the top 10 percent.

And given the growth of health and pension benefits, industrial workers secured a measure of life security never before enjoyed by blue-collar Americans.[48]

None of this gave General Motors management a pass. In 1953 when President Eisenhower appointed GM president Charles E. Wilson to his cabinet, the auto executive appeared before Congress to defend his views and qualifications. When asked if there was any conflict between his career as a corporate officer and his new governmental duties, Wilson famously replied that what was "good for the country, was good for General Motors, and vice versa."

Congress eventually confirmed Charles Wilson as secretary of defense, but his bold declaration generated a howl of outrage that has not quite lost all its voltage even after more than half a century. Wilson's quip might have been arrogant, but it was controversial precisely because there was a plausible case for making it.[49]

So too at Wal-Mart, which argues that the company's downward squeeze on prices raises the standard of living of the entire U.S. population, saving consumers upwards of $100 billion each year, perhaps as much as $600 a year at the checkout counter for the average family. A McKinsey Global Institute study concluded that retail-productivity growth, as measured by real value added per hour, tripled in the dozen years after 1987, in part due to Wal-Mart's competitive leadership of that huge economic sector. "These savings are a lifeline for millions of middle- and lower-income families who live from payday to payday," argues Wal-Mart CEO H. Lee Scott. "In effect, it gives them a raise every time they shop with us."[50]

But why this specific, management-imposed trade-off between productivity, wages, and prices? Henry Ford used the enormous efficiencies generated by the deployment of the first automotive assembly line to double wages, slash turnover, and sell his Model T at prices affordable even to a tenant farmer. As historian Meg Jacobs makes clear in *Pocketbook Politics: Economic Citizenship in Twentieth-Century America*, the quest for both high wages and low prices has been at the heart of America's domestic politics throughout much of the nation's recent history. And when social policy tilts toward the left, as in the Progressive era, the New Deal, and on the World War II home front, workers and consumers find their interests closely aligned. They see the relationship between wages and prices as a fundamentally public, political issue and not merely a dictate of corporate management or the interplay of market forces.[51] Thus, as late as 1960 retail wages stood at more than half those paid to autoworkers, in large part because the new unions and the New Dealers had sought to equalize wages within and across firms and industries. But by 1983, after a decade of inflationary pressures had eroded so many working-class paychecks, retail wages had plunged to but one-third of those earned by union workers in manufacturing, and to about 60 percent of the income enjoyed by grocery clerks in the North and West. And this is just about where retail wages remain today, despite the considerable rise in overall productivity in the discount sector.[52]

Indeed, if one compares the internal job structure at Wal-Mart with that which union and management put in place at GM during its mid-twentieth-century heyday, one finds a radical transformation of rewards, incentives, and values. GM workers were often lifetime employees, so factory turnover was exceedingly low: these were the best jobs around, and they were jobs that rewarded longevity. Auto industry turnover is less than 8 percent a year, largely a result of normal retirements. At Wal-Mart, in contrast, employee turnover approaches 50 percent a year, which means it must be even higher for those hired at an entry-level wage. Turnover at Kmart is somewhat lower, and Costco, which provides even higher wages and benefits, reports a turnover rate of only 24 percent.[53] The workers are voting with their feet.

The hours of labor, the very definition of a full workday, constitutes the other great contrast dividing America's old industrial economy from that of its retail future. Since the passage of the Fair Labor Standards Act in 1938, most Americans have considered an eight-hour workday and a forty-hour week the nominal standard. Employers are required to pay time and a half to most nonsupervisory workers when their hours exceed forty per week. But the reality of our work lives has not always conformed to this standard. Industrial managers at General Motors and other high-benefit firms have frequently insisted upon a longer workweek, perhaps forty-eight or fifty-two hours, in order to meet production goals. Most workers dislike such mandatory overtime, but neither the unions nor the government can do much about it because, from the employer's perspective, the total cost of each additional hour of work has been relatively low. General Motors and other unionized firms have never been required to pay overtime on that large slice of their labor cost that consists of health and pension "fringe benefits." But at Wal-Mart and other low-benefit firms it is a near capital offense for store managers to allow workers to earn overtime pay. Indeed, at Wal-Mart a thirty-two-hour workweek is considered "full-time" employment. This gives managers great flexibility and power, enabling them to parcel out the extra hours to fill in the schedule, reward favored employees, and gear up for the holiday rush. But the social consequences of this policy are profound: unlike General Motors, Wal-Mart is not afraid to hire thousands of new workers each year, but employees' attachment to their new job is low, and millions of Americans find it necessary, and possible, to moonlight with two part-time jobs.[54]

GM and Wal-Mart have also generated extraordinarily divergent pay hierarchies. During its heyday, factory supervisors at GM—hard-driving men in charge of between two thousand and three thousand workers—took home about five times as much as an ordinary production employee. At Wal-Mart, district store managers—in charge of about the same number of workers—earn more than ten times the pay of the average full-time hourly employee. And when one calculates the ratio of CEO compensation to that of the sales floor employees, the disparity in pay becomes even greater at these two template corporations. In 1950 GM president Charles E. Wilson, who was one of the most well-paid executives of his era, earned about 140 times more than an assembly line worker; while H. Lee Scott, the Wal-Mart CEO in 2003, took home at least 1,500 times as much as one of his full-time hourly employees.[55]

Reforming the Wal-Mart Template

The fight to change the Wal-Mart business model, and in particular its labor policies, is part of a larger struggle to democratize our economic life. In China and elsewhere this requires a political transformation of the first order. When authoritarian governments preside over an era of massive, sustained proletarianization, an eruption of considerable magnitude cannot be far behind. China's transformation into the workshop of the world is therefore generating the flammable social tinder that might well explode, along lines first glimpsed at Peterloo in 1819, Lowell in 1912, even Shanghai itself in 1927. When this eruption takes place, the shock waves will force companies like Wal-Mart to rethink their wager on the transpacific supply chain and the global sweatshop.

At home our ambitions involve the effort to revive a social democratic ethos within American politics, policy, and work life. The fight is not against Wal-Mart per se, on aesthetic or consumerist grounds, but against the reactionary squeeze the corporation has been able to mount against the wages and income of all who labor within, compete with, or depend upon the new retail-centered political economy. This road leads to politics, especially in those bicoastal states where Wal-Mart now seeks a large retail foot-print. The roar that greeted GM president Wilson's claim that what was good for GM was good for the country generated a set of real constraints upon America's most prof-itable and efficient auto corporation. GM could have put Chrysler into bankruptcy and pushed Ford to the wall had it chosen to expand its market share beyond the 45 percent it enjoyed during the years after World War II. But it correctly feared federal antitrust action had it chosen to pursue such an overtly aggressive pricing strategy. Instead, GM maintained a price umbrella under which smaller competitors might shelter and autoworkers win higher take-home pay.

Wal-Mart's competitive strategy has been just the opposite, which, not unexpectedly, has generated a howl of outrage from the unions, from small business, and from those communities that see the company's low prices as a threat to Main Street vibrancy. Site fights in California and elsewhere in the coastal United States may well signal the start of an era in which Wal-Mart's business template is subject to much greater political challenge and constraint. Wal-Mart's major worries derive not from the competition mounted by Target or Home Depot, but from angry voters, hostile government officials, and skillful class-action lawyers.

This is not unique in American history: powerful firms have often been forced to alter their business model and their labor policies, even without the passage of new legisla-tion or the unionization of their employees. Even before the passage of antitrust legisla-tion, muckraking journalists put John D. Rockefeller's Standard Oil on notice that it would have to curb its predatory pricing strategy. U.S. Steel was forced to abandon the punishing twelve-hour day in 1924 after clergy, reformers, and Commerce Secretary Herbert Hoover lobbied the autocratic steel men who then led America's largest com-pany. IBM put its entire blue-collar workforce on salary in 1959 to avoid unionization in an era when organized labor seemed to be winning a guaranteed annual wage for factory workers. In the post–civil rights era we have seen how corporations have enshrined "di-versity" as a core human resource principle. And in China, Central America, and else-where a set of nongovernmental organizations, often backed by students and unionists in the U.S., have put a spotlight on the sweatshop labor employed by the contractors who supply the goods sold in the apparel and toy departments of so many American stores.

Today, Wal-Mart faces legal challenges on a variety of fronts, from the exploitation of illegal immigrants and the violation of child labor laws to discrimination against its female employees. If successful, these suits will have a material impact on Wal-Mart labor costs, bringing them somewhat closer to those of its competitors. Perhaps even more important, Wal-Mart's labor policies are coming under attack from a wide variety of elected officials, as well as unionists and academics, who argue that the company's ability to pay such low wages is possible only because state and federal tax, welfare, and health care programs subsidize the living standards of Wal-Mart employees far more than those of other U.S. workers.[56] In California researchers at UC Berkeley found that Wal-Mart wages—about 31 percent below those in large retail establishments as a whole—made it necessary for tens of thousands of company employees to rely on public "safety net" programs, such as food stamps, Medicare, and subsidized housing, to make ends meet. The Berkeley study estimated that reliance by Wal-Mart workers on public assistance programs in California cost state taxpayers about $86 million annually, in part because the families of Wal-Mart employees utilized an estimated 40 percent more in taxpayer-funded health care than the average for families of all large retail employees. In Connecticut and Alabama the findings were similar if not so dramatic. In Georgia, offspring of Wal-Mart employees were by far the largest participants in Peach-Care, the state's medical insurance plan for poor children.[57]

The challenge, therefore, is to channel this critical wave into a broad coalition that can begin to transform the nature of work at Wal-Mart and the whole business model under which the big-box retailers are now restructuring so much of the economic world. If Wal-Mart's ambitious expansion plans are thwarted, then Wal-Mart management might begin to realize that a higher-wage, higher-benefit employment model may well be only way that it can escape from these populist constraints. And when workers at Wal-Mart see that they may have a lifetime career at the company, then they will be much more likely to look to the trade union idea to give to their work life the democratic dignity and sustaining income it deserves.

TWO

Woolworth to Wal-Mart: Mass Merchandising and the Changing Culture of Consumption

Susan Strasser

"We must have cheap help or we cannot sell cheap goods," wrote Frank W. Woolworth to his store managers in 1892, when his business was still young and many of the managers were not employees but old friends and mentors, full partners in their branch stores. "When a clerk gets so good she can get better wages elsewhere, let her go—for it does not require skilled and experienced salesladies to sell our goods. You can get good honest girls at from $2 to $3 per week and I would not give $3.50," he went on. "It may look hard to some of you for us to pay such small wages but . . . one thing is certain: we cannot afford to pay good wages and sell goods as we do now, and our clerks ought to know it."[1]

Wal-Mart is not unusual among big retailers in basing low prices in part on low wages. As Frank Woolworth discerned, mass merchandising depended from the start on sacrificing workers' interests to low prices. Nor was Wal-Mart the first amazingly dominant retailing firm, a description that could easily apply to other predecessors, including the Sears, Roebuck mail-order business, and the A & P grocery chain, as well as to Woolworth. Like Wal-Mart, the early mass merchandisers—the department stores, chain stores, and mail-order houses of the late nineteenth and early twentieth centuries— lured customers away from neighborhood shopkeepers they may have known all their lives. Like Wal-Mart, the successful leading firms of mass merchandising's first fifty years spawned organized resistance because they threatened local grocers and small merchants as well as large regional and national wholesalers and manufacturing corporations. Even the Wal-Mart greeter has precedents: the manual for the Riker-Hegeman drug chain, which had 105 stores in New York in 1914, instructed the store manager to stand at the entrance and welcome every customer who entered. Wal-Mart, in other words, can best be understood at least in part as a highly successful exemplar of the principles of mass merchandising, exhibiting patterns that have operated for more than a century. Still, this contemporary juggernaut differs from its predecessors in some critical ways, which are also essential to understanding the Wal-Mart phenomenon.[2]

Controlling costs was crucial for Frank Woolworth, who built his business on fixed prices. As in today's dollar stores, everything literally sold for a nickel or a dime at his 5 (and later 5&10) Cent Stores, so there was no way for him to make up for increased costs by raising prices. The burgeoning consumer economy of the 1890s offered few of the brokers of closeouts, factory seconds, and excess merchandise from other retailers that service the dollar stores, although undoubtedly manufacturers attempted to get whatever money they could from selling their surplus. Woolworth's strategy for preserving his pricing plan lay in seeking out and promoting small, cheap goods—the safety pins, combs, mops, and other quotidian products newly made possible by that growing mechanizing and industrializing economy. The low wholesale prices of the massive depression that began in 1893 enabled him to add new lines such as leather goods to his stock. Now a nickel or a dime could buy belts and pocketbooks as well as stove polish, hairpins, and knitting needles. Everybody could use these products, and most people could afford them. Building big stores in downtown locations, Woolworth's company grew by servicing a wide range of urban workers and suburban consumers who shopped in city centers. In 1924, when Woolworth became one of the first two retailers to join the list of corporations whose stock prices went into the Dow Jones Industrial Average, the company comprised 1,356 stores.[3]

Men like Frank Woolworth, Richard Sears (the guiding spirit of the other Dow Jones retailer), and the A & P grocery chain's John Hartford were pioneers of mass merchandising. During the last decades of the nineteenth century and the first decades of the twentieth, they established innovative methods and systems that could handle the huge new output of mechanized factory production and organize distribution across a continent, among thousands of manufacturers and millions of consumers. As the United States shifted from an agricultural to an industrial society, modern organizational systems and advanced technologies for production and distribution transformed industry itself. Standardized, uniform products that cost money were manufactured in highly mechanized factories, many of them organized for efficiency as defined by Frederick Winslow Taylor and Henry Ford, and operated by large corporations that sold goods over long distances. Decision making at those companies was increasingly driven by marketing more than by production. Industrial managers learned from the developing advertising profession that they could make more money by creating demand, not merely by manufacturing products and then trying to sell what they had made.[4]

Markets were growing in any case because of demographic change: population increase (much of it from immigration), urbanization, and a decrease in household size. These trends alone could account for substantial market growth in consumer goods. Simply put, the more people and households, the more demand for household goods, and people in cities had less time and space for home production. The economic effects of these demographic changes were compounded with a general rise in disposable income, with the rising expectations and standards of living promoted by the new products and by the developing advertising industry, and with the triumph of a culture of mass consumption.

Increasingly, Americans satisfied their needs entirely through the market. It was literally a consumer culture, in the anthropological sense. People's daily routines involved making fewer things and purchasing more, while shopping and planning for consumption became important activities, pursued both as part of household work and for pleasure. Factories poured out goods that had once been made at home. New classes of human activity became commodities as folk culture was commercialized, and experiences became something to buy. The young adopted new ways sooner than the old, and the rich quicker than the poor, but the new culture came to encompass everybody. Even the families of low-paid urban workers, who had little land for gardens and insufficient time for handcrafts, joined the expanding market for manufactured goods, and people in the most remote rural areas shopped from the Sears and Montgomery Ward catalogs.

As production moved out of households and artisans' shops, an ever expanding market for manufactured goods was not only an economic abstraction. New products from new companies—indeed, new kinds of products from new kinds of companies—found their way into those stores, and into people's homes and daily routines. Prepared foods, ready-made clothes, and factory-made furniture and utensils altered the texture of daily life. They replaced the various makeshifts of most people's subsistence, and began to substitute for much of the massive productive and maintenance work once done by housewives and servants. Electric and telephone wires, and pipes for water and gas, literally joined the private household to the public world. New technologies made old ones obsolete, as, for example, electric lights replaced oil lamps. Americans of all classes began to use products that nobody had ever made at home or in small crafts shops—products like toothpaste, cornflakes, safety razors, and cameras. These provided the material basis for new habits and the physical expression of a genuine break from earlier times.

The foundation for this transformation had been laid throughout a long period of change. Beginning with the textiles of the Industrial Revolution, new products came sooner to the cities than to the farms, and wealthy people enjoyed more benefits from economic growth than did the poor. But in both city and countryside, economic development had brought an ever greater proportion of Americans into the money economy. Business cycles brought depressions regularly, each graver than the one before, as more people depended on wages and manufactured products and as more businesses engaged in trade over longer distances.

As long as production was generally local and small-scale, distribution could be carried out by rural peddlers and general stores, by single-line urban shops (such as grocery, dry goods, hardware, or shoe stores), and by the wholesalers who serviced these retailers. Big wholesaling firms held the power in this arrangement. They took bids from manufacturers on unbranded soap or tenpenny nails, and they decided what and how much choice to offer the shopkeepers who were their customers. Wholesalers' traveling salesmen crisscrossed the country on the railroads; they visited the corner grocer, the Main Street hardware dealer, and the crossroads general-store keeper, introducing these retailers—and, through them, their customers—to the thousands of new products. Eventually, the increased flow of merchandise from high-output factories to individual kitchens and parlors, and the new advertising, branding, marketing, and retailing techniques that developed to handle that flow, created new retailing and wholesaling institutions that grew big enough to overtake the old ones.

Beginning in the 1880s, branding altered the balance of power in the chain of distribution, offering manufacturers a new kind of control by establishing direct relationships with end users. Previously, wholesalers took bids for white soap from manufacturers and promoted what they bought to retailers, who sold it to their customers. But when customers and retailers began to ask for Ivory, a product that could be obtained only from Procter and Gamble, wholesalers had to buy from that company. To the extent that manufacturers could convince people to rely on advertising rather than on grocers' opinions, branding offered them a more predictable and controllable market, with protection against competition and industry price fluctuations. By 1910, many now familiar national brands—Ivory, Kellogg's, Colgate, Singer, Heinz, Kodak, Wrigley's, and others—were established in American consumers' minds.[5]

Branded, standardized products came to represent and embody the new networks and systems of factory production and mass distribution, the social relationships that brought people the things they used. Formerly *customers*—purchasing the objects of daily life from familiar craftspeople and storekeepers in networks of relationships based in villages, small towns, and big-city neighborhoods—Americans became *consumers*. Buying and using factory-made goods, they participated in a complex network of distribution, a developing global market that promoted individuals' relationships with big, centrally organized companies. They got their information about products not from the people who made or sold them, but from advertisements created by specialists in persuasion. These changes were accelerating processes that had taken firm hold on the American way of life by the time the economy crashed in 1929.

It was in the context of these decades of cultural change that mass merchandisers—department stores, mail-order houses, chain stores, and supermarkets—developed the many successful methods of operation that Sam Walton was to inherit in 1945 when he opened his first Ben Franklin variety store franchise. Those methods, in turn, rested on such fundamental principles as fixed prices, rapid stock turn, low overhead, and low markup—principles that are at the core of all mass marketing.

Department Stores: The First Mass Merchandisers

The first tenet of mass marketing to develop historically—a rule of operation easy to take for granted today, but an essential principle for employers who rely on low-paid workers—was fixed prices. Nobody bartered or bargained with Woolworth or Sears.

Nineteenth-century peddlers and general-store keepers had often traded teakettles, packages of pins, clocks, and other manufactured goods for eggs, animal skins, medicinal herbs, and other products of farm and wilderness, or for recyclable materials like rags and bones. Country general stores continued to barter well into the twentieth century; 87 percent of those reporting to a 1919 Harvard study exchanged cash, merchandise, or credit for farm produce, especially eggs and butter. In urban downtowns before the Civil War, and in immigrant neighborhoods to the end of the century, merchants more often bargained for cash; they marked goods with secret price codes to remind them of their own buying prices as they haggled, often with customers who had grown up bargaining at European markets.[6]

Bargaining and bartering, however, could be entrusted only to the most reliable employees. "The old dicker and bargain policy" of the old-fashioned store, wrote marketing professor Paul Nystrom in 1915, "required salespeople with considerable skill in handling customers." New York City's A.T. Stewart, proprietor of a huge dry goods emporium, the "richest dry goods house in the city," was one of the first retailers to institute the one-price system, at least as early as 1846, when he opened his four-story "Marble Palace" at Broadway and Chambers Street. Stewart was explicit about the relationships between fixed prices and cheap labor. "Not one of them has his discretion," he maintained, referring to the thousand clerks who staffed the new store he opened at Ninth Street and Broadway in 1862. "They are simply machines working in a system that determines all their actions."[7]

Stewart's establishment, which served tens of thousands of customers a day during the 1860s, has sometimes been described as the first department store. More accurately, it was a departmentalized dry goods store, with both merchandise and clerks organized into departments that sold only textiles and clothing. During the 1860s and 1870s, other successful dry goods stores did evolve into full-fledged department stores, both in the United States and in Europe. Rowland H. Macy, for example, began to expand his stock beyond dry goods around 1860. By 1877, his twenty-four departments sold china, toys, house furnishings, flowers, and books, among many other goods.[8]

For Macy, as for Stewart before him and the many department-store owners who followed him, departmentalization offered a structure for developing specialized buyers and clerks and sophisticated accounting systems. By putting different kinds of merchandise in separate departments, merchants could audit the contribution that individual departments and even single pieces of merchandise made to overall profits, and they could drop unprofitable goods and lines of goods. Departments also helped managers to compare employees, evaluating them and their departments with numerical measures of performance.

Macy's and other big-city department stores, writes historian Neil Harris, represented "mass encounters with the art and objects of the modern world, dramatic, persuasive, self-consciously designed to produce a maximum effect." For the affluent women of the "carriage trade," these stores offered levels of service, luxury, and excitement that have prompted historians to describe them as "dream worlds" and "palaces of consumption." Department stores drew crowds with their displays, using mirrors, electric lighting, and colors to create a festive atmosphere. By the turn of the century they provided customers with an array of services never before offered even by the most exclusive single-line shops: lunchrooms, tearooms, and other restaurants; public telephones, as well as telegraph and post offices; beauty parlors, child care, first aid, and lost-and-found departments. Some department stores featured live music, some sponsored lectures and plays, and some housed branch libraries. Telephone service and delivery made it possible to extend the dream world to customers' homes. In 1907, Wanamaker's in Philadelphia took orders around the clock.[9]

Less has been written about the development of department store services for the "shawl trade," the immigrants who patronized the bargain basements more easily recognized as Wal-Mart progenitors, than the upstairs departments. Marshall Field's inaugurated the bargain basement in 1879; Boston's Filene's made basement shopping central to its mission, opening its "automatic" basement thirty years later—the first air-conditioned space in the store, decorated with a colored glass floor and mirrored ceilings. Historian Susan Porter Benson describes the new basements of the early twentieth century as a "device for turning an unattractive area into a revenue producer." But selling bargains was not new with the basements, nor was opening the store to a clientele that included both rich and poor. A.T. Stewart had introduced the clearance sale as a means of moving old stock as early as 1837, when depression conditions pressured merchants to innovate or close their doors. Stewart also sold fabric remnants that were said to bring poor women elbow to elbow with the affluent.[10]

Selling old stock and bringing in new goods was the essence of rapid stock turnover, another crucial principle of mass merchandising developed by Stewart and the department store merchants. Small storekeepers tended to let unsold goods sit on the shelf for months or years. Successful mass merchandisers, in contrast, understood that shelf space could be used over and over again by stock that sold quickly, and that capital tied up in unsold wares could reap continual profits if it was invested instead in things that people would buy. A simple textbook explanation of turnover concerned a pushcart peddler; if he sold his goods by noon, reinvested his money in more stock, and sold out again by the end of the day, his original investment earned twice as much. The concept was a profound departure from the basic idea of marking up merchandise enough to cover a proportion of expenses and yield a profit. By increasing turnover, mass merchandisers made fortunes not from high markups on individual products, but from volume sales of products with lower markups.[11]

Rapid turnover of massive quantities of stock created economies of scale. The biggest department stores were huge: the stores that Marshall Field's and Macy's completed in 1902 each had over a million square feet of floor space, more than four times the size of a Wal-Mart supercenter. Such stores had thousands of employees; in 1904, Marshall Field's employed eight thousand to ten thousand workers and served a quarter of a million customers a day in high season. Department store merchants therefore also had massive buying power. They could and did serve as their own wholesalers, and some also became middlemen for small-town merchants; Marshall Field's, especially, was one of the biggest general wholesalers to the developing West.

Small, single-line urban merchants understood that they could never compete with huge companies that were economic forces in themselves. During the 1880s and 1890s, some urban retailers tried to keep department store growth in check, demanding taxes on, or laws that would restrict, the number of lines of merchandise a store could handle. These efforts, easily defeated by the department store merchants and their friends in government, presaged more popular and powerful protests, conducted later against mail-order houses and chain stores, which would call on the loyalty of small-town customers to small-town merchants.[12]

More successful campaigns were waged against department store labor policies. Like A.T. Stewart in the middle of the nineteenth century, many of the managers of these big operations treated sales workers as "machines working in a system that determines all their actions." Department store saleswomen earned low wages in comparison with other jobs available to them; they spent many hours on their feet; they were strictly disciplined with inspections, fines, and dismissals; and their employers based this treatment on the widespread assumption that women workers only worked temporarily. In 1890, the New York City Consumers' League was founded by a group headed by Josephine Shaw Lowell, described by historian Kathryn Kish Sklar as "New York's most politically powerful woman." At an early mass meeting of the league, packed with fashionable women, a charismatic department store clerk named Alice Woodbridge described long hours of standing, compulsory overtime without pay, and bosses who rewarded "fidelity and length of service [with] only the reward of dismissal," in the words of Maud Nathan, a leader of the league. The next year, the Consumers' League began to issue a "White List" of department stores that met the "standard of a fair house," avoiding the legal difficulties of blacklisting and boycotting. It published the list—compiled with regard to wages, hours, physical conditions, management-employee relations, and child labor—in New York newspapers. The New York organization was instrumental in creating the National Consumers' League; under the energetic Florence Kelley, who came to New York to head the national group in 1899, the department store White List evolved into the famous White Label campaign, a twenty-year-long movement against sweatshop production.[13]

The Consumers' League was not alone in investigating department store working conditions. Other women's social reform organizations, including the Women's Trade Union League and the Young Women's Christian Association, helped to develop a bill of particulars that encompassed bad ventilation and unsanitary toilets, grueling systems of rules and discipline, and low pay. "The critique of the department store," writes Susan Porter Benson, "became so widespread and was so easily verified by the concerned public that even relatively favorable articles included the Consumer League's indictment of department-store practices." In response to this pressure, as well as to internal financial demands, the more progressive store executives instituted new policies that promoted training and decent treatment, lunchrooms and other welfare programs, and various kinds of bonuses and incentives that rewarded sales in the pay envelope.[14]

Mail-Order Houses: The Technology of Retail Factories

Mail-order businesses, not dependent on expensive downtown display space, offered an even wider range of products than department stores, although the distinction is not precise, because most big department stores issued their own mail-order catalogs. Montgomery Ward, the first of the big firms that initially sold only by mail, began in 1872 as a way to eliminate middlemen and get good prices for members of the Grange, the leading national farmers' organization. In a nation with a substantial agricultural population—in 1900, three-fifths of the population still lived in places defined by the census as rural—the success of the mail-order merchants rested on making the entire range of new factory-produced goods available to people who could not get to stores. Ward's 1884 catalog ran 240 pages and listed nearly ten thousand items; that number had more than doubled by the early 1890s, thanks to a new warehouse. By that time the company had serious competition from Sears Roebuck, which was eventually to surpass it. Sears's 1897 catalog, 786 pages long, claimed, "Nearly everything in merchandise can be found in this book." [15]

Mail-order houses offered what Internet shoppers would now recognize as a convenient, private shopping experience; these stores provided no services, only products. But for mail order to succeed, people had to learn to visualize merchandise without actually seeing it—photographic reproduction was still far too expensive for use in catalogs—and to put their trust in merchants they had never met. "Any one who has had experience in learning to read a plan or blueprint or in forming a mental conception from written words," a popular magazine writer explained in 1916, "will realize how difficult it has been to accustom those who were used to buying after actual inspection of the thing bought to make their choice from a catalogue." At the outset, Montgomery Ward sent merchandise on a cash-on-delivery basis, and customers paid only if they were satisfied with what they had received. "Send No Money," Sears advertised, so often that one of the firm's leading executives used the phrase to title his memoirs. [16]

Even the skeptical might well be tempted to try the mail-order houses because—as at Wal-Mart—their prices were so low. The 1897 Sears catalog offered sewing machines, for example, at $15.55 to $17.55, and Ward's prices were approximately the same. In contrast, Singer and the other big-name firms sold machines on the installment plan for at least double, and often many times, that price. Alvah Curtis Roebuck, who soon left the business although his name remains, remembered that during the depression years of 1894 and 1895, the two partners discussed the possibility of cutting prices radically, but did not believe they could increase sales sufficiently to do so. By

September of 1897, however, they were ready to slash the middle-priced machine by more than $3. The standard scholarly history of the company tells a tale with distinct parallels to Wal-Mart strategies:

> Orders deluged the company . . . Sears was intoxicated. He persuaded the manufacturer to lower his price to the company by one dollar per machine, down to $9.50. Then Sears, Roebuck likewise dropped its price—to $12.50. In October 19,000 orders made their way to the company; even after cost of advertising and order-handling this represented a profit of $19,000.

Prices were consistently lower in the catalogs. A 1916 estimate suggested that at local retail stores, consumers paid average markups of about 75 percent over the prices charged by manufacturers; those who purchased the same goods from "an honest and well-managed retail mail order house" paid only 37 percent more than the manufacturer's price.[17]

The big mail-order houses did not simply squeeze manufacturers; they owned many of them. To some extent, their lower prices could be attributed to vertical integration. Richard Sears, especially, had developed a strategy for getting merchandise in the large quantities he needed: he helped finance the expansion of manufacturing firms that promised to sell him their entire output, loaning them money and purchasing shares in initial public offerings. By 1906, Sears held a major interest in sixteen manufacturing plants, including factories producing stoves, furniture, agricultural implements, plumbing equipment, and cameras.[18]

Like Wal-Mart, the great mail-order houses achieved low prices also by applying technology and system to the distribution process, at a level that most contemporary Americans imagine had to wait for the invention of the computer. In 1906, Sears moved to a new distribution plant in Chicago. It covered forty acres, with miles of pipes, wires, railroad tracks, and underground tunnels connecting the buildings. The building where the merchandise was handled included a clothing factory, and could receive a sixty-car train. Railroads, telegraph companies, the express companies, and the post office all managed branches on the grounds. The goal was to achieve a smooth flow of goods through the system, much like a factory adopting conveyer belts to move goods through the production process. Two thousand people processed more than nine hundred sacks of mail every day. With the scheduling system inaugurated at the new plant, Sears could ship merchandise within forty-eight hours of receiving an order. Special machines opened twenty-seven thousand letters per hour; the factory was equipped with "elevators, mechanical conveyors, endless chains, moving sidewalks, gravity chutes, apparatus and conveyors, pneumatic tubes and every known mechanical appliance for reducing labor," in the words of the 1905 catalog. As early as 1911, Sears maintained a card index that showed what every customer had ever bought, and used it to decide who would get which specialized catalog. By 1915, Sears and Montgomery Ward kept files on 4 million to 6 million customers.[19]

When the Sears plant opened in 1906, the company employed nearly eight thousand workers, a hundred times the staff of 1895. Personally influenced by Chicago's famous social reformer Jane Addams, personnel manager Elmer Scott turned Sears, Roebuck into one of America's model firms for employee welfare. The company established a plant hospital, disability benefits financed by employee contributions, a night school, five restaurants, employee discounts, paid vacations, and other benefits. Nonetheless—and despite an official policy against night and Sunday work (the standard workweek was fifty-seven hours)—department managers regularly violated the overtime rules, and, according to the standard history, "the company paid wages only as high as necessary to maintain its work force."[20]

Like Wal-Mart, mail-order houses met considerable opposition from local business interests and attacks in local newspapers. Small-town businessmen organized "trade-at-home" clubs, and during 1906 and 1907, midwestern commercial associations banded together in the Home Trade League of America. In 1912, in the middle of an Iowa winter, the Cedar Falls Commercial Club paraded through town, marching to band music under banners that proclaimed, "We thought we were buying cheaper, but we know better now." After the parade, club members converged on the town square for a catalog bonfire. Other groups fought in the marketplace: Peabody, Kansas, merchants urged customers to bring their catalogs to the stores so that merchants could match mail-order prices.[21]

Some historians have described the protests as inevitably futile, the ineffectual actions of men whose old-fashioned way of life was threatened by technological and organizational change in a developing economy. But small-town businessmen usually led their communities' forces for local economic development. Their associations promoted road building, sewer systems, train depots, and irrigation projects; they crusaded not only against mail-order houses but also against peddlers and other less-established businesspeople. They attempted both to defend their immediate financial interests and to expand their horizons. Still, they failed to see that the good roads they promoted and the mass-merchandising techniques they attacked were two sides of the same coin, a sweeping cultural transformation.[22]

The protests were effective enough to demand a response from Sears and Montgomery Ward. Both companies courted consumers directly. "This book tells you just what your storekeeper at home pays for everything he buys," the cover of the 1899 Sears spring catalog stated, "and will prevent him from overcharging you." In 1902, Ward's catalog reprinted an agricultural paper's declaration that farmers were "tyrannized over by the country merchants." Sears promised in 1908 that goods would arrive from Chicago in plain wrappers because "many people object to having the name of the shipper spread across every box or package, so that when it is unloaded at the station or express office everyone can see what they are getting and where they buy it. . . . We have learned that thousands of our customers need the protection that the omitting of our name affords. This applies especially to townspeople."[23]

The Chaining of America: System and Opposition

Two decades later, shopkeepers joined a campaign in opposition to chain stores that echoed the anti–mail order protests, with local merchants again urging patrons to trade at home, battle big business, and save the American way of life. The mail-order houses had remained a generally rural phenomenon until the 1920s, when Sears and Montgomery Ward built bricks-and mortar stores in urban areas. Along with chain stores selling groceries, drugs, variety merchandise, and other specialties, these new outlets again threatened the businesses that lined small-town Main Streets and urban neighborhood shopping streets. As historian Lizabeth Cohen has shown for Chicago, chains did not conquer urban retailing all at once. At least until the Depression made the expanding chains' low prices irresistible, immigrant communities stayed loyal to ethnic businesses, the face-to-face personal relationships that went along with retail credit, and the delivery and other services that small retailers provided.[24]

In some states, chains enjoyed tax advantages unavailable to independents, a major

Chain stores attracted customers with low prices. Herrin, Illinois, 1939. Photograph by Arthur Rothstein.

FARM SECURITY ADMINISTRATION/OFFICE OF WAR INFORMATION, LIBRARY OF CONGRESS

issue for legislative reform as opposition to chain stores developed. In others, opponents attempted to enact legislation specifically taxing chains. The first such bill was introduced in Missouri in 1923 but did not pass; four years later, antichain bills were introduced in thirteen states, and succeeded in Maryland, North Carolina, Georgia, and Pennsylvania. The chains went to court, and while the cases were on appeal, more states passed taxes on chain stores. The Supreme Court accepted such taxation in 1931, prompting the introduction of hundreds of bills in state legislatures; the peak was 1933, when 225 antichain bills were introduced in forty-two states, and thirteen passed. During the same period, the Federal Trade Commission, directed by the Senate to investigate the chains in 1928, issued thirty-three interim reports; its final statement, issued in 1935, confirmed many allegations against the chains. The Roosevelt administration also initiated antitrust actions, most notably in 1939, when the Justice Department filed a suit against A & P, which the company lost seven years later.[25]

Both sides of the chain-store debate mobilized public opinion during this period of legislation and litigation. During the late 1920s, home-grown trade-at-home campaigns were organized in small towns; the first antichain mass meeting was held in Petersburg, Virginia, in 1926. The owner of a Louisiana radio station, with sufficient wattage to broadcast his opinions across the Midwest and the South, organized a national group, the Merchants' Minute Men, which coordinated local trade-at-home campaigns in more than four hundred towns by 1930. That year, chain stores were the national college and high school debate topic. To combat the small merchants and their organizations, the chains hired public relations firms. The National Chain Store Association funded a campaign that targeted more than four hundred thousand editors, marketing teachers, state officials, legislators, and libraries. Other chain groups, and individual chains, mounted public relations efforts over the next decade, culminating in a three-year publicity program that A & P began in 1937.[26]

A & P—the Great Atlantic and Pacific Tea Company—was the largest, oldest, and best established of the chains. In 1930, it reached a peak of 15,737 outlets, more than four times the number of Wal-Marts (including supercenters and Sam's Clubs) in the United States in 2004. That year, its sales totaled $1.066 billion, more than 1 percent of the gross domestic product. The next largest chain grocery, the Kroger Grocery and Baking Company, had peaked the year before at a fraction of A & P's size, with 5,575 stores and $286 million in sales.[27]

A & P founders George F. Gilman and George Huntington Hartford had opened their New York tea store in 1859; by 1865 they ran twenty-five stores as well as a widely advertised mail-order tea and coffee business. They began to expand into other grocery lines during the 1880s and 1890s, and by the turn of the century, A & P operated nearly two hundred grocery stores in twenty-eight states and the District of Columbia. Other grocery chains remained much smaller; for example, the Great Western Tea Company of Cincinnati—later the Kroger Grocery and Baking Company—was founded in 1882 and ran thirty-six stores in 1902. Nongrocery chains also began during the same period. Frank Woolworth opened his first successful five-cent store in 1879, had fifty-nine stores in 1900, and purchased thirty-seven more in 1904, in a significant expansion. McCrory's had twenty stores in 1900, and Kress had eleven, but S.S. Kresge, which would become the second largest variety chain, was still a single store. Drug chains lagged behind, probably because many pharmacists considered themselves professionals more than businessmen. Still, at the turn of the century, distribution was for the most part confined to single stores operated by individual merchants, and chain operations were small by later standards.[28]

By 1912, the biggest chains (especially A & P and Woolworth) had grown significantly and were under attack as part of the Progressive movement to protect the public from the excesses of big business. Critics charged that Wall Street interests dominated the chains. Indeed, Woolworth's directors included Henry Goldman of Goldman, Sachs and Company; Philip Lehman of Lehman Brothers; and the chairman of the board of the Chase National Bank. These three men also served together on the boards of Sears and two other companies. "When a man with a business investment of three thousand dollars is told to compete with a man having a business investment of three million dollars—he is told to do the impossible," a representative of the National Association of Retail Druggists told a Senate committee. "Unrestricted competition . . . is nothing short of a cruel joke."[29]

Like department stores and mail-order houses—and like Wal-Mart—chains depended on innovative systems that rested on the fundamental principles of mass merchandising. Unlike most small stores, they practiced modern accounting, organized their merchandise into departments, and turned stock frequently. The United Cigar Stores, with more than nine hundred outlets in 1914, required daily reports from each store; men from headquarters appeared without notice to check on their accuracy. The company claimed to turn the stock fifty times a year, in contrast to even the most prosperous and up-to-date independent tobacco stores, which turned stock fifteen or twenty times. Chain-store locations were chosen systematically, and real-estate specialists negotiated sales and leases. Child's restaurants, with eighty outlets around the country, waited as long as five years for specific locations, chosen on the basis of detailed data. United Cigar employees stood on street corners counting pedestrians; the company's real-estate subsidiary bought whole buildings to secure good locations, and reaped substantial income renting office space. Inventory management enabled chains to know what was selling and to move it efficiently from boxcar to shopping basket. By the interwar period, A & P managers filled out standardized order sheets twice a week, to be processed at warehouses that arranged the goods in the order they were listed on the sheet.[30]

Unlike mail-order houses, which built massive plants staffed with workers who interacted more with management than with the public, chain stores brought the principles and techniques of centralized mass merchandising to many stores in multiple locations, operated by clerks and low-level managers working far from company executives. Still, like A.T. Stewart in the mid-nineteenth century and Wal-Mart today, the chains developed methods that enabled them to operate with low-cost labor. "The Philadelphia grocery chains," reported the weekly advertising trade journal *Printers' Ink* in a 1914 series on chains, "hire immigrants at low salary . . . because the work has been methodized to the point where it requires the least possible amount of instruction, supervision and personal initiative."[31]

Intent on controlling their systems and keeping labor costs low, the chains at first resisted unionization. The union movement, in turn, joined forces with the chains' opponents. But, suggests historian Richard Tedlow, the grocery chains (already under attack by so many levels of government during the New Deal) eventually chose to court unions in order to garner political support. A & P signed collective-bargaining agreements with American Federation of Labor unions in 1938 and 1939. In return, the unions—representing large numbers of members who were also consumers, interested in low prices—opposed antichain legislation. Centrally managed chains were formidable, but could be organized more easily than tens of thousands of small stores. The president of the Amalgamated Meat Cutters claimed that chains paid better and were easier to work with than independent merchants, and pointed out that unions would be threatened by the demise of the chains because old-fashioned independent proprietors had fewer employees.[32]

Systematized and massive buying power enabled chains to make new kinds of demands on manufacturers and wholesalers. Like Sears and Montgomery Ward, some chains eliminated wholesalers completely, and invested in manufacturing plants. When they bought merchandise from others, they asked for and got extra discounts; they demanded—and sometimes simply took—extensions of time for payment, financing operations in part on the credit of the wholesalers and the manufacturers. The creditors "don't like it," wrote the *Printers' Ink* investigators, "but what would you have them do? Once they have tasted the chains' money, it is twice as hard to refuse." As critics charged, chains had access to Wall Street financing. And like Sears, the biggest chains integrated backward into manufacturing: A & P's subsidiaries baked bread, ran canneries, packed beans and cereals, and in 1930 functioned as the world's largest coffee merchant.[33]

Such financial advantages enabled chains to offer better prices than independent merchants on branded, nationally advertised products, threatening manufacturers' power and alarming small retailers forced to sell identical goods at higher prices. Price-cutting challenged the central marketing strategy used by successful mass producers, who aimed to establish brand loyalties strong enough to overcome price sensitivity, belief in the qualities of Kellogg's or Ivory that would convince customers to pay whatever they cost. If the 10¢ cornflakes sold for 8¢, they feared, consumers might conclude that Kellogg's was worth no more than cheaper brands.

Not all chains cut prices. The five-and-tens rarely followed the practice; drug chains all did. While A & P "is not a rabid price-cutter," *Printers' Ink* wrote in 1914, most other grocery chains were. In theory, chains could advertise trademarked goods as loss leaders, and then encourage clerks to "substitute," pushing private brands at the counter by claiming that the unadvertised products (on which the merchants made more money) were just as good. But, the authors explained, most chains did not substitute; independents were far more guilty of the practice.

> The chain theory of merchandising is to give the public exactly what it wants. If it can satisfy the customer and bring him back again and again, it will make many profits that will outweigh the one large one that might possibly be secured from substitution. . . . The Owl Drug Company, of San Francisco, has a sign posted in its stores threatening with dismissal any clerk who shall substitute. . . . This is contrary to the general impression of chain methods, but it is thoroughly in line with modern merchandising principles.

Still, after the sale was made, the Owl clerk was supposed to suggest the private brand for the customer's *next* purchase.[34]

Concerned that their brands would be undermined, some manufacturers refused to sell to chains that cut prices, and had to defend themselves when chain stores filed suit. Other manufacturers mobilized small retailers and their organizations into support for a policy called retail (or resale) price maintenance, whereby manufactures set prices not only to wholesalers, but also to retailers and consumers, sometimes by printing a price on the package. Known as fair trade to its friends and as price-fixing to its foes, price maintenance has a legislative and legal history that is long, complicated, and still ongoing. The Supreme Court ruled it illegal under the Sherman Antitrust Act in 1911, in a case concerning the Dr. Miles Medical Company, a patent medicine firm. Almost all of the states passed legislation permitting price maintenance within their borders during the early years of the Depression. These laws were reinforced by the Miller-Tydings Act (1937), which amended the Sherman Act to give federal sanction to retail price maintenance in interstate trade. Along with the Robinson-Patman Act (1936), which limited the discounts available to chain stores, this law built the antichain legal edifice. In 1975, Miller-Tydings was repealed by the Consumer Goods Pricing Act, which legitimized the pricing practices of Wal-Mart and other discount stores and was essential to their further expansion. But the details of price maintenance were still being debated (and part of the law was once again reversed) as late as 1997, when the Court held that manufacturers could set maximum prices in *State Oil Company v. Barkat U. Khan.*[35]

The Rise of Self-Service

For all its many outlets and its efficient warehouses, A & P did not operate supermarkets until the late 1930s. Its small stores were run by clerks who stood behind counters and retrieved goods for the customers. During chain merchandising's first decades, most chain groceries offered the same services that independent groceries typically provided: credit, delivery, and telephone ordering. Although top management was unlikely to help rural districts through bad harvests or workers through strikes the way the old-fashioned grocer or general storekeeper did, in other ways chain stores resembled the independents in the early years. Many chains supplemented store income by operating peddler wagons, and later automobiles; as many as twenty salesmen worked out of each store, soliciting sales on commission. A & P had thousands of peddler routes, Grand Union more than 3,500.[36]

In 1912, A & P instituted "Economy Stores," an innovation that would kindle the rapid expansion of the chain. Operated by one manager and one assistant—who closed the store to go to lunch—Economy Stores eliminated services and functioned strictly on a cash-and-carry basis. The resulting savings were passed on to shoppers, who paid

Shopping at Woolworth's, 1941. Photograph by John Collier.
FARM SECURITY ADMINISTRATION/OFFICE OF WAR INFORMATION, LIBRARY OF CONGRESS

lower prices at the new, uniform red-fronted stores than at older A & P outlets. Under the new policies, the company opened hundreds and even thousands of stores every year until it reached its peak in 1930. But while some other chains followed suit and abolished credit and delivery, many still offered these two essential (and typical) services of turn-of-the-century independent grocery stores.[37]

At least as early as 1909, writers in business magazines were suggesting that the old-fashioned method of hiring clerks to wait on customers was less than ideal. An expert on store fixtures dreamed of "a fixture from which the customer can select goods without assistance, pay the cashier and leave the store." The first successful self-service operation is generally credited to Clarence Saunders, who opened his Piggly Wiggly store in Memphis in 1916. The next year he was granted a patent on the design: customers carried baskets through a maze of aisles that exposed them to all the merchandise, and they exited at checkout stands. The Piggly Wiggly chain ultimately had 2,660 stores, and by 1926 sales at the average Piggly Wiggly were well over twice those at the average A & P.

Supermarkets, which brought the advantages of self-service to fruition, were a direct result of the Depression. As Richard Tedlow writes, "The supermarket was built on price appeal." Although there were earlier precedents, several variations on what are now recognizable as supermarkets began business during the 1930s. Their imaginative entrepreneurs understood the new conditions of a consumer culture in crisis: a population accustomed to branded goods, increasingly equipped with automobiles and refrigerators, and looking for low prices as the Depression deepened. Supermarkets were built outside major urban areas, on big tracts of cheap land or in empty factory buildings. In their huge spaces, manufacturers mounted big displays that made self-service an effective merchandising technique for branded, packaged goods. With ample acreage devoted to parking lots, supermarkets could serve customers from miles away. With carts on wheels—a significant innovation over baskets—and with cars to carry groceries home, shoppers were not constrained by the amount they could carry. With refrigerated storage in their kitchens, they could buy even perishables in great quantities, contributing to the supermarkets' high volume and fast turnover.[38]

By the 1950s, half of American grocery purchasing was done in supermarkets, but numerically they were still only 5 percent of the grocery stores. The successful chain grocery companies had converted into supermarket chains; A & P had made this strategic decision in 1938. Their stores grew by broadening the merchandise mix, expanding to include lines of merchandise carried by variety stores. Many of the successful independents, in contrast, now served in essence as nonchain convenience stores. Individual proprietors were willing to work long hours, and small neighborhood stores provided frequently used, highly perishable foods—especially milk and bread—within walking distance.[39]

During the 1950s, new kinds of discount stores applied supermarket principles to more lines of goods; with the exception of E.J. Korvette, most were too short-lived to be remembered by name. Making money by means of volume and low overhead, and despite low markups, they specialized in brand-name semidurable goods such as luggage, sporting goods, cameras, jewelry, and appliances. Discounters assailed state and federal fair trade laws in word and in deed, selling branded goods below the manufacturers' "suggested retail price." They operated with minimal labor and offered minimal service, growing by expanding their merchandise lines to encompass most of those retailed by department stores, which were opening outlets without bargain basements in suburban malls. Some "closed-door discounters" charged membership fees and courted particular groups, such as government employees or union members.[40]

In 1962, two huge variety store companies, Kresge and Woolworth, inaugurated discount chains Kmart and Woolco; a Minnesota department-store chain opened its first four Target stores; and Sam Walton started the first Wal-Mart in a sixteen-thousand-square-foot building in Rogers, Arkansas. Twenty-five people worked there. Clerks earned considerably less than minimum wage. The logo included the slogans "We sell for less" and "Satisfaction guaranteed." Advertisements explained that Wal-Mart could lower prices because it bought directly from the manufacturer, and indeed, the store charged as much as 50 percent off items like Sunbeam and General Electric appliances, and Polaroid cameras. The grand opening drew "tens of thousands" of customers, according to Walton. The success in Rogers almost immediately fostered expansion, for both the store and the company.[41]

What's New About Wal-Mart?

History, Mark Twain reputedly declared, does not repeat itself, but sometimes it rhymes. Sam Walton stood on the shoulders of retail giants. We comprehend his achievements better if we recognize theirs; we understand his company's success better if we grant its similarities to its predecessors. Still, Wal-Mart is without doubt a unique retailing phenomenon. What, then, is new and different about it?[42]

First, sheer size. In 2004, the company's annual revenues were 2.3 percent of the

United States' gross domestic product; it did 20 percent of the retail toy business, and sold 14 percent of all groceries; it was the world's largest corporation. Wal-Mart was so vast, investment banking adviser Peter J. Solomon explained in 2004, "that the principal strategic question for every American retailer and consumer goods manufacturer is: 'What's my relationship to Wal-Mart?' " Arguably, this was once equally true of A & P and the packaged-food industry, but never before has one retailer so dominated retailing and manufacturing in virtually *all* consumer goods lines, nor have the dealings of a single retailer so impacted the entire economy.[43]

Along with the other discount giants that also emerged in 1962, Wal-Mart had the advantage of timing, expanding initially during a period of prosperity that promoted the flowering of a culture of consumption. Americans simply have—and buy—more stuff than they had when Woolworth and Sears were in their heyday, and vastly more stuff than during the Civil War years, when A.T. Stewart was at his peak and A & P was first getting started. We no longer make our clothing or prepare a large quantity of our food, nor do we know the people who do it for us. Purchasing and amassing standardized products, individual consumers create "lifestyles" that come as close to fulfilling their needs and representing their tastes as their budgets, and their time and tolerance for shopping, allow.

While many of the marketing methods and consumption patterns of the early twenty-first century are extensions of earlier trends, the world of consumer goods retailing is qualitatively different than it was a century ago. Retailing has become more standardized; the business districts of small towns and urban neighborhoods once reflected regional differences, ethnic heritages, and distinctive personalities. Consumption is held to be a source of identification and satisfaction that surpasses work for most people, and rivals it for everybody. Clothes are labeled on the outside; consumers advertise beer and vacation resorts on their T-shirts. Brands have become individual statements about status with respect to other individuals, whether ghetto youth flaunting their sneakers or Wall Street traders brandishing their watches.

In such a culture, consistently low prices on a wide range of products are a powerful draw for most people, who never earn enough to satisfy their desires. And while the Wal-Mart shopping experience may appear to be the opposite of the luxurious dream-worlds of early-twentieth-century department stores, the chain distinguished itself from the start by its similarly customer-oriented policies toward both merchandise and workers. It attunes its stock to its clientele; its supercenters enable working families to do one-stop shopping. In other words, customers are powerful at Wal-Mart. As one Minnesota woman wrote to her local paper, she could "come out with a cart full top and bottom" for the same amount of money that would fill only a bag or two at other stores. "How great that feels."[44]

The company has many time-honored strategies for keeping overhead low. Like Frank Woolworth, who let good clerks go when they could get better wages than he was willing to pay, Wal-Mart managers have favored customers' financial interests over those of their workers. Like Richard Sears, who bought and sold his suppliers, Wal-Mart is famous for squeezing manufacturers, sacrificing good relations with producers on the altar of low price. Like the mail-order companies, which were publicly subsidized by rural free delivery beginning in 1901 and parcel post in 1912, Wal-Mart has developed extraordinary expertise at getting government subsidies. It builds stores and distribution centers with public assistance: help with land purchases and financing deals; infrastructure construction, such as water lines, sewers, and access roads; property tax breaks, state corporate income tax credits, and tax-exempt bond financing; enterprise zone status; and job training and worker-recruitment projects.[45]

The company developed during—and has helped contribute to—a change in the power structure of distribution. By the time Sam Walton started Wal-Mart in 1962, retail price maintenance was effectively in decline, as a variety of discount outlets simply ignored manufacturers' price limitations. From the start, Wal-Mart distinguished itself by offering low prices on branded goods. After the 1975 Consumer Goods Pricing Act legally ended retail price maintenance, warehouse discounters flourished, and were increasingly able to pressure manufacturers for good deals based on their size. More recently, Wal-Mart has held additional power with respect to manufacturers simply because manufacturing has become less important to the American economy—a trend that Wal-Mart has contributed to, by forcing manufacturers to go offshore.[46]

In part, the power shift has resulted from the company's control of information. Like Sears and A & P, Wal-Mart has effectively applied technology to problems of merchandising. It did so during a period accurately described as an information revolution. It was one of the first companies to adopt Universal Product Code scanning, and was thereby able to gather (and manipulate) information about merchandise and about consumers instead of depending on manufacturers' market research. In 1988, Wal-Mart completed the largest private satellite communication system in the United States, linking all stores and distribution centers with the Arkansas headquarters, with two-way voice and data transmissions and one-way video. More recently, the company has ordered its top suppliers to invest in radio frequency identification (RFID) technology, applying tags to pallets and cases so that merchandise can be tracked at every stage in the distribution process.[47]

Finally, Wal-Mart has done an exceptionally good job of targeting particular markets. As clearly as the mail-order houses went after the rural market during the 1890s, Wal-Mart set out to serve small towns in poor areas. A 2000 study by economist Andrew Franklin found "a significant negative relationship between median household income and Wal-Mart's presence in the market." In the words of the lead plaintiff in the sex-discrimination case against the company, "They are promoting themselves to low-income people . . . They don't lure the rich . . . They know the haves and have-nots. . . . They don't put Wal-Mart in high-end parts of the community. They plant themselves right in the middle of Poorville." Within that market segment, the company has done a particularly good job of creating a retail environment attractive to working women with families, who can buy everything they need in one place at good prices, saving both time and money.[48]

Successful companies not only drive weak competitors out of business; they foster new competition. "The last dominant retailer to have such influence," Peter J. Solomon explained in 2004, was Sears. As that company expanded during the 1920s from a catalog house into a bricks-and-mortar chain sanctified by Dow Jones, local department stores merged to create such major new competitors as Federated Department Stores, which still operates many department store chains, including Macy's. Similarly, wrote Solomon, "Wal-Mart's success is stimulating countervailing forces," mergers among Wal-Mart suppliers. He did not mention the many other kinds of opposition developing as he wrote, from unions and community groups.[49]

Those groups have developed a critical analysis of Wal-Mart that ranges from low wages to gender discrimination to the cultural impoverishment of communities dominated by big-box stores. As Wal-Mart opposition has developed, it has focused increasingly on globalization, incorporating pressing issues of the environment, the global labor force, and human rights. History provides no simple answers or explanations for the questions raised by these critiques. Indeed, a historical perspective generally complicates matters. But it also provides a viewpoint from which we may evaluate the present: things change, it was not always like this, and what we see now will develop into something different. Companies have life cycles; they are transitory phenomena; they rise and fall. Both a "template for twenty-first-century capitalism" and a spectacularly successful practitioner of nineteenth-century principles of mass merchandising, Wal-Mart is no more eternal than the Sears catalog, which dominated American merchandising in its day. But it is also part of an enduring trend, the development of a culture of consumption dominated by giant enterprises.

THREE

It Came from Bentonville: The Agrarian Origins of Wal-Mart Culture

Bethany E. Moreton

Back in 1999, when *Fortune* magazine was celebrating the turn of the millennium, it went looking for the "Businessman of the Century." The ultimate victory of the sentimental favorite was never in doubt: who but Henry Ford, pioneer of mass production, could plausibly stand for the entire international economic order of the previous one hundred years? On the way to the winner's circle, however, the editors highlighted contenders from other sectors of the economy, including semifinalist Sam Walton, the founder of Wal-Mart.[1] Three years later, Wal-Mart topped the magazine's annual rankings of the world's largest corporations, and it may well be that when the magazine is selecting its Businessman of the Twenty-first Century, it will have to reach back to Walton for a belated tribute. In the meantime, the contest encapsulates our current analytical dilemma: Ford, we can all agree, set a paradigm for an entire social formation in the earliest decades of this past century. Its constituent parts, its long-term consequences, and its ultimate demise have been around long enough to attract deep, nuanced analysis; but what came next?

As Supreme Court justice Potter Stewart so arrestingly remarked of obscenity, we may not be able to define it, but we know it when we see it. It's the service economy: fast-food nation, McWorld, the consumers' republic. It's globalization: the Lexus under the olive tree, the lasers in the jungle, the Tibetan pilgrims following the Chicago Bulls. It's post–Cold War American hegemony: the new world order, the end of history, the

57

clash of civilizations.[2] In some circles, it travels under the nom de guerre of "post-Fordism," presenting us with a rare instance of harmony between the readers of *Fortune* and the readers of imprisoned Italian Communist Antonio Gramsci. The period from 1914 until 1973, they agree, was characterized by mass production and mass consumption of consumer durables; planned power sharing on the part of big business, big government, and big labor; and social standardization through bureaucratic institutions, nuclear families, and a homogenizing nationalism. The period since 1973 has relied increasingly on the "niche" production and consumption of ever more disposable items, a retreat from the state regulation and social safety nets that stabilized the boom-and-bust business cycle, highly flexible labor markets and work arrangements, an explosive acceleration of circulating capital and credit, and a social and cultural emphasis on difference.[3] But the term "post-Fordism" itself suggests the limitations of the concept: it is a negative definition, tempting us to measure the new terrain by the norms of the familiar one. "Wal-Martism" can plug this conceptual hole in the middle of post-Fordism. The specific case of the auto industry drew analytical attention to components of modernity—the regimentation of time, for example, or the creation of consumer desire. Wal-Mart deserves a hearing on the same terms. We should ask not just how it differs from Ford or GM, but what original inputs created the "Wal-Mart Way."

This essay—part of a larger project—considers one of those key inputs: the company's actual geographical home in the Ozark Mountain region of Northwest Arkansas. It argues that Wal-Mart did not halt the march of industrial modernity with *Hee-Haw* anachronisms. Even at its supposed midcentury zenith, the high-wage manufacturing sector depended on a host of informal economic arrangements that have outlived it, and none more successfully than Wal-Mart.[4] The supposed paradox of Wal-Mart—the riddle of the high-tech hillbillies, the mystery of rustics who can tote a Bible in one hand and an electronic scanner in the other—actually masks a genuine historical problem: how did the world's largest corporation grow from the most violently antimonopoly section of America? How, in fact, did the "red" and "blue" actors in this drama switch sides?

In the 1930s, two of today's most vociferous Wal-Mart critics—*The Nation* magazine and the retail union—helped lay the groundwork for Wal-Mart's future dominance, while the small Arkansas towns that epitomize the company fought tooth and nail to prevent its advent. For Wal-Mart to thrive, it had to overcome a pair of entrenched local objections to its business model: suspicion of the captain of industry, and loyalty to republican manhood. In meeting these twin challenges, Wal-Mart pioneered a managerial culture that has proved downright cutting-edge.[5]

The Wal-Mart Paradox

Today, even the most casual reader of the national press has encountered some version of this formula: Wal-Mart is the biggest company on the planet. Its sales on a single day recently topped the GDPs of thirty-six sovereign nations. If it were the Independent Republic of Wal-Mart, it would be China's sixth largest export market, and its economy would rank thirtieth in the world, right behind Saudi Arabia's. And then the punch line: it's from a little bitty town in Arkansas where you can't even buy a beer![6] Bentonville, Arkansas, always rated this kind of mention in the business press as the unlikeliest of places to produce a world-class player. "The paradox," marveled one representative commentator in 2002, "is that Wal-Mart stands for both Main Street values and the efficiencies of the huge corporation, aw-shucks hokeyness and terabytes of minute-by-minute sales data, fried-chicken luncheons at the Waltons' Arkansas home and the demands of Wall Street."[7]

A more useful interpretation of the "Wal-Mart paradox" comes from within its own management. In Wal-Mart circles, no single story of the company's early years was more treasured than that of the Chicken Report. Since the early 1970s, Wal-Mart had courted investors with laid-back annual meetings featuring fishing trips and barbecues, and by the mid-eighties the national analysts could not ignore the home office's overtures. The result was an irresistible audience of slightly bewildered city folk, struggling to comprehend the company's magic. With encouragement from Walton, Senior Vice President Ron Loveless elaborated on one of management's typical in-house gags and presented it to the attentive crowd. "People often ask us how we predict market demand for discount merchandise," Loveless began, "and you've heard a lot of numbers today. But there is more to it than that. We raise a good many chickens in Northwest Arkansas, and we've come to depend on them for what we call the Loveless Economic Indicator Report. You see, when times are good, you find plenty of dead chickens by the side of the road, ones that have fallen off the trucks. But when times are getting lean, people stop and pick up the dead chickens and take 'em home for supper. So in addition to the traditional methods, we try to correlate our advance stock orders with the number of dead chickens by the side of the road." With elaborate graphs, Loveless demonstrated the entirely fictitious relationship, gravely explaining the peaks and valleys of chicken mortality, describing one anomalous spike as a misleading head-on collision between two chicken trucks outside Kosciusko, Mississippi, and projecting slides of a uniformed "Chicken Patrol" inspecting a bird's carcass on a two-lane country road. "And the audience sat there nodding and frowning and writing it all down!"[8]

Wal-Mart delighted in playing up the supposed contrast between hillbilly Arkansas and high-tech big business. But if we read this juxtaposition as paradoxical, we deserve the drubbing that the Chicken Patrollers dished out. In fact, the reputed "antimodernists" have shown a consistent talent for innovation. The rural South embraced distance commerce back when it meant mail-order catalogs and global cotton markets.

An Ozark farm in the late 1970s. Small-scale farms supplied many of Wal-Mart's early employees, both in management and in hourly positions.

COURTESY OF SHILOH MUSEUM OF OZARK HISTORY, SPRINGDALE, ARKANSAS

Fundamentalist preachers first seized the new technology of radio and then cable television to create a deterritorialized community of the faithful. The Moral Majority mastered direct mail to build a new political constituency. And, indeed, the small-town retailer set the technological standard for a global industry.[9] These Sunbelt enigmas are not examples of some odd hybrid, "half . . . defender of traditional lifestyle, half entrepreneurial innovator."[10] They are in fact unadulterated innovators, for their carefully cultivated traditionalism itself represents a radical new creation. Like every such invented tradition, it clothes itself in stridently archaic imagery. To accept this version at face value, however, is to seriously underestimate its capacity. Wal-Mart and its host culture indeed embody many paradoxes, but they do not include fried chicken and terabytes.

The Ozarks: Wal-Mart Country

If nothing much springs to mind when you hear the term "Ozark Mountains," you are probably not a country music fan. The world's largest country attraction outside of Nashville is Branson, a Missouri Ozark town that caters to retirees looking for a good surf-and-turf combo and a mid-afternoon show by the Oak Ridge Boys. A spin through Branson will quickly alert you to a related Ozarks trait: the area's extraordinary ethnic homogeneity. Northwest Arkansas and southern Missouri have historically been among the whitest places in the country—over 95 percent white as late as 1996. The African American proportion of the population in Wal-Mart's Benton County has stayed under 1 percent since the close of the Civil War.[11] Moreover, the oldest waves of American immigration predominated—eighteenth-century English and Scotch-Irish, pre–Civil War Germans. Like much of the South's rural interior, the region remained virtually untouched by the southern and eastern European immigration waves of the late nineteenth and early twentieth centuries, the Catholics and Jews who made up the industrial workforce in the North.[12] In the wake of that immigration, during the high tide of American eugenicist sentiment, the Ozarks enjoyed a brief vogue as a reserve supply of "old-stock Anglo-Saxons" who needed only to be taken off ice to reinvigorate the nation with traditional republican virtues of thrift, self-sufficiency, hard work, and quaint Elizabethan speech patterns.[13]

Like the Appalachian counties farther east, Wal-Mart's Ozark homeland avoided the pathologies of widespread tenancy and monocropping that characterized the South's old plantation zones. On the better lands, a diversified farm economy built around grain, fruit, and livestock obviated the need for extensive holdings and massive labor reserves that commodity row crops demanded: family labor and modest capital could suffice to coax a stable living out of a 125-acre farm.[14] But the success of this economy depended on the constant out-migration of surplus adults and the low consumption levels of those who remained behind: measured in access to electric power, farm machinery, running water, phone service, or automobiles, the Ozarks in 1930 ranked at the bottom of America's consumer hierarchy.[15]

The penetration of railroads in the 1870s meanwhile began a long process of transforming the mountains: the unlovely economic bases of lead mining and timber clearcutting denuded hills and removed the forest game reserves that had supplemented small-scale farming on thin soil. Pell-mell extraction produced a " 'quick-rich, long-poor' " pattern of underdevelopment, and the families on marginal farms became a reliable source of part-time labor in their struggle for solvency.[16] This one-foot-on-the-farm strategy had proved its utility in many previous settings where labor-intensive innovations sought a toehold: the earliest textile mills in the United States explicitly targeted the unmarried daughters of New England farmers. Twentieth-century boosters of the New South likewise assured restless northern industries that low wages suited their citizens just fine, since the family collard patch could make up the difference.[17]

Ozarkers stood outside the major currents of international migration until very recently, but they played a major role in circulating domestic migrants. Route 66, the storied highway that carried "Okies" and "Arkies" into the San Joaquin Valley, passes right through Wal-Mart country.[18] Though the area earned its reputation by flushing landlocked white folks downstream toward the Golden State, the Ozarks also diverted the stream inward to its own counties. While the "sick old people from Iowa" poured into 1920s Los Angeles, the Ozarks of the same era attracted hardier midwestern "city clerks and tradesmen" who had wearied of "the precariousness and routine" of indoor occupations. Many of these migrants responded to romantic promotional brochures that touted the restorative virtues of the self-sufficient rural idyll. Marshalling their life savings, these enervated desk sitters bought marginal land sight unseen, then went bust trying to plant apple trees in chert.[19]

But there was more to the Ozarks' appeal than just slick PR. The midwesterners responded to the powerful pull of the independent farm at a time when the perils of large-scale bureaucratic enterprises were all too apparent. In a 1934 travel article, celebrated muralist Thomas Hart Benton christened the area "America's Yesterday." With the country's today grim and its tomorrow uncertain, this paean to a preindustrial, pre-urban, pre-immigrant America located our collective past in a decreasingly representative white rural enclave. If the Ozarks sheltered "the very last of our fathers' America," then our fathers must all be Scotch-Irish farmers—not slaves, not immigrants, and not factory hands.[20]

World War II put an end to the dream of small farm independence for all but the most ideologically committed. Pricey new chemical, mechanical, and biological inputs—herbicides, automatic tomato pickers, hybrid corn—took up the temporary slack in the labor market and made farming so capital-intensive that only increased acreage could support the great leap forward in mechanized production.[21] But for those who did not need to wrest a living out of their acreage, farming could still serve as an attractive "lifestyle choice," especially now that it came equipped with flush toilets. Thus by the 1960s the Ozarks had become one of the country's few four-season retirement destinations, a back-to-the-land Florida without the bikinis. Retirement communities fueled the area's staggering 81 percent population increase between 1960 and 1998, and its oldest resort town, Bella Vista, Arkansas, served as something of a national prototype for this new industry.[22] Weary midwesterners forwarded their Social Security checks to their new addresses near the region's artificial lakes, courtesy of the Army Corps of Engineers.

These migrations to Wal-Mart country drew people who disrupted some local patterns and exaggerated others, but who at least could plausibly imagine the Ozarks as their yesterday. The first serious crack in the region's monochromatic demographics came only very recently. Between 1990 and 2000, the two-county heart of Northwest Arkansas saw an almost tenfold increase in Mexican and Central American immigrants attracted by the boomtown construction pattern and the ubiquitous poultry-processing plants.[23] The plants are only the most visible tip of an agribusiness revolution uniquely suited to the area's small-farm allegiances: contract chicken growing. In this system of mass protein production, farmers receive tens of thousands of day-old chicks, raise them in a computer-controlled climate according to a rigidly standardized schedule, and then return the broilers and fryers to Tyson Foods for processing by Spanish-speaking immigrants—a kind of factory farming for the outsourced era. As one such grower put it, "This isn't farming. It's going to a job in your back yard."[24]

Contract farming nevertheless testifies to the enduring appeal of the landowning dream. In the Ozarks, far from both plantations and steel mills, the vision of independent country living remained a plausible goal for native-born whites in the twentieth century. The economic substance may have drained from the farm, but at least the form remained, and the money would have to come from waiting tables during the high season in Branson or hauling chicken nuggets to California. Low consumption, constant movement, and a long commute to off-farm waged labor were the price you paid to live in the country and work anywhere but a factory.

What's the Matter with Arkansas? Antimonopolism in Wal-Mart Country

Potential obstacles to Wal-Mart's success may suggest themselves in this quick sketch of Wal-Mart country, but we do not need to deduce them on our own. The area's inhabitants made their objections explicit in the regional tradition of antimonopolism. At the turn of the twentieth century, large-scale enterprises like Wal-Mart scored abysmally low marks in its future territory's estimation of social worth. Upland Arkansas, southwest Missouri, and the eastern sections of Oklahoma, Kansas, and Texas all hosted the nation's most vigorous popular protests against huge economic "combinations." The strikes and rebellions of 1886 that posed the nation's greatest collective challenge to industrial capitalism spread out of Sedalia, Missouri, future home of an early Wal-Mart.[25] The People's Party likewise grew up in the giant retailer's backyard. From towns like Searcy, Arkansas, and Cleburne, Texas—future sites of Wal-Mart's automated distribution centers—Populists demanded a variety of government mechanisms to prevent the growth of corporations and trusts.[26]

While the central hero in this struggle was the farmer, the small country merchant enjoyed a brief but dramatic moment as the emblem of rural virtue. The vehicle for his symbolic career was the anti–chain store movement of the 1920s and 1930s. The movement provoked a policy battle that claimed headlines around the country and ultimately spawned New Deal legislation that could have ended Wal-Mart's career before it even began.[27]

Understanding the anti–chain store movement as anything but an outbreak of protectionist crankery requires grounding it in the antimonopolist tradition. Its ideological origins lie in the nineteenth-century Populist critique of the new industrial economy. Well into the nineteenth century corporate charters remained a privilege rather than a right: the limited liability and diffusion of ownership they represented could claim legal protection only insofar as they served the public interest. But as mass production demanded increasingly vast organizations of capital and management in the 1880s and 1890s, the Supreme Court vested corporations with legal personhood under the Constitution and established a new category of protected property in the form of expected return on investment. The corporation entered the twentieth century as an immortal supercitizen.[28]

This cataclysmic reorganization did not proceed unopposed. Though rural Americans had never dwelt in an Eden of subsistence farming, the world of commercial agriculture at least retained an aura of noble Jeffersonian independence—all the more so as the seemingly endless supply of "vacant" land abruptly ran out in 1890 and the nation's population tipped from rural to urban. The successive waves of agrarian revolt that swept the South and West ever more sharply identified the industrial "combinations" as illegitimate actors, expressing a general distrust of distant corporations in the folk idiom of economic evil: malevolent international cabals, adulterated money, shady dealings. Congressional hearings and muckraking journalists regularly demonstrated that such charges often had a depressing basis in fact, but at the end of the day even the most rigidly law-abiding corporation could eat a Jeffersonian yeoman for lunch. A cooperative of indebted farmers could not match the capital-generating capacity of a publicly traded company.

Yet antimonopolism did not expire on the marginal back forties around Cleburne and Searcy. Though their electoral victories in local and state elections were short-lived and ultimately overshadowed by their defeat in the presidential campaign of 1896, the Populists endowed much of subsequent Progressive-era policy with their agenda. Professional economists might have been extolling the virtues of big industry, but legislators and congressmen were dancing to the farmers' tune. In the compromised versions of the antitrust acts, the agrarians' antipathy became national law just in time for the production demands of World War I to legitimate massive corporations in fact if not in principle.[29]

Tolerating corporate industry as a necessary evil was nevertheless a far cry from accepting it as a positive good. Although the dynamo had its bards among both socialists and capitalists, the republican yeoman ideal was firmly enshrined in the national mythos. The early twentieth century saw intense concern with maintaining the countryside as a healthful wellspring of national virtue, endlessly resupplying cities with fresh-faced Anglo-Saxon plowmen and milkmaids. In good times and bad, the countryside retained an emotional claim upon the nation that the teeming industrial cities could not equal. In the various forms that the periphery's agrarian challenges took, the economic villains remained relatively stable: distant northeastern bankers and megacorporations with a stranglehold over the country's credit and distribution systems. The challengers saw their cause not as impinging on a competitive free market but in fact as preserving competition by denying the combinations their unfair economies of scale. In a society of self-identified producers, this logic commanded wide loyalty.

Small country merchants walked a fine line in this cosmology. While early Farmers' Alliances classed them among the producers, their relationship to monopoly distribution could tip them into the villain's role in agrarian morality tales.[30] Moreover, until the Federal Reserve system and the Farm Loan Act ushered in a liberalization of credit in the 1910s and 1920s, rural merchants often doubled as informal banks, a position ripe for abuse among the South's many innumerate sharecroppers.[31] Looking back on the career of the small-business stratum from the vantage point of 1951, C. Wright Mills pointed out that while farmers' moral authority had produced the federal giveaway of land through the Homestead Act, Congress had never undertaken national regeneration through the distribution of small retail stores.[32] Thus the small merchants' bid for yeoman status was in part a conscious appropriation of their farmer customers' own sterling reputation. In the century's early decades, after all, even giant monopolies strove to clothe themselves in the mantle of rural producerist virtue and put a human face on their superhuman economic organization. To hitch their star successfully to the farmer's wagon, the anti–chain store activists had to convince a broader base than merely the movement's immediate beneficiaries. Their success in winning support—particularly in what later became Wal-Mart country—illuminates an important chapter in that company's prehistory.[33]

The Chain Menace

Seen in the *longue durée* of American economic history, the fact that requires explanation is not the coming of chain stores but rather the persistence of small shops into the twentieth century. Like the family farm, the corner store was already a visible throwback to observers in the 1920s. Since the advent of widespread railroad and telegraph access in the nineteenth century, the trend in distribution had moved steadily toward greater efficiency, standardization, and central control. Inevitably, efficiency meant compressing various points in the distribution chain. First wholesalers and their representatives displaced innumerable small peddlers, then after the 1870s themselves felt the pressure of mass retailers large enough to deal directly with manufacturers. Depending on where you stood in this process, the charge of monopolism and unfair dealing sounded salient at different historical moments.

The urban department stores, the first mass retailers of any influence, faced cries of foul play from their small, single-line competitors in industrial cities of the Gilded Age. Reeling from the cataclysmic depression of 1893, Chicago's small merchants used their influence in the city council to fight giants like Marshall Field's, but like their counterparts in New York and Massachusetts, they ultimately failed to carry their argument in state legislatures. Wal-Mart country played little part in this first debate over centralized distribution, since the department stores were confined to larger cities. A decade later the mail-order companies challenged southern and midwestern country stores. Despite fierce nationwide opposition from rural shopkeepers and wholesalers, the catalogs' future was assured with the congressional approval in 1912 of extended parcel post service, by which taxpayers underwrote rural consumption.[34]

The anti–chain store movement of the late 1920s and early 1930s offered vigorous and, for a time, effective resistance, dwarfing all previous attempts to arrest mass distribution. And while today the opposition to Wal-Mart comes from "blue" stalwarts, in this earlier battle the positions were reversed. Wal-Mart's unique contribution to post-Fordism rests on this genuine paradox.

Attack of the Independents

In 1929, the year of the Crash, the antichain movement could claim over four hundred local organizations, with dozens of issue-specific newspapers and radio stations as well as traveling lecturers in the pattern of the Farmers' Alliance—or, more ominously, on the subscription plan of the revived Ku Klux Klan.[35] A poll from 1936 found that 69 percent of the public had a negative impression of chains, with the highest proportion of ire in the South and Midwest. The "chain store menace," marveled *The Nation,* was "the question most talked of below the Ohio."[36] Between 1925 and 1937, 916 antichain bills were introduced in state legislatures, and fully 50 became law. After this outcry produced two separate high-profile federal investigations of chain practices, congressmen from Arkansas and Texas sponsored the federal antichain bills that passed in 1936 and 1937. An additional bill that would have essentially taxed large chain operations out of existence—called by its supporters the "community preservation bill" and by its detractors the "death sentence bill"—came close to passing several times before falling victim to wartime changes.[37]

Much of the organized opposition to chains came, unsurprisingly, from small merchants themselves, but what is striking about the movement of the early Depression years is how much public support it garnered in other quarters as well. Though the agitation predated the Crash, the economic calamity that followed focused hostile attention on the machinations of big business of all stripes, granting a second wind to the previous generation's antimonopolism. The small merchants' hostility, like that of the farmers themselves, rested on a specific vernacular definition of monopoly. Small-scale commercial growers insisted that their family farms merited public protection against the predatory efficiencies of the factory farm, regardless of the effects on consumers' food bills; the independent merchants likewise drew the focus away from consumer choice and substituted the suite of symbols bequeathed to them by the nineteenth-century fight against railroads.[38] In the long run, this fundamental conflict of interests between low-budget shoppers and small-scale retailers was resolved in favor of the former; but with the citizen not yet fully transmogrified into a consumer first and foremost, the question could remain in debate for most of the decade.[39]

Just as the small retailers' case was made by many outside their ranks, so the chains could call on allies from the rational champions of progress. *The Nation* magazine announced in 1930 that "a new battle on evolution is raging in the South" in which the small merchant represented the "fundamentalist position" against the chains, exemplars of "modernism."[40] Reason was clearly on the side of the latter, in *The Nation's* opinion, and small-town shopkeepers needed to come to grips with their own extinction: "In the age of greatest efficiency there must be three classes of people, the consumer, the producer, and a minimum number of citizens involved in distribution."[41] Certainly there might be some problems along the way, *The Nation* conceded, but the market would handle those: "The wages in chain stores for employees other than managers are inadequate and will eventually be raised. The chains will realize that it is to their own advantage to pay their labor well."[42]

The choice of metaphor—evolution versus fundamentalism—serves as a timely reminder that the progressive opinion makers were quick to see slack-jawed backwardness in arguments that today sound downright radical. Writing of the literal antievolutionary sentiment of the early twentieth century, historian Ed Larson points out that theories of natural selection were widely used to justify "laissez-faire capitalism, imperialism, and militarism." Eugenicists were proud to claim Darwinian theory, the fundamentalist position, by contrast, defended the weak and the economically superfluous that rational science would render obsolete. The textbook at stake in the 1925 Scopes "Monkey Trial," *Civic Biology,* calmly pointed out that if the retarded, the insane, the criminal, and the epileptic members of the human family were animals, "we would probably kill them off to prevent them from spreading."[43] Similarly, the small-town independents were expected to understand that their continued existence represented a drag on the natural economic order, and if a few eggs got broken on the way to maximum efficiency, so be it. They could always get a job at the A & P.

And when many of them did, they had a good chance of being represented by a union. Among the major opponents of the federal antichain "death sentence" bill were the two unions representing retail stores. Patrick Gorman, president of the Amalgamated Meat Cutters and Butcher Workmen, convinced the American Federation of Labor to come out against the bill in 1939 by pointing out that "in the southern states . . . for years we failed to organize the smaller grocery men and meat market men. In the South they chased us out of their stores." But now A & P had signed contracts in over a dozen southern cities—more proof that chain executives could be counted on to see reason.[44]

In contrast to this enthusiastic support, the heart of the antichain critique comprised two cherished Populist tropes. One axis of argument grouped various suspicions of "foreign"-owned big business generally, with "foreign" implying not international but simply distant and unfamiliar. While the idiom could easily slide into paranoid anti-Semitism and racism, the distrust was often honestly come by. The sections of the country that opposed chains most vociferously had suffered at the hands of northern railroads, eastern banks, and industrial monopolies that demonstrably extracted wealth in a semicolonial relationship with the hinterlands.[45] "I don't want to be bolshevistic," wrote one Texan in support of Depression-era antichain legislation, but "it certainly is no permanent relief or progress for the government to create temporary jobs and distribute money and in a few days it all wind up in Chicago or New York City in the hands of a few extremely wealthy men, owners of the chains and utilities."[46] The leading congressional champion of the independents pointed out that while 200 companies controlled more than half the country's corporate wealth, fully 180 of them were located in the North, leaving only 11 in the West and a mere 9 in the South: "How a true Texan can favor ownership and control of local business by Wall Streeters, I cannot understand."[47] Members of the Ku Klux Klan in Clarke County, Georgia, railed against the chain owners as a "Little Group of Kings in Wall Street" and warned that Jewish and Catholic immigrants were using the chain to pauperize native-born white Protestants.[48] Employing a familiar metaphor for rural Protestants, a 1937 ancestor of the *Left Behind* books cast chain stores as evidence of the imminent Apocalypse.[49]

The suspicion of distant "foreigners" was echoed in charges of shady business practices: mere efficiencies of scale were not thought sufficient to produce the price differentials between chains and the "independents," as the owner-operated stores tellingly dubbed themselves. Such savings must come either from sly, thumb-on-the-scale tricks of the constantly relocated "gypsy" chain managers, or from the kind of illegal collusion that had brought on the original antitrust legislation at the turn of the century. Referring to the evidence of volume discounts publicized by a Federal Trade Commission inquiry into the A & P chain, a wholesaler made the connection explicit: "Some years back the railroads indulged in this practice, making secret concessions to the larger shippers, giving them an advantage over the average man. . . . ANY CONCERN LARGE AND POWERFUL ENOUGH TO EXACT CONCESSIONS

THAT CANNOT BE EXTENDED TO EVERYONE HAS NO RIGHT TO EXISTENCE."[50]

The other polestar of antichain agitation likewise derived from the symbolic power of yeoman independence. The original political virtue of the landowning head of household lay in his literal self-possession: he could participate in the public sphere because he called no man master. The implicit corollary to his independence was the legal *dependence* of the other members of his household: women, children, and in various times and places, servants, tenants, or slaves. By the 1920s, with independent farming a distinctly minority occupation in the United States, the independence could adhere in other forms of proprietorship, provided the illusion of self-command remained. Thus the chains, owned by stockholders and managed "scientifically" according to the standardized principles of Taylorism, raised the specter of "a nation of clerks." The least industrialized sections of the country might see their sons fall prey to the same dehumanizing factory discipline as the immigrant masses of the North and East, working for the Man rather than epitomizing him.

Thus a generation before the man in the gray flannel suit offered a bogey of the standardized postwar salary man, middle-class Americans could gaze with horror on the specter of the permanent retail clerk. This man-boy would be relegated to the lifelong status of a "helper," classed by one outraged observer alongside such effeminate professionals as typists, stenographers, and secretaries. Chain-store employment could potentially strip him of political manhood in the form of the franchise, through constant mobility that prevented registering to vote. Even his physical masculinity could fall victim to the chains' downward pressure on wages, for he could not earn enough "to marry and have a wife and children, and thus must miss ninety-nine percent of nature's program of life."[51]

The economic logic of mass distribution demanded that many nineteen-year-old clerks would stay in that lowly condition throughout their productive years, never becoming the pop of a mom-and-pop. "[Chains] stifle opportunity for local boys," charged a proponent of chain taxes in the classic middlebrow organ, the *Reader's Digest*. "Their clerks stay clerks. . . . [A chain] doesn't want bright boys—it wants plodders, dutiful machines."[52] Klansmen warned that chain monopolies, by shutting out the option of small-business ownership, were enslaving American children and turning young men into "automatons."[53] An Arkansan wrote his senator, "Do you really believe rugged individualism can be revived without legislation to destroy the 'Octopus' movement" of chain retailers?[54] Decked out in an apron, subjected to time-and-motion studies, trapped behind the produce counter of the Piggly Wiggly—the sturdy yeoman was indeed imperiled.

Wal-Mart, an economic colossus exemplifying unprecedented industry domination, thus arose in the heartland of fiery antimonopolism; from the massive railroad strikes of the Gilded Age, through Populism and the chain-store battles of the Second New Deal, the Southwest cast its lot with the ideal of small-scale agrarian independence. In order to make its home in the old Populist countryside, Wal-Mart had to overcome the twin objections to chain distribution: its remote, faceless ownership and its threat to white rural manhood. In successfully meeting these challenges, Wal-Mart shaped the Sunbelt service sector and claimed Henry Ford's national mantle.

The Boss as Everyman

The American hinterlands had long personalized their resentment against the megacorporations as hostility to the individual robber barons of the Northeast. To rid the corporate structure of its conspiratorial associations, the Sunbelt needed to put a different human face on the company. In the Sunbelt's boom years, Northwest Arkansas produced many examples of the boss as Everyman, the multibillionaire captain of his industry who made a point of wearing his egalitarianism on his sleeve. Conspicuous underconsumption marked the rise of Ozark chicken king John Tyson, whose son and grandson dressed in the khaki uniforms of their employees. The region's mighty trucking empires were founded by men in overalls with grade-school educations. These successful Ozarkers pointedly declined to acquire trophy wives as their fortunes grew, and instead publicly credited their original spouses as full partners in the family business. This was often no more than the literal truth: Mrs. Helen Walton's family money, for example, bankrolled the original discount stores, and her degree in economics was a solid asset in all the Waltons' enterprises. As urban, coastal America came to look less and less like Northwest Arkansas, these entrepreneurial titans insisted ever more firmly on their Ozark identities. In the local phrase, they never forgot what they came from.

This populist stance went a long way toward humanizing some of the world's biggest corporate fortunes. During the heyday of the Fordist economy, auto companies poured vast resources into the fledgling PR field in an effort to make a gigantic corporation into "something personal, warm, and human"; advertising strove to convert AT&T into a "friend and neighbor" or the GM headquarters into "the family home."[55] In contrast, the down-to-earth Mr. Sam was himself an ad for Wal-Mart, not least of all in the financial markets. Wal-Mart wooed stockholders and analysts with home-style barbecues, canoe trips, and bus tours of the stores. Warren Buffett promoted Wal-Mart stock early and often, in his Reagan-era role as the wholesome old-stock Nebraska populist to Michael Milken's corrupt urban insider.[56] Little Rock's Stephens Inc., the largest investment bank outside of Wall Street and an IPO underwriter for all four major Ozark firms,

Making a sale, Lake Dick, Arkansas, 1938. Photograph by Russell Lee.

FARM SECURITY ADMINISTRATION/OFFICE OF WAR INFORMATION, LIBRARY OF CONGRESS stressed its own farm-boy roots and Arkansas loyalties. Rather less was said of its original business in speculating in guaranteed municipal bonds during the Depression.[57] At least these fortunes were not running off to build libraries in Pittsburgh or business schools in Boston. They stayed within sight of the old home place.

As with so many Sunbelt success stories, these resolutely humble men could represent their companies in part because they initially headed entrepreneurial rather than corporate empires. With their family members, they owned and controlled the businesses in lieu of stockholders and salaried managers. Walton took pains to describe the decision making of Walton Enterprises as a family gathering, evoking an idealized kitchen table to Americans who increasingly dined alone at the drive-through window: "Sometimes we argue and sometimes we don't," he wrote, but decisions were made in the private sphere. Moreover, since "everybody gets the same" share, economic justice was achieved in one family.[58] Likewise, Walton's aversion to publicity for the company was figured as resenting an intrusion into the family's private business; ExxonMobil would have had a hard time making the same argument. As the visible creations of individual families, the Ozark companies remained plausible carriers of the myth of the independent producer. Each firm wore a family surname proudly: no "General" this or "International" that for Tyson Foods, Jones Truck Lines, or Walton's Family Centers.[59]

Founding Father

While the entrepreneurial pattern of "local boy made good" went far to answering one populist critique, it actually fit the other Ozark magnates much better than it did Mr. Sam.[60] The Walton family history exemplified the Southwest's growth pattern, in which government largesse turned into individual virtue by the addition of sweat equity. Walton's father and grandfather served as postmasters, a form of federal patronage that provided a steady if hardly munificent wage amid the vagaries of farming. His uncle staked out a free land grant when the federal government drove Indian owners out of Oklahoma and made white settlers a gift of the territory. Homesteading, the federal subsidizing of the yeoman ideal, laid the basis for what was to prove a much longer-lived wealth engine in the future Sunbelt: not small-scale farming but land speculation. Two generations of Waltons profited from the loans and mortgages that underwrote land booms, taking time out to farm only when World War I guaranteed a government market for their crops at peak prices.[61] For their part, the Waltons worked hard with the capital their government furnished and became legendary for thrift: "He could squeeze a Lincoln until the president cried," exclaimed one longtime employee of Sam's father.[62] The family inspired more respect than affection, driving relentless deals, yet never crossing the line into dishonesty. And while their living was more comfortable than most, it was hardly extravagant.

Walton's biography of finance, inherited security, and public inputs is hardly the stuff of a convincing Horatio Alger tale. Clearly the Walton past would have to change to meet the needs of the present. A host of mythologizers relentlessly forced Walton's personal history into the threadbare rags-to-riches plot line. Typically a "family tradition of hard work and thrift" stands in for actual material hardship.[63] The national economic disaster of the Depression and the regional one of the Dust Bowl are elided into Walton's personal biography. "While still a child, Walton moved with his family from one town to another in Missouri, where he observed Dust Bowl farms. He promised himself he would never be poor."[64] Though his father was in fact repossessing those farms for the family mortgage company, Walton's childhood somehow converges with that of the busted farmer, not the moneylender. "It pained Thomas Walton [Sam's father] to have to take a man's land from him when the crop failed to come in," one hagiographer hazarded, though "these defaults added up to thousands of acres of land under the Walton name."[65] In 1989, when Walton's judicious division of $7.2 billion among his four children dropped him from number one to number twenty on the annual *Forbes* list of the four hundred richest Americans, fully 40 percent of his fellow superrich had inherited their money. A billionaire with a job helped maintain the legitimacy of the entire category.[66]

Since Mr. Walton's passing in 1992, when both presidential candidates paused to offer tribute, Wal-Mart has made a conscious policy of reinforcing its identification of founder with company. Banners in the company auditorium repeat the sayings of Chairman Sam. His handsome visage smiles gravely down from the walls, and clips of his firsthand advice are played for employees and stockholders alike. Former employees speak of him with unfeigned warmth, and even union-minded workers argue their case as an attempt to "restore the respect for the employees that was Mr. Sam's vision."[67]

The streak of fond paternalism is not confined to company insiders. Elsewhere, the family analogy successfully replaced the managerial one. Walton's best-selling 1992 "autobiography" debuted to a million-dollar Father's Day promotional campaign with life-sized Sam Walton cutouts, patriotic window dressings, and radio ads during *Country Countdown*.[68] The 1995 novel *Where the Heart Is*—an Oprah's Book Club selection and later a successful movie—features seventeen-year-old Novalee Nation, pregnant, deserted, and broke, who makes her home in an Oklahoma Wal-Mart. She lives there clandestinely for two months, keeping a careful log of what she owes Wal-Mart for the canned goods and toiletries she uses, and dramatically gives birth to "Americus Nation" in the store. Sam Walton subsequently visits the madonna and child in the hospital, and in the absence of the baby's father, he ensures their economic future. Explaining that the publicity has been good for the company, Walton absolves the single mother of her consumer debt and promises her a job in the Wal-Mart itself once she recovers.[69]

Not many of the superrich would be welcome at a young mother's bedside, but Walton was "no Donald Trump," an *Arkansas Gazette* reviewer pointed out in 1990.[70] "A billionaire everyone can love" declared *USA Today*.[71] "A televised version of Walton's life would resemble the 'Andy Griffith Show,' not 'Dallas.' "[72] Tourists on their way to Branson make a pilgrimage to the Wal-Mart Visitors' Center, the exquisitely restored five-and-dime that Walton operated on the Bentonville Square in the 1950s. Many become visibly emotional at the sight of Walton's 1979 Ford pickup. Reports one of the center's longtime docents, " 'The comment I hear most is 'Oh, I wish I could have met Mr. Walton.' "[73] Eat your heart out, Bill Gates.

The identification of Wal-Mart with Sam Walton allowed his personal reputation to stand in for the company's. Walton very publicly cultivated company policies that stressed transparent procedural ethics. Wal-Mart's buyers could not accept so much as a paper clip from a manufacturer's representative. In the waiting room at the Bentonville headquarters, visitors and employees alike can help themselves to a cup of diner coffee, but they are expected to insert 15¢ in a box to pay for it. Rather than install a coin-operated dispenser, the company makes its point by charging on the honor system. In expressing their distrust of an economic *structure*—monopoly corporate distribution—the prewar critics of chains had used the idiom of conspiracy: "sharp dealers" who struck backroom bargains in the shadows of skyscrapers. The postwar solution was a sober, thrifty, churchgoing Anglo-Saxon, the ideal patriarch of our fathers' America.

Redeeming a Nation of Clerks

But what of the other populist nightmare, the impotent, servile clerk?

From the earliest days of the chain menace, some independent merchants had sought to join the chain rationalization of storekeeping rather than beat it. Indeed, A & P's fifteen thousand–plus stores began as a single tea shop in New York, Woolworth in a five-hundred-square-foot vacancy in Lancaster, Pennsylvania.[74] Only a few early, well-capitalized innovators could surf the wave of the retail revolution, however; for the rest, the path to strength in numbers lay in banding together. Their solutions echoed earlier attempts to meet big distribution with self-organization. Nineteenth-century farmers had organized rural cooperatives, some of them explicitly socialist, to bypass the parasitical merchants. By the 1920s, the impulse had moved further down the distribution chain. Organizations like the Independent Retail Grocers Association and the Rexall Drug network joined together multiple small stores to bargain with wholesalers for the same volume discounts and advertising budgets as chains; even some cooperatives gave up the nonprofit fight and affiliated with these "voluntary chains."[75]

Wal-Mart's own direct ancestor, Butler Brothers, followed a related path. Having grown from a Boston dry goods store into one of Chicago's dominant wholesalers of general merchandise for the central and western states, Butler Brothers joined an increasing number of wholesalers who operated retail franchises to compete with variety chains. To the prospective franchisees, the firm offered management services that mirrored the chains' own central planning: a location bureau to scout out likely store sites; start-up loans to outfit the new store; circuit-riding "experts" to advise the merchant on every detail of operation from window dressing to bookkeeping. Butler's massive Chicago warehouse even housed a model store on its thirteenth floor, which its retailers could visit for an object lesson in modern, chain-style presentation.[76] These innovations built upon the "Success in Retailing" guides the firm had long published for their customers, making the element of control more concrete.[77]

Whether the voluntary associations stretched up from existing retailers into the wholesaling function or down from established wholesalers into stores, however, the catch was the same. The price of survival was submission to chain managerial practices. The proprietor's independence gave way incrementally to distant, salaried experts who monitored every detail of his operation and even provided the start-up loans to enter the business. The distinctions between working *for* a chain and working *like* one became harder to discern, narrowing to the point of a vague gesture of respect for the franchisee's self-mastery. "Each Ben Franklin store owner is given advice, help, suggestions and service from Butler Brothers," ran one labored argument from 1957, "but still each owner is free to carry out his own individual ideas and store policies, as long as they do not violently disagree with the Ben Franklin policies or standards. . . . Dealing with each voluntary chain member as a separate store owner with ideas and a mind of his own is a far cry from that of a national chain where power of control is absolute."[78] In a move familiar to Cold War logic, the authoritarian regime prospered by contrast to the totalitarian one.

Even this soft regimentation irked Ben Franklin's largest franchisee, Sam Walton,

Springdale, Arkansas, Wal-Mart in the 1970s, probably just before Halloween. Note the clutter and the manual electric cash registers.

who with his brother James ("Bud") had built up sixteen of the stores in small towns around the Ozarks.[79] Walton, a talented and experienced merchant with a degree in business, flouted many of the Butler Brothers rules designed to ease the entry of new shopkeepers into the field. The break between them came when Butler Brothers resisted the postwar discount store, a new format that relied on high turnover and low overhead to offer national brands at cut rates. The company's resistance was hardly surprising, given its fundamental identity as a wholesaler. Butler Brothers refused to finance Walton's discount experiment. Instead, using his wife's family land and her trust fund as collateral, he borrowed enough money from a Texas bank to open the first discount store himself.[80] To duplicate its success, Walton would have to employ the dreaded nation of clerks.

During the Depression, the New Deal's economic administrators had referred to the independents as the "Mama, Papa, and Rosy stores."[81] The owner, in other words, managed the labor of his female dependents. This model in turn grew out of traditional agrarian economies, in which the household was the productive unit and its male head legally owned the labor of all its members. The uneven advance of women's legal rights to their own earnings left the home-based business in limbo. Generating income in a family enterprise was akin to domestic service, which the law still assumed a woman owed her husband.[82] In a mom-and-pop store, Pop was management, Mom was labor. And when the chain removed ownership, it substituted and exaggerated this psychological wage of male mastery.

The industrial management model traced its ancestry back to the nineteenth-century military innovations that coordinated and supplied mass mobilization, with a correspondingly male command hierarchy. But the decentralized service sector provided a different structure: hundreds of widely scattered male managers supervising women and young men. Rather than taking orders from machines, like the deskilled factory operatives, or from other men, like the "generation of bureaucrats" that so alarmed commentators in the fifties, these men gave the orders. A Wal-Mart store replicated not a Prussian army division but a farmhouse: dozens of waged women in smocks, overseen by a salaried store manager in a tie. The men could hold the symbolic position of Papa while the women remained Rosy.

"Like a Family"

When many hourly veterans of Wal-Mart's early years speak of their working lives, one sentiment recurs with startling regularity: "I loved working at Wal-Mart," they say emphatically. "It was like a family."[83] This simile is not generic: pressed for examples, a woman might mention the personal support she received upon the death of a parent, or the constant round of break-room baby showers.[84] Children and husbands were such frequent visitors to the stores that everyone knew who went with whom; special events like in-store fashion shows or craft fairs pulled into service every family member old enough to walk. The company could win an employee's bedrock loyalty by accommodating her hours to her children's school day—a perk few parents would take for granted in any field. In the context of small towns, extended families, and long-term marriages, women compared Wal-Mart's stable, sociable hourly jobs to the lonely monotony of ironing or chicken processing, not to the brutal schedules and constant mobility of Wal-Mart's well-compensated male managers. And while it took a federal court battle to force Walton to pay even minimum wage to his stores' staff in the Ben Franklin days, many employees from Wal-Mart's biggest growth years found the pay competitive if not munificent. Moreover, the constant stock splits rewarded the same stability that they valued themselves.[85] Raised on farms that were rapidly losing their viability, many women of Wal-Mart saw the company's terms as a reasonable bargain that allowed them to stay close to home and accorded with their own essential conceptions of their responsibilities.

But to treat the enthusiasm for a familial workplace as a purely economic choice among limited options is to miss the power of Wal-Mart culture. Despite free-market neoliberalism's infatuation with *homo economicus,* this autistic rational actor would be turned down cold for a job as a Wal-Mart greeter. A service economy patterned on a pastoral family is not supposed to make sense in the arid pseudoscientific fantasies of economics, in which every human being is imagined as a profit-maximizing, rights-bearing isolate.[86] Rather, the agrarian model resonates with an entire worldview that figures the family as the divinely sanctioned plan for any human structure—the church, the nation, the law.[87] When Wal-Mart CEO Lee Scott defends the company's low wages by asserting that few employees are trying to support a family on them, he admits what many of his critics themselves have argued: outside of the desert island that neoliberal economics assumes, we all conduct our survival strategies within a web of human relations.[88] If for many the ideal unit of analysis is the family, figured as an intrinsic whole made up of complementary differences, then paradoxically the champions of communitarian social policy wound up arguing for the lonely, isolated, self-interested individual. No wonder their message often fell on skeptical ears.[89]

Thus with managerial authority naturalized as a gender trait, the paradigmatic company of the service economy sidestepped labor conflict. Many women experienced important elements of their work as caregiving, a valued if underpaid skill within the family ideal, and the manager's substantial salary mirrored the domestic arrangement.[90] Nowhere was this conflation of management functions and adult masculinity more obvious than in the occasional moments of ritualized inversion—the store turned upside down for "Ladies' Day." As celebrated in the Elton, Missouri, Wal-Mart in 1975, Ladies' Day featured elections among the hourly employees for the women in their ranks to assume the positions of store managers and assistant managers.

> The first business of the day was coffee made by Jesse Lutz, in place of the ladies. . . . The regular Friday morning meeting was conducted by Karen and her [elected] assistants . . . for one day the ladies were to be addressed as Mrs. or Ms. . . . Windows were washed by Jerry Pate, Assistant Manager, and the refrigerator was defrosted and destroyed by Ray Olive, another Assistant Manager. . . . Approximately 25 red light specials were conducted by Mr. Olive and Mr. Lutz. They also, complete with smocks, ran the cash registers when business increased. . . . Thanks to the co-operation and sportsmanship from the men at No. 44, Ladies day was a huge success![91]

On other special occasions the shared common sense of gender difference was reinforced with exaggerated symbols of rural patriarchal authority. Men found an extraordinary array of costumes that allowed them to arm themselves with dummy weapons from cowboy pistols to SWAT automatic assault rifles. Hardly a month passed without the display of a trophy deer, a birthday shotgun, or a champion bass. Rather than feminizing the nation of clerks, Wal-Mart provided a stage on which to perform the contrast between men and women.

The current class-action lawsuit charging pervasive gender discrimination at Wal-

Mart focuses on the company's record in the past five years. But using data going back to 1975, one of the plaintiff's experts concludes that, at the end of the twentieth century, Wal-Mart store management remained more overwhelmingly male than its competitors a quarter century before. "Such long-term persistence," wrote economist Marc Bendick, "is further evidence that the shortfall in female employment observed in 1999 reflects attitudes and practices deeply embedded in the organization's corporate culture."[92] A lawyer concurred: "Wal-Mart is living in the America of thirty years ago."[93]

Or is it thirty years ahead of the curve instead? Wal-Mart is not a throwback, dragging its feet on an inevitable modern road to a sex-neutral economy. To the contrary: seen in a broader context, the North Atlantic's brief experiment with stable, high-wage industry and rights-based culture was the exception, whose future remains uncertain at best. Thirty years ago, the economic hybrids that had grown up in Fordism's shadow began to flourish in the full sunlight of deindustrialization. The unwaged household labor and part-time work that supported the American breadwinner ideal came out from the shadows, and the rural families of the South and West entered the new economy with a patriarchal cosmology ready. By adapting the management/labor dyad to a "natural" male/female hierarchy, Wal-Mart simply performed another of the Sunbelt's classic sleights of hand. Like postwar evangelicalism, the country music industry, or the Republican Party's "Southern Strategy," the region's service sector spun traditional straw into radical new gold.

To meet the region's populist objections to corporate capitalism, Wal-Mart pioneered an economic breakthrough that Saskia Sassen argues undergirds globalization generally. Whereas historically the workers in the nation's leading economic sector—let alone its leading company—have constituted its natural "labor aristocracy," the Arkansas discount store broke this connection.[94] Today the patriarchal organization of work ranks as a hallmark of the global economy, from maquiladoras of young Honduran women embroidering swooshes on shoes to the immigrant-owned family motels and convenience stores that dot the United States. While snowbound capitalists and communists alike raised the assembly line to the status of cultural icon, the South was looking for the next new thing. Managers retooled their agrarian birthright as the symbolic heads of household, the Jeffersonian "masters of small worlds," and the Sunbelt service sector added one more brick to the edifice of the new world order.[95]

FOUR

Growth Through Knowledge: Wal-Mart, High Technology, and the Ever Less Visible Hand of the Manager

James Hoopes

Wal-Mart is one of the most highly disciplined firms in the history of business. To find another big company managed with so passionate a commitment to cost control it might be necessary to go back to the origins of the large business firm in nineteenth-century America. "Watch the costs," Andrew Carnegie is supposed to have said, "and the profits will take care of themselves." Nineteenth-century managers at the likes of Carnegie Steel, operating equipment of unprecedented capital intensity, focused relentlessly on control.

But in the early twentieth century cost control lost some of its favor as a managerial method. As large organizations took shape in less capital-intensive, more labor-intensive parts of the economy such as light assembly, the growing importance of what was called "the human element" made management seem more a matter of inspirational leadership and less a matter of control, at least among fashionable management gurus. (Fashion, of course, was one thing and factory reality another.)[1] Ever since, softer management styles emphasizing employee empowerment, participation, teamwork, and so forth have been comme il faut among management theorists.

Cultural and political values helped give currency to the twentieth-century preference for softer management styles. Bottom-up management offered a superficial similarity to the democratic values of American society and made corporate life easier on the consciences of both managers and employees than it might otherwise have been. The boss became the "leader," running the firm not through top-down dictatorship but by serving as a moral exemplar and leader who inspires others to work with a will. But as Wal-Mart shows, wishful thinking cannot change the reality that business corporations are ultimately top-down organizations, undemocratically managed by a powerful few for their own benefit as well as, in theory and not too infrequently in fact, the benefit of shareholders.

And then there are employees. On the whole, workers' economic well-being has been much improved by a century and a half of modern corporate life, but not in proportion to the benefits enjoyed by managers and owners. In recent years, the disparity has widened, with top management rewarding itself at a rate hundreds or even thousands of times that of the pay of frontline employees. The business corporation is becoming even more clearly what it has always been in American history: often useful to the many and extraordinarily good to the fortunate few. Like their historical predecessors, today's corporations simultaneously support and subvert democratic values. No contemporary company better illustrates the tension than Wal-Mart.

To understand Wal-Mart's place in the history of business it is useful to consider a subfield of economics called the theory of the firm. Theorists of the firm attempt to explain the seemingly incongruous existence of business firms in a free market. If the free market were always the most efficient way of organizing economic activity, there should be no firms, no managers, and no employees. In a perfectly free market, each of us should be self-employed free agents, maximizing our economic interests by buying and selling our autonomously produced goods and services. But in fact, relatively few of us work freely in the marketplace. Most of us are employees working under the control of large organizations, regardless of how successfully the managers of those organizations hide their undemocratic authority—often even from themselves—by minimizing overt displays of power.

What explains this contradiction between the theory of the free market and the reality of the unfree firm? The most widely accepted explanation for the existence of business firms in free markets is the concept of transaction costs introduced by the Nobel Prize–winning English economist Ronald Coase in his still influential 1937 essay, "The Nature of the Firm." Observing that there are costs associated with market transactions, Coase theorized that firms arise whenever managerial power inside an organization can produce and distribute goods and services at less cost than the market.

Coase quoted D.H. Robertson's characterization of firms as "islands of conscious power" which arise in an "ocean of unconscious co-operation like lumps of butter coagulating in a pail of buttermilk."[2] The milk is the market and the lumps of butter are companies. Where managerial authority inside an organization can achieve lower production and distribution costs than are attainable by transactional relations among autonomous individuals, the free market gives way to those "islands of conscious power" otherwise known as business firms.

Coase theorized that the size of the firm is naturally limited because just as market transactions have a cost, so does management. Small firms easily raise their profitability through growth, which spreads management and other costs across more units of product. But as the firm increases in size it also increases in complexity, creating more opportunity for managerial error. Every firm would therefore seem to have an optimal size beyond which the risk of loss from mismanagement more than offsets the chance of gain from economies of scale.

The great business historian Alfred Chandler corrected Coase's brilliant but somewhat static hypothesis with a more dynamic understanding of management. Chandler asserted that it is necessary "to relate administrative coordination to the theory of the firm."[3] Optimal firm size is at least partly conditioned by management's ability to coordinate relations among different parts of the organization. A well-designed organizational structure plus intangible elements of leadership and skillful human relations may expand optimal firm size by increasing management's effectiveness. And a still more basic factor in determining optimal firm size is the level of technology available to management.

Among his many contributions, Chandler showed that modern management arose because of technological change. The nineteenth-century transportation and communication revolutions lowered the cost of management or "administrative coordination" within firms. Therefore, said Chandler, "the visible hand" of the manager replaced Adam Smith's invisible hand of the market in large portions of modern economies.

By pairing Coase's argument with Chandler's, it is possible to arrive at a more general theory of the firm's optimal size and its relation to technological development in any particular era. New technology that reduces the cost of a company's transactions reduces the firm's optimal size. But new technology that reduces the cost and increases the effectiveness of management *increases* the firm's optimal size. Obviously, technological development is likely to affect *both* management costs and transaction costs. The impact of technology on the optimal size of any particular firm is therefore the net balance of technology's effect on the efficiency of management versus technology's effect on the efficiency of the market.

During the second Industrial Revolution, technological change clearly favored managerial power over the free market. The telegraph, railroads, and heavy machinery increased optimal firm size in many industries by enabling managers to lower corporations' internal costs for communication, distribution, and production. While transaction costs were appreciably reduced by this same technology, they did not fall nearly as

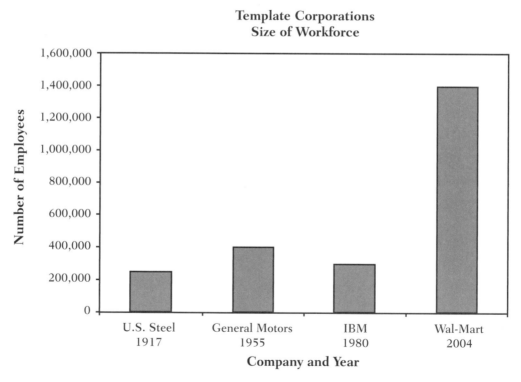

Template Corporations
Size of Workforce

Source: Richard Tedlow, *Giants of Enterprise: Seven Business Innovators and the Empires They Built* (New York: Harper Business, 2001); 2005 Wal-Mart annual report.

dramatically as management costs. Therefore, the economic advantage of the new technology went to large management-intensive firms.

This relative drop in the cost of management versus the cost of market transactions led to the rise of mass marketers such as Marshall Field's, Macy's, and Sears. All these companies built managerial hierarchies whose administrative coordination of the flow of goods within the firm replaced many of the market transactions that would have otherwise been needed to move merchandise across great geographical distances to its ultimate consumers. Hence also the integration of production and marketing processes—previously the work of separate firms—within great manufacturing corporations such as Standard Oil, Du Pont, and General Motors, the last of which Nelson Lichtenstein aptly characterizes as a "template" company for the era of heavy industry.

But now, in our "knowledge economy," high technology is exponentially reducing the cost of collecting and analyzing vast quantities of information. Transaction costs, which include information costs, are accordingly falling. If transaction costs alone determined optimal firm size, companies should be getting smaller. Conventional wisdom among management theorists for the past couple of decades has therefore favored such ideas as flattened hierarchies, reengineered processes, learning organizations, and knowledge management. Although the creators of such theories often reject the unsavory label "downsizers," their common effect has been to promote the idea that competitive advantage today lies with firms of reduced size.

And many of today's large firms are smaller than they would otherwise be without information technology, especially the large manufacturing firms that were the highest organizational achievement of the second Industrial Revolution. General Motors, for example, though still the world's largest automaker, now outsources to suppliers many parts of the car that it would formerly have manufactured within the firm. From GM's point of view, modern information and communication technology mean that the efficiency obtainable from more focused suppliers is no longer lost to high transaction costs formerly involved in dealing with outside firms.

Many other factors are of course involved in outsourcing, including lower wages in overseas regions of the global economy. But even within the American economy, lower transaction costs mean that many items that were formerly cheaper for GM to make on its own are now cheaper to buy from another firm. GM today is a smaller company than it would have been without the revolution in information technology.

Yet our era has also seen the rise of a new template company, Wal-Mart, which is not getting smaller but larger thanks to information technology. Not only is Wal-Mart now the world's largest firm in terms of sales, but it is still growing rapidly by every other meaningful measure, including profit, productivity, geographical scope, and number of people employed. Wal-Mart is rapidly approaching 1.5 million "associates," just within the United States. Within a few years Wal-Mart will employ 2 million Americans. And it is successfully penetrating the Asian, European, and Latin American markets while growing ever more dominant in the U.S. Seven cents out of every dollar spent in a store in America last year were spent in a Wal-Mart.

Despite its antediluvian size, Wal-Mart is clearly good for our democratic society in some respects, generating social mobility for at least some employees. Although Wal-Mart's low wages are a national problem and its discrimination against women employees is a disgrace, the retailer's human-relations policy is in at least one respect a model of democratic values. An unusually high percentage of Wal-Mart managers, probably a higher percentage than at any other large company in the world, started in low-paying jobs and lack a college or university degree.[4] Were it not for Wal-Mart's sex discrimination, the company could fairly claim to embody one of the old rallying cries of democracy, the career open to talent. For males at least, breaking into management at Wal-Mart is more a matter of ability and performance than it is a matter of educational credentials, which are increasingly an instrument of privilege in America.

Recruiting managers without college degrees may have been a matter of necessity when Wal-Mart was starting out in the Ozarks. But the company has turned its hard-won skill at developing managers without higher education into a competitive advantage. Many new managers at Wal-Mart are unencumbered with business school theories that might interrupt the company's steady focus on the bottom line. Perhaps just as important, many Wal-Mart managers do not understand the importance of perfect haircuts, expensive clothes, luxury cars, and Montblanc pens.[5] Such rough-cut managers are likely to have a tough time jumping to more conventional competitors who place a premium on polish. Wal-Mart can therefore pay its managers less, sparing itself and its customers some of the bloated managerial costs all too typical of American capitalism.

Wal-Mart serves the democratic interest of America by lowering prices and raising the standard of living of the working-class and middle-class customers who are its main clientele. A famous study of 2002 by the McKinsey consulting firm showed that 25 percent of the gains in productivity in the U.S. economy from 1995 to 1999 were due to Wal-Mart. Thanks to the Arkansas company, retailing trumped the high-tech industry as a contributor to the late twentieth-century productivity surge.[6]

But of course high technology is crucial to Wal-Mart's success. Its satellite and computer network links store managers, regional managers, and top managers in a dense web of information. Wal-Mart managers use this information to coordinate operations and lower costs to a degree unprecedented in the history of retailing.

In terms of the theory of the firm outlined above, information technology is expanding the optimal size of firms in some industries by reducing management costs even more rapidly than transaction costs. In particular, the costs of coordinating relations among people are greatly reduced by the information revolution. Therefore, in today's knowledge economy as opposed to the second Industrial Revolution, corporate gi-

Wal-Mart distribution center, Temple, Texas. Photograph by Matt Wright.

antism finds its natural home in relatively labor-intensive industries like retailing, not capital-intensive industries in the manufacturing sector.

Wal-Mart is a living, breathing behemoth of a top-down corporation despite the assertion, found in much fashionable management theory, that such companies are dead dinosaurs. Information technology has made Wal-Mart superbly efficient not in spite of but because of its gargantuan size and highly centralized organization. Fleeter of foot than the smaller firms with flattened hierarchies that are supposedly the nimblest competitors in the knowledge economy, Wal-Mart shows that high technology is fostering its own form of the huge, highly centralized corporation run with ruthless, hierarchical efficiency.

Wal-Mart's communications system lowers costs by facilitating efficient scheduling of the flow of goods within the supply chain. Skillful use of information technology enables Wal-Mart to coordinate deliveries to its distribution centers so well that many goods are "cross-docked." That is, the goods never enter a Wal-Mart warehouse but only arrive there, cross the loading dock to a waiting truck, and are sent on their way to a store. After the truck makes its store delivery, Wal-Mart's information system may route it to a nearby supplier so as to "backhaul" goods to the distribution center rather than run empty.

Spread and Growth of Wal-Mart

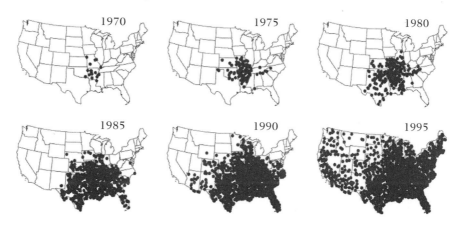

Source: Emek Basker, University of Missouri.

The retailer's internal operations are no less dependent on technological coordination and no less efficient than its supply-chain management. A quarter century ago, Wal-Mart pioneered point-of-sale collection of data that allows real-time tracking of inventory and automatic replenishment of orders throughout the company. Thanks to this technology, Wal-Mart is a master of inventory "turnover," increased speed of which not only reduces the cost of capital tied up in stocked goods but lowers other costs. For example, less handling of inventory also means less damage to inventory.

Wal-Mart managers skillfully mine computerized data on sales for exploitable patterns of customer behavior. A famous example was the company's discovery that sales of beer and paper diapers rose in tandem on Fridays. By stocking the two items near each other, Wal-Mart made it easier for a parent picking up diapers on the way home from work to celebrate the weekend's arrival with a six-pack.

Wal-Mart's position at the downstream end of the supply chain gives it an informational advantage on demand levels vis-à-vis suppliers. Therefore the giant retailer is sometimes able to manage its suppliers, or at least some of their departments, better than they could do for themselves. For example, Wal-Mart may experience a pickup in the demand for paper diapers that will affect not only its own operations but those of Procter and Gamble, manufacturer of Pampers, and also the operations of 3M, which supplies the sticky tapes that keep the diapers closed. Rather than all three companies allocating managerial resources to the decisions involved in meeting the demand surge, it makes sense for Procter and Gamble and 3M to delegate authority over some of their processes to Wal-Mart.[7] This system, called vendor-managed inventory (VMI), is often touted as requiring new levels of trust among firms. And indeed, suppliers report that Wal-Mart is an honest customer and keeps its word.

Delegation of internal management decisions to outside firms is scarcely new in business history. But the information revolution has at least partly reversed the direction of delegation. For example, retailers have often delegated stocking decisions to perishable-goods suppliers because of their superior knowledge of product shelf life. Now, however, it is the other way around, with suppliers delegating managerial authority to Wal-Mart because of its superior knowledge of demand.

It is widely asserted that Wal-Mart's thirty thousand suppliers resent the retailer's strong-arm negotiating tactics and pressure on profit margins. That is no doubt true in many cases. In a now famous incident, Wal-Mart was able to squeeze Vlasic down to a cent or two of profit on a $2.97 gallon-sized jar of pickles by threatening to stop buying the company's other products.[8] The gallon jar of pickles was so successful at Wal-Mart that Vlasic lost sales in higher-margin channels. Although it is generally agreed that the episode was not decisive in Vlasic's subsequent bankruptcy filing, it scarcely helped the company.

The story of Vlasic—a premium brand in the grocery business—illustrates a little-noticed way in which Wal-Mart benefits consumers at the expense of at least some high-end suppliers. Wal-Mart drives down the price premium for "branding" or creating noneconomic value in products. For many brands, shelf space at Wal-Mart is a mixed blessing at best, undoing years or even decades of marketing effort that established the product's cachet and premium price. Anticorporatists aiming to "debrand America" have an ironic ally in the world's largest company.

Yet Wal-Mart is undeniably good for its suppliers in some respects, including dissemination among them of improved management techniques and cost discipline. In data processing alone, Wal-Mart has used its market power to enforce standard protocols among suppliers that ultimately lower not only Wal-Mart's costs but those of the corporate economy in general.[9] Wal-Mart is a powerful force for imposing efficiency and focus throughout the American and world economies.

Wal-Mart is a master not only of managerial technique but of managerial strategy. Some of its shrewdest moves have been counterintuitive. Wal-Mart, it has been said, "spreads like molasses." Despite its phenomenally rapid sales growth, Wal-Mart only slowly achieved a national geographic presence, coming in under the radar of competitors. By filling up one geographic region before moving on to another, Wal-Mart makes maximum efficient use of the capital invested in that region's distribution facilities before investing yet more capital in a similar infrastructure in a new region. Wal-Mart's strategy of creeping across the landscape has differed markedly from that of other fast-growing retailers, who have entered new markets with all possible speed.

Another counterintuitive but shrewd strategy is the company's practice of overpopulating regions with stores—as many as eighty or even a hundred stores within three hundred miles of a single distribution center—which then cannibalize each other's sales. But what looks foolish from the lay perspective is a smart move from management's. Some cannibalization of individual store sales ensures maximum regional sales, creating the volume that allows maximum productivity and profitability to emerge from Wal-Mart's superbly efficient internal operations and supply-chain management.

By melding its low-cost operations with a strategy of genuinely competing by low prices, rather than the mere promise of them, Wal-Mart has achieved a rare coherence of corporate strategy and "mission." Competing on price means less spending on national advertising, so Wal-Mart does not feel under pressure to be in every market as soon as possible. That in turn allows for a still more disciplined focus on low costs and efficient growth, which are the essential ingredients in Wal-Mart's low-price strategy.

Although Wal-Mart's supply-chain management gets a great deal of press, the company's financial statements suggest that skillful management of internal operations remains essential to its competitive advantage. Two indicators of retailing efficiency are the percentage of sales revenues consumed by cost of goods sold (CGS) and by expenses for selling and general administration (SGA). CGS is an indicator of the effectiveness of the firm's relations with its suppliers and SGA of the efficiency of internal operations. Here are those numbers, expressed as a percentage of sales, for Wal-Mart and some of its competitors in 1993.

	WAL-MART	WEIGHTED AVERAGE OF COMPETITORS (KMART, TARGET, CALDOR, BRADLEES, AND OTHERS)
CGS	75.1	72.8
SGA	18.1	24.6

Source: Stephen P. Bradley and Pankaj Ghemawat, "Wal Mart Stores, Inc.," Harvard Business School Case 9-794-024, exhibit 6, p. 20. My thanks to my Babson College colleague John Stamm for calling my attention to this case and sharing his copy with me.

Wal-Mart's low SGA is not entirely attributable to efficient internal operations. The company's sophisticated supply-chain management may push into cost-of-goods-sold outlays that in more traditional retailers would show up as expenses for selling and general administration. For example, Wal-Mart is a pioneer of radio frequency identification (RFID) technology that will allow speedy and accurate tracking of goods both within the firm and within the supply chain, further speeding turnover and lowering handling costs. Wal-Mart's importance as a customer means that it is able to require its suppliers to invest millions of dollars in the RFID technology. Although RFID will eventually improve operating efficiency and lower SGA for both the suppliers and for Wal-Mart, some of the suppliers' cost for the technology will probably be passed back to Wal-Mart in the form of higher prices, at least initially, and show up in the retailer's CGS.

Yet the company's impressive achievement over the last decade in driving down the cost of internal operations, as represented in SGA, seems to be at least as important as efficient supply-chain management in maintaining its competitive advantage. Comparisons between 1993 and 2003 are tricky because by the latter year Wal-Mart had become not only the world's largest retailer but also the world's largest grocer. Grocers, even more than discount retailers, operate on narrow margins, a fact which probably accounts for Wal-Mart's high CGS in the chart below. And Wal-Mart's success in driving competitors out of business also means there are fewer large discounters against which a comparison can be made. Yet Wal-Mart's SGA number for 2003 is so much better than the competition's that there can scarcely be any doubt that the company continues to derive much of its competitive advantage from getting ever more productivity out of its internal operations.

	WAL-MART	**TARGET**
CGS	77.0	67.4
SGA	16.8	22.3

Source: "Hoover's Online: The Business Information Authority," http://www.hoovers.com, accessed May 25, 2004.

Wal-Mart's low SGA—a large part of which is wages—helps to explain the increasingly schizoid nature of the company's reputation. In the business press, Wal-Mart perennially shows up at or near the top of lists of the world's most-admired companies. These lists reflect the opinion of managers in other firms who admire and envy Wal-Mart's efficiency and cost discipline. Meanwhile, the mass media run stories suggesting that Wal-Mart sweats its efficiency out of oppressed workers via contracts with suppliers employing illegal aliens, by forcing unpaid or "off-the-clock" overtime on defenseless workers, and by massive amounts of sex discrimination—to cite only the most prominent accusations in a seemingly infinite stream of recent bad publicity for Wal-Mart.

There is no necessary contradiction between Wal-Mart's status as a widely admired and widely reviled company. It is a well-known economic principle that there are two ways of raising workers' productivity. It is admirable for a company to equip employees with better technology that will enable them to do more work with the same effort. It is contemptible to use managerial power to squeeze work out of employees. Wal-Mart does both.

Another increasingly widespread and largely justified critique of Wal-Mart is that it is bad for the social fabric. In half a century we have gone from General Motors as the country's largest employer, paying union scale, to Wal-Mart as the largest employer, paying poverty-level wages and allegedly helping to create a caste-ridden "two Americas." Wal-Mart's competitive advantages in scale and technology are so well entrenched that it could be a leader in moving the service industries closer to paying livable wages. The company's failure to embrace such a role voluntarily is not exceptional corporate behavior. Lawsuits by aggrieved employees, government regulation, labor organizing, and so forth—not managers' moral leadership—are a necessary push factor if Wal-Mart's superb skills in producing wealth are ever to be put to the service of social justice for its employees.

Wal-Mart is an example of how the Enron scandal only touched the surface of the ethical shortcomings in contemporary corporate life. Despite foolish claims made for moral leadership in much management literature, executives can abuse their power in many other ways than simple theft. The business world's current post-Enron drive to restore trust in corporate America is profoundly mistaken and undemocratic. In a democratic society all forms of power, and especially corporate power, should be suspected rather than trusted. Paradoxically, only managers who know and acknowledge that they have no claim on our trust deserve our moral respect. Those who openly claim the mantle of moral leadership need watching. Wal-Mart exemplifies the fundamentally undemocratic moral compromises inherent in the business corporation, which improves human life through the creation of wealth while, as a corollary, reducing freedom by exercising arbitrary managerial power.

The giant retailer has also been accused of ravaging the landscape of rural and small-town America. Wal-Mart, it is alleged, ruthlessly destroys the achievements of mom-

and-pop entrepreneurs, leaves Main Street a desolate row of empty storefronts, and creates unsightly sprawl at the new big box on the edge of town. Whether or not this critique is overblown, it poses a large political threat to the company by giving the public an impression that Wal-Mart is a unique enemy of some traditional, quintessential America. The company's belated public relations response, on TV and in the newspapers, seems ineffective so far. Wal-Mart is meeting increasingly effective resistance to its attempts to open new stores, not just in the countryside but in urban areas, including even impoverished neighborhoods that one would have thought stood to gain from any development at all.

It was not always thus. Sam Walton, who founded the company in 1962 and died in 1992, seemed during his lifetime to be an entrepreneurial hero. "Mr. Sam," as he was known, drove a pickup truck to work, lived out his life in a modest house in Bentonville, sponsored buy-American programs, enriched loyal employees through stock vesting, got Wal-Mart on lists of best companies to work for, and assiduously tried to avoid being known as a fabulously rich man. (If Sam were had been alive a decade after his death, with his fortune in his sole possession rather than divided among his five principal heirs, his net worth of $100 billion would have made him twice as rich as Bill Gates, with his measly $50 billion.)[10] And he raised the wealth of his community. The low-wage jobs now viewed as the scourge of modern workers were more than welcome when Sam began to create them by the thousands forty years ago in the Ozarks.

Equally welcome in rural and small-town America were Wal-Mart low prices. The anguish of small-town businesses in the face of competition from giant firms is a recurring theme in American history, marked a century ago by the coming of chain stores, half a century ago by the arrival of edge-of-town malls, and in recent years by big oil's massacre of independent gasoline stations. But when big business offers lower prices, customers are seldom numbered among those who mourn the quaint charm of small shops. It is a terrible thing for a shopkeeping family to lose its store, but it is also wrong to romanticize small-town businesspeople, who are as mixed a lot as any other human group. Some are models of entrepreneurial energy and skill but others laze along on a bit of inherited capital or some other small, unearned advantage over their neighbors. Some are largehearted, while others are as unscrupulous as any big-city master of the universe, as Sam knew from personal experience.

As a young entrepreneur in Newport, a small Arkansas town in the late 1940s, Sam lost his first business—a successful variety store—thanks to his mistake in signing a lease with no renewal clause. When the lease expired in 1950, the avaricious landlord refused to renew it, but instead he took the store that Sam had built up with five years of hard work and gave it to his son. In 1969 Sam opened a Wal-Mart in that same town and drove his former landlord's son out of business. Walton claimed that revenge had no part of it.[11] Maybe it didn't. As Wal-Mart began to put not only small but also large competitors out of business, Sam would rebuke gloaters among Wal-Mart managers, remind them that families were suffering. He often ordered them to hire employees of the bankrupt firm.[12]

In the early years, Wal-Mart was a relatively good place to work, as work goes in our post-Edenic world. In the 1960s a minimum-wage job in rural Arkansas, where both per capita income and the cost of living were less than half the national average, was no bad thing, especially with a stock-vesting plan that gave all long-term employees a chance to share in the company's financial success. The company accommodated workers' family needs through flexible work scheduling and gave employees pride in their work. Wal-Mart's relentless cost cutting reflected not only Sam's personal values but the values of many of his employees, who grew up like him, not exactly poor but taught to stretch a dollar beyond the imagining of the urban middle class. If in those days there was little indignity in working at Wal-Mart, it was because there was little false dignity in Sam Walton.

In some ways Sam's spirit lives after him. It's not just that Wal-Mart employees still earn low wages but that managers, too, still earn less than their counterparts at other companies. Only by hanging on for nine years and getting vested in the stock-sharing plan do Wal-Mart managers begin to have a chance at big money. Wal-Mart office workers reportedly still use both sides of a sheet of paper, so a handwritten memo is likely to have an old one scribbled on the back, addressed to the sender of the new one. And the cheaply paneled walls at Bentonville headquarters are still decorated with neckties that Wal-Mart's buyers, in a typically unwitting castration ritual, have gleefully scissored from suppliers' representatives.

Wal-Mart employees have a tradition of high morale that still lives among many of them. At annual meetings held in the University of Arkansas basketball arena, which seats seventeen thousand people, employees participate as enthusiastically as shareholders. With entertainers such as Halle Berry dancing the twist and Patti LaBelle singing "Somewhere over the Rainbow," the events seem more like pop concerts than corporate meetings.

In the stores, too, there is no denying the high morale of many Wal-Mart employees. A Wal-Mart worker recently told me that though he personally feels humiliated by the daily Wal-Mart cheer, invented as a morale booster by Sam, where employees wiggle their rear ends on management's cue, many employees enjoy and are energized by it. Management's success in eliciting high performance and a sense of shared responsibility from employees is clearly a major reason for the company's success.

Yet it is scarcely clear that a business model good for the Ozarks in the 1960s is good for America and the world in the early twenty-first century. There is no question, of course, that Wal-Mart is good in many respects for the U.S. and world economies. But even though Wal-Mart's efficiencies, low prices, and use of uncredentialed managers reflect democratic values, in other respects Wal-Mart is a worse-than-average corporate tyrant, bad for democracy.

Some commentators tell us not to worry over the fact that the country's largest employer pays poverty-level wages and that it makes health insurance available to employees only at a price that many of them cannot afford. The argument is that most Wal-Mart employees do not need a living wage and good benefits because they are young, because they are old, because they are supplementing another family member's higher income, and above all because they are starting their climb up the allegedly still intact ladder of social mobility.

Beyond the fact that the majority are women who are not proportionally represented in management ranks, we do not know as much about Wal-Mart employees as would be useful in answering its defense of poverty-level wages. It is not known how many Wal-Mart workers have real prospects of moving on to better-paying jobs, how many have working spouses or partners, how many are single, how many are supporting children, how many are pensioners supplementing Social Security, how many live below the poverty line, how many are homeless. A study answering those questions would be a great contribution to understanding our society today.

Yet we know enough to say that as Wal-Mart has grown from a rural upstart to a dominant player in urban markets as well, it has come to employ substantial numbers of the working poor. Critics of Wal-Mart's low wages increasingly use the economic concept of "externalities" or costs shifted from inside the company to the rest of society. One study has found that taxpayers annually subsidize Wal-Mart to the tune of $2,103 per employee in the form of food stamps, school lunches, Medicaid for uninsured workers, housing assistance, low-income energy assistance, et cetera.[13] That amounts to a total taxpayer subsidy for Wal-Mart of nearly $3 billion a year.

It is a mistake, though, to argue against Wal-Mart's low wages strictly on the basis of externalities and social costs. From the taxpayer's perspective, social savings from better pay and benefits for Wal-Mart employees would be at least partly offset by losses from higher prices. Wal-Mart would pass on to customers at least some of the cost of higher wages. Some of the money that taxpayers saved from reduced welfare costs for Wal-Mart employees would be lost when taxpayers shopped at the new, more socially responsible Wal-Mart.

The real argument against poverty-level wages in a democratic society is not just economic but moral and political. In our putatively free country there is far too little freedom for the working poor. They do not get the material rewards that are the main compensation corporations offer other citizens for compromising their freedom and going to work for a manager. The comfortable classes at least live in relative freedom outside the workplace. The working poor, however, fall under the control of additional managerial bureaucracies, either charitable or governmental, which "give" them the necessities of life their work should have earned.

Yet some sort of governmental intervention seems essential to whatever level of social justice is possible in a corporate and global economy. The relevant question, probably unanswerable in any absolute sense and not even provisionally in this essay, is What is the best model for government intervention so as to support social justice while minimizing restraints on the ability of the corporate economy to create wealth? But it is at least certain that a beginning in answering that question cannot be made without open acknowledgment that companies like Wal-Mart, paying wages that deny a fair number of employees the ability to live with dignity and autonomy, subvert the democratic principles of justice and freedom.

The working poor are also, of course, less able to resist stringent management in the workplace. It seems clear that Wal-Mart now manages its employees more harshly than it did formerly. The company was surely not idyllic when Sam was alive, and for many employees it is scarcely hellish today. Yet the "family" metaphor, so terribly abused by much of corporate America, rings ever more false at the world's largest company. A manager who fires a Down syndrome employee for helping herself to a candy bar from a store shelf (I know the employee's sister) may be true to Wal-Mart's policy of zero tolerance for theft, but at what expense to his soul? The manager's refusal to indulge in so slight an act of humanity as a second chance raises the possibility that he acted less out of righteousness than fear for his own job. "Family," it is certain, had nothing to do with it.

Employee lawsuits and allegations of abuses charged by the media and government are too numerous to dismiss as the inevitable friction involved in any large organization. There is a disturbingly predictable pattern following any negative media coverage of Wal-Mart. After some shameful abuse is alleged to have occurred in the stores, a public relations officer at corporate headquarters announces that the incident, if true, was a local aberration that does not reflect the company's "values." Whether the company even knows its real values, as represented in its fierce top-down cost discipline, and whether those values put unreasonable pressure on store managers that leads to abuse of employees, are questions in which top management has indicated little interest.

Barbara Ehrenreich's account of her experience as a frontline employee supports charges that for a substantial portion of employees there is little dignity, let alone joy, in working at Wal-Mart. Rather, there is a good deal of harsh control and even more than usual of the corporate world's customary attempts at psychological manipulation by managers or, rather, "servant leaders." For some "associates," perhaps many, the Wal-Mart "family" is mean- and small-spirited. Self-righteously enjoining employees' momentary respites as "time theft" may enhance Wal-Mart's economic efficiency.[14] But such moralistic oppression is an abuse of power and for some employees undermines the psychological strength needed to resist tyranny, whether managerial or political.

It is customary to blame the declining prospects of American workers on the fierce competition of the global economy. But the modern managerial corporation and its masterful use of high technology should not get off the hook. Though firms in the past two centuries have improved the lives of the many, they continue just as much as in the past, or maybe even more, to be managed by the few and for the few. This hard truth is ever ignored by management theorists who long to understand the firm as a democratic instrument.

For the past couple of decades, the conventional wisdom among management theorists was that the big, vertically structured firm was finished thanks to information technology. Hosannas were sung to the democratic virtues of the small, flat organizations that were supposedly going to dominate the new economy. Now that it is evident that big business is not going away anytime soon, cutting-edge management theorists predictably claim that information technology is "harnessing democracy" inside huge firms by making it possible to blend economies of scale with local control: "the benefits of centralization are often the benefits of bigness, not benefits of centralization itself. And, in many cases, when communication gets cheap enough, you can afford to decentralize in a way that gives you both the benefits of bigness, like scale economies, and the benefits of smallness, like motivation and flexibility." [15]

But at least at Wal-Mart it has not worked out that way. Wal-Mart's success depends on using high technology and low-cost communication to realize not the benefits of both bigness and smallness but the benefits of both bigness and top-down centralization. Although Wal-Mart store managers are famously allowed control over price and stocking decisions in order to permit quick responses to local situations, their results are monitored closely on a weekly basis thanks to information technology and the near-Orwellian supervision that it makes possible.

To put it in terms of the theory of the firm, high technology has greatly reduced the risk of mismanagement in huge organizations by tremendously expanding what the business texts of several generations ago called, with refreshing frankness as compared to today's management speak, "the span of control." At Wal-Mart, information technology has increased, not reduced, management power and worker subjection. Today's hope for what might be called information technology democracy in the workplace seems as destined to defeat as the dreams of "industrial democracy" a few generations ago. [16]

Even recently announced reforms are indicative of Wal-Mart's top-down centralization. Top management has vowed to promote women in direct proportion to their percentage of the applicant pool for managerial positions (scarcely an objective test, since managers can manipulate the composition of the pool by encouraging male applicants and discouraging females). Top managers have pledged that if they fail to deliver on their promise they will cut their own annual bonuses. [17] It is no doubt good for top management to put its own compensation on the line, to be measured against results. But management's confidence in doing so in this case amounts to a tacit admission that responsibility for the company's past gross injustices belongs right at the top of the organization.

Wal-Mart has also promised reforms in pay and working conditions that point to more, not less, management control through information technology. Although the details have not been announced at the time I write, promised pay reforms seem likely to amount to token increases while removing frontline managers' ability to discriminate against women workers. Thanks to companywide communication systems, Wal-Mart will relieve local managers of responsibility for pay rates and merit raises.[18] Similarly, the idea of ensuring that cashiers get work breaks by using a centralized computer program to shut down their cash registers testifies to Wal-Mart's continuing reliance on information technology to manage with ever greater hierarchical controls.

The firms that Coase thought of as "islands of conscious power" are now continents. Their managers exert power across great organizational distance and at great remove from the affected workers. Of course, it does not take sophisticated information and communications technology for the organizationally powerful to profoundly affect the lives of the weak. Top managers a century ago often made single decisions that shaped, for good or ill, the lives of thousands of workers. But those were big decisions with big consequences—the decision, say, to open or close a factory. Workers' routine operations within the factory were still controlled by immediate supervisors.

Now, a Wal-Mart employee can be affected not just by epochal decisions in the life of the firm but by routine, daily decisions made by managers working in another state rather than by an immediate supervisor. Admittedly, the store manager or a subordinate manager still decides that, for example, an employee will operate a cash register during busy selling hours and then, in the ensuing slow period, move to women's wear to re-hang clothes that customers tried on but did not buy. But the pressure under which the employee works depends not just on the mercy of her immediate supervisor but on centralized decisions emanating from Wal-Mart headquarters and the computers that tell the individual store managers how many (or rather, how few) person-hours they are expected to use that week. The possibility not just for callous indifference but for simple ignorance by the managers who determine those working conditions is greater than ever before.

Now, let us return to the metaphor of the visible hand of management that Alfred Chandler thought had replaced Adam Smith's invisible hand of the market in many parts of the economy. Modern management is developing its own invisibility because Wal-Mart workers never see the managers at regional, national, and international headquarters whose decisions affect them, not just in large ways, but on a routine daily basis. Millions of employees will therefore labor under increasingly invisible managerial control as the Wal-Mart template is inevitably adopted by more and more companies. Management invisibility is further increased by the tendency for firms at the downstream end of the supply chain to use technology to manage operations in upstream suppliers (e.g., Wal-Mart and the diaper manufacturers mentioned earlier in this paper).

Invisible management seems likely to be increased, not decreased, by technological change now on the horizon. New sensor technology such as "smart dust" will inexpensively monitor truck drivers, salespeople, field-service technicians, and other off-site personnel who have traditionally worked at a distance from their bosses. The cost of personnel management seems likely to continue to fall faster than the cost of market transactions.

In light of the theory of the firm outlined at the start of this chapter, the decreasing cost of managing labor-intensive business can be expected to continue to raise the potential size of firms like Wal-Mart. As a corollary, the number of citizens who work under harsh supervision can only be expected to rise. As managerial power is increasingly exercised with distant but scalpel-like precision over large numbers of employees, the hand of management will become ever less visible to those most immediately affected by it.

In industries such as retailing where centralized management power is increased, not decreased, by the information revolution, democratic political institutions are likely to be employees' main recourse against the widening disparities of the modern economy. Some look to labor unions to organize Wal-Mart employees as well as workers at other new corporate giants.[19] But unless labor can achieve more organizational unity and centralized leadership than it has ever done previously, unions are likely to remain weak reeds against managerial power that is increasingly consolidated and made more effective by information technology. At minimum, labor is likely to need to find governmental assistance via democratic political action, as happened in the New Deal. Alternatively, the lower tier of American society may eventually meet its human needs through a renewed birth of welfare statism, but that too would require democratic political action. Perhaps the future will open other possibilities unimaginable to us now.

Or perhaps we will continue on what seems the present path to a two-tier America with a smaller middle class. Many other nations fear that modern information technology and the global economy it supports are making them more like America, with what they see as a vapid culture and garish middle-class values. But the process may also be working the other way around, making America a little more like the world's least envied societies, where the many are dominated by the few.

What is clear at present is that high technology is not always, as it is often portrayed by management seers, a force for egalitarianism and freedom in our economic organizations. For the foreseeable future, democratic societies eager to enjoy the undeniable material benefits of the business corporation will have to deal with a greater, not smaller, contradiction between the theory of the free market and the reality of the unfree firm.

A Global Corporation

FIVE

Making Global Markets: Wal-Mart and Its Suppliers

Misha Petrovic and Gary G. Hamilton

Introduction: The Wal-Mart Effect

In the 1990s, as Wal-Mart became the biggest world retailer, its effect on the U.S. economy came under much scrutiny. At first, the "Wal-Mart effect" represented little more than the heightened competition between mass retailers, forcing many of them to merge, acquire other firms, declare bankruptcy, or overhaul their supply chains. But as Wal-Mart revenues grew from $33 billion in 1991 to $191 billion ten years later, some observers argued that the Wal-Mart effect had become an economy-wide phenomenon, even one of global porportions.[1] Economists have pointed out that low retail prices help suppress inflation while saving American consumers billions of dollars. As the biggest private employer in the U.S., Wal-Mart creates more than a hundred thousand jobs a year, and as the leader in the implementation of information technology, it is responsible for a significant share of the economy's productivity growth. At the same time, numerous political activists, union leaders, and scholars have attacked Wal-Mart for holding down wages, driving small retailers out of business, and accelerating the shift of manufacturing jobs overseas. And the jobs it does create, they argue, merely cannibalize the jobs once offered by Wal-Mart's higher-waged competitors.[2]

The net economic impact of any company, even one as big as Wal-Mart, is notoriously hard to measure, mainly because of the difficulties in specifying how the effects of corporate performance reverberate through the rest of the economy. Thus, we should not expect the arguments about the Wal-Mart effect to be resolved anytime soon. Moreover, even if Wal-Mart's overall impact could be calculated precisely, we would still be left with more difficult issues such as its impact on local communities, quality of life, and the environment.

In this chapter, we examine the Wal-Mart effect from a different angle. Instead of focusing on standard measures of corporate performance, such as profits and sales, we emphasize Wal-Mart's ability to shape the institutional structure of the economy. More specifically, we explore Wal-Mart's relations with its suppliers, both domestic and foreign. While this topic has often been addressed in the business and popular press and recently even attracted some attention in the academic literature, what is typically missing from the current discussion is a description of various aspects of the retailer-supplier relation in terms of a broader framework of the creation and reproduction of market institutions. Thus, our main goal is to describe Wal-Mart's treatment of its suppliers—from negotiations about price to product development, and from arm's-length transactions to long-term partnerships—as an aspect of its *market-making* activities.

Market making refers to all activities oriented toward creating and reproducing opportunities for trade, from pricing and contracting, to finding and retaining trading partners, to getting the products into and through the market. Wal-Mart's ability to make markets—to define the shopping environment, the assortment of merchandise, and the "everyday low price" for its customers, and to specify the rules of conduct and standards of performance for thousands of its global suppliers—is the most profound of all Wal-Mart effects, revealing how the corporation has reshaped the global market for consumer goods during the last twenty years.

At the same time, we should note that our present focus on Wal-Mart should not be taken to imply that this company's market-making efforts are somehow unique or unprecedented. While its size and global influence may indeed be exceptional, Wal-Mart is just the most outstanding example of the new brand of retailers that have recently come to play a dominant role in creating and shaping global markets for consumer goods. Wal-Mart may have the starring role, but it is surrounded by a very talented cast that includes Carrefour, Aldi, Metro, Royal Ahold, Tesco, Ito-Yokado, Kingfisher, and IKEA, as well as Home Depot, Costco, and Best Buy. And these large retailers are joined by a supporting crew of brand-name marketers and assemblers, such as Nike, Gap, VF Corporation, the Limited, Louis Vuitton, Otto Versand, Dell, Hewlett-Packard, and many other similar firms.

Our analysis of Wal-Mart as a market maker should be seen as part of a larger historical narrative that brings together three trends in the global economy. The first is the shift in the balance of market power from manufacturers to retailers, a process that so far has developed to the greatest extent in the United States, but is also starting to accelerate elsewhere. The second trend refers to the rise of new global manufacturers, especially in East Asia, and the concomitant decline of international competitiveness of many American manufacturing firms. The third trend is the growing power of consumers in shaping marketing and production choices throughout the distribution channel. All three trends represent a shift in *market power relations,* and in all three, large American retailers have played the crucial role. Since the late 1970s, they have provided market mechanisms by which the competitive advantages of foreign manufacturers have been translated into lost orders for American firms. At the same time, their access to consumer purchasing information and their control over marketing channels have not only increased retail power over their suppliers but also generated a greater sensitivity to consumer preferences, which is often somewhat misleadingly interpreted as an increase in "consumer power."[3]

Market Making and Retail Power:
A Conceptual Overview

Since the late 1970s, an increasing number of industry observers have been describing the shift in market power from manufacturers to retailers. They have identified several causes of such a power shift, including the retailers' ability to use point-of-sale data to directly assess consumer preferences, the increase in retail concentration, the decrease in effectiveness of mass media as marketing channels, and the proliferation of store brands. Large retailers, they argue, are increasingly able to squeeze their suppliers and induce various forms of price concessions.[4]

However, empirical studies of the performance of retailers and their suppliers in this period show no clear evidence of systematic differences or a shift in their profitability. Moreover, manufacturers who sell only to large retailers that dominate particular markets do not necessarily have lower profit margins than those that do not, or even than those powerful retailers themselves.[5] Instead of trying to explain away such findings, we propose to sever the link between the notion of market power in the distribution channel and the profitability of retailers and their suppliers. Thus, we define vertical competition and, by implication, the power distribution between retailers and manufacturers, in terms of their respective abilities to shape the conditions of trade. These abilities cannot be reduced to mere bargaining about prices and quantities. Market negotiations also include issues such as how and when the product will be delivered, who will take the responsibility for packaging and presentation, advertising and warranty provisions, and even product character and composition. In other words, retailers and manufacturers compete not only to determine the outcomes of market negotiations, but also to set the rules and mechanisms by which these outcomes are typically determined.

The Evolution of the Retail Power, 1960–1990

Before the late 1970s, there was little talk about the power of retailers over their suppliers. A few giant retailers, such as A & P and Sears, have had an undeniable power over their vendors for the better part of the twentieth century, but they were treated as exceptions rather than indications of industrywide trends. In the postwar era, the economic power of large American manufacturers seemed unassailable. They were seen as paragons of technological sophistication and organizational efficiency, in marked contrast with the labor-intensive, low-tech retail sector still dominated by relatively small firms and segmented markets.

The relations between retailers and their suppliers started to change in the early 1970s as a result of three major factors: retailers' ability to deploy new information technologies to assess consumer demand; increased concentration in the retail sector; and the rise in global competition in suppliers' industries. While the impact of these three was felt throughout the 1970s, it was not until the early 1980s that they converged to bring about a dramatic change in the retail power and enable the new generation of big-box retailers to become a major driving force in shaping the American economy. For the first time since the 1920s, and perhaps since the emergence of the modern industrial enterprise, it was the merchant, not the manufacturer, who led the drive to rationalize market institutions. From the diffusion of bar codes and scanning devices, to electronic data interchange, direct store delivery, and quick replenishment, to integrated logistics solutions and vendor-managed inventory, the rationalization initiatives and technological innovations flowed from large retailers to their suppliers.

Although less well recognized, the impact of the big U.S. retailers on their foreign suppliers and on the growth of their host economies was no less powerful. Retailers did not just buy products in developing countries; they also organized and rationalized global supply chains, established trade standards and logistics solutions, and even ventured into product development. The rapid growth of East Asian economies in the 1970s and 1980s would have been inconceivable without the strong U.S. demand for manufactured goods, and the paramount role of big retailers in organizing and channeling that demand.[6]

The retailers that emerged as industry leaders in the 1980s were not the same ones that dominated the top ranks of the industry between the 1930s and 1970s. Instead of traditional department stores, national mass merchandisers (Sears, Montgomery Ward, and JCPenney), and grocery chain operators, the new industry leaders came from the ranks of full-line and specialty discounters. Wal-Mart, Kmart, and Target, the "big three" of the discount industry, all started their operations in 1962; Home Depot, Costco, Best Buy, Office Depot, Gap, Limited, and Nike are of an even more recent vintage. In order to understand the sources of the retail power in the 1980s, then, we first need to go back to the 1960s and the emergence of the discount retailing.

In its 1961 annual report, the Woolworth Company, then the seventh largest retailer and for several decades the largest variety chain operator in the United States, depicted a worldwide revolution in retailing which "reveals consumer willingness to dispense with certain services in exchange for cash savings and the shopping for all manner of goods under a single roof, with self-selection and checkout counters." Responding to this trend, the company announced that it would establish, beginning in early 1962, "a chain of mass-merchandise, self-selection, low-margin, high-quality Woolco Department Stores" in the United States and Canada.[7]

By the time Woolworth decided to join the ranks of discounters, the "discounting revolution" that had started only a couple of years earlier was in full swing. The success of the pioneer hard-good discounters of the 1950s, such as E.J. Korvette, Vornado, Zayre, and Arlan's, revealed that massive inefficiencies could be squeezed out of traditional retailing. Apart from the grocery sector, where supermarkets had driven the rationalization trend since the 1940s, and the automotive and gasoline sectors, where distribution was tightly controlled by large manufacturers, other retailing firms enjoyed the benefits of the seller's market, with high gross margins, little direct price competition, and little incentive to innovate.[8] Thus, the first discounters were able to offer standard, mostly branded consumer goods at prices 10–25 percent less than what other stores were charging, simply by cutting their operating costs and accepting lower profit margins. By the late 1950s, discounting became sufficiently well established to attract the attention of large chain operators, mostly of variety and junior department stores, whose entrance into the field signified the beginning of the discount revolution. These included Dayton Hudson's Target stores, and Treasure Island stores operated by JCPenney, as well as Woolworth's Woolco and Kresge's Jupiter and Kmart stores. In 1962 alone, more than twenty retail chains, including Wal-Mart, started discount operations, prompting *Fortune* to publish a comprehensive study of the new trend, spanning four issues of the magazine and titled "The Distribution Upheaval."

The buying power of these chains and their experience in managing large numbers of establishments pushed the discounting sector to a new level of competitive advantage. The merchandise assortment was not only expanded but also systematized, coming to resemble that of a department store. The new chains repudiated the hodgepodge assortment of cheap merchandise associated with many early discounters, and several operators decided to call their stores promotional rather than discount, while nonetheless upholding the principles of self-service and discount prices.

Woolworth's 1961 annual report had captured the major elements of the format that, by the end of the decade, was to emerge as the discounting mainstream: the large, freestanding store that provided easy access and ample parking; the breadth of merchandise that paralleled that of the department store and allowed one-stop shopping; the replacement of the labor-intensive model of "full" customer service with rationalized and automated forms, ranging from new ways of tracking and packaging goods to store designs that relied on shopping carts and electronic cash registers; and, of course, the emphasis on low prices. The format itself was hardly new; in fact, it represented little more than the application of the supermarket model, introduced in the late 1930s, to nongrocery retailing. What was new, however, and what perhaps is most deserving of being labeled a revolution, was how rapidly the discounting format was adopted in the general-merchandise sector and also how rapidly, once the adoption reached a critical mass in the early 1970s, those new discounters emerged as the leaders in technological and market-making innovation.

The favorable macroeconomic climate of the 1960s generated a lot of room for growth in the discounting sector, and the competition stayed relatively low, with few bankruptcies and few mergers recorded before the mid-1970s recession. The full-line, medium-sized discount store, represented by Kmart, Woolco, and Gibson's stores, became the dominant format of the discount sector. The revenues of general-merchandise discounters had surpassed those of department stores by 1970, but this was mostly the result of the rapid decline of the independent department store; at the same time, department store chains and mall-based specialty retailers experienced strong growth.

Consolidation and intense competition characterized the 1970s. Many pioneer operators, including several top ten chains, such as Korvette and Vornado (Two Guys), folded during the decade. The recessions of 1980 and 1981 led to another wave of bankruptcies, including Fed-Mart, JCPenney's Treasure Island stores, and Woolco, the second biggest discount chain. At the same time, the second half of the 1970s saw a flurry of acquisition activity, led by Kmart, which by 1977 operated one thousand stores, had over $10 billion in revenues, and had passed JCPenney to become the third biggest retailer in the United States. Wal-Mart and Target were among other major buyers of the period, and by 1982 they joined Kmart to form the big three of the discount world, controlling 35 percent of the sector's $70 billion in sales.[9]

The rapid consolidation, while certainly accelerated by the turbulent macroeconomic conditions, betrayed a more fundamental shift in the nature of discounting. As large discounters expanded their merchandise assortment and achieved economies of scale in purchasing, their pursuit of operational efficiency shifted to more sophisticated strategies rationalizing their internal operations. Kmart, Wal-Mart, Zayre, and Target emerged as industry leaders in developing two major technological innovations of the period, the use of computers for inventory management and stock replenishment, and the automated distribution center. By the end of the 1970s, this small group of leading discounters managed to surpass all other retailers, even the supermarket chains, in technological and organizational integration.

The 1980s brought a rapid proliferation of discounting formats, including their penetration into specialty retailing. At the beginning of the decade, nineteen out of twenty top discounters carried full lines of general merchandise; at its end this was true for only

ten of them.[10] Warehouse clubs, off-price retailers, and specialty discounters in electronics, toys, office products, and "home-improvement" merchandise all joined the
ranks of industry leaders in the late 1980s. At the same time, mass merchandisers such
as Sears and Montgomery Ward; department stores such as Dillard's, Ames, and
Mervyn's; and apparel and footwear chains such as Melville Shoe, the Limited, and
Gap, came to operate on the same principles as the discounters. By the late 1980s, the
line between the discount industry and other retailers had blurred to the point that the
very notion of discounting lost any distinctive meaning. This led to more competition
and, hence, to a major wave of consolidation. Among the top ten discounters of 1980,
only four—Wal-Mart, Kmart, Target, and failing Caldor—were still in operation in
1992. Of the forty-two department store chains operating in 1980, only twenty remained in the business a decade later. Fully 80 percent changed hands during that
time.[11]

Even the big three discounters had their problems. Kmart debuted two off-price apparel chains, the upscale Designer Depot in 1983 and the more basic Designer Rack
the following year, and Target followed with its own version, Plums, the same year; but
all three proved unsuccessful and folded by the late 1980s. Wal-Mart had its own share
of failures with dot Discount Drugs (started in 1983, sold in 1990) and Helen's Arts and
Crafts (1984–1988).

The strategies of the big three diverged in the mid-1980s. Kmart, still the biggest of
the three, went aggressively into specialty retailing, acquiring Waldenbooks, Payless
Drug, Builder's Square, the Sports Authority, Office Max, and Borders. At the same
time, it pursued a private brand apparel strategy in its discount stores and expanded its
national advertising presence. While Kmart initially shunned the warehouse club and
the combo grocery-discount formats, it entered this segment in 1987 with American
Fare hypermarket, followed shortly with Pace Membership Clubs and Kmart supercenters. This intense expansion and diversification strategy took its toll, however, in the
1990s, when, unable to complete a massive renovation of its discount stores, Kmart di-
vested most of its specialty holdings and went through several waves of reorganization.

Target, the smallest of the big three, pursued a different strategy. Its parent, Dayton
Hudson, acquired Mervyn's chain of junior department stores and the stores of the
bankrupt Ayr-Way and Fed-Mart, but sold its B. Dalton bookstores as well as its controlling interest in nine regional shopping malls. Instead of diversifying, Target there-

after successfully focused on apparel and household furnishings, establishing an image of an upscale discounter.

While Kmart was emulating Sears's diversification strategy and Target aligned itself with Penney and the department store chains, Wal-Mart, the most efficient and fastest growing of the three, led the development of warehouse and combination (grocery and general-merchandise) formats. The first Sam's Wholesale Club opened in 1983, and by 1991 Wal-Mart became the leading warehouse operator (only to lose the first place to the newly merged Costco and Price Club in 1993); its first hypermarket—Hypermart USA—opened in Dallas at the end of 1987 and the first supercenter followed in 1989. But Wal-Mart's expansion strategy, in terms of market scope as well as merchandise assortment, remained extraordinarily cautious, especially for a company that averaged 40 percent growth a year in the late 1970s and the early 1980s. Most of its stores were still in small towns, and even in 1990, when it surpassed Kmart and was one year away from passing Sears to become the world's biggest retailer, it operated in only twenty-eight states. David Glass, the CEO from 1988 to 2000, described the development of Sam's Club stores as a result of investors' pressure to diversify, adding that "[i]t complemented the Wal-Mart store: We can put them side by side; they get different customers. Sam's was also more of a metro strategy than what we were doing in Wal-Mart."[12] Similarly, the supercenter format was a direct extension of the idea of one-stop shopping and it required little more, at least from the consumer's perspective, than putting a supermarket and a discount store under the same roof.

Even before it became the largest U.S. retailer, Wal-Mart had established itself as the undisputed leader in defining the mainstream form of general merchandising. With Sears and Kmart aggressively pursuing diversification and struggling to define their core merchandising strategy, and Target and Penney repositioning themselves as leaders in basic fashion and soft goods, Wal-Mart remained the only major general merchandiser to clearly emphasize the more traditional, full-line discount approach. The proliferation of new products in the 1970s and 1980s made this strategy increasingly precarious. Compared to the Sears of the 1950s and 1960s, let alone to the early twentieth-century department store and the Sears general catalog, the assortment of merchandise in the Wal-Mart discount store has always represented only a minuscule share of all goods available to the consumer. The rapid rise of specialty retailers in the 1980s seemed to indicate that consumers were looking for more choice and more depth in each merchandise category rather than the convenience of one-stop shopping for a wide variety of goods. Wal-Mart's subsequent performance demonstrated that the American retailing landscape still had a place, and indeed a sizable one, for an enlarged version of the old variety store.

INFORMATION TECHNOLOGY AND LEAN RETAILING

Discounters' implementation of information technology (IT) in the 1980s was only the third wave of IT innovation in the retail trade, but the first one to have a substantial influence on the manufacturing sector as well.[13] Starting in the early 1960s, retail applications of IT were at first limited to a small number of financial and inventory-management tasks, slowly expanding to incorporate other aspects of the business process. In the early 1970s, the main objectives of IT deployment became the integration of systems for reliable tagging and automatic identification of products, on the one hand, and the point-of-sale (POS) scanning and recording devices such as electronic cash registers, credit card, and check ("electronic fund transfer") readers on the other. The development of the Universal Product Code (UPC) system by a number of major food manufacturers and grocery chains in the mid-1970s marked the first successful convergence of the two systems. This created an opportunity for efficient integration of the front-end, financial, and inventory-management aspects of the business process.

The cost of implementing a new system of automated checkout counters equipped with bar code scanners was considerable, and the advantages of the new system could be realized only when a substantial proportion—estimated in the business literature at the time to be 70 to 85 percent—of the products were coded. With strong support from the food industry, this objective was reached in the supermarket sector as early as 1976, only two years after the first implementation of the system, creating a substantial advantage for the early adopters.[14] In the general-merchandising sector, the development was slower, hampered by a much higher number of stock-keeping units and by a greater diversity of suppliers. Moreover, the need for speed at the checkout was less pressing than in the grocery sector, since most purchases consisted of only a small number of items. Instead of bar codes, department stores and mass merchandisers used tickets with standardized type, usually generated in-house, and optical character recognition

(OCR) devices ("wands") for scanning. The lack of standardization meant that the innovation was more dispersed than in the grocery sector, and first adopters were often smaller department store chains such as Mervyn's and Dillard's. By the end of the 1970s, most major chains relied heavily on the use of wands, with Sears the sector's heaviest user.[15]

The situation changed dramatically during the 1980s, with momentous consequences for the retailing industry as well as for transportation and manufacturing. The supermarket industry ceased to be the innovation leader, and the big discounters, led by Wal-Mart and Kmart, emerged as the champions of the UPC, driving its diffusion along their supply chains. Supermarket chains had both less incentive and less opportunity to innovate outside their own industry. Unlike general merchandisers, they faced a small, highly concentrated group of large domestic suppliers, in the food, tobacco, and health care industries, that had no significant foreign competition. At the same time, the competition between supermarket chains was quite limited. The major "national" chains operated in segmented local markets, competing mainly against smaller chains and independents.[16]

In contrast, the discounters relied upon a more atomized set of supply industries, most of whom faced a significant degree of import penetration. Not only was their power to shape supplier markets much greater than in the grocery sector, but they also had more incentive to innovate, because of the intense competition in the general-merchandise retailing sector. By 1980, therefore, leading discounters recognized that major promises of IT could be realized only by the reorganization of the entire supply chain. Kmart and Wal-Mart, as well as a group of leading apparel retailers such as Gap and the Limited, started pressuring their suppliers to tag all their products *before* the delivery, and to develop capabilities for rapid and efficient delivery to the retailer's highly automated distribution centers. By 1986 the practice was well established, and the benefits became obvious enough to require more concerted action by the industry leaders.

Hence came the Voluntary Interindustry Commerce Standards (VICS) initiative led by general discounters, department stores, and apparel retailers, but also including distributors and manufacturers. Despite its name, VICS demanded somewhat less than voluntary compliance with its suggested standards, the first of which was the general adoption of the UPC throughout the supply chain. The first marketing message that retailers sent to their suppliers about the UPC requirement was, in the words of the the chief information officer of Wal-Mart Bob Martin, "pretty positive." [17] It had the familiar picture of a bar code, accompanied by a message: "The fastest route between the two points is the straight line." The fine print read: "Universal Product Codes are required for all items BEFORE ORDERS WILL BE WRITTEN." "When companies did not comply," Martin continued, "a little bit stronger message, more than a marketing campaign but still polite, was needed." Using the same picture and the fine-print statement, the main message now simply asserted: "If you don't draw the line, we do." [18]

The UPC requirement was the first VICS recommendation. There soon followed electronic data interchange (EDI) standards and codes for shipping containers and intermediate products. By 2000, over 90 percent of the entire nonfood consumer goods industry in the U.S. (in terms of volume), as well as a large number of global companies, were members of VICS and promulgated its standards. The result was a new, rationalized system of production and distribution. Frederick Abernathy and his associates have summarized the technological requirements of this new system, which they call "lean retailing," in terms of four building blocks: UPC, tags, and scanning devices; computerized inventory management; automated distribution centers; and adoption of communication standards throughout the supply chain.[19]

Through their adoption of lean-retailing techniques, Wal-Mart and other large discounters were able to induce suppliers—trading companies, manufacturers, shippers, and fast-freight forwarders—to rationalize their own operations in accordance with the retailers' requirements. These measures created an awareness of the seminal importance of the supply chain itself. Before the 1980s, the links between manufacturers and retailers were conceptualized from the manufacturers' point of view, as distribution channels. With the advent of lean retailing, the perspective shifted to that of the retailers. As Philip Schary and Tage Skjott-Larsen put it, the supply chain now identifies "the complete process of providing goods and services to the final user," and conceptualizes "all parties and logistics operations from supplier to customer" to be part of a single system, a system that is evaluated in terms of the "performance of the chain as a whole." This system includes "procurement, production and distribution operations, . . . extends across organizational boundaries, [and] is coordinated through an information system accessible to all members." [20]

Since the early 1970s, a substantial share of the merchandise carried by discounters has been imported from East Asia. This started in the 1960s, with a flood of cheap housewares, consumer electronics, and small motorcycles imported from Japan and apparel imported from Hong Kong. In the 1970s Taiwan and South Korea joined the ranks of major exporters. By 1972, as Japan increasingly shifted toward exporting cars and other high-technology goods, the imports from this group of Asian economies accounted for two-thirds of the value (and a substantially higher proportion of the quantity) of all U.S. imports of apparel and small electric appliances, 57 percent of kitchenware, and 80 percent of consumer electronics.

These already impressive numbers continued to increase during the 1970s, but they tell only one part of the story. Perhaps more important, the increasing share of imports from Asia was paralleled by the increasing share of the total imports in domestic consumption. As we can see in figure 1, this increase was particularly dramatic between 1965 and 1975, with electronics, sporting goods, footwear, and leather products leading the way.

Cheap imports from Asia shifted the power balance between discounters and their domestic suppliers. Throughout much of the 1960s, discounters scrambled to fill their stores with quality merchandise, typically conceding to suppliers' terms. By the mid-1970s, however, they not only were able to demand quantity discounts and other concessions based on their control over a substantial share of the consumer market, but also threatened to circumvent uncooperative suppliers in favor of their foreign competitors.

An account of how they established linkages with Asian manufacturers is described at length in another location.[21] It is sufficient here to say that most Asian manufacturers had little or no access to the American market except through retailers and merchandisers, and therefore willingly adapted to the exchange requirements placed on them by specialty and discount retailers, as well as such brand-name merchandisers as Nike. Because different Asian manufacturers had different production capabilities, American buyers quickly became quite sophisticated about where and with whom they would place their orders. For instance, long runs of standardized mass-produced items, such as microwave ovens and television sets, were ordered from Korean and Japanese manu-

FIGURE 1. SHARE OF IMPORTS IN THE APPARENT U.S. CONSUMPTION OF SELECT CATEGORIES OF CONSUMER GOODS, 1965–1995

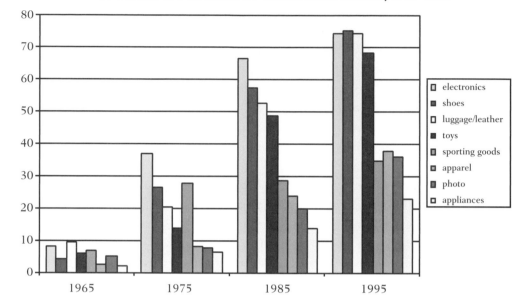

Source: U.S. Department of Commerce, *U.S. Industrial Outlook,* various years.

facturers, whereas short runs of batch-produced items, such as women's fashion appar-els, were given to Taiwanese and Hong Kong firms. Companies having a line of differ-entiated products, such as Nike or Gap, would match their orders with the firms having capabilities to produce those products. Repeat orders of different kinds of products, as well as similar products targeted to different niche markets, helped to build diversified manufacturing capabilities across Asia, so that, by the late 1970s, buyers could order al-most any type of consumer product from somewhere in Asia and have it made accord-ing to their specifications. As Asian firms improved their ability to respond to buyers' demand, American manufacturers found themselves increasingly losing whatever lever-age they may have had in earlier decades.

By the mid-1980s, the United States' imports of consumer goods from East Asia reached their peak, with more than 70 percent of imported nonautomotive consumer goods in those years coming from a select group of East Asian economies (Japan, Taiwan, South Korea, Hong Kong, and Singapore). A very large proportion of these goods, from apparel and footwear to consumer electronics to toys and sporting goods, were sold by the largest, most cost-conscious American retailers. Concerned that the trade deficit was too high and that U.S. manufacturing was losing its competitive edge, the U.S. government negotiated with the governments of Japan, Taiwan, and South Korea to allow their currencies to float upward by around 40 percent versus the U.S. dollar. The agreement, known as the Plaza Accord (it was signed at the Plaza Hotel in New York City), was reached in September 1985 and led to a thorough reorganization of Asian manufacturing.

Faced with the sudden increase of the dollar value of their factor inputs, and eager to keep their prices low and thus maintain their contracts with American retailers, Asian businesses quickly began to diversify. Most of Taiwan's light industries (garments, footwear, low-end consumer electronics) moved to locations where property and labor were much cheaper than in Taiwan, primarily to mainland China, but also to Southeast Asia. Many of these firms established low-end mass-market production lines in China, and retained high-end niche market batch production in Taiwan.[22] Large segments of Japanese export-oriented industries moved to Southeast Asia.[23] In addition some firms, such as Toyota, Honda, and Sony, established portions of their business in North America. South Korean business also moved labor-intensive operations to Southeast Asia, as well as to other developing countries in Latin America and central Europe. In each place that they established their new businesses, low-price supplier networks began to form.

At the same time, the East Asian businesses that remained at home either made core component parts for export to their overseas factories, upgraded their existing lines of products, or started manufacturing entirely new products. Fortuitously, from the late 1980s through the 1990s, high-technology industries created completely new product worlds (e.g., personal computers, cell phones, compact-disk and DVD players) based on components that Asian and not U.S.-based firms manufactured from the beginning.[24] These new industries more than replaced the export volume of the older industries that had moved overseas. By the early 1990s, Asian firms were making both the high-end and low-end products in most consumer goods categories.

Both in high-technology industries at home and in light industries that had moved to other countries, Asian manufacturers began to implement supply-chain techniques that American retailers and trade-name merchandisers required. A consequence of this reorganization was that a smaller numbers of Asian firms began to produce larger quantities of goods destined to be sold in fewer chain stores in the U.S. and around the world. Such companies as Dell, the Limited, and Nike worked through exclusive networks of producers, often selecting lead Asian firms to coordinate their supply and production lines. Large American retailers also developed overseas offices that concentrated on buying particular products in particular places from particular firms. As a result, many of their Asian subcontractors and suppliers grew very large and began to adopt vertically integrated, economy-of-scale production systems to meet their orders.

The reorganization of supplier networks in Asia was not always smooth, but still created intense global competition in consumer goods industries that further reduced the competitiveness of the U.S.-based suppliers. The latter increasingly found themselves unable to make existing low-end products at the price points required by American retailers, match the quality of high-end Asian manufactures, or enter into the new industries where Asian manufacturing firms had advantages from the outset.

Wal-Mart and Its Suppliers

WAL-MART'S GROWTH IN THE 1990S

In the 1970s and 1980s, Wal-Mart was a rising power among other U.S. retail powers. But by the early 1990s, Wal-Mart outgrew the retailing context to become a major force in restructuring large sectors of the domestic and, increasingly, the global economy. In 1987, Wal-Mart was still an upstart, an unusually successful regional retailer with a strong presence in twenty states (and a few stores in another three) that dominated small-town markets. Its technological savvy and its phenomenal growth rate, averaging over 30 percent a year in the 1980s attracted a lot of attention from the business press as well as from competitors. Moreover, the Buy American campaign initiated in 1985 was hailed as a paragon of corporate patriotism, overshadowing protests of local merchants against opening of new Wal-Mart stores in their communities.[25] Still, in 1987, with its one thousand discount stores and eighty-four warehouse clubs generating almost $16 billion in sales, Wal-Mart was only the fifth biggest retailer in the U.S., one-third the size of Sears.

Only five years later, in 1992, Wal-Mart had already become the established leader of the industry, having surpassed Kmart in 1990 and Sears in 1991. Its two thousand discount stores (including new supercenters) and 256 Sam's Clubs, now spread over forty-five states, Puerto Rico, and, as the first international venture, Mexico, generated sales of over $50 billion. Its newly acquired wholesale distribution subsidiary, McLane Company, distributed groceries to over thirty thousand convenience and independent stores (generating almost $3 billion in sales), and its trucking fleet and system of distribution centers were the biggest in the country.[26]

This, however, was only the beginning of the new phase of Wal-Mart's growth spanning the rest of 1990s, a phase represented by two trends that departed from Wal-Mart's previous strategies: its rapid expansion into grocery retailing, driven by its supercenter format, and its first efforts at global retailing.

Supercenters and the Reorganization of American Retailing

The supercenter format seemed a logical next step in the evolution of one-stop shopping, combining a supermarket-sized grocery section with the standard assortment of discount merchandise. However, the earlier attempts to create such "combo" stores, including Wal-Mart's own experiment with Hypermart USA, were only moderately successful, and the business press often dismissed them as lacking merchandising focus or being inappropriate to the American shopping culture. It was not until 1992 that Wal-Mart's management realized that the supercenter format could be the mainstay for the company's future growth. Unlike hypermarkets, which were located in metropolitan areas where they experienced intense competition from category killers and established supermarket operators, supercenters followed Wal-Mart's proven strategy of small-town expansion and "geographic fortification,"[27] and were often based on existing discount stores, with their already established customer base. Supercenters were such an immediate success that even Wal-Mart's management was surprised. Discovering that adding grocery departments to existing stores typically increased sales of nonfood merchandise by 30 percent, Wal-Mart accelerated the conversion of discount stores into supercenters. In 1994, supercenters represented the majority of newly opened stores (figure 2). At the end of 2004, there were more than 1,600 supercenters in the United States, a number that is likely to double in the next five years.

The ascendance of supercenters and warehouse clubs dramatically changed the nature of retail competition in the United States and led to the integration of general-merchandise, specialty retailing, grocery, and drugstore sectors. By 2003, this newly integrated sector accounted for $1.5 trillion in retail sales. Figure 3 shows the relative performance of its main retail formats, both discount and nondiscount ones. Wal-Mart supercenters, the most formidable retailing force of the last decade, capture around 7 percent of the total sector sales, and industry analysts predict this share to triple in the next six years.

The Wal-Mart supercenter defines the very core of this new field of integrated merchandising. Other giant retailers—Target and Costco, Kroger, Safeway, and Albertson's, Walgreens and CVS, the newly merged Sears and Kmart, and even Wal-Mart's own Sam's Club—increasingly position themselves in relation to supercenter retailing, some trying to emulate it, others emphasizing what they do better or differently. Consolidation in each of the four major formats that compete directly with supercenters—warehouse clubs, supermarkets, drugstores, and discount department stores—left only a

FIGURE 2. GROWTH OF WAL-MART STORES IN THE 1990S

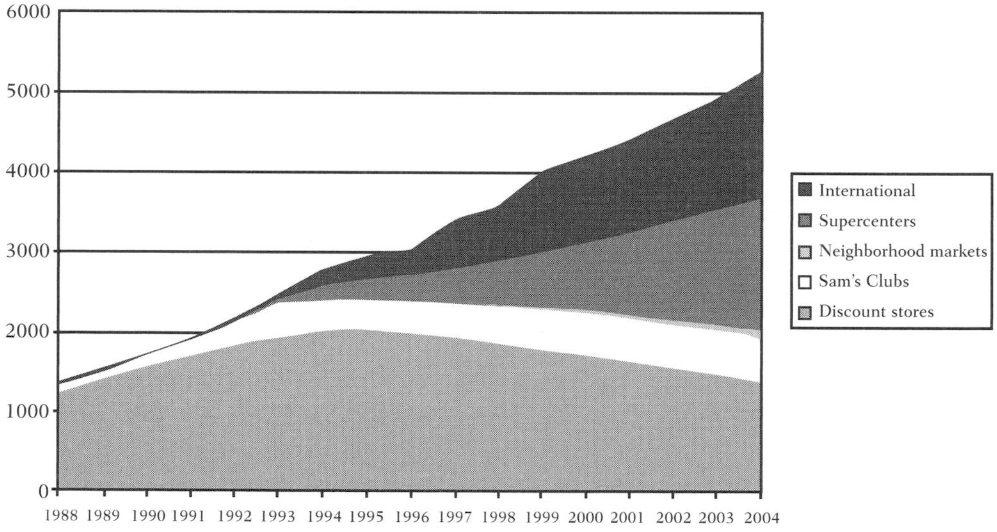

Source: Wal-Mart Corporation annual reports, various years.

FIGURE 3. REVENUE SHARE OF VARIOUS STORE FORMATS, INTEGRATED GENERAL MERCHANDISE SECTOR*, 1992–2003

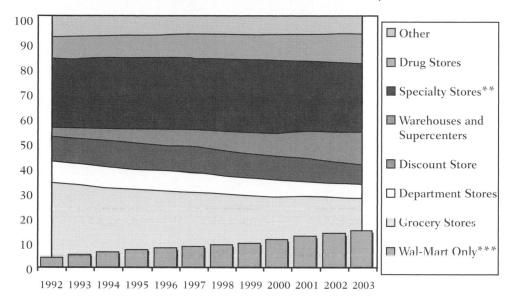

Legend:
- Other
- Drug Stores
- Specialty Stores**
- Warehouses and Supercenters
- Discount Store
- Department Stores
- Grocery Stores
- Wal-Mart Only***

* Integrated general merchandise sector is a combination of general merchandise, food and beverage, and beauty and health care stores (see text for more details)
** Includes apparel, furniture, home furnishings, electronics, appliance, sporting goods, books, jewelry and other specialty stores
*** Wal-Mart stores revenues are also included in the "warehouses and supercenters" and "discount stores" categories

Source: U.S. Census Bureau, Current Business Reports, Series BR/03-A, *Annual Benchmark Report for Retail Trade and Food Services: January 1992 Through February 2004* (Washington, DC, 2004).

handful of major competitors with a lion's share of the market (see table 1 for a list of the biggest American retailers).

Further toward the periphery, yet still well within this field of competitive forces, are specialty apparel retailers such as Gap and the Limited, off-price apparel discounters such as TJX, and department stores, including JCPenney, Kohl's, and Dillard's. As their overall share of the soft goods market continues to shrink under the assault of big discounters, they are forced to pursue diversification strategies, competing on style, service, assortment depth, and the quality of merchandise. Specialty retailers in other

TABLE 1: TOP AMERICAN RETAILERS, ORGANIZED BY THEIR POSITION IN THE INTEGRATED GENERAL MERCHANDISE SECTOR*

RETAIL CATEGORY/ RETAILER/RANK**	REVENUES 2003 (BILLIONS OF DOLLARS)	STORES 2003
Wal-Mart Supercenters (1)***	100	1471
Warehouse Clubs		
Costco (5)	42.5	420
Sam's Club (1)	34.5	538
BJ's Wholesale Club (38)	6.7	150
Discounters and Mass Merchandisers		
Wal-Mart Discount Stores (1)***	74	1478
Target (4)	48.1	1553
Kmart (14)	23.4	1515
Sears (6)	41.1	1970
JCPenney (15)	17.8	1077
Grocery Chains and Drugstores		
Kroger (3)	53.8	3774
Safeway (7)	35.5	1817
Albertsons (8)	35.4	2305
Walgreen (9)	32.5	4227
Ahold USA (11)	26.9	1489
CVS (12)	26.6	4179
Department Stores		
Federated Department Stores (20)	15.2	450
May Department Stores (21)	13.3	1124

Apparel Specialty

Gap (18)	15.8	3022
TJX (22)	13.3	2062
Limited (34)	8.9	3911

Other Specialty

Best Buy (13)	24.5	1767
Staples (23)	13.2	1559
Office Depot (24)	12.4	1099
Toys 'R' Us (26)	11.6	1500

HOME IMPROVEMENT CENTERS

Home Depot (2)	64.8	1707
Lowe's (10)	30.8	952

* Select retailers from the list of fifty largest retailers (by revenue), 2003
** Rank by revenue
*** Estimated from total Wal-Mart stores revenue

Source: Stores (www.stores.org), July 2004

categories, from Best Buy, Office Depot, and Staples to Toys 'R' Us, Barnes & Noble, and Blockbuster, follow similar marketing strategies in an attempt to distinguish their merchandise assortment from the standard supercenter offering. Even those sectors that until recently had been impacted only marginally by the reorganization of the general-merchandising sector in the 1990s, such as home-improvement centers, auto parts stores, and gasoline station/convenience store operators, find themselves increasingly drawn into the new regime. Finally, of course, we should also mention the possible revolution in general merchandising, Internet-based retailing. While still of modest size compared to their brick-and-mortar counterparts, Internet-only retailers are already making a big splash with their incredible market capitalization and innovative business models. In 1996, Wal-Mart was among the first large retailers to join the e-commerce trend, and it has recently announced significant expansion plans for its Internet retailing unit.

Global Expansion

Wal-Mart's successful entry into grocery retailing was one major aspect of its 1990s expansion. The second, and somewhat slower to develop, was its international expansion. Since the 1970s, Wal-Mart has been selling imported goods sourced by U.S. brand-name merchandisers and, to a lesser degree, directly by its purchasing agents in Hong Kong and Taiwan.[28] Estimates of the percentage of both type of imported goods sold in Wal-Mart ranged upwards of 40 percent in the 1980s. Despite their extensive involvement with suppliers in Asia, Wal-Mart always seemed to be one step behind its competitors. "In going to Asia and then into China, department stores always beat us," remembered one retired Wal-Mart executive. "A lot of people were there long before we were. But it was part of the strategy to let them go through the initial tortures. [Wal-Mart would] step in when all the groundwork had been laid."[29]

Following the precedents set by other firms, such as Royal Ahold and Carrefour, Wal-Mart in the early 1990s began to use its global supply chains to enter consumer markets outside the United States. The first Wal-Mart store to open abroad was its Club Aurrera (modeled on Sam's Club) warehouse in Mexico City, operated as a joint venture with Mexican retailer Cifra. In the following two years, more stores were added in Mexico and Puerto Rico, and Wal-Mart entered an agreement to supply Japanese retailers Ito-Yokado and Yaohan with its private label merchandise, which the latter would market in Japan, Singapore, Hong Kong, Malaysia, Thailand, Indonesia, and the Philippines. In 1994, the expansion accelerated with the acquisition of 122 Woolco stores in Canada and the opening of three Sam's Clubs in Hong Kong. Table 2 presents a chronology of Wal-Mart's international expansion.

That expansion's early phase, which lasted until 1998, was characterized by focused expansion in North America and very cautious and generally not very successful steps elsewhere. From this early expansion, Wal-Mart managers found out that retailing in foreign markets, especially those that differ significantly from the U.S. domestic market, requires a considerable learning period and numerous adaptations of the merchandising model. It also became apparent that Wal-Mart's operational efficiency required a considerable economy of scale and significant market share in order to be successfully replicated abroad.

After 1999, however, Wal-Mart's global expansion efforts became much bolder, marked by large acquisitions: the British retailer Asda (1999), Interspar hypermarkets in

TABLE 2: A CHRONOLOGY OF WAL-MART'S INTERNATIONAL EXPANSION

1991	Mexico City, Mexico (joint venture with Cifra)
1992	Puerto Rico
1993	Wal-Mart International division formed with Bobby Martin as president
1994	Canada: acquisition of 122 Woolco stores; Hong Kong: 3 stores
1995	Argentina (3 units); Brazil (5)
1996	China (through a joint-venture agreement); Indonesia; exits Hong Kong
1997	Acquisition of dominant interest in Cifra (Mexico); Germany: acquisition of 21 Wertkauf stores
1998	South Korea (4 units, joint venture); Germany: acquisition of 74 Interspar stores
1999	United Kingdom: acquisition of 229 ASDA stores
2001	Wal-Mart moves its main global distribution center (global sourcing center) to Shenzhen, China
2002	Wal-Mart becomes world's most global retailer (measured by sales outside of the home market); Japan: minority stake in Seiyu
2003	Brazil: acquisition of 118 Bompreco stores

Source: Wal-Mart Corporation annual reports, various years.

Germany (1999), a stake in Japanese retailer Seiyu (2002), and the Bompreco chain in Brazil (2004). At the same time, Wal-Mart began to open stores in China, following a "greenfield" strategy similar to its early U.S. expansion. As a result, Wal-Mart is currently not only the biggest global retailer, with almost $60 billion in sales outside the U.S. market, but also the biggest retailer in Canada and Mexico, the third largest in the UK and Brazil, and likely soon to claim a top spot in China and Japan. In all these countries, its entry triggered a substantial reorganization of the domestic retail market, similar in scope and direction to the one that occurred in the U.S. in the 1990s. Even its less successful entry in Germany led to an intense price war and the consolidation of the domestic market. The sheer possibility of its entry into France provoked a merger between Carrefour and Promodes in 1999, thus creating the world's second biggest retailing firm.

Beside Wal-Mart, very few American big-box retailers have ventured beyond the North American market, Costco, Staples, and Toys 'R' Us being the major exceptions. Similarly, the presence of foreign retailers in the American market has been relatively limited and has decreased in recent years. Thus, Wal-Mart's global competitors are mainly foreign firms, all of them with substantial experience in grocery retailing and with longer and more extensive international retailing experience; the battle for a share of the $4 trillion general-merchandise-and-food global market is being waged outside of Wal-Mart's home turf. At the same time, retail concentration in most developed countries, and even many developing ones, is significantly higher than in the American market, and the development of big-box specialty retailing is considerably weaker, creating more intense competitive conditions.

Wal-Mart's transformation in the 1990s had a significant impact on its supply chain. Its entry into grocery retailing brought an increasing number of large manufacturers of packaged consumer goods into the orbit of its major suppliers. The effects were felt on both sides, as the manufacturers experienced a strong pressure to adapt to Wal-Mart's business model and increase their operational efficiency, and the retailer further rationalized its supplier base. The global expansion of Wal-Mart stores created the much bigger challenge of creating a new global sourcing infrastructure of a size and complexity well beyond what any multinational firm had attempted before. Wal-Mart now operates as a major exporter as well as importer in several large regional markets, shuffling tens of thousands of products around the world to meet the local demand in its 3,600 domestic and 1,600 international stores. While this creates a whole new set of opportunities for its major partners, which can now gain unprecedented access to global consumer markets, it also creates even more pressure to continuously shape and adapt their business models to Wal-Mart's strict demands.

SIZE MATTERS

Wal-Mart, so the press asserts, has the power to "squeeze" its suppliers, reducing their profit margins, imposing cost-cutting measures, and, in the case of the U.S. firms, forcing them to turn to outsourcing. Such power is generally traced to its size or, more precisely, to its market share. Wal-Mart controls about 15 percent of the domestic sales of general merchandise and food, and in some categories such as household staples and basic apparel its share is closer to 30 percent. Even for the biggest manufacturers of packaged consumer goods, from Procter and Gamble to Clorox and Revlon and from Del Monte to Nabisco and Sara Lee, the amount of business with Wal-Mart—typically ranging between 15 percent and 30 percent of total shipments—creates a significant dependency on the retailer's demands. And such dependency can, of course, be much higher in the case of smaller firms among Wal-Mart's twenty thousand global vendors, and in particular for those supplying the retailer with its private brand merchandise.

While Wal-Mart's market power is undeniable, and for many manufacturers unavoidable, becoming a Wal-Mart vendor is a highly sought prize because the retailer's size generates an opportunity to reach such a huge number of global consumers. Wal-Mart stores are today, arguably, the biggest marketing channel for consumer products in the world: the 20 million customers who shop at Wal-Mart on an average day represent a bigger market than could be reached by any traditional mass media promotion.[30]

Wal-Mart's size also implies that severing a relation with even major suppliers has little effect on the retailer's side.[31] Indeed most of Wal-Mart's vendors receive no guarantees that their business relationship with the retailer will be a long-lasting one. Wal-Mart's famous "Plus One" principle—that for each of the hundreds of thousands of products it handles either the price should be lowered or the quality improved every year—puts intense pressure on its suppliers to stay ahead of their own competition. Thus, partnering with Wal-Mart holds both the promise of reaching major global markets with minimal advertising and promotional outlays, and the danger of adapting one's business model to the retailer's strict demands only to find out that the resulting lowered profit margins and the efficiency pressure are more than one's organizational capacities can bear.

The fact that more than five hundred large vendors have established permanent sales offices near Wal-Mart's Bentonville headquarters, and that tens of thousands of global suppliers attend its global purchase fairs, shows that many manufacturers consider the prospect of becoming a Wal-Mart partner worth the gamble. From the retailer's side, the partner-selection process is based on two main dimensions: the ability of a vendor to offer an everyday low supply price, and its operational and technological compatibility with Wal-Mart's own business process.[32]

THE PURSUIT OF EVERYDAY LOW SUPPLY PRICE

Most accounts of Wal-Mart in the popular press tell of the retailer's relentless pursuit of the lowest purchase price. These accounts, however, give little information about how Wal-Mart's overall pricing model shapes the business strategies of Wal-Mart's suppliers. The "everyday low price" standard means that Wal-Mart's buyers are not bargain hunters, trying to locate and close an extraordinary deal. Nor do they push for a discount on the prevailing market price.[33] Instead, they base their estimate of the purchasing price on the suppliers' cost structures and operational efficiency. Competitive bids may, of course, help to reveal the cost structure, but they are not the only means to do so. Wal-Mart often requires suppliers to open their books and submit to a rigorous cost analysis. Once a cost structure for a product is established, Wal-Mart requires the suppliers of that product to accept the retailer's own business strategy: low profit margins, rapid turnover, and high sales volume. Unlike other retailers, Wal-Mart demands of suppliers no elaborate trade promotions and no slotting allowances paid to the retailer in exchange for obtaining shelf space for products.[34] Instead, the cost of trade promotions and direct-marketing campaigns is typically deducted from the wholesale price, and the savings are passed on to the consumer. For example, John Fitzgerald, a former vice president of Nabisco, remembers Wal-Mart's reaction to his company's plan to offer a 25¢ newspaper coupon for a large bag of Lifesavers in advance of Halloween. Wal-Mart told Nabisco to add up what it would spend on the promotion—for the newspaper ads, the coupons, and handling—and then just take that amount off the price instead. "That isn't necessarily good for the manufacturer," Fitzgerald says. "They need things that draw attention."[35]

For the manufacturer, consenting to Wal-Mart's requirements for everyday low supply price holds the promise of gaining market share at the expense of the profit margin, the same outcome that it may also pursue through consumer and trade promotions. The main difference between these two strategies is that partnering with Wal-Mart entails losing a great deal of control over the pricing of one's products. Dealing with Wal-Mart, in other words, means accepting the structure of a highly rationalized market exchange with little space for strategic maneuvering.

Wal-Mart has developed a number of initiatives to help its suppliers deliver a quality product at a low cost and in a timely manner. Its "Vendor Information Manual" contains contracting instructions, specifies EDI requirements, and outlines the proper way to ship and deliver goods. The famous Retail Link gives vendors a direct insight into inventory levels of each product at each Wal-Mart store. Its data warehouse, which both provides internal operational data and serves as the backbone for the Retail Link, is by far the largest private collection of data in the world, second only to the Pentagon's. Currently, it contains over five hundred terabytes of data. It collects and organizes data from 140,000 POS systems around the world and records 20 million customer transactions each day. Several hundred thousand data-mining questions are sent to it every week. This elaborate infrastructure for product management is directly available to Wal-Mart's thousands of vendors, which can use it to reduce their own inventory-management costs, enhance operational efficiency, and test the potential of new products in a way that is more precise and less costly than the standard product-marketing tools. One such marketing strategy, often referred to as "micromarketing," includes placing a new product in a small sample of Wal-Mart stores and assessing the demand for it dynamically. Market demand can be fully tested in as little as four weeks, a process that with traditional marketing campaigns often took six months or more.[36]

Vendors' ability to use this infrastructure requires that they conform to Wal-Mart's logistics requirements, which are among the most rigorous in the industry. Wal-Mart not only manages hundreds of millions of items in its 5,500 stores around the world, but also adjusts the inventory levels of all these products according to local demand forecasts. To manage these products Wal-Mart depends on the strict cooperation of its suppliers with the needs of its logistical system.[37] Delivery of the right amount of product at the right time—the window of delivery to the distribution center is generally around fifteen minutes—is the key aspect of this process, but the additional product-related requirements can also be quite elaborate. For instance, Wal-Mart, and not the suppliers, specifies the display features of floor-ready products, features that come as additions to basic labels, source codes, and other identifying elements.[38]

Behind the ever evolving technology of product management stands an even more complex negotiation over which side has the power to define the final product that consumers buy. Wal-Mart's efficiency in managing consumer markets implies that it is able to translate its competence in assessing the shape of consumer demand (what consumers want, at what price point, in what quantities, and at what time) into defining the shape of the product that will be produced and delivered by its vendors. This leads us beyond Wal-Mart's two standard partner-selection criteria that we just discussed—the cost structure and the operational efficiency—to two more ambiguous aspects of its buying "philosophy" that also have significant long-term impact on the structure of its supply base.

BUYING DIRECT

The principle of buying direct from the manufacturer and thus reducing or eliminating the role of the wholesaler has been a driving force in discount retailing's rationalization of the consumer goods market. As retailers grew in size, they recognized that either they or the manufacturers could more efficiently perform many of the "value-adding" functions typically done by wholesalers. These functions depended on the industry and the historical distribution regime, but the persistence of attempts to eliminate the middleman spurred many comments about the decline and ultimate disappearance of the wholesale sector.[39] Yet, far from being squeezed out of business by the joint assault of retailers and manufacturers, wholesalers maintained a fairly stable share of income and corporate profits over the second half of the twentieth century. Rather than eliminating the role of wholesalers, the drive to rationalize consumer goods markets kept redefining which specialized wholesale functions add value to the supply chain, continually creating opportunities for the firms that establish a core competence performing these functions.

The commitment to buying direct, then, especially in Wal-Mart's case, is based on utilizing economies of scale that eliminate operational inefficiency in the supply chain. Like most other large chain retailers, Wal-Mart has acquired a broad set of capabilities that resemble those of a typical wholesaler.[40] Thus, even an efficient wholesaler that is able to match Wal-Mart's low-profit, high-volume business philosophy and can provide useful intermediation services still puts itself in a more vulnerable position by partnering with Wal-Mart than does a manufacturer having corresponding qualities. Moreover, this vulnerability is not limited to traditional wholesalers, but can be experienced by all types of intermediaries, including many firms that are commonly recognized as manufacturers, but whose core competences have shifted to marketing and supply-chain management. In order to become vendors to such large retailers as Wal-Mart, these firms rely on developing their own capable, low-cost suppliers; yet this puts them in danger of eventually being bypassed in favor of these same suppliers. In short, the principle of buying direct generates a constant pressure on Wal-Mart's vendors to define their own core competences as complementary to, rather than competitive with, those of the retailer, with wholesaling, marketing, transportation, and supply-chain management being the most commonly contested areas.

MANUFACTURER BRANDS, STORE BRANDS

The competitive pressure that Wal-Mart's strategy of buying direct puts on many of its vendors is similar to the pressure that Wal-Mart's private-label brands puts on brand-name manufacturers. The strong commitment to store brands is a relatively new development at Wal-Mart, closely related to both its entrance into the grocery sector and its global expansion. Since its founding, Wal-Mart has been known as a store that sells national brands, a merchandising strategy crucial to building a reputation as a low-price leader. As Wal-Mart's reputation grew in the 1980s, the discounter was able to add more prestigious national brands to its assortment, especially in apparel, while keeping its low-price image. However, after Loblaw proved successful with its President's Choice brand in 1991, Wal-Mart launched its own premium Sam's Choice brand, followed two years later with an economy offering, Great Value. Today, Wal-Mart manages a portfolio of several hundred of its own brands covering most merchandise categories and accounting for around 40 percent of total sales.[41]

These numbers, however, tell only a part of the story. Store brands have become a crucial part of Wal-Mart's global expansion strategy. Since few manufacturer's brands have a true global presence, Wal-Mart stores and their price-leadership image may prove to be the best marketing channel for building strong, value-priced, global brands. Wal-Mart's popular Great Value brand of packaged grocery items is already sold in most international Wal-Mart units, including those in Germany and China. Its George line of apparel, the leading clothing brand in the UK, is now also offered in the United States, Canada, and Germany. In the global context, Wal-Mart's brands have an advantage over manufacturer-controlled and manufacturer-advertised brands for two reasons: first, although manufacturer brands may sell well in some regional markets, store brands can easily be established as their value-priced complements in all markets where Wal-Mart operates; second, Wal-Mart's shopping and consumption models redefine an increasing range of products as standardized cheap consumables for which the very concept of branding may become less significant.

For its suppliers, therefore, the impact of Wal-Mart's store-brand strategy is ambivalent. On the one hand, the limited number of items in each product category in Wal-Mart stores, especially compared to other big-box specialty retailers, clearly favors big national brands and store brands over smaller, second-tier brands. The national brands are needed to attract a broad range of consumers and to provide the basis for low price claims; the store brands attract price-sensitive shoppers, generate higher profit margins, and create negotiating power over brand-name manufacturers. Indeed, the growth of stores brands at Wal-Mart can threaten even the best-established national brands. From dog food and garden fertilizer to painkillers and vitamins, many Wal-Mart store brands are now national sales leaders, surpassing their better-recognized and more heavily advertised competitors.

Although the rise of store brands may not spell the demise of nationally advertised, manufacturer-controlled brands, it may gradually transform them into niche, high-end, high-margin players. However, those manufacturers that want to avoid such a fate may have little choice but to follow Wal-Mart's lead in defining the shape and the dynamics of the global "product world," thus ceding a substantial amount of control over brand development and advertising. Although many manufacturers may try to preserve their best-known brand names, it is likely that an increasing share of their productive capacity will go to supplying Wal-Mart with its own store-branded goods.

THE EVOLUTION OF WAL-MART'S RELATIONS WITH ITS SUPPLIERS

The evolution of Wal-Mart's relationship with its suppliers demonstrates how the company has established a market-making supremacy throughout its supply chain. In the 1960s and early 1970s, as a regional discounter with modest buying power, Wal-Mart bought mostly national brand merchandise, searching for the lowest prices in the market, including closeout deals and similar bargains. Like most other retailers at the time, it had to accept manufacturers' power to define the terms of trade, which stretched from product development, branding, and advertising to logistics issues and, through resale price-maintenance statutes, even to some aspects of retail pricing. Some major retailers, such as A & P, Safeway, and Sears, evaded manufacturers' power by maintaining a broad assortment of store brands, but the new discounters typically accepted manufacturers' market-making strategies, defining their own business model in terms of the efficient distribution of nationally advertised goods.

But from the mid-1970s to the mid-1980s the balance of market-making power shifted decidedly in favor of big discounters. Using their growing buying power, and the access to an increasing supply of cheap foreign manufactures, they pitted their suppliers against each other in order to achieve the lowest purchase price. The consequent decline of domestic consumer goods industries was rapid, and import penetration soared to unprecedented levels. Wal-Mart, Kmart, Target, and a number of other big discounters were among the main beneficiaries of this process, using foreign sourcing both to maintain their low-price appeal and to increase their leverage vis-à-vis their domestic suppliers. By the end of this period, almost half of all merchandise sold at Wal-Mart stores was imported, and the retailer was able to force an increasing number of its domestic suppliers to accept its everyday low price business model.

In the mid-1980s, the transition to a new phase of retailer-supplier relationships occurred; adversarial relations and intense competition between retailers and their domestic suppliers gave way to a new climate that forged cooperative links and partnerships. As we have seen, the appreciation of major Asian currencies based on the Plaza Accord and the consequent rapid, albeit temporary, decline of the competitiveness of Asian manufacturers brought only short-lived relief to domestic manufacturers. American suppliers benefited much more from the retailers' realization that the most effective way of using their market-making power was by reorganizing their supply chains, rather than simply extracting concessions from them. Since these efforts were based on the diffusion of new information technologies, American suppliers were generally able to benefit from their proximity to the emerging national infrastructure of IT products and services.

Through its early adoption of the UPC code and EDI tools, development of automated distribution centers, and leadership in the VICS initiative, Wal-Mart emerged as the undisputed industry leader of supply-chain rationalization. Even its much hailed

Buy American campaign, is best understood in the context of such rationalization efforts. The stories of domestic suppliers who benefited from the Buy American campaign typically reveal that Wal-Mart went beyond simply offering to buy their merchandise on favorable terms. The retailer also participated in product design and development, suggested improvement in the supplier's overall business process, and managed the logistics of distribution.

Wal-Mart's efforts to develop a new group of technologically capable suppliers that would adopt the retailer's own business model resulted in the creation of stable relationships with several large manufacturers of packaged consumer goods. The leading example of such a relationship is Wal-Mart's much heralded partnership with Procter and Gamble, which started in 1988. In the 1990s, with the retailer's entry into grocery retailing, these partnerships became commonplace. Minimal requirements for establishing such relationships included transparency of pricing and contracting, as well as a degree of technological sophistication and operational efficiency. During the 1990s, supplier relationships evolved to include the coordination of product development and vendor-managed replenishment procedures (facilitated by the Retail Link system). Many large suppliers established permanent offices in Bentonville with teams fully dedicated to furthering their partnership with Wal-Mart.

Doing business with Wal-Mart became the main operational mainstay for hundreds of suppliers. The retailer's extraordinary growth in the 1990s, however, meant that it did not need to make equal commitments to all of its "partners." Its growth, of course, generated extraordinary opportunities for some; yet it also pushed them to adapt to the retailer's insistent demands for technological and logistical competence and to the rapidly changing dynamics of the consumer markets it helped create. From the Retail Link to the adoption of RFID, Wal-Mart became the major driver of technology-based productivity gains in the American economy. At the same time, the success of its store brands generated an intense pressure on major manufacturers to improve their product lines and develop new ones. However, the potentially biggest challenge and biggest opportunity for its suppliers came from Wal-Mart's global footprint. Its expansion efforts in Japan and China, and the recent announcement by Wal-Mart CEO H. Lee Scott that the company is considering growth opportunities in India and Russia, promises to create a completely new retailer-supplier regime, based on integrated global sourcing for a worldwide set of retail markets.

Conclusion: The Coming Era of Global Procurement?

Wal-Mart executives know that in order to sustain the remarkable rates of growth expected by its shareholders, Wal-Mart must continue with aggressive international expansion. In the United States, its same-store sales growth has been sluggish in the last few years, both compared with its historical rates and with the growth of its international division. Of course, the American market remains the world's largest, and even the most pessimistic prognoses allow that the number of Wal-Mart domestic supercenters may double before reaching the saturation point. In the international arena, Wal-Mart has already achieved the dominant position in Canada and Mexico and is still growing in the United Kingdom. Germany, where Wal-Mart has yet to turn a profit, and Japan, which is still dominated by small stores, represent other main expansion opportunities. In the long run, however, it is the understored, virgin markets of developing countries such as China, India, and Russia, with their rapidly expanding consumer purchasing power and low levels of retail competition, that hold the main promise for Wal-Mart's future growth.

The less well understood aspect of Wal-Mart's global expansion is how it will affect its suppliers. On the one hand, the retailer's expansion into new markets certainly represents a tremendous growth opportunity for those suppliers that can meet the global consumer demand. On the other hand, these suppliers will increasingly have to rely on Wal-Mart, and a small number of other global retailers, to assess, interpret, and shape global consumer demand and to translate it into specific product and service requirements in supplier markets. From the suppliers' perspective, the globalization of retailing poses the issue of retail power even more starkly than before. Increased retailers' control of global consumer markets may entail further decline of manufacturer control over product development, branding, and pricing, and a new wave of increased consolidation and competition in consumer goods industries, as occurred recently with the merger of Procter and Gamble with Gillette.

Although a fundamental economic transformation triggered by the globalization of retailing power may still be in the offing, we can look at some recent developments in Wal-Mart's global sourcing strategy for a hint of its general outline. Since 1999, Wal-Mart's Global Sourcing group has been developing mechanisms to help Wal-Mart stores around the world with their buying tasks. The group does not buy merchandise.

Instead, it refers to itself as "a service organization that aids in the procurement and execution of strategic initiatives developed by merchants."[42] It researches sources of supply, identifies new products, specifies import opportunities, and shares knowledge about merchandising practices within the Wal-Mart organization. Most of its recent successes involve introducing new private-label (store-brand) products, such as Alcott Ridge wines (made by Gallo) and George apparel, to all of Wal-Mart's international markets. The globally standardized products go hand in hand with globally standardized sources of supply. From apparel and wine to copy paper and light bulbs, the number of private label suppliers has been reduced in order to "deliver consistent quality around the world."[43] In addition to promoting global sourcing initiatives, Wal-Mart has increasingly relied on its largest global suppliers for insight on how to handle its international expansion. These partnering efforts have recently evolved into the creation of an elite group of fifty top suppliers that serve as advisers for Wal-Mart's global venture, providing operating models on the basis of their own extensive international experience.

Perhaps an even better sign of the times to come is Wal-Mart's renewed emphasis on sourcing products from China. While Wal-Mart has been buying in China since the early 1970s, first through American and Japanese importers and later through its purchasing partners from Hong Kong, it only recently established direct buying offices in Shenzhen (2001) and Tianjin (2003). The Shenzhen office was in the meantime promoted into Wal-Mart's global purchasing headquarters, clearly indicating the retailer's strategic orientation toward Chinese suppliers. While the current level of Wal-Mart's buying in China, at over $18 billion in 2004, is huge both in absolute terms and in terms of its share of U.S. imports from China (10 percent) and of total foreign buying in China (30 percent), it represents only 10 percent of the retailer's overall purchasing budget, a proportion significantly lower than that of many other major U.S. retailers. Thus, the main significance of Wal-Mart's sourcing initiatives in China lies not in its rationalization of the buying process, but rather in the fact that it has been buying relatively little from Chinese suppliers and that this amount is likely to increase substantially in the near future.

These recent developments indicate not only a probable future trajectory for Wal-Mart's global expansion, but also provide a model that other global retailers will likely adopt. So far, only a few other mass retailers have developed a major global presence and a strategy of integrated global procurement, most notably Carrefour, Metro, Ahold, and Tesco. None of these has yet approached the level of Wal-Mart's logistical and technological sophistication. However, as the share of the global retail market captured by Wal-Mart and a handful of other global retailers continues to increase, we can expect that in the next ten years a small group of these retailers will dominate the making of consumer markets in all major economies around the world.

This concentration of global retailing will certainly have a powerful impact on the shape of the global supplier markets. Will the power of retailers over their suppliers continue to increase? Although we cannot give a definitive answer to this question, we conclude that such a trend is quite likely, for at least two reasons. First, the concentration of global retailing is still at a very low level compared to most manufacturing industries, and thus we can expect leading retailers to continue to increase their market share and their buying power. The second, and perhaps more profound, reason is that our notion of the "natural balance of power" between retailers and manufacturers may have been distorted by the long period in which mass manufacturers enjoyed global economic prominence. For the better part of the twentieth century, the giants of the steel, petrochemical, automotive, electronic, and packaged consumer goods industries dominated the corporate landscapes of their national economies and captured the imagination of business observers and the general public. They not only created a new world of standardized and affordable goods, but also pioneered new techniques advertising, packaging, selling, and servicing these goods, thus assuming responsibility for making the modern consumer market. Moreover, these big producers represented the first crop of the "multinationals" that started the post–World War II wave of economic globalization.

In the broader historical context, however, the prominence of manufacturers is an anomaly. Until the end of the nineteenth century, the making of large-scale markets, including global ones, was predominantly the task of merchants, rather than producers, and it was merchants, and not manufacturers, who established the largest and most powerful businesses. In this sense, what we observed in the second half of the twentieth century as the shift of market-making power from manufacturers to retailers may be less a novelty than the restoration of the traditional division of labor between market makers and producers.

SIX

The Wal-Mart Effect and the New Face of Capitalism: Labor Market and Community Impacts of the Megaretailer

David Karjanen

> The cities will be part of the country. I shall live 30 miles from my office in one direction, under a pine tree; my secretary will live 30 miles away from it too, in another direction, under another pine tree. We shall both have our own car. We shall use up tires, wear out road surfaces and gears, consume oil and gasoline. All of which will necessitate a great deal of work; enough for all.[1]
>
> —Le Corbusier

Le Corbusier served as the standard-bearer of modernism; his dream of a "radiant" city, planned with central streets, infrastructure, and enough work for all, symbolizes the optimism of postwar modernist thought. The reality of American postwar urban and rural areas, however, has been profoundly different. The transformation of the urban landscape, as well as smaller towns and the rural countryside, has been changed dramatically by the spatial expanse of capital. Sprawl, suburbanization, and migration out of central cities have shaped not only where Americans live and work, but also where they shop. Retail development has been an integral part of this process as stores follow consumer demand out of the central city and into the suburbs and exurbs.

In this transformation of the built environment, no institution has been more controversial than Wal-Mart. While the actual impact of a Wal-Mart store on commerce, traffic, labor, and community life will vary from region to region and town to town, there is little doubt that this firm stands in the vanguard of those forces reshaping the world, both of space and work, in which a majority of Americans live.[2] To understand this transformative impact, this chapter first looks at the historical relationships between corporations and communities during key stages in the development of U.S. capitalism. It then examines the effect Wal-Mart's expansion has had on a variety of contemporary communities in the United States. We conclude that spatial and structural inequalities are enhanced when the megaretailer transforms a regional economy.

It is vital to clarify the historical relationship between corporations and communities in order to understand the contemporary dimensions of the "Wal-Mart effect." During the last two centuries, the transformation in the character of American capitalism has been integral to the rise and continual reconfiguration of the American city and its rural hinterland. In the era of commercial capitalism (1840–1890), or what historian Sean Wilentz has called "metropolitan industrialization," large port cities like New York, Philadelphia, Boston, and Baltimore, as well as Chicago, Cincinnati, and St. Louis, flourished because of their location at the confluence of a network of river, rail, and seaborne commerce. The vitality and complexity of such cities arose out of the multitude of functions they performed: as financiers and processors of the flow of commodities generated by the hinterland, as sites of numerous small manufacturing enterprises, as transport and transshipment hubs, and as centers of entertainment, culture, and consumption.[3]

Chicago may well have been the preeminent commercial center of this sort, at least during the first half century of its extraordinary growth. As William Cronon has shown in his magisterial *Nature's Metropolis: Chicago and the Great West*, the commercial success of the nation's second city was dependent upon a symbiotic, ecologically integrated relationship between the city and its vast hinterland. Chicago's railroads, banks, agricultural equipment manufacturers, grain elevators, and Board of Trade auction pits were all necessary to transform a continent of wheat into the foodstuffs consumed by hungry urbanites. The city's dominance in meatpacking, mail-order merchandising, and railroad construction and finance were tributes to the intimate, reciprocal connections between Chicago and its regional clients.[4]

The rise of the giant corporation and the emergence of an industrialism based upon both mass production and mass consumption transformed the nation's commercial cities between 1890 and 1960. In this second era of capitalist growth, which some historians and sociologists have denominated "Fordist," cities like Detroit, Pittsburgh, Bridgeport, Akron, and Winston-Salem became identified with the mass production of a single product, while other metropolitan regions, including New York, Chicago, Buffalo, Philadelphia, and St. Louis, saw the emergence of a set of large manufacturing firms which added bulk and muscle to their commercial economic infrastructure. Thus during the early twentieth century there was a clear spatial dimension to the economy of places: a proximity between consumers, producers, and distributors was critical to an expanding regional economy and a well-integrated civic life.

The Fordist cities of the early twentieth century were not necessarily large, because U.S. manufacturing was quite decentralized, often sited in medium-sized towns like Lynn, Flint, Rochester, Erie, Utica, Toledo, Grand Rapids, and Camden. One such manufacturing town was Pittsfield, Massachusetts where the anthropologist June Nash found that General Electric had achieved a near hegemonic influence during the early twentieth century, when both the company and the town enjoyed rapid growth. GE's cultural and political dominance was based upon that corporation's civic engagement, its generation-long support for local schools and charities, and a "social contract" between business and labor which ensured a family wage for white male workers. From the 1930s through the 1970s the New Deal state legitimized the labor-management accord and generalized its social achievements, through Social Security, minimum-wage standards, and other welfare-state entitlements, throughout the community.[5]

Although the era of Fordist industrialism was not without intense class conflict and racial subordination, it did generate a certain spatial stability. In Pittsfield and other sites of mass production, corporate investment remained relatively stable, even if employment fluctuated in a highly cyclical fashion during the post–World War II decades. Corporations like GE generated a set of nearby satellite firms which often hired those workers temporarily unemployed during recessions and seasonal layoffs. Downtown business districts served both the working class and those higher up the income scale, with a standard set of retail firms, like Woolworth, JCPenney, Sears, A & P, and numerous local specialty shops, catering to a stratified but geographically proximate set of consumers. The white working class became increasingly homogeneous, residing within a well-defined set of neighborhoods, whose stability was enhanced by Progressive era/New Deal innovations in city planning (zoning), home finance, and school construction. Overall, the Fordist era left a distinctive mark on the American urban land-scape: towns and cities dominated by a stable set of well-capitalized industries, sur-rounded by lattices of class-stratified housing and smaller businesses, ringed by a set of suburbs that were truly "bedroom" communities, i.e., dependent geographically and economically upon the vibrancy of the urban industrial core.[6]

Post-Fordism: Transforming Consumers and Communities

> Capitalist development must negotiate a knife-edge between pre-serving the values of past commitments made at a particular place and time, or devaluing them to open up fresh room for accumula-tion. Capitalism perpetually strives, therefore, to create a social and physical landscape in its own image and requisite to its own needs at a particular point in time, only just as certainly to undermine, dis-rupt, and even destroy that landscape at a later point in time.
>
> —David Harvey

Capitalist development is an ongoing process, observes David Harvey, and the inter-action between capital and communities is one of continual variation as new forms of settlement, development, and growth occur in cycles that generate decline and trans-formation. The current era, which began during the economic trauma of the late 1970s, has sped up these processes. Social scientists often describe these past forty years as one of post-Fordism, a historical period characterized by the globalization of produc-tion, extreme capital mobility, and high levels of employment insecurity and stratifica-tion.[7] Concurrently, the transformation of America's communities—from the urban cores to the suburban fringes and from the mill towns to the small farms—directly re-flects these underlying changes in the political economy, both within the U.S. and throughout the world.[8]

Sociologist Manuel Castells has emphasized the extent to which post-Fordism has generated a spatial and structural polarization within the urban world.[9] As central cities have lost their manufacturing facilities, more-affluent residents have migrated to the suburbs, sometimes as a function of a racially motivated "white flight" but also because a sizable slice of the working population now finds its livelihood centered well beyond the old business and factory districts.[10] In this way, the Fordist city—one with an old downtown and set of main shopping streets surrounded by manufacturing plants—has shifted toward a more spatially polarized urbanism with more affluent commuters living and working in freeway-dependent suburban or exurban communities, while the poor and minority populations remain trapped within a jobless central city.[11]

Simultaneously, there is a major structural shift toward postindustrial employment and the attendant expansion of the lower-wage service sector.[12] This structural shift is primarily seen in the move from manufacturing employment toward service-sector employment, which produces an "hourglass" economy wherein high-wage information-technology jobs grow rapidly, middle-income occupations contract violently, and most

TABLE 1. TEN OCCUPATIONS WITH THE LARGEST JOB GROWTH IN THE U.S. ECONOMY, 2002–12

OCCUPATION	EMPLOYMENT (THOUSANDS)			
	2002	2012	%	MEDIAN HOURLY WAGE
Registered nurses	2,284	2,908	27	$24.53
Postsecondary teachers	1,581	2,184	38	$16.55
Retail salespersons	4,076	4,672	15	$8.82
Customer service representatives	1,894	2,354	24	$12.79
Combined food preparation and serving workers	1,990	2,444	23	$7.05
Cashiers	3,432	3,886	13	$7.68
Janitors and cleaners	2,267	2,681	18	$8.98
General and operations managers	2,049	2,425	18	$35.86
Waiters and waitresses	2,097	2,464	18	$6.79
Nursing aides, orderlies, and attendants	1,375	1,718	25	$9.98

Source: Bureau of Labor Statistics, employment and occupational projections, 2002–12.

new employment growth occurs at the bottom of the wage scale, where retail and other service-sector jobs proliferate.[13] The Bureau of Labor Statistics estimates that during the decade 2002–12, the occupations with the largest growth in the U.S. economy will be in higher-wage technical trades, such as registered nurses, postsecondary teachers, and general managers, while the rest of employment will tend toward lower-wage jobs (under $10 per hour). Very little job growth is expected in the U.S. economy among middle-income occupations—those paying between $10 and $15 per hour.

The growth of the hourglass economy is also closely related to the industrial shift toward retailing and service-sector employment. As table 2 indicates, retail trade plays a significant role in these structural changes, as retailing will account for over 2 million of the new jobs created between 2002 and 2012. Indeed, retail as a segment of the economy has grown dramatically over the past twenty-five years, increasing from 16 to 31 percent of all wage and salary employment in the United States.[14]

Retail trade growth continues to be one of the largest areas of new industry employment, and much of the occupational growth tends to be in the lower-wage jobs such as sales, cashiers, food service and so forth. As table 3 shows, the earnings of employees in the retail sector is far lower than in other industries, with a median hourly wage of $9.71. Adjusted for inflation, the real value of wages in the retail sector fell between 1970 and 2004, and median hourly wages in general merchandise stores, the sector of the retail industry that Wal-Mart and other discounters are categorized, is even lower—$8.66 per hour in 2003.[15]

Given that the retail industry has one of the lowest median hourly wage rate of all industries, its continued expansion exacerbates the already growing income inequalities in the hourglass job market—contributing to the rapid expansion of the bottom of the wage distribution. Moreover discount retailing, which has flattened the job hierarchy and simplified the complex staffing pattern that once characterized full-service department stores like Macy's and Bloomingdale's, has eliminated many of the career ladders that once enabled clerks to become higher-wage specialists, buyers, and managers.[16]

The Wal-Mart Effect

How should we examine the community impacts of this mega-retailer? The very term "community impacts" is a broad category, encompassing a variety of different topics:

economic, social, and environmental. Urban planners, land-use consultants, economists, and environmental experts use a variety of indicators and methods to assess the effects of a new commercial development on a particular community or region. Many of these indexes overlap, and the overall impact of retail restructuring in the United States varies widely.[17]

Wal-Mart's impact on local business proved an early subject of research. The work of

TABLE 2. INDUSTRY SHIFTS, U.S. ECONOMY, 2002–12

INDUSTRY	EMPLOYMENT	
	PERCENT CHANGE	NUMERIC CHANGE
Construction	15.1	1,013,700
Manufacturing	-1.0	-157,300
Wholesale trade	11.3	638,200
Retail trade	**13.8**	**2,082,000**
• Department stores	18.1	309,400
Transportation/distribution	21.7	914,100
Information	18.5	631,900
Finance and insurance	10.1	590,000
Real estate	18.4	373,700
Professional services	27.8	1,864,300
Administrative and support	37.0	2,807,400
Educational services, private	28.6	759,200
Health/social work	32.4	4,385,600
Arts/recreation	28.0	497,000
Lodging/food services	16.1	1,638,200
Other services	15.7	959,900
Government	11.8	2,529,400

Source: Bureau of Labor Statistics, Employment and occupational projections, 2002–12.

TABLE 3. MEDIAN HOURLY EARNINGS BY INDUSTRY, 2004

INDUSTRY	MEDIAN HOURLY WAGE
Utilities	$24.80
Professional, Scientific, and Technical Services	$21.90
Management of Companies and Enterprises	$20.87
Information	$20.12
Public Administration	$18.22
Mining	$17.70
Educational Services	$17.32
Finance and Insurance	$17.01
Transportation and Warehousing	$16.99
Construction	$16.71
Wholesale Trade	$15.75
Manufacturing	$15.07
Health Care and Social Assistance	$13.80
Real Estate and Rental and Leasing	$12.39
Other Services (except Public Administration)	$11.16
Administrative Support and Waste Management and Remediation	$10.48
Retail Trade	$9.71
Arts, Entertainment, and Recreation	$9.56
Agriculture, Forestry, Fishing, and Hunting	$8.27
Accommodation and Food Service	$7.71

Source: U.S. Bureau of Labor Statistics, Occupational and Employment Statistics National Industry Data, 2004.

Kenneth Stone, an agricultural economist at the University of Iowa, drew national attention by demonstrating that Wal-Mart's dramatic expansion during the 1970s and

1980s was having a pervasively adverse impact on existing small-town retailers and on the fabric of community life in which those local businesses had long existed. Stone found that in the first decade after Wal-Mart peppered small-town Iowa with nearly a hundred large stores, the state lost 555 grocery stores, 298 hardware stores, 293 building-supply stores, 161 variety stores, 158 women's apparel stores, 153 shoe stores, 116 drugstores, and 111 men's and boys' apparel stores.[18] In a more recent analysis of Mississippi, Stone and his colleagues found that Wal-Mart supercenters, which sell groceries as well as general merchandise, captured most of their food sales from existing grocery stores within the county where the supercenter was located. Consequently, other food stores experienced average annual declines in sales from 10 percent after the first year to nearly 17 percent five years later. But Stone also found that counties without a supercenter managed to maintain grocery store sales at a fairly steady level after the opening of a supercenter in an adjacent county. Moreover, furniture stores in counties with a Wal-Mart actually experienced an increase in sales for most of the years following the opening of a supercenter, but building-material stores saw average sales

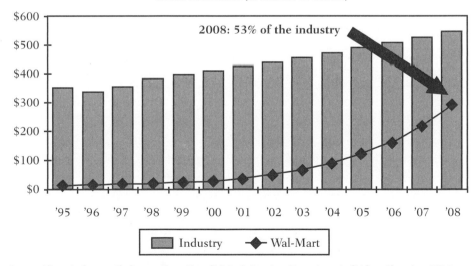

Wal-Mart Will Have a Majority of the Entire Retail Food Industry by 2008

Retail Food Sales (in billions of dollars)

Source: Alissa Anderson, Sheheryar Kaoosji, and Victoria Ramirez, Department of Urban Planning, UCLA.

declines of 8 percent to 12 percent. Overall, Stone's Mississippi study concluded that Wal-Mart supercenters capture substantial amounts of miscellaneous retail trade from other retailers, ranging from 3 percent the first year to over 9 percent by year five.[19]

An additional finding taken from the community economic development literature is that locally owned businesses may have a greater catalytic effect than national chains such as Wal-Mart. Local firms generate more economic growth per dollar of sales because they usually source more goods and services from local suppliers than do the larger multinationals, whose supply networks are international and whose distribution centers—Wal-Mart has more than a hundred throughout the United States—bypass even regionally produced commodities.[20] This multiplier effect—the additional amount of economic activity generated from a dollar of expenditures—typically varies between 0.7 and 2.0.[21] In other words, expenditures in local businesses generate an additional 70¢ to $2, while expenditures by local customers at the national chain stores generate something close to zero. Thus Wal-Mart rarely advertises in the local newspapers of the communities in which it locates its stores, and there is some evidence that it discourages suppliers from advertising independently of Wal-Marts ads. Unlike its old-line grocery-store competitors, which were a mainstay of local newspaper advertising, Wal-Mart relies far more upon television and direct mail, the national, atomizing media most characteristic of the post-Fordist world.[22]

While in the previous era of Fordist capitalism, corporations and communities were symbiotically related, with local producers and consumers, with supply and demand spatially close, in the post-Fordist era the liquidity of capital disrupts this connection. Wal-Mart boasts that it does $137.5 billion in business with sixty-eight thousand U.S. suppliers, representing "more than 3.5 million supplier jobs."[23] But such domestic sourcing is detached from traditional distribution channels, breaking the links between community businesses and the economic success of the local Wal-Mart store or even of the regional distribution center which supplies it. Wal-Mart does not manufacture or source locally, but merely acts as a global commodity supply chain, distributing globally sourced goods to local markets.

One of the most politically contentious issues surrounding Wal-Mart is that of job loss, or job replacement. It is clear that Wal-Mart is a driving force behind the transformation of the human resource practices in the retail industry and has changed the face of employment within the retail world. To date, the impact of Wal-Mart on the overall employment level is a mixed one: while many jobs are created by Wal-Mart's rapid expansion into specific communities, a difficult-to-determine number are displaced or permanently lost.[24] Although Wal-Mart creates about one hundred thousand new jobs per year, the retail industry, facing competition from the megaretailer and other discount chains, has cut frontline sales staff between 10 and 30 percent in the years since 1990.[25] University of Pennsylvania economist Edward Shils has determined that Wal-Mart's direct cannibalization of other retailers has caused the loss of 1.5 jobs for every 1 created by the giant discounter.[26] Some small towns have lost their entire Main Street, and with it the jobs attached to a host of smaller retailers. In Nowata, Oklahoma, for example, downtown retailers were driven out of business by the location of a suburban Wal-Mart, which became the only retailer in the local market area. The loss of these downtown commercial tenants had a ripple effect throughout the town's economy: wholesalers, suppliers, and banks were shut down as commercial properties left town. Then, twelve years after it opened, Wal-Mart closed its Nowata store, devastating what remained of the community and leaving something close to a ghost town in its wake.[27]

Of course, Wal-Mart's economic impact has rarely been so dramatic, which is why Emek Basker's rigorous, nationwide study of the company has proved so valuable. She found that after a Wal-Mart store entered a preexisting market, overall retail employment increased by one hundred jobs in the first year, but then half of this gain disappeared during the four years that followed. Because of the company's extreme vertical integration, wholesale employment declined by approximately twenty jobs, and Basker found little spillover job creation within those retail sectors in which Wal-Mart does not directly compete, suggesting that Wal-Mart does not create agglomeration economies in retail trade at the county level. Echoing the analyses of Stone and others, Basker found that Wal-Mart's long-run job-creation effects are indeed minimal; she calculated that as other retail establishments exit or contract, Wal-Mart generates a statistically significant net gain of approximately fifty jobs after five years.[28] Overall, studies of both regular Wal-Mart stores and of the grocery-cum-general-merchandise supercenters have shown that the company's market share often comes at the expense of competitors.[29] The determining factor is whether the local retail market area has a surplus or shortage of retail space. When Wal-Mart enters an oversupplied town, retail markets lose small businesses; undersupplied markets are less likely to do so.[30]

As important to the job creation/destruction problem is that of job quality: wages and benefits. This is one of the most highly contentious issues that divide Wal-Mart and its critics. As of early 2005, the company claimed that "Wal-Mart's average national wage is around $10 an hour," and that "74 percent of Wal-Mart associates work full time." According to Wal-Mart CEO H. Lee Scott, the company therefore "spends more broadly on health benefits than do most big retailers, whose part-timers typically are not offered health insurance."[31] But much evidence, both anecdotal and statistical, indicates that the world's largest company pays wages and benefits that are much lower than the existing grocery industry and even lower than most paid in the discount retailing sector itself. Until 2003, when the Impact Fund's gender-discrimination suit forced Wal-Mart to make public nearly a decade of payroll data, evidence for low Wal-Mart wages was largely journalistic and anecdotal. Bob Ortega, the *Wall Street Journal* reporter who wrote a 1998 corporate history, estimated Wal-Mart's starting wages at between $6 and $7 per hour. The writer Barbara Ehrenreich, who worked in a Portland, Maine, Wal-Mart in 1999, reported her pay at $6.50 an hour; and the in-house publication of Ralph's supermarkets reported that in 2003 Wal-Mart employees averaged $7.62 an hour, while Ralph's employees, largely unionized, earned $13.61 an hour.[32]

The wage data pried loose by the Impact Fund, and then analyzed by statistician Richard Drogin, provided researchers with their first accurate look at the Wal-Mart employment profile. A 2004 briefing paper from the University of California, Berkeley, Center for Labor Research and Education found that Wal-Mart's wages were significantly below retail industry standards. In California Wal-Mart workers earned on average 31 percent less than workers in large retail companies (one thousand or more employees), with wages of $9.70 per hour compared to the $14.01 average per hour earnings for the retail sector as a whole, which includes unionized grocery stores. The Berkeley study also found that 23 percent fewer Wal-Mart employees were covered by employer-sponsored health insurance than those employed by large retailers as a whole. As of 2001, only 48 percent of the Wal-Mart workforce was enrolled in the company's own health plan, largely because of low pay, high turnover, high co-payments, and a yearlong waiting period for full-time workers. In contrast 95 percent of unionized grocery workers in the San Francisco Bay Area are covered by an employer-based health care program.[33]

Military-base closures and the out-migration of manufacturing jobs are devastating to local economies not only because of the unemployment they bring, but also because of the erosion of local wage standards. In the case of Wal-Mart, the issue is how the decline in the number and proportion of higher-paying jobs may affect the local economy. Much of the research on this topic has centered on the California market, as it stands to lose tens of thousands of unionized, higher-paying grocery store jobs in the face of supercenter competition from Wal-Mart. A 1998 study of how an influx of superstores into San Diego County would impact the regional economy found an annual decline in wages and benefits of between $105 million and $221 million, and an increase of $9 million in public health costs.[34] The region was also expected to lose pensions and retirement benefits valued at between $89 million and $170 million per year. Likewise, a 2004 Bay Area Economic Forum study found that if big-box grocery stores obtain a 6–18 percent market share during the next several years, the Bay Area wage/benefit payroll will fall by some $353 million to $677 million per year. And because of multiplier effects, the net economic impact of this wage and benefit reduction is likely to double the direct loss.[35]

Because of Wal-Mart's low wages, its employees use public assistance programs in California, and elsewhere, to a far greater extent than better-paid workers in the service sector. The UC Berkeley study, "Hidden Cost of Wal-Mart Jobs," estimates that the cost to California taxpayers is $86 million annually; this comprises $32 million in health-related expenses and $54 million in other assistance.[36] Similar findings were reported by the Democratic Staff of the House Committee on Education and the Workforce, which estimated that every two-hundred-person Wal-Mart store costs federal taxpayers more than $400,000 per year, or about $2,103 per employee.[37] Good Jobs First, a public interest organization specializing in state and local economic development, found that in eleven of the twelve states where it could obtain good information, the children of Wal-Mart employees were the single largest participant in the taxpayer-funded state programs that provide Medicaid coverage for families with poverty-level incomes. In Tennessee, 25 percent of Wal-Mart's entire workforce participated in TennCare, the state's health plan for the poor, uninsured, and disabled. And in Georgia more than ten thousand children of Wal-Mart employees participated in PeachCare for Kids, the state's health insurance program for low-income working families. This was more than ten times the number of employees of the company that stood in second place.[38]

One of the main reasons cities actively court large retailers like Wal-Mart is that the stores generate lots of sales-tax revenues. In an era of declining revenue, municipalities are keen to find any means of generating new sources of income, particularly if the money goes directly to the city's general fund and is not earmarked for state, county, or special budgetary purposes. Sales-tax rates vary widely, but in many instances planners and city officials view Wal-Mart's presence as an excellent income source because of the sheer size of retail sales that the typical store will generate. Wal-Mart's grocery super-stores produce even more revenues, despite the fact that most grocery items are not taxable. This is because these supercenters generate an increased volume of cross-marketed and spillover sales. A typical hundred-thousand-square-foot Wal-Mart retail store will have a sales volume of $325 per square foot, which translates into millions of dollars in annual revenues for the city, state, and county.[39] The final revenue total, how-ever, depends on the ability of a new Wal-Mart to bring in new taxes, not simply take them from a nearby retailer. With the retail market already saturated in the United States, however, most stores will simply draw sales from the rest of the existing market.[40]

Industrial plants and facilities typically generate greater property-tax revenues than commercially zoned land. However, because of the paucity of urban industrial acreage in the U.S. and the rise in vacancy rates on such properties, most city officials now see commercial development as the best alternative to nonresidential land usage, in order

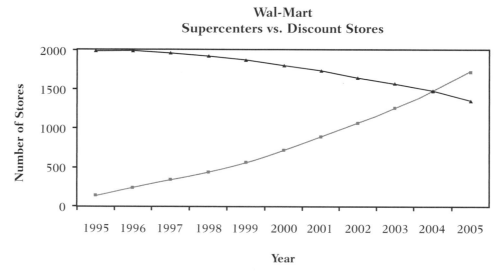

Wal-Mart
Supercenters vs. Discount Stores

Source: Alissa Anderson, Sheheryar Kaoosji, and Victoria Ramirez, Department of Urban Planning, UCLA.

to generate the necessary revenue for their public service needs.[41] But the capacity of a new Wal-Mart to increase property taxes must be considered in relation to the decline in the tax revenues generated within adjacent residential districts, whose values are adversely affected by increased traffic, commercial sprawl, and the resulting loss of aesthetic value. And there is always a chance that a Wal-Mart store might be abandoned, in which case the company keeps the parcel as part of its real estate holdings, which prevents competitors from moving in and capitalizing on the vacant commercial space.[42]

A Wal-Mart store is often purported to generate positive catalytic effects—that is to say, spillover traffic and economic growth due to increased commercial activity. However, recent research indicates that catalytic effects are very limited across other industrial sectors, and in areas where Wal-Mart absorbs market share at the expense of other small businesses, it often acts as a barrier to market entry.[43] The reasons for limited catalytic effects vary widely and depend on local market conditions, but they reflect several characteristics of Wal-Mart's impact on local economies. First, Wal-Mart sources many of its goods through the home office in Bentonville, Arkansas—wholesale suppliers locally are not used—and as a result, these local firms do not gain from the arrival of Wal-Mart, and in fact may lose out as the retailers they supply go out of business or relocate due to competition from the megaretailer. Second, in areas that are already adequately served by retailers, Wal-Mart may simply cannibalize sales from existing firms, putting them out of business.[44] Other firms, particularly nearby food-serving businesses and other stores that do not directly compete with Wal-Mart, may have increased demand due to the numerous shoppers that are attracted to the stores.[45] But overall, it is clear that the expansion of Wal-Mart into a local market area will not necessarily result in the revitalization that some economic models predict; there may be increased retail traffic, new tax revenues, and an increase in revenue from the property tax if the local market conditions are very poor to begin with; otherwise the store may simply take the place of existing retailers, and have little effect when all the impacts are taken into consideration.

Finally, an infrequently discussed element of Wal-Mart's business model is the company's aggressive pursuit of public assistance when developing new stores and distribution centers. Wal-Mart's real estate operations are now among the largest of any company in the world, and it is very active in locating subsidies for store development. Typically, Wal-Mart seeks out every possible form of business incentive when making site-selection decisions. These include direct public assistance in the form of tax breaks, low-cost financing, land write-downs, land transfers, site assembly, fee reductions or waivers, and infrastructure improvements. In some instances a single Wal-Mart anchor receives as much as $14 million.[46] In 2001, for example, Ohio slated $10 million in tax breaks for Wal-Mart to establish distribution and manufacturing facilities in the state. These incentives were promised despite the fact that Wal-Mart's food-distribution centers, which could only serve stores within a 150-mile radius, were almost certain to locate in Ohio; indeed, construction had begun on one project even before the incentives were approved.

Wal-Mart has been aggressive and persistent in seeking to reduce its fixed costs, including both land and capital assessments. For example, in 1997 in Florida, Wal-Mart challenged Hernando County's method for setting the value of the furniture, fixtures, and equipment—also known as tangible property—in its local stores and in a nearby distribution center. At Wal-Mart's Hernando County distribution center, the county had set the tangible property value at $14.18 million, but the company sued to lower the valuation and thereby win a tax refund of some $775,000. The circuit court rejected Wal-Mart's suit, but the company did not give up, doggedly returning each year to challenge the validity of its tax bill.[47]

National studies show that Wal-Mart has also benefited from many state subsidy programs. In a 2004 study, Good Jobs First found that more than 90 percent of the company's ninety-one extant distribution centers had received some form of economic development subsidy. The values of these state and local subsidy deals for individual Wal-Mart distribution centers were as high as $48 million (with an average of $7.4 million), while for retail outlets the largest was $12 million (with an average of $2.8 million).[48] Additionally, state subsidies for Wal-Mart were found in thirty-five states, with the largest number in California, Illinois, Missouri, Texas, and Mississippi. In total dollar terms, Louisiana, Florida, and New York also ranked high.[49] The subsidization of the world's largest company raises the question of not only why it is necessary, but what the potential loss to municipal and state governments is in times of tight revenues. Wal-Mart maintains that the new taxes and jobs generated within the local economy more than pay for these subsidies. Yet, the fiscal payoff is hard to calculate and may not always materialize.

One of the reasons that Wal-Mart has been so attractive to so many cities has been the need to revitalize old malls and shopping districts, often referred to as "Greyfields."

Wal-Mart's real estate division has been very active in seeking out underutilized and undervalued properties, particularly those that are in redevelopment project areas that could generate public assistance and subsidies. Thus, both hard-pressed municipalities and Wal-Mart have an interest in capitalizing on these underutilized properties and redeveloping them.

Although Wal-Mart's urban real estate operations may generate capital for inner-city properties, this same capital fluidity also allows for the cyclical use and abandonment that characterizes the company's retail operations. For instance, in some cases vacancy rates remain high after a Wal-Mart store or Sam's Club anchors a revitalized Greyfield property. Indeed, small business owners and local Business Improvement District members may view the presence of a Wal-Mart store as a barrier to entry for smaller competitors in the local market.[50] As a result, vacancies and economic blight may continue, which proved the case in San Diego County's heavily subsidized College Grove Redevelopment Project anchored by a Wal-Mart and Sam's Club employing nearly five hundred workers. There, none of the thirty-two businesses that compete in the same category of retail goods as the Wal-Mart and Sam's Club stores attributed any increased business activity due to the College Grove revitalization; indeed, the local retail submarket maintained the second highest vacancy rate in San Diego.[51]

Although Wal-Mart probably builds about two hundred stores per year within the United States, it also vacates about half that number each year. The company claimed that in 1998 it sold or leased 10 million square feet of what it calls "once-occupied" stores, but the 1999 inventory of Wal-Mart Realty's "available buildings" indicated that the company had about 20 million square feet of empty store space on the market for sale or lease.[52] As of 2003 there were some 390 vacant or soon-to-be-vacated Wal-Marts in the United States, amounting to over 30.3 million square feet of unused retail space, plus thousands of acres of unused parking.[53] Wal-Mart describes this store "recycling" as part of the company's natural "evolutionary process," but such property churning clearly stands in significant contrast to the staid Main Street retailers whose department stores of old seemed such permanent, iconic features of the urban landscape.[54]

Sprawl and Wal-Mart have become synonymous in many parts of the country. Environmentalists and smart-growth advocates have been increasingly concerned about the growth of exurban megastores and the abandonment of the urban core of so many cities and towns. Aesthetic issues are important but so too are social and economic efficiencies. First, the infrastructure cost and service needs of large retail centers are far greater than those of the smaller, denser city core.[55] Big-box stores and supercenters are generally located on the fringes of urban areas, primarily because the amount of land needed for development makes it cost-prohibitive to build closer to the city center.[56] Consequently, unless special efforts are made to extend some form of public transit to these sites, access is predominantly by car. Furthermore, the distance from residential neighborhoods and the lack of walkways near the store or through the parking lot make big-box stores and supercenters less accessible to pedestrians. Locating public infrastructure on the edge of a town therefore increases long-term maintenance costs to the municipality and increases the public service costs for police and firefighters.

In virtually every community where Wal-Mart locates, traffic is a significant concern because the company's business model requires a high customer turnover to support a high level of sales per square foot. Typical Wal-Mart stores generate several thousand average daily car trips (ADTs).[57] Supercenters in regional shopping centers can generate as many as twenty thousand ADTs depending on location and demographics.[58] Stand-alone Wal-Mart stores can generate between three thousand and nine thousand customer car trips per day.[59] Thus, the movement of Wal-Mart and other large discount retailers to suburban and exurban areas accelerates sprawl, and in the process the proliferation of big-box stores leads to increased traffic, higher infrastructure costs, and other problems associated with the dispersal of residences from jobs, recreation, and shopping.[60]

The Wal-Mart Effect in Historical Perspective

> Commercial accumulation tended to generate uneven development among buyers and sellers. . . . Because different socioeconomic groups were living and working closely together in the Commercial Cities, these spreading inequalities became more and more physically evident. . . . this evidence of inequality generated popular protest against it. Because these protests frequently had political effect, they tended to limit opportunities for further commercial accumulation.
>
> —David Gordon

Economist David Gordon aptly describes current conflicts between Wal-Mart and numerous localities, yet he was here referring to political developments that first appeared in the 1820s and 1830s. Current controversies surrounding the company are therefore not entirely new, but reflect past social protests resulting from capitalism's own structural and spatial development. A comparative historical perspective helps understand these changes because, as the early part of this chapter emphasized, the history of capitalism within the context of a defined community is also the history of particular modes of production, distribution, and consumption.

The compact, centralized early twentieth-century city, with mass transit lines converging on a vibrant downtown district, was the perfect environment for department store growth. In 1904 over ten thousand people would shop daily at Macy's in New York, and up forty thousand people per day entered Marshall Field's in Chicago, Macy's flagship store was the largest commercial building in the United States, with over 1 million square feet, larger than any industrial plant in existence at the time.[61] These urban retail configurations reflected therefore key characteristics of the Fordist economy, which flourished until well into the post–World War II era.

Wal-Mart did not create the post-Fordist world, but it clearly embodies the contradictions and dichotomies of that new stage in the history of capitalist development. As the world's largest multinational it can generate massive economies of scale and leverage huge capital flows to invest in undercapitalized communities, regions, and whole nations. Thus Wal-Mart claims that it saves U.S. consumers upwards of $100 billion per year.[62] But this business model can flourish only by externalizing many of its most important social and economic costs, which are displaced onto a relentlessly squeezed supply chain, an underpaid retail workforce, and those many thousand communities and municipalities which have been forced to absorb so many of the intangible expenses generated by a spatially discontinuous commercial environment that requires significant infrastructure and public service costs.

Wal-Mart is a reflection of a new form of capital accumulation, a global company that now functions not so much as a producer or manufacturer, but instead as a global commodity chain and logistics operation. In contrast to the large enterprises of the Fordist era, which required, or at least tolerated, the regulatory hand of an intrusive welfare state, Wal-Mart and other labor-intensive retailers have abandoned the Keynesian project and now seek complete flexibility to employ labor and source their product within a highly segmented and inequitable market. Bypassed in this process are the cumulative effects of economic development we have witnessed over the previous century, a spatial environment, both political and economic, that puts workers, consumers, and capitalists in contact, producing both conflict and community.

Today, Wal-Mart's presence merely brings the commodity to the market through a business model that depends on high-volume sales, car-dependent shoppers, and land uses that contribute to sprawling development. As a driver of the retail economy, it dramatically expands employment in the lower wage segment of the retail industry. As a template for multinational enterprise within a global economy, Wal-Mart reflects both the changing content of capitalism itself, a form of flexible accumulation where capital moves detached from the spatial confines of local labor forces and consumption patterns, and the changing relationship between corporations and communities. Taken as a whole, these developments accelerate what Manuel Castells describes as the spatial and structural polarization of urban life. By catalyzing the expansion of lower-wage labor within the world of commodity distribution while at the same time reconfiguring the geography of the post-Fordist city, Wal-Mart has generated a spatial discontinuity within the built environment and a structural inequity within the world of labor.

SEVEN

Wal-Mart and the Logistics Revolution

Edna Bonacich
with Khaleelah Hardie

In the fall of 2002 the West Coast ports of the United States were shut down for ten days. During a contract-renewal dispute the Pacific Maritime Association (PMA), a powerful employer group, locked out the ten thousand West Coast unionists belonging to the International Longshore and Warehouse Union (ILWU). The president of the United States, George W. Bush, threatened to take dockworkers out of the jurisdiction of the National Labor Relations Act (NLRA) and put them under the more restrictive Railway Labor Act (RLA), to bring in the National Guard to handle commercial vessels under the guise that this was a wartime emergency, and/or to break up the system of coastwise bargaining used by the ILWU and compel each port to bargain separately. Clearly all of these proposals were aimed at drastically weakening the union by presidential fiat. In the end, none of the threats were implemented, and the president terminated the lockout by taking the risky pre-midterm-election step of invoking the Taft-Hartley Act for the first time in decades, and forcing the ports to open again. Clearly this was no ordinary labor strife.[1]

Why was the closure of the ports deemed so important that it required presidential intervention? What relevance does this episode have for Wal-Mart? This West Coast ports lockout provides a window on a major change that has been occurring over the last thirty years in the way goods are produced and delivered. We refer to this change as the logistics revolution, a revolution that has been led by Wal-Mart Stores Inc.

163

The term "logistics" has two, interrelated meanings. On the one hand, it refers to the nuts-and-bolts distribution functions that a firm must undertake, namely, transportation and warehousing. On the other hand, it can mean the management of the entire supply chain, including relations between retailers, their producers/suppliers, and their carriers/transportation providers. The latter meaning has become more important with the creation of flexible and dispersed production systems, including offshore production, requiring high levels of coordination to bring products to the market in an accurate and timely fashion.

Our purpose in this paper is to examine how Wal-Mart's practices have affected production and distribution, and the workers who are employed in these fields. Most of the criticisms of Wal-Mart have focused on its impact on its competitors in retailing (how it destroys Main Street), and on its own employees (its sales workers) and the workers of its competitors (especially in the food sector with the emergence of Wal-Mart supercenters). This paper shifts attention to the firms and workers who make the products Wal-Mart sells, and to the transportation companies and workers who move these products to Wal-Mart's distribution centers and stores. We focus primarily, but not exclusively, on the ports of Southern California and their surrounding logistics systems because of the tremendous growth in manufactured imports from Asia, and their importance to the giant retailers such as Wal-Mart. The fight over the ILWU contract is one example of the importance of logistics workers in the Wal-Mart supply chain.

The Growth of Manufactured Imports to the United States

International trade has grown enormously over the last twenty to thirty years. Goods that used to be manufactured domestically are increasingly being produced offshore. The U.S. used to be the leading producer and exporter of manufactured products, but this has changed since the mid-1980s. Table 1 shows the rise of U.S. exports and imports, both in general and for manufactured goods alone. As can be seen, imports to the U.S. have grown hugely, especially in recent decades. In 1970, manufactured imports were valued at $27.3 billion. By 2000, their value had grown to $1.013 trillion, an increase of about 3,700 percent. In 1970, manufactured goods accounted for 68 percent of total imports. By 2000 they were 83 percent of the total. In 1970 the U.S. exported

$4.4 billion more manufactured goods than it imported. The balance of trade in manufactured goods deteriorated until it became negative in 1983. By 2000, the U.S. had a total trade deficit of $436.1 billion and climbing, and manufactured goods made up 74 percent of the deficit.

The United States is the world's leading trader, in terms of both exports and imports. In 2000, the value of U.S. merchandise exports reached 12.3 percent of global exports. In the same year, the U.S. imported 18.9 percent of the world's total imports.[2] In 2000, 39.5 percent of U.S. imports came from Asia, 21.9 percent from Western Europe, 18.1 percent from North America (Canada and Mexico), 13 percent from the rest of Latin America, and the remaining 7.7 percent from the Middle East, Africa, and Eastern Europe. Imports from Asia totaled $469.3 billion.[3]

Table 2 shows U.S. imports from Asia during the five-year period 1999–2003. The big story is the rise of China. Over the five-year period, China's imports to the U.S. grew by a staggering annual rate of 16.8 percent. They accounted for over 12 percent of total U.S. imports in 2003, and over 33 percent of U.S. imports from Asia. The table reveals a shift in import leadership from Japan to China. Of course, Japan remains a major importer to the U.S., now ranked number four, and continues to be a formidable source of

TABLE 1. U.S. EXPORTS AND IMPORTS,
TOTAL AND MANUFACTURED GOODS, 1970–2000 (IN $ BILLIONS)

YEAR	TOTAL			MANUFACTURED		
	EXPORTS	IMPORTS	BALANCE	EXPORTS	IMPORTS	BALANCE
1970	43.8	40.4	3.4	31.7	27.3	4.4
1975	109.3	98.5	10.8	76.9	54.0	22.9
1980	225.7	245.3	-19.6	160.7	133.0	27.7
1985	218.8	336.5	-117.7	168.0	257.5	-89.5
1990	393.6	495.3	-101.7	315.4	388.8	-73.5
1995	584.7	743.2	-158.7	486.7	629.7	-143.0
2000	781.9	1,218.0	-436.1	691.5	1,012.7	-321.3

Source: U.S. Census Bureau, *Statistical Abstract of the United States: 2003*, table 1295.

manufactured products, and of the trade deficit. Still, the table clearly shows that over the last five years, China has overtaken Japan as a source of imports to the U.S. The switch occurred in 2002, and the gap is widening.

TABLE 2. U.S. MERCHANDISE IMPORTS FROM ASIAN COUNTRIES, 1999–2003 ($ BILLION)

COUNTRY	1999	2000	2001	2002	2003	AVG. ANN. GROWTH
World	$1,024.8	$1,216.9	$1,142.0	$1,163.5	$1,259.4	5.3
Total Asia	$391.2	$454.7	$410.5	$431.0	$460.2	4.1
China	$81.8	$100.1	$102.3	$125.2	$152.4	16.8
Japan	$131.4	$146.6	$126.6	$121.5	$118.0	-2.6

Source: U.S. International Trade Commission Web site, 2004.

The Rise of the West Coast Ports

The West Coast ports have grown with increased Asian imports to the United States. Table 3 shows the containerized trade (imports and exports) flowing through the nation's three largest container ports. New York, which used to be the country's largest port, has dropped to third place. Each of the two Southern California ports ranks as the first or second largest container port in the nation, and together they are the third largest container port in the world, behind Hong Kong and Singapore.

The relative decline of New York reflects the shift in predominant trade routes from the Atlantic (trade with Europe) to the Pacific (trade with Asia). However, greater proximity to Asia does not entirely account for the rise of the West Coast ports, since Asian products can be transported through the Panama Canal to the East Coast, which is still the economic heartland of the nation. The growth of the West Coast ports also depended on technical and legislative changes.

Of vital importance was the development of the container. The containerization of ocean shipping began to take hold slowly in the 1960s, and is still expanding around the world. Containers are like truck trailers without wheels. They allow for the development of intermodal freight transportation, whereby goods can be packed into a con-

**TABLE 3. CONTAINER TRAFFIC THROUGH THE
NATION'S THREE LARGEST CONTAINER PORTS, 1995–2003 (TEUs)***

PORT	1995	2000	2003
Los Angeles	1,890,184	3,233,284	4,709,339
Long Beach	2,116,149	3,270,817	3,114,221
LA/LB	4,006,333	6,504,101	7,823,560
New York	1,537,416	2,242,372	2,819,407

* TEUs are twenty-foot equivalent units, the standard measure for containers. Most ocean containers are forty feet in length, or two TEUs.

Source: Jack Kyser, *International Trade Trends and Impacts: The Southern California Region; 2003 Results and 2004 Outlook* (Los Angeles: Los Angeles Economic Development Corporation, 2004), 22.

tainer at an Asian factory, transported by truck (using attachable wheels, called "chassis") or rail to a seaport, stacked on an ocean vessel, removed from the ship at a U.S. port, placed on a truck and/or train (double-stacked), and delivered to a warehouse or distribution center somewhere in the U.S.—all without being opened, and under a single bill of lading. The West Coast ports can be used as the entry point for goods bound for Chicago by rail. This kind of rail move is called "landbridge." It enables ocean vessels to avoid the longer time it takes to traverse the Panama Canal.

Containerization drastically changed the character of dock work. Before containers, packages would have to be placed on pallets and carefully stowed in the hold of a ship. This was heavy work that took a long time. The shift to containers greatly increased the productivity of dock work, reducing the time in the port to a fraction of what it was under the old "break bulk" system. The change required the ocean carriers to negotiate with the powerful ILWU, leading to the adoption of the Mechanization and Modernization (M&M) agreement of 1960, brokered under the leadership of Harry Bridges.[4]

The shift to containers and intermodalism also enabled ships to grow larger and larger. By 2004, the largest vessels could carry over eight thousand TEUs (twenty-foot equivalent units, the standard measure of number of containers). The typical container is forty feet long, and weighs around thirty tons when loaded. These giant ships are a sight to behold, as they sail into port loaded to the gills with these big boxes. Longshore workers operate giant cranes that zip back and forth over the ship, discharging and re-

Containerized shipping has revolutionized international trade during the last thirty years.
PORT OF YOKOHAMA

loading the cargo at astounding speeds of twenty and even thirty containers per hour. It now takes a day or two to turn the ship around, ready for its next voyage. Watching the discharging of a giant container vessel gives one a visual sense of the massive and continuous flood of imports into the United States from Asia.

The bigger container vessels can no longer pass through the Panama Canal, and are described as post-Panamax. Panama is considering expanding the canal, and some East Coast ports have expanded to receive all-water service from Asia via the Panama or Suez Canals. Even so, neither an expanded canal nor the East Coast ports pose a serious threat to the West Coast ports, given the continually growing volume of imports from Asia.

Among the West Coast ports, Los Angeles and Long Beach (LA/LB) are the clear leaders. Measured in terms of weight, the ports of LA/LB handled 164 million tons of goods in 2003, 58 percent of total trade through the West Coast ports. Tacoma ranked second with a 9.7 percent share, showing that no other West Coast port comes close to the volume handled by the twin ports of Southern California.[5] The reasons for this concentration are multiple, not the least of which is the size of the local market.

Most import data measured by value are collected for the customs district rather than the ports, a larger category that includes airports.[6] The total value of goods entering through the Los Angeles Customs District in 2003 was $167.3 billion. Of this amount, $60.2 billion, 36 percent, came from China, easily the largest importer to Southern California. Second was Japan, with 17.7 percent of the total, and third and fourth were Taiwan and South Korea, with 5.8 percent each. While some of these imports were brought by air freight, 81 percent of the total, and 91 percent from China, arrived via ocean transportation.[7]

Intermodalism did not only depend on containerization. It also required the deregulation of the various transportation modes. Trucking and the railroads were deregulated starting in the late 1970s and reaching full momentum in the 1980s. Rates, which had been under government control, were now allowed to respond to the market. Deregulation also freed the trucking companies and railroads to compete both within and between their industries, and allowed them to cooperate and to buy each other. Ocean shipping was also deregulated in the 1980s, permitting the steamship lines to engage in and control intermodal moves from door to door, using trucks and rail.[8]

The Logistics Revolution and the West Coast Ports

A paradigm shift in the way goods are produced and sold has been developing over the last thirty years. The system of production and distribution has shifted from a "push" to a "pull" model.[9] The push system was dominated by large consumer goods manufacturers. It involved long production runs to gain efficiencies of scale and minimize unit costs. It led to inventory surpluses which were pushed out to retailers.[10] Under the pull system, consumer behavior is tracked through the retailer, which then transmits consumer preferences up the supply chain. Replenishment is put in motion almost immediately. Suppliers are required to meet short lead times and to make more frequent deliveries of smaller lots, based on what is actually selling, thereby reducing retailer inventory. This system can be described as just-in-time (JIT) for retailers, or "lean retailing."[11]

Pull production and distribution were made possible by the development of the bar code. Bar coding, which identifies products down to the stock-keeping unit (SKU) level, allows retailers to collect point-of-sale (POS) data so that they can instantly keep track of exactly what is selling. This enables them to make electronic connections with their suppliers and service providers to order replenishments in a timely manner. It also increases the power of retailers relative to manufacturers, who now must often gear all aspects of their production to the increasingly stringent demands of giant retailers.

The importance of the West Coast ports is also linked to this pull system, because the speed of product delivery has become much more important. JIT delivery systems have much more difficulty dealing with interruptions in delivery flows, because firms that use it do not maintain the same levels of inventory. The mass retailers of today rely on the constant and predictable flow of goods, which allows them to save on the cost of maintaining inventory.

The bottom line for the West Coast ports is that it was estimated that the country lost almost $2 billion a day for every day that the ports were shut down during the 2002 lockout.[12] True, this estimate was developed in a study sponsored by the PMA, and was used to try to persuade the president to intervene. The union argued that the estimate was grossly exaggerated for precisely this reason, presenting alternative figures that showed a much more modest impact.[13] Regardless of the precise figures, retailers we interviewed complained about delays resulting from the ten-day closure.

Wal-Mart's Logistics Expertise

Wal-Mart has played a leading role in developing the logistics revolution. As one logistics consultant told us: "Wal-Mart wrote the book, and it keeps rewriting it every day."[14] In a 2003 *Fortune* article Wal-Mart is described as "the company that almost single-handedly made the bar code ubiquitous by demanding 20 years ago that suppliers use it."[15] Its mastery of logistics has been deemed by numerous authors to be the cause of its success.[16] According to Peter Tirschwell, editor of the *Journal of Commerce,* "Wal-Mart has set the pace by expanding the definition of logistics practices." He points out that because Wal-Mart and the other big-box chains compete so aggressively on price, margins in the retail sector are razor thin, which forces the industry to give top priority to logistics.[17]

Wal-Mart has streamlined logistics by sharing data electronically with its suppliers, and by driving out unnecessary middlemen, all to the purpose of offering rock-bottom prices to its customers. The importance the company attaches to logistics is shown in its leadership: both David Glass and Lee Scott, previous and present CEOs, came out of logistics.[18] For example, current CEO Scott was elevated by Glass from the Transportation Department.[19] As a result, Wal-Mart has been able to maintain lower inventory levels than its competitors. It can reorder quickly and be sure when the goods will arrive. By 1983 it spent less than 2¢ per dollar on distribution, the lowest rate in the retail industry.[20]

Wal-Mart decided to own and control its own trucks and computer systems, treating these as core competencies of the company. The company invested heavily in information technology and bought a fleet of trucks.[21] It bought a satellite system for $24 million in the early 1980s. By 1988 it had the largest privately owned communications network in the country.[22]

The techniques that Wal-Mart developed are now being copied by its competitors and by others in unrelated industries. Wal-Mart introduced at least four key concepts, according to one logistics textbook: the strategy of expanding around distribution centers (DCs), using electronic data interchange (EDI) with suppliers, the big-box store format, and "everyday low prices."[23] The advantages of these four innovations are as follows:

- Wal-Mart enters a region by building a new DC in a central location, and opening a group of new stores around it. This enables the company to add new stores at little additional cost.
- The use of EDI with suppliers cuts the transaction costs of ordering products and paying invoices, since these functions are handled electronically. In addition, Wal-Mart gains control over the scheduling and receiving of products, ensuring a steady and accurate flow of products to its stores.
- The big-box format allows Wal-Mart to combine a store with a warehouse in a single facility. The big box holds large amounts of inventory, and saves on the shipment of goods from a warehouse to the store.

- "Everyday low prices" enable Wal-Mart to forecast sales more accurately and smooth out demand swings associated with special sales events.

Wal-Mart also developed a system of replenishing its stores twice a week, while its competitors were replenishing twice a month. This limited the time period for which store managers had to forecast sales, increasing their accuracy. More frequent replenishments led the company to pioneer the cross-docking system as a means of reducing the cost of small lot replenishments. Cross-docking is a system where truckloads from a particular producer arrive at the DC and are unloaded, and their contents are broken down into smaller lots and combined with the smaller lots of other trucks bound for the same destination. DCs that cross-dock enable products to flow faster through the supply chain. Moreover, the costs of handling are reduced, since storage and retrieval are no longer necessary. However, cross-docking does demand a high degree of coordination, and is difficult to accomplish in practice.[24]

Wal-Mart is known for forming effective partnerships with its vendors. The case that is touted as the ideal model of such retailer-manufacturer partnerships is the relationship between Wal-Mart and Procter and Gamble. P&G was known as a tough company that was able to dominate its market and its retailers. It used its own research on consumer buying to argue with retailers for increased shelf space. P&G was widely viewed as a self-aggrandizing bully.[25]

The logistics revolution turned this kind of power relationship on its head. The collection of POS data put power into the hands of the giant retailers. They knew what consumers were buying, which prices were most effective to maximize sales, when products gained and lost popularity, and demographic and regional differences in buying patterns. They could use this knowledge to tell their suppliers what to produce, when to produce it, how to deliver it, and for what price.

At first the relationship between Wal-Mart and P&G went through hard times. "P&G would dictate to Wal-Mart how much P&G would sell, at what prices, and under what terms. In turn, Wal-Mart would threaten to drop P&G merchandise or give it poorer shelf locations."[26] The relationship began to change in the mid-1980s, and they managed to work out a partnership based on sharing information to increase sales and lower costs for both companies.[27]

The two companies developed a sophisticated EDI link, which gave P&G the responsibility for managing its Wal-Mart inventory. P&G received continuous data via satellite on sales, inventory, and prices, enabling it to replenish goods rapidly, often directly from the factory to individual stores. The two firms use electronic invoicing and electronic transfer of funds. The order-to-delivery cycle has been speeded up, and stock-outs have been almost entirely eliminated. Meanwhile, various costly processes, such as order processing and billing, have been rendered unnecessary, and errors have been reduced. As of 1996, Wal-Mart was P&G's largest customer, generating more than $3 billion in revenues or about 10 percent of P&G's total.[28]

Wal-Mart is leading the retail sector in the implementation of other logistics innovations, including greatly increasing the demands that retailers place upon their suppliers. These retailers, Wal-Mart included, are pushing activities that they used to perform back onto their suppliers. These include such requirements as putting the final price labels on goods, placing garments on hangers before they are shipped to the retailer, ensuring that labels are placed in the exact spot on the box that the retailer requires, and packing boxes to the retailer's precise specifications. Wal-Mart and other giant retailers have the power to impose these and other requirements on an accept-the-terms-or-you-will-be-dropped-as-a-vendor basis. In addition, they can impose costly consequences for the tiniest of errors, such as charging a $25-per-box fine if one label is crooked. During 2003 the specificity of the requirements and the financial penalties intensified.[29]

Two new logistics initiatives are being pursued by Wal-Mart at the time of writing. One is known as Collaborative Planning, Forecasting, and Replenishment (CPFR), a best-practices system developed by Voluntary Interindustry Commerce Standards (VICS). More recently VICS has developed the Collaborative Transportation Management system. These are systems for increasing the sharing of information among all the participants in a supply chain, including the transportation providers.[30]

A second innovation, which has created turmoil among Wal-Mart's vendors, was the demand that its top one hundred suppliers put Radio Frequency Identification (RFID) tags on all their cases and pallets by January 2005. RFID is an improvement over bar coding, enabling more information to be fed more quickly and with less handling into information systems. Undoubtedly it will ultimately increase efficiency, but in the short run it is both an expensive and unperfected technology, and Wal-Mart has been forced to set back the time-line for implementation. Moreover, some analysts expect Wal-Mart to save \$8 billion a year, mostly in labor costs, but it is unclear how the vendors will benefit.[31] The ability of the company to insist on such a change is an indication of its power over manufacturers.[32]

The Good, the Bad, and the Ugly

There is no doubt that Wal-Mart has displayed a form of genius that has provided some major benefits to U.S. society. It has forced its competitors and suppliers to become more efficient, has removed unnecessary middlemen from the system, and has single-handedly kept inflation at bay.[33] The overall cost of logistics declined from 14.5 percent of nominal GDP in 1982 to 8.5 percent in 2003.[34] Customers have received the benefits of low-cost products. Some of Wal-Mart's suppliers have thrived under its hegemony, making up for a drop in prices with guaranteed high-volume sales.

Nevertheless, as is widely known, critiques of Wal-Mart have been on the rise.[35] These have come from a variety of sources, including Main Street, where small stores complain that they are being driven out of business; trade unions, which contend that not only is Wal-Mart fiercely antiunion toward its own employees, but that it undercuts unionized competitors and forces them to lower labor standards (as in the Southern California supermarket strike of 2003–4, led by the United Food and Commercial Workers, or UFCW); employees, who receive low wages, substandard medical benefits, and are currently suing over sex discrimination;[36] local government officials, who see the company as arrogantly trying to bypass regulations, and forcing down living standards for workers in their communities (as in the case of Inglewood, California, which successfully fended off an attempt by Wal-Mart to pass a referendum that would deny the city's right to regulate the company); and probably others.

Our focus is on another source of criticism, namely from vendors (including manufacturers) and logistics providers, and their employees. While the professional logistics literature praises Wal-Mart for its excellent communications with vendors, there is another side to this picture. Yes, Wal-Mart helps to make its vendors more efficient. But it also exercises its considerable power to make their lives miserable. In the course of this research, we found ourselves collecting such stories, and they were certainly easy enough to find. Everyone seemed to have their own horror stories of how they had been abused, or knew of others who had suffered at the hands of the "the big gorilla." These stories did not come from angry leftists who resented the triumphs of capitalism. Rather, they came from the business community.

Let us give an example, recently told us by a logistics consultant. Wal-Mart sells Huffy bicycles, which are made in China. Wal-Mart tells Huffy to import fifty thousand bicycles and store them in its distribution center. Wal-Mart asks that these bikes be delivered in small lots on a JIT basis to its stores. If, by the end of the season, Wal-Mart sells only thirty thousand, Huffy is stuck with twenty thousand bikes that it must scramble to sell to someone.

Why would any company put up with this kind of treatment? Wal-Mart is certainly not a monopoly, and does not exercise monopoly power to drive prices up. Rather, in many industries, it comes close to being a monopsony. At least, in several major industries, such as food and clothing, it is the major seller in the world. Many vendors find the company hard to avoid. For example, Dial Corporation, maker of Dial soap, does 28 percent of its business with Wal-Mart. If it lost that account, it would have to double its sales with its next nine customers in order to maintain the same level of business.[37]

Another horror story concerns Vlasic Pickles. Briefly, Wal-Mart got Vlasic, the number one brand, to sell a gallon jar of pickles for $2.97, an unprofitable price. This proved to be a very popular item that was selling at 240,000 jars a week at Wal-Marts around the country. But Vlasic's non–Wal-Mart business fell. According to Fishman,

> The gallon jar reshaped Vlasic's pickle business. It chewed up the profit margin of the business with Wal-Mart, and of pickles generally. Procurement has to scramble to find enough pickles to fill the gallons, but the volume gave Vlasic strong sales numbers, and a powerful place in the world of pickles at Wal-Mart. Which accounted for 30% of Vlasic's business. But the company's profits from pickles had shriveled 25% or more.[38]

Vlasic begged Wal-Mart for relief, but the retailer refused. Vlasic said it would raise the price, and Wal-Mart said it would stop buying all Vlasic products. Most telling was a reported comment by a Wal-Mart representative when the company finally decided to allow Vlasic to raise the price somewhat: "We've done to pickles what we did to orange juice. We killed it. We can back off."[39]

Wal-Mart is known to force its suppliers to redesign everything from their packaging to their computer systems, and does not hesitate to tell them what it will pay. It is known to insist on examining the private financial records of a supplier, and to claim that the margins are too high and must be cut.[40] Wal-Mart is also reputed to insist that its suppliers shave 5 percent off of their prices each year. If they do not comply, they are dropped.[41]

Wal-Mart is playing a role in moving production offshore, especially to the low-cost manufacturing center of the world, China. An article in a prizewinning *Los Angeles Times* series reported: "By squeezing suppliers to cut wholesale costs, the company has hastened the flight of U.S. manufacturing jobs overseas. By scouring the globe for the cheapest goods, it has driven factory jobs from one poor nation to another."[42] Fishman makes a similar point:

> Of course, U.S. companies have been moving jobs offshore for decades, long before Wal-Mart was a retailing power. But there is no question that the chain is helping accelerate the loss of American jobs to low-wage countries such as China. Wal-Mart, which in the late 1980s and early 1990s trumpeted its claim to "Buy American," has doubled its imports from China in the past five years alone, buying some $12 billion in merchandise in 2002. That's nearly 10% of all Chinese exports to the United States.[43]

In 2003, Wal-Mart imported $15 billion worth of goods from China, accounting for nearly 11 percent of the U.S. total.[44]

An example of pressure to move offshore is a Chicago household-products manufacturer, Lakewood Engineering and Manufacturing. Wal-Mart was selling Lakewood box fans for $20, the same price they sold for ten years prior. Wal-Mart wanted Lakewood to lower the price further. Lakewood automated and pressured its suppliers to lower their prices. But none of this was enough, and in 2000, Lakewood was compelled to open a factory in Shenzhen, China, where workers earned 25¢ an hour compared to the $13 earned by their Chicago employees. Lakewood's owner reports that all the retailers he deals with, including Home Depot and Target, are hard bargainers, but none is as tough as Wal-Mart.[45]

The pressure to lower prices does not stop at the U.S. border. Wal-Mart is equally tough with its global suppliers, thereby playing an important role in creating the global sweatshop problem and the well-known "race to the bottom" of competition between countries to offer global retailers the cheapest prices. Producers in developing countries who wish to enter the U.S. market are dependent on the big retailers. The director of international trade for the American Textile Institute described the situation like this: "You don't tell Wal-Mart your price. Wal-Mart tells you."[46] This can lead to illegal practices. Neil Kearney of the International Textiles, Garment and Leather Workers Federation (ITGLWF) describes how sweatshops are created:

> These [multinational] companies adopt codes of conduct, some of them in very nice language, but then they negotiate deals which make it impossible for their contractors to honor the codes. The companies say to the contractor, "Please allow for freedom of association, pay a decent wage," but then they say, "We will pay you 87 cents to produce each shirt." This includes the wage, fabric, everything.[47]

It was this kind of practice that enabled the National Labor Committee, led by Charles Kernaghan, to embarrass celebrity Kathie Lee Gifford for having her name attached to a Wal-Mart line of clothing that was being produced under sweatshop conditions in Honduras and New York.

The monopsony-type role that Wal-Mart plays in relation to some U.S. industries and companies extends, in some cases, to entire developing countries. For example, Wal-Mart is the most important customer of Bangladesh. However, by continually reducing its prices, it threatens the well-being of the country.[48] By the end of 2003, Wal-Mart used over three thousand supplier factories in China, a number that was expected to rise. Wal-Mart has played a significant role is making southern China the fastest-growing manufacturing region of the world. "The marriage between the world's largest and most efficient retailer and China's low-cost factories is setting a new global 'cost standard' for manufactured products, according to consulting firm Deloitte Touche Tohmatsu."[49]

Apart from pushing production offshore, another complaint, which we heard about from a logistics consultant, is a phenomenon called the "Bank of Wal-Mart." The company sets terms for payment to the vendor of (for example) thirty days after delivery, but sells the goods well before it has to pay, holding on to the vendor's money in between.

About 70 percent of goods are now sold before the supplier is paid, and Wal-Mart aims to get that figure to 100 percent.[50]

Manufacturers are not the only vendors who find themselves squeezed by "the big gorilla." Indeed, we first heard that description from a company that provided logistics services for Wal-Mart.[51] We have interviewed various members of the international transportation community, including steamship lines, railroads, port trucking companies, and warehouse operators. While they generally would not want to be quoted, few had anything good to say about Wal-Mart, and some were unable to control cursing, even in front of an aging woman academic for whom they would normally (though incorrectly) feel compelled to clean up their language. One owner of a port trucking company stated: "I won't work with people like that, no matter how much business they control." Another man, who ran a third-party logistics operation for Wal-Mart, told us his wife made him quit the job because his health was suffering from the constant stress he was under because of the ceaseless pressure he faced from Wal-Mart representatives.

The biggest shippers (importers),[52] of which Wal-Mart is the very biggest, are able to use their huge volume and the threat of shifting that volume to other carriers to achieve the lowest rates from the ocean carriers.[53] The rates the steamship lines receive reverberate throughout the freight transportation industry, since intermodal moves must be paid for out of that basic rate. If Wal-Mart squeezes a steamship company, that company must squeeze its port trucking firms and other land carriers.

In sum, while good things can be said about Wal-Mart's logistics innovations, it can also be demonstrated that many of its suppliers and logistics providers experience the company as an extremely powerful and unavoidable bully that forces them to cut prices beyond what is possible to achieve by increasing efficiencies to the maximum. So far we have looked only at business relations with Wal-Mart. We need to consider what this does to labor. But first, let us return briefly to the question of international trade and transportation.

The Importance of Retailers in Ocean Shipping

The role of Wal-Mart in pushing production offshore is revealed in the corporation's import practices. Wal-Mart is the largest importer of containerized cargo to the United

Retail Store 2003 Revenues
(In Billions)

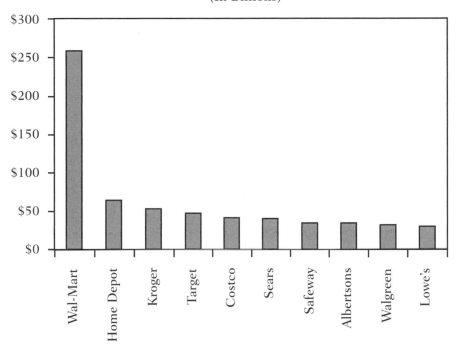

States, by far. Other retailers have also risen in prominence in this trade. Table 4 presents the top twenty importers involved in ocean container trade, as measured primarily by PIERS (Port Import/Export Reporting Service) of the *Journal of Commerce.*[54] These data provide us with a sense of who actually controls this trade.

Wal-Mart is clearly at the top of the heap, followed by Home Depot and Target. These three giant retailers accounted for about 45 percent of all top twenty importers' TEUs in 2003. Thirty-two of the top one hundred importers were retailers. A grand total of 14,053,048 TEUs were imported to the U.S. in 2003, and Wal-Mart accounted for 3.3 percent of them.

Wal-Mart does not use only the ports of LA/LB for its containerized imports from Asia. In fact, since the West Coast ports lockout of late 2002, Wal-Mart has made sure to diversify its ports usage by building DCs near several East Coast ports. Nonetheless,

TABLE 4. TOP TWENTY IMPORTERS TO THE UNITED STATES VIA OCEAN CONTAINER TRANSPORT, 2003

RANK	IMPORTER	TEUS	% OF TOP 20
1	Wal-Mart Stores Inc.	471,600	22.3
2	Home Depot Inc.	267,100	12.6
3	Target Corp.	208,400	9.9
4	Dole Food Co.	171,300	8.1
5	Chiquita Brands Int'l Inc.	108,600	5.1
6	Lowe's Cos.	96,500	4.6
7	Kmart Corp.	86,400	4.1
8	Heineken USA Inc.	77,700	3.7
9	Interbrew SA	65,400	3.1
10	Ikea International A/S	60,200	2.8
11	Payless ShoeSource Inc.	56,800	2.7
12	Ashley Furniture Industries	53,400	2.5
13	Matsushita Electric Corp. of America	52,800	2.5
14	Sony Corp. of America	50,700	2.4
15	American Honda Motor Co.	50,400	2.4
16	General Electric Co.	49,300	2.3
17	Toyota Motor Sales USA Inc.	49,050	2.3
18	Pier 1 Imports Inc.	47,300	2.2
19	Big Lots Inc.	46,000	2.2
20	LG Group	44,700	2.1
	Total, Top 20	2,113,600	100.0

Source: *Journal of Commerce*, May 21, 2004.

it remains a major user of the ports of Southern California, with a gigantic 2.7-million-square-foot import campus of four DCs in Mira Loma, an unincorporated community in the western part of Riverside County.

As the nation's premier gateway for Asian imports, Southern California has developed into a major logistics center, where goods are placed on rail and shipped to the rest of the country, and where they are transloaded from ocean containers to domestic containers and truck trailers, for regional as well as national deliveries. Port truckers haul containers on chassis both to rail heads and to warehouses and distribution centers. A huge DC complex has formed on the eastern outskirts of Los Angeles, in the western Inland Empire (consisting of Riverside and San Bernardino counties), which accepts, sorts, stores, and delivers imports from the ports. These DCs are typically giant, windowless structures with a capacity to unload and load containers and trailers with efficiency and speed. The Wal-Mart DC is part of this complex.

Impact on Labor

Wal-Mart is lowering labor standards, not only for its own employees,[55] but also for the employees of all its competitors and potential competitors. This threat was the principal cause of the supermarket strike in Southern California, because the major chains feared Wal-Mart's stated intention to open forty supercenters in California. Wal-Mart is well known as a viciously antiunion company that does not hesitate to stretch the limits of the law to eliminate employees who show any tendency whatsoever to get organized. Its competitors use Wal-Mart's ability to keep unions out as a bargaining ploy against their own unions, which are faced with accepting concessions, or losing their jobs altogether to this mighty undercutter.

Apart from the sales workforce, other segments of the working class are also affected by Wal-Mart's practices, namely production and transportation/logistics workers. Above, we focused on Wal-Mart's impacts on its manufacturers/suppliers and its logistics providers, i.e., its *business* partners. But, of course, squeezing at the business level inevitably translates into squeezing the employees of these businesses. We already hinted at this in the discussion of Wal-Mart's role in pushing manufacturing offshore in search of the world's lowest wage labor. This creates the double whammy of increasing

Rail and Trucking Routes from the Ports of Southern California

Tonnage
_____ 0 to 500,000
_____ 500,000 to 1,000,000
_____ 1,000,000 to 10,000,000
_____ 10,000,000 to 50,000,000
██████ More than 50,000,000

joblessness in the U.S., and importing low-cost goods that undercut what remains of domestic manufacturing, leading to a ratcheting down of labor standards.

Let us look at this squeezing of production and logistics workers more closely, with special emphasis on the latter. Wal-Mart is not the sole cause of these developments, but the logistics revolution and the rise of retailer power as epitomized by Wal-Mart are certainly important factors in these developments. We have detected three major trends that have contributed to the deterioration of conditions for these workers: increased contingency, weakened unions, and racialization of labor. Let us look at each of these a little more closely.

Increased Contingency. There has been a rise in outsourcing and contracting out. Layers of intermediaries have been created between the "ultimate" employer (which we call the parent firm) and the workers. The parent firm uses a network of producers/suppliers which is constantly shifting. This produces instability and unpredictability for the supplying companies and their employees. This is shown in the rise in temporary and part-time workers, independent contractors, and piece-rate systems of pay.

For example, port truckers used to be unionized workers, organized by the International Brotherhood of Teamsters (IBT), but they have been transformed into "owner operators" who are paid per haul (a form of piece rate). Because they are technically independent contractors, even though in practice they work for port trucking companies, which in turn work mainly for steamship lines, which in turn work for shippers like Wal-Mart, they are subject to antitrust suits if they should try to organize or join a union.

Among the Inland Empire DCs, temporary-work agencies and employee-leasing firms have sprung up, making it much easier for the direct employer, the DC, to switch to those that will give it the best, i.e., cheapest, lowest-wage deal. It also enables the DCs to get rid of the workers or the entire temp agency should anything like organizing develop among the workforce.

Weakened Unions. Contingent relations make union busting much easier, since the parent company can shift work away from contractors who show any signs of labor trouble. Indeed, whole regions and countries can be abandoned because their workforces are too politically mobilized. This is what has happened to seafarers, who used to have strong unions on the West Coast. Now the entire Pacific trade is run by foreign steamship companies, and they often use "flags of convenience." FOCs allow them to register ships in countries (like Liberia) with a minimum of regulations and labor standards. And the liners can search the world for crews that are least likely to place any conditions on the terms they are offered. The loss of an IBT presence near the docks as the organizer of port truckers is another example of this deterioration.

Racialization. Racialization of labor refers to a process whereby a group of people is cordoned off for special, exclusionary treatment, typically based on a combination of physical appearance and putative ancestry. The process usually involves the denial of full citizenship rights to members of the racialized group, coupled with a belief that they form an "undeserving other," less worthy of a decent standard of living, or of one comparable to that of the person making the judgment. While the motivations behind racialization may be complex and varied, one motive stands out: the more effective exploitation of the labor of the racialized group. When group members are denied basic citizenship and other commonly accepted rights, they can be subjected to excessively exploitative labor regimes. Higher levels of surplus can be extracted from racialized workers, who have limited recourse for defending themselves.

In the U.S. today, such racialization is technically illegal, yet it persists in various hidden guises, including the denial of citizenship rights to undocumented immigrants, who become easy prey for unscrupulous employers, who propagate an image of Mexican and Central American workers as "poor, unskilled, illegal, and unworthy"; and continuing to view African Americans and other groups as less than full and equal members of the society. Moreover, workers employed offshore in low-wage jobs are often seen in racial terms by both their employers and by competing workers. The term "China-Mart" has been used to attack Wal-Mart, not so much to get it to stop exploiting Chinese workers, but to insinuate that those Chinese workers are responsible for stealing American jobs.

Both seafarers and port truckers fit the racialization mold. In the first case, the sailors are from the poorest, least-developed countries, and must put up with conditions that no American sailors and their unions would tolerate. The port truckers, at least in Southern California, are overwhelmingly Latino immigrants, mainly from El Salvador and Mexico. A certain proportion of them are undocumented, but in addition, as a group, they fall under the blight of the state's anti-Latino sentiment, and occasional legislation.

The longshore workers are a glorious exception to these processes. They have managed to hold on to a powerful union, have fought (not always completely successfully) against the outsourcing of their jobs, and have managed to continue to be treated with respect and decent pay even though their membership is now more ethnically diverse (it used to be overwhelmingly white). The very fact of their racial diversity must add to the fury of the employers over the union's power, since there is an unacknowledged assumption that workers of color should not be making that much money or exercising that much power. The ILWU has been a clear obstacle to the goals of Wal-Mart and the other big-box retailers.

The Politics of the West Coast Ports Lockout

Beliefs about the good of the economy do not emerge unaided in the president's mind. Interests make themselves known. In the case of the West Coast ports, the major actor was a newly formed organization called the West Coast Waterfront Coalition (WCWC).[56] The WCWC was composed of shippers. In fact, most of the members were retailers, and Wal-Mart was prominent among them.

Prior to 2002, retailers had not played an active role in the negotiations between the

PMA and the ILWU. But as the significance of imports has grown, so has retailers' interest in improving the flow of cargo through the West Coast ports. The WCWC had other interests besides labor relations, but it certainly was concerned with weakening the power that the ILWU was able to exercise over port operations. They believed that 2002 was the showdown year, in which concessions had to be forced upon the union. Not only did the WCWC work closely with the PMA, but it was able to get the ear of the president. As it turned out, the PMA made a significant blunder. Because the ports were shut down as a result of an employer lockout rather than a strike (although the PMA claimed it locked the workers out because they were engaged in an undeclared slowdown "strike"), the union could claim it was eager to return to work, whereas the employer was the one that resisted a negotiated reopening of the ports. The result was that while the ports were forced open, the PMA and the WCWC did not get all the concessions they had hoped for.[57] But we can be sure that this was not the last chapter in this conflict.

Implications for Fighting Back

The labor movement is in decline around most of the world. This problem cannot be solved merely by greater effort, such as trying to re-create the welfare state, focusing on organizing the unorganized, changing labor law, comprehensive campaigns, or increased union democracy. These are all good things and very important in their own right, but they are not enough.

We need to acknowledge fully the changes that are occurring. The labor movement needs to absorb the reality of the logistics revolution and the power it has given to retailers like Wal-Mart. We need to use these changes, instead of vainly trying to move backward. We need an equivalent paradigm shift in social struggle. The fact is that the economy has changed dramatically as a result of the logistics revolution, and worker organizing needs to change along with it. In most industries it has become almost impossible to organize one plant or firm, because it will disappear. Parent companies will shift their business away, and the company will go out of business.

This reality has led U.S. unions to move away from manufacturing, and to focus their organizing efforts on services, including public sector functions, that clearly cannot leave the country. It is no accident that the Service Employees International Union

(SEIU) is the largest and most powerful union in the United States today. While this approach may be practical in the short run, it avoids a confrontation with the most vital and powerful sectors of capital. To the extent that organizing is occurring, it is at the periphery of the economy and not in its heart.

Looking at this system of production and distribution, what are its weaknesses and vulnerabilities? Some are clearly evident, including extended supply chains and networks which can potentially be cut; JIT delivery, whose interruption can be devastating; nodes, like ports and airports, through which goods must flow; some more stable relationships that are easier to pressure; links to the global workforce, which open the possibility of international supply-chain campaigns; branding of the retailers, who are then vulnerable to increasing public exposure and criticism; and the fact that the giant retailers like Wal-Mart deal directly with consumers, who are also workers and citizens. The international trade community is aware of some of these vulnerabilities, especially the first three, framing the danger as the threat of a terrorist attack, rather than labor disruption.

Some of these types of struggle are already occurring, for example, the Inglewood revolt, and similar organized efforts to keep Wal-Mart and other big-box retailers out of urban communities; citizen backlash against the pollution and congestion effects of global trade on local gateway communities; the activities of United Students Against Sweatshops (USAS); and the new class-action suit against Wal-Mart for discrimination against women. Again, these are worthwhile and difficult campaigns, but do they get at the heart of the matter?

We realize that organizing under conditions created by the logistics revolution is not easy. It may require campaigns of a scale that we have never seen, and may demand a consolidation of resources and of interunion cooperation and coordination that has never been tried before. The labor movement may also have to abandon its standard approach of trying to win a contract with a single large employer. For example, "flexible organizing" may need to be considered—in which membership in the union does not depend on stable employment in one location. And unions may have to develop their own form of JIT strategies—where they have the flexibility to take advantage of vulnerabilities that show up unexpectedly, by acting rapidly to capitalize on a weakness.

Another clear implication of this analysis is the central significance of the transportation and warehousing unions. They cover workers who serve as the circulatory system of global capitalism. Global production and distribution thrusts them into prominence as strategically vital actors. The challenge for them is not only to get their own unions in order and to struggle for gains for their membership. Their challenge also lies in recognizing the role they could play in gaining the power necessary for workers and working-class communities, here and abroad, to place serious demands on global capital. They have the potential power to change a corrupt and unsustainable system that is increasing inequality and misery for millions of people. This is the opportunity that the logistics revolution affords. Is the U.S. labor movement prepared to take on such a challenge?

EIGHT

Wal-Mart in Mexico: The Limits of Growth

Chris Tilly

Introduction

Wal-Mart, the fast-growing retailer from Bentonville, Arksansas, has achieved notorious success in Mexico. Wal-Mart, which only entered the Mexican market in 1991, boasts 696 Mexican stores and 2004 sales of 140 billion pesos (close to $12 billion),[1] eclipsing the 111 billion pesos earned by its three closest competitors combined.[2] The retail giant has prompted headlines describing it as a "Goliath"[3] or "Leviathan"[4] that has "invade[d],"[5] "trounc[ed] the locals,"[6] and "transform[ed] the Mexican market,"[7] and is decried as a "threat to sovereignty."[8] With roughly 101,000 employees, it is the country's largest private employer. Seemingly, Wal-Mart de México is unstoppable.

Or is it? In this chapter, drawing on a combination of reviews of literature and press, analyses of public data sources, interviews with retail actors and consumers, and collective bargaining contracts, I argue that Wal-Mart achieved a powerful first-mover advantage in Mexico by acquiring Cifra, the leading chain of self-service stores, and by introducing several innovations perfected in the United States (in pricing and the management of inventory, labor, and suppliers). However, three factors are beginning to impose limits on that advantage. The first is the rapid modernization of a portion of the Mexican retail sector—in many cases through imitation of Wal-Mart. Second, the polarized Mexican income structure limits the population of consumers able to shop at Wal-Mart and its subsidiaries. Finally, repeated economic crises and stagnation have driven many Mexican consumers back to traditional and informal retail outlets.

A key reason for caring about Wal-Mart's future in Mexico is its impact on employment. In addition to the impact on its own numerous employees, a business of Wal-Mex's size and visibility also has spillover effects on other jobs in the retail sector (which employs about one Mexican worker in five outside of agriculture) and on low-skill jobs in general. Wal-Mart in the United States has a reputation for providing low-wage, exploitative jobs.[9] But again, the Mexican story is more complex. Wal-Mart pays wages slightly above the Mexican retail industry average, and offers pay and benefits comparable to its competitors' (though with some notable differences). Many Mexican Wal-Mart stores have union representation, although unions in Mexican retail generally do very little for their members. There may be important reasons to fear negative impacts of Wal-Mart's explosive growth in Mexico, but most of those reasons appear to apply with equal force to the rest of the retail sector.

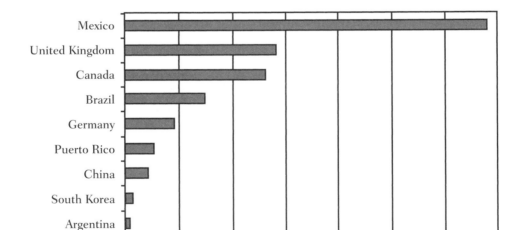

Wal-Mart International

Number of Stores

Source: Wal-Mart annual reports.

In the next section of the chapter, I set the context for discussion of Wal-Mart's Mexican adventure by contrasting the retail sectors in Mexico and the United States, particularly as regards employment. The following section lays out evidence on Wal-Mart in Mexico, and the last section offers brief conclusions.

Retail Employment: Comparing Mexico and the United States

Table 1 profiles similarities in the retail industry as an employer on both sides of the border. Retail is a large employer in both countries, accounting for more than one nonagricultural private sector worker in five. This makes retail comparable to manufacturing in employment size—somewhat smaller in the United States, somewhat larger in Mexico. Retail is also a predominantly—though not overwhelmingly—female job in both countries. The feminization of retail is particularly striking in Mexico, where the proportion of workers who are women stands 44 percent higher than the economy-wide proportion.

As is often the case with "women's" jobs, retail employment pays below-average wages both north and south of the border. The gap between retail wages and the economy-wide median looms larger in the United States, at 32 percent. But the 12 percent difference in Mexico is more significant than it appears. Only two of eight other major industries (construction and agriculture and fisheries) pay less. Moreover, the "commerce" category shown for Mexico includes higher-paid wholesale workers. And

TABLE 1. SIMILARITIES BETWEEN RETAIL EMPLOYMENT IN THE UNITED STATES AND MEXICO

	U.S.	MEXICO
Retail as proportion of nonagricultural private employment	21.2%	21.0%
Women as percentage of retail workforce	52.5%	51.5%
Ratio of percentage of women employed, retail/all industries	1.11	1.44
Median retail wage as percentage of wage for all industries	68.2%	87.9%

Sources: U.S. data from Bureau of Labor Statistics, http://stats.bls.gov. Mexican data from Mexico's Instituto Nacional de Estadística, Geografía y Informática (INEGI, http://www.inegi.gob.mx). Figures for various years, 1998–2001.

the Mexican earnings figure shows earnings *per day,* and therefore is elevated by the long hours that Mexicans work in retail trade.

As table 2 shows, it is in hours of work that we begin to see a divergence between retail employees in the two countries. In the United States, as is well known, retail has a huge (though minority) part-time workforce, bringing weekly hours below the economy-wide average. In Mexico, in contrast, the average retail worker plies his or her trade for fifty-one hours per week, significantly above the average. The explanation for the long hours becomes clear when we realize that the majority of Mexican retail workers are self-employed or unpaid (the unpaid category in Mexico includes family members, but also *meritorios,* meaning interns or apprentices)—a far cry from the 5 percent of U.S. retail workers falling in these categories. In the United States, a retail worker is 26 percent *less* likely to be self-employed or unpaid than the average; in Mexico, to the contrary, retail employees are 60 percent *more* likely to have one of these statuses. Completing this picture, the average Mexican retail business had two employees in 1998—

**TABLE 2. DIFFERENCES BETWEEN RETAIL EMPLOYMENT
IN THE UNITED STATES AND MEXICO**

	U.S.	MEXICO
Average weekly hours in retail	28.9	50.8
Average hours as percentage of average hours for all industries*	84.5%	120.4%
Self-employed or unpaid as percentage of retail workforce	5.4%	55.7%
Ratio of percentage self-employed or unpaid, retail/ all industries	0.74	1.60
Average employment per retail establishment	14.5	2.2
Ratio of average employment per establishment, retail/all private	0.89	0.38

*Hours ratio is for weekly hours in the United States, annual hours in Mexico.

Sources: U.S. data from Bureau of Labor Statistics, http://stats.bls.gov. Mexican data from INEGI, http://www.inegi.gob.mx. Figures for various years, 1998–2001.

little more than one-third the size of the average establishment economy-wide. North of the border, in contrast, retail businesses are nearly as large on average as other establishments.

Thus, retail work has not been proletarianized in Mexico to anything like the extent it has in the United States. Indeed, the statistics in tables 1 and 2 refer only to establishments with fixed locations, but a huge number of retail workers toil in the Mexican informal sector, estimated by the National Institute of Statistics, Geography, and Informatics (INEGI) to employ 29 percent of the Mexican nonagricultural workforce, of whom nearly a third work in commerce and restaurants.[10] Retail is second only to domestic service in the percentage of workers classified as informal.[11] At the same time, interestingly, Mexico still has a significant state retail sector, including 394 stores of the Institute for Security and Social Services for State Workers (ISSSTE), employing eleven thousand,[12] and over twenty-two thousand rural DICONSA (Distributor of the National Company for Popular Subsistence) stores, which typically employ one person apiece.[13] Overall, the retail industry is dominated by mom-and-pop operations that recall a bygone era in the United States. It's not that corner stores operated by one or two people have disappeared in the United States (retail establishments with one to four employees make up 46 percent of all retail sites),[14] but they have long since been overshadowed by supermarkets and department stores that account for the bulk of employment and sales. Moreover, in Mexico food stores account for 50 percent of retail employment, compared to only 20 percent in the United States.[15]

The Mexican retail industry's structure reflects—and reinforces—Mexican shopping habits. The average U.S. family shops for food 4 times per week.[16] According to a poll carried out by Mexico's retailer association, the National Association of Supermarkets and Department Stores (ANTAD) in association with the Gallup Organization, the average Mexican family makes 4 weekly trips to the supermarket, 8.8 trips to neighborhood grocery stores, and 7.5 trips to markets or specialized stores (such as *tortillerias* or butcher shops), for a total of 20 weekly food shopping trips.[17] This number, stunning to U.S. eyes, results not just from cultural traditions such as that of buying fresh tortillas daily (a habit reported by 56 percent of Mexican respondents), but also from the fact that many Mexicans have neither a car nor a large refrigerator. Rita Schwentesius and Manuel Angel Gómez[18] described the five main channels for food retailing in Mexico:

1. open-air, public markets, generally in city centers and managed by city governments; the retailers sell from small stalls;
2. mobile street markets (*tianguis*) that change location from day to day; communities and city neighborhoods typically have a day of the week ("plaza market
   day") when the *tianguis* shows up and sells a variety of products similar to that
   of a supermarket, but usually of lower quality and with negotiable prices;
3. traditional small shops that sell a limited line of products; the types and quality
   of products they carry depends on the incomes and tastes of the neighborhood;
4. specialized stores (such as fruit shops); these are of little importance in Mexico
   as the consumers prefer to buy perishables from *tianguis*;
5. self-service stores, including supermarkets and modern convenience stores.[19]

Schwentesius and Gómez reported that 58 percent of Mexicans prefer to shop for fresh
fruit and vegetables at open-air markets or *tianguis,* while only 21 percent prefer supermarkets. Researchers Jorge Mendoza, Fernando Pozos, and David Spener found that in
retail sales of new clothing, similarly, retail enterprises include department stores, self-
service stores (where consumers shop without the assistance of clerks), and specialized
clothing stores but also open-air markets, *tianguis,* street vendors, and *aboneros,* who
sell clothing and other goods door-to-door. They estimated that in 2000, department
and self-service stores accounted for about one-third of clothing sales, specialized (usually small) clothing stores another third, and the less formal outlets one-third.[20] Another
estimate, for dry goods more generally, puts self-service stores at 28 percent, department stores at 16 percent, and specialty retailers at under 5 percent, with the remaining
52 percent claimed by the informal sector.[21] In contrast, nonstore retailing accounts for
a tiny 0.3 percent of U.S. retail employment.[22]

In brief, as retail analysts are fond of saying, Mexico is "understored."[23] This does *not*
mean that Mexican consumers lack access to retail outlets; the combination of large
stores, neighborhood stores, and the informal sector appears to meet consumer needs.
But it does mean that Mexicans, at least until recently, had relatively few modern, large-
scale stores. Into this relative vacuum has entered Wal-Mart.

Wal-Marts in Mexico look similar to those around the world. Shown here is a store in Mexico City. Photograph by José Luis Álvarez Galván.

Wal-Mart in Mexico

SECRETS OF SUCCESS?

Wal-Mart first stuck its toe into Mexico in 1991 through a joint venture with Cifra, Mexico's leading retail company, initially limited to developing Sam's Club warehouse stores in Mexico. The tremendous success of the first Sam's Club stores and the impending passage of the North American Free Trade Agreement encouraged further collaboration, and Wal-Mart and Cifra expanded their joint venture through the 1990s. Wal-Mart purchased a majority stake in Cifra in 1997.[24] Prior to the joint venture, Cifra's lineup included Aurrera *autoservicios* (superstores selling food, clothing, and a variety of other items), Superama supermarkets, Suburbia department stores, and Vips restaurants. To this roster, Wal-Mart added Wal-Mart superstores (shifting Aurrera to a budget niche and relabeling its stores Bodega) and Sam's Club warehouse stores, and introduced two new restaurant formats. Wal-Mart–Cifra had fewer *grocery* stores (though more stores of all formats) than either of competitors Gigante and Comercial Mexicana as of 1993, but had overtaken them by 2000[25] and today has 326 Wal-Mart, Aurrera, Sam's, and Superama stores. Wal-Mart controlled 49 percent of Mexican supermarket sales in 2001.[26]

Wal-Mart's success is particularly striking in comparison with the performance of other international entrants. As table 3 shows, Wal-Mart's presence dwarfs that of every other major foreign retailer. The one partial exception is 7-Eleven, but a convenience store has one-twentieth the employment of a superstore, and within the convenience-

TABLE 3. WAL-MART AND OTHER RECENT INTERNATIONAL RETAIL ENTRANTS IN MEXICO

CHAIN	COUNTRY	FORMAT	YEAR ENTERED	MEXICAN STORES IN JULY 2004
Wal-Mart	U.S.	Self-service	1991	646 (326 grocery stores)
7-Eleven	U.S.	Convenience	1971	"More than 500" (compare OXXO/Femsa with "over 3,000")
Auchan	France	Self-service	1997	Exited in 2003 with 5 stores
Carrefour	France	Self-service	1994	27; exited in 2005
HEB	U.S.	Self-service	1997	19
Inditex (Zara)	Spain	Department	1992	100
JCPenney	U.S.	Department	1995	Sold its 6 stores to Grupo Sanborns in 2003

Sources: Number of stores and related information from company Web sites. Year of entry from Rita Schwentesius and Manuel Ángel Gómez, "The Rise of Supermarkets in Mexico: Impacts on Horticulture Chains," *Development Policy Review* 20, no. 4 (2002): 487–502, except 7-Eleven, Inditex, and JCPenney from company Web sites. News of Carrefour's exit from Gabriel de la Garza, "Arranca venta de Carrefour," *La Reforma*, February 4, 2005.

store niche 7-Eleven is swamped by Mexican competitor Oxxo (combined with Bara and Six, its sister chains within the Femsa Group). Thus, Wal-Mart's success does not reflect general success by U.S. or multinational companies in Mexico; rather, it appears to be distinctive.

What, then, can explain Wal-Mart's phenomenal track record in Mexico? The conventional explanation is that it has brought a set of superior management techniques and technologies. Press accounts have emphasized Wal-Mart's low-price strategy, high-technology distribution network, and intense pressure on suppliers for discounts[27]— "the same formula" as in the United States, according to *New York Times* reporter Tim Weiner.

Wal-Mart rolled out its "every day low prices" (EDLP) policy in Mexico in 1999–2000, once inflation had diminished to the point where meaningful price comparisons were possible.[28] The chain marked tens of thousands of items down as much as 14 percent, and it has also passed on further savings, for example when currency shifts decrease an item's cost to the company. Wal-Mart also began to post price comparisons with other chains, a practice that in 2002 got it expelled from ANTAD, Mexico's retail association. "EDLP has been extremely successful for us in Mexico," commented Wal-Mart International CFO Charles Holley.[29]

Wal-Mart de México also has connected with and replicated the U.S. company's huge, automated distribution network. With NAFTA eliminating most trade barriers, Wal-Mex has direct links to U.S.-based distribution centers, but also has built twelve distribution centers within Mexico.[30] In addition to heightened efficiency, this multiplies Wal-Mex's power as a purchaser, since Wal-Mart consolidates orders for all goods from outside the United States. "I buy 20,000 plastic toys, and Wal-Mart buys 20 million. Who do you think gets them cheaper?" asked Francisco Martinez, chief financial officer of Wal-Mart rival Comercial Mexicana.[31]

As in the United States, Wal-Mex uses that buying power to drive down prices. According to an unhappy executive of a small clothing manufacturer I will call Ropinta:

> Wal-Mart has driven many suppliers out of business. Wal-Mart maintains its profit margin. . . . They never reduce *their* margin. They *do* pass on savings in price, but at the expense of the manufacturer. You can increase efficiency a certain amount, but . . . For example, they may tell you, "We're going to sell shirts

at a discount of 40 percent—you, the manufacturer, have to cut your price 40 percent." So the consumer benefits, but they're driving out of business the manufacturers that provide *jobs*.[32]

Observers argue that another contributor to Wal-Mex's success is its use of a wide range of formats to appeal to varied classes of consumers, and particularly lower-income consumers.[33] Executives of competing Mexican companies also referred to Wal-Mart's use of minutely prescribed systems and procedures. "There's a sign on the Wal-Mart headquarters saying 'Ordinary people coming into a company to do extraordinary things,'" commented an executive of another chain. "With the right systems, training, and tools, ordinary people *can* do extraordinary things."

LIMITS TO THE SUCCESS STORY

There is some truth to these interpretations. But I argue that (1) they overlook a number of conjunctural advantages difficult to replicate in other times and places; (2) competitors are now successfully imitating these strategies, diminishing the Wal-Mex advantage; and (3) the polarization of Mexican society limits retail strategies aimed primarily at a middle market.

Wal-Mart's conjunctural advantages were several. First of all, "they bought the business [Cifra] that was already the leader," as one department store executive commented. Shortly after Wal-Mart launched its joint venture with Cifra, the dramatic peso devaluation of 1994–95 offered the U.S. company a unique opportunity to buy a controlling share of Cifra at an extremely low price (though Wal-Mart deserves credit for having the foresight to invest in Mexico rather than pulling out, as Kmart and Sears did).[34] More broadly, Wal-Mart gained first-mover advantages by arriving in a Mexico that was "understored," where other retailers were still using traditional high/low pricing (based on periodic discounts rather than consistently low prices), still depending on suppliers for most deliveries, and little accustomed to demanding discounts from suppliers.

Mexican retailers have proven to be quick studies. All three of the main national *autoservicio* chains competing with Wal-Mart now offer some version of its EDLP formula. (A number of retail executives and managers commented that a pure EDLP strategy is not yet feasible, since Mexican consumers still expect periodic sales.) Comercial Mexicana and Soriana now aggressively publicize price differences with Wal-Mart and Aurrera. In addition, some of the larger suppliers (especially soft drink and snack food manufacturers) have begun to print suggested prices on their packages, deterring retailers from charging more. Wal-Mart's competitors insist that there is now no significant price difference, and many Mexican consumers seem to have drawn the same conclusion. "In terms of service, prices, assortment, they're all pretty much the same," commented a Guadalajara cabdriver.[35]

Similarly, squeezing suppliers has become commonplace for large Mexican retailers. The Ropinta apparel supply executive quoted above described in some detail retailers' process of negotiating a "*contrato leonino*":

> First, they ask you for a discount. Then, on top of that, they say, "We want a graduated volume discount"—1 percent off for this much sales, 1 percent more off for that much. And then they ask for a "confidential discount"—confidential because nobody puts it in writing—for another 1–2 percent. And if you don't provide *promotores* [stock handlers to stock merchandise in the store], *another* discount. And on the anniversary of signing the contract, another discount . . . And if you send the wrong amount, not enough, they fine you. In some cases, the fine erases your whole profit margin. . . . And then they have provisions when they're opening a new store, that if you send the wrong amount, the whole order is free.

However, this account is not about Wal-Mart, but its competitor Soriana, which he described as the most predatory of the major self-service chains "right now" (in mid-2004). An industry consultant offered the opinion that Gigante, yet another chain, was actually squeezing suppliers hardest. Comercial Mexicana, Gigante, and Soriana have now also boosted their market power by forming a buying alliance, Sinergía, which may be a step toward more extensive cooperation against Wal-Mart. Although Mexico's Federal Competition Commission originally ruled the pact illegal, it reversed itself in July 2004 and allowed it to proceed.

Executives from competing chains report that they have also begun to shift toward centralized, highly automated distribution and tracking systems, and to create detailed

Bodega Aurrera is Wal-Mart's budget brand in Mexico. Shown here is a store in Mexico City. Photograph by José Luis Álvarez Galván.

procedure manuals. What's more, Gigante and Comercial Mexicana, Wal-Mart's largest rivals, have created multiple store formats (three in the case of Gigante, four in the case of Comercial Mexicana) and have through acquisition or joint venture accumulated constellations of retail outlets (Comercial Mexicana has Costco and the California chain of restaurants; Gigante has Office Depot, Radio Shack, Price Smart, and the Toks restaurant chain) (information from company Web sites). The net result of Mexican chains' emulation of Wal-Mart is that Wal-Mex's share of sales among the top five Mexican retailers has remained steady for the last two years.[36]

There is also growing evidence that the Wal-Mex advantage does not translate well to other contexts. Wal-Mart has failed to reproduce its Mexican success elsewhere in Latin America. Historian Julio Moreno noted that Wal-Mart's success in Brazil has been modest, and its experience in Argentina "disastrous."[37] In Brazil, where Wal-Mart recently reached sixth place among retailers, the discounter confronted other entrenched retailers already using the low-price strategy, and made early missteps that tarnished its reputation with consumers. In Argentina, Wal-Mart entered without a joint-venture partner, maintained a strategy predicated on high incomes despite Argentina's prolonged descent into recession, and encountered difficulty in securing local suppliers (because of pressure from other retailers seeking to box them out, Wal-Mart charged).

Closer to home, Wal-Mart has struggled in northern Mexico, particularly the Monterrey area.[38] Executives of another chain offered several analyses of Wal-Mart's difficulties in the region. Soriana and the Texas-based HEB were already entrenched by the time Wal-Mart arrived. Wal-Mart made some early merchandising mistakes, opening no frills Bodegas that had done well in central Mexico but left more sophisticated northern customers cold. One executive suggested that Wal-Mart stumbled when it turned management of the northern stores over to Aurrera, whose more hierarchical style frustrated employees. And one attributed the ensemble of problems to Wal-Mex's increasing geographic dispersion: "Just to be spread out causes problems. With a lot of dispersion, it's hard to concentrate on regional marketing."

Finally, as polarization between rich and poor increases in Mexico, Wal-Mart's approach of selling to a broad middle faces structural limits. Robert Buchanan, an analyst at NatWest Securities, commented: "Mexico is a land of haves and have-nots. It's a poor bet for an American broad-lines retailer that is mostly aimed at the middle class."[39] *Chain Store Age,* writing shortly after the 1994 devaluation, said that Mexican retailing had "become overdeveloped in some sectors, particularly self-service retail (including discounters), shopping malls, and high-end stores all competing for the small share of the population with medium to high purchasing power (estimates range at 10–30%)."[40] Despite Wal-Mart's domination of the supermarket sector, it still accounts for only 7 percent of Mexico's total retail sales.[41]

Table 4 helps explain why.[42] This comparison, based on price checks in Wal-Marts in the United States and Mexico in January 2005, demonstrates that while some Mexican prices are lower, others are roughly equal, and a few are considerably higher. To gauge the accessibility of these prices to low-income consumers in both countries, table 4 converts the prices to the number of hours of work at the applicable minimum wage it would take to purchase each item. Given that the Mexican minimum wage was less than one-tenth of the U.S. minimum on an hourly basis, the price difference in "minimum wage hours" is striking. A Mexican minimum-wage earner must expend from three to twenty-five times as many hours as his or her U.S. counterpart to buy the same

TABLE 4. COMPARING PRICES IN MEXICAN AND U.S. WAL-MARTS

	MEXICAN PRICE AS % OF U.S.	HOURS OF WORK AT MINIMUM WAGE TO PURCHASE ITEM		MEXICO/U.S. RATIO
		MEXICO	USA	
Merchandise item				
1 kg pinto beans	47%	1.6	0.3	4.9
1 kg rice	68%	1.5	0.2	7.1
1 l corn oil	77%	3.1	0.4	8.0
Small can tuna	137%	1.2	0.1	14.2
1 gallon whole fresh milk	103%	5.6	0.5	10.9
Cheerios, 425 g box	101%	5.0	0.5	10.5
Tostitos corn chips, 500 g	24%	1.9	0.8	2.5
Bleach, 3.8 liters	108%	3.2	0.3	11.3
30 kitchen-size trash bags	85%	6.1	0.7	8.8
Toilet paper, 12 rolls	50%	5.4	1.0	5.2
Huggies diapers, pack of 34	127%	18.1	1.4	13.2
Pine fragrance cleaner, 2 liters	56%	3.8	0.7	5.8
Liquid laundry detergent, 2 liters	235%	7.3	0.3	24.5
Men's T-shirts, pack of 3	171%	20.6	1.2	17.7
Hand soap, 4 cakes	143%	3.9	0.3	14.9

Source: Price comparisons in January 2004 (see note 42).

items; for most items the ratio falls between five and fifteen. In short, Wal-Mart is far less affordable in Mexico than in the United States. As one reporter put it, "For the average Mexican consumer a trip to a Wal-Mart supercenter is a high-end experience."[43]

Economic polarization and impoverishment have worsened over time, with predictable results for shopping patterns. The percentage of Mexicans who state an overall preference for shopping in a supermarket dropped from 75 percent in 1993 to 56 percent in 2000[44] and 34 percent in 2003.[45] On the other hand, analysts agree that the informal sector—accounting for something like half of Mexican retail sales—has grown because of economic crisis. According to analyst Chris Albi of Valores Banamex,

> During the crisis, Mexicans got used to shopping more in municipal food markets and the informal street markets known as *tianguis*. For washing machines or European-tailored suits, department stores are basically the only alternative. But for food, regular clothing and general merchandise, Mexicans have other lower-cost options than the established retail chains.[46]

Similarly, Mendoza, Pozos, and Spener concluded that small-scale and informal apparel sellers are likely to retain a significant share of the retail clothing market, serving moderate- to low-income customers.[47] In addition to offering lower costs, neighborhood retailers are more likely to offer informal credit and flexibility in quantities sold. "We sell to people in the very low classes, including many who are unemployed," reported the proprietor of a new family-run corner store in an outlying urban area. "It's hard for us, because we thought we would sell a whole box of cookies or a whole package of diapers, but instead we're selling them one by one."

Indeed, Antonio Chedraui, then president of ANTAD, pointed to consolidation in the *informal* sector as one outcome of the economic crisis, which leads to growth in bargain-seeking customers as well as an increased supply of jobless people in search of a means of survival. "We're not talking about one vendor with a stand on the street corner anymore, but someone who has 100 stands or more and hires a staff to work them," he said.[48] And as the Mexican economy slumped once more in 2001 because of the U.S. recession, Mexican toy manufacturers contracted with street vendors to sell their toys to offset declining store sales.[49] Of course, inability to accurately measure the size of the informal retail sector makes any broad conclusions somewhat speculative, and some

Tianguis (street market) in the city of Morelia, Mexico. Photograph by Chris Tilly.

analysts have recently offered the contrary view that Wal-Mex is now stealing market share from the informal sector.[50] But many of the Mexican consumers I spoke to in early 2004 continued to tout the affordability of the *tianguis* and public markets in comparison with self-service stores.

WAL-MEX JOBS

I assess job quality based on pay and benefits as tabulated in selected union contracts from the cities of León and Guadalajara, where I obtained contracts for Wal-Mart and two competitors for each city.[51] Comparison of union contracts with interview findings in the two cities suggests that contractual pay rates constitute a floor for actual pay rates, and contractual benefits appear to be a generally accurate representation of actual benefits received.

Despite Wal-Mart's reputation as a low-paying company in the United States, and journalistic claims that it offers low pay in Mexico, it appears to offer pay levels comparable or superior to those in other chains (table 5). Other useful comparisons are Mexico's minimum daily salary, which was 43.73 in Guadalajara and 42.11 in León in 2004,[52] and the national average of daily compensation in retail, which I estimate at 66 pesos in 2003 (far below the economy-wide average of 160 pesos); by these yardsticks as well, Wal-Mart offers decent pay. The problem is not low pay at Wal-Mart in particular, but rather low pay in the retail sector in general. (To get a sense of the purchasing power of these salaries, note that Wal-Mex customers were paying about 8 pesos for a kilo of rice, 9 for a kilo of beans, 18 for a liter of corn oil, and 31 for a gallon of pasteurized milk.)

In fringe benefits, Wal-Mart lags somewhat behind other chains (table 6). Wal-Mart offers a year-end bonus twice that required by law, but otherwise offers only those benefits required by Mexico's national labor law. Comercial Mexicana (in Guadalajara), Soriana, and Gigante all offer somewhat more generous packages. Gigante stands out, providing more vacation days, double the vacation pay, and its own pension plan. But

TABLE 5. WAL-MART DAILY PAY RATES (PESOS) COMPARED TO THOSE IN OTHER CHAINS, 2004

	WAL-MART (LEÓN, GUADALAJARA)	COMERCIAL MEXICANA (LÉON)	COMERCIAL MEXICANA (GUADALAJARA)	SORIANA (LEÓN)*	GIGANTE (GUADALAJARA)*
Assistant janitor	67	—	—	75.62	75.03
Sales, general merchandise	75.30	54.59	71.23	71.24	75.03

*Imputed from 2002 rates of pay by applying the percentage increases implemented by Comercial Mexicana in León. Based on pay at four months at Soriana and six months at Gigante (other chains do not list pay differences by seniority).

Source: Collective-bargaining contracts from the Juntas Locales de Conciliación y Arbitraje, Guadalajara and León.

with that exception, Wal-Mart compensation does not appear far out of step with other chains. Moreover, given high employee turnover rates in retail, differences in vacation times and pension plans for senior employees will affect only a small proportion of the retail workforce. ANTAD estimated third-trimester supermarket staff turnover at 30 percent in 2004, implying an annual turnover rate of 90 percent.[53]

Also noteworthy, in comparison with the United States, is the fact that Wal-Mart has union contracts at all in Mexico. According to Marco Antonio Torres of the Center for Labor Studies, Wal-Mex simply "pays an organization to negotiate collective contracts to comply with labor laws" and "keeps the contracts on hand to meet legal requirements."[54] But in fact, Mexican retail unions *as a rule* appear to offer only minimal protection to their workers. Economists José Alfonso Bouzas and Mario Vega analyzed

TABLE 6. WAL-MART BENEFITS COMPARED TO THOSE IN OTHER CHAINS, 2004

	WAL-MART (LÉON, GUADALAJARA)	COMMERCIAL MEXICANA (LÉON)	COMERCIAL MEXICANA (GUADALAJARA)	SORIANA (LÉON)	GIGANTE (GUADALAJARA)
Days of pay in year-end bonus (*aguinaldo*)	30	30	30	30	30
Vacation days after 2 years	8	8	8	8	10
Vacation pay as % of regular pay	25%	25%	30%	25%, to 30% after 2 years	50%
Pension plan beyond social security?	No	No	No	No	Yes

Source: Collective-bargaining contracts from the Juntas Locales de Conciliación y Arbitración, Guadalajara and León.

Gigante contracts and concluded that they were *contratos de protección* (sweetheart contracts) designed to protect the company from serious union organizing rather than to defend workers.[55] In my interviews, managers referred to unions as "white" or even "white paper," and few unionized workers (outside of the ISSSTE, which has a strong public sector union) were even aware that they were represented by a union. Like its compensation policies, Wal-Mex's labor-relations approach seems to place it squarely in the mainstream of Mexican retailers.

Conclusions

A closer look at Wal-Mart's performance in Mexico indicates that it is neither invincible nor exceptionally exploitative. Though Wal-Mex has indeed scored impressive growth since 1991, this spurt rested on a specific set of circumstances. Imitation by competitors, income polarization, and economic hardship that steers consumers toward the informal sector will limit Wal-Mart de México's reach in the future. Already, Wal-Mart has stumbled in Brazil, Argentina, and northern Mexico for related reasons.

Wal-Mart's pay roughly equals or exceeds that of its competitors; all pay less than twice the minimum wage for entry-level jobs. The company's approach to labor relations also appears comparable to that of other large retailers. Wal-Mart does trail in fringe benefits, but in most cases the differences are small.

All of this does not mean that Wal-Mart's entry is purely beneficial for Mexico. Critics charge that Wal-Mart drives small retailers out of business, weakening community fabric in the process. Wal-Mart's recent opening of a store in the archaeological zone of Teotihuacán, the site of 1,500-year-old pyramids, crystallized this issue, uniting local merchants, economic nationalists, and historic preservationists in an attempt—ultimately unsuccessful—to stop the store. Critics also argue that Wal-Mart is in the process of bankrupting many small suppliers, flooding the country with cheap imports that further undermine domestic production, and threatening Mexican sovereignty by heightening U.S. domination of the Mexican economy. But as the example of pay levels illustrates, the key issue may not be that Wal-Mex is playing a distinctively negative role, but rather that Wal-Mex is representative of problems that characterize much of the retail sector.

It is worth taking a moment to draw up a balance sheet of the broader impacts of retail modernization in Mexico, and indeed in much of Latin America and the developing world.[56] There is some evidence that Wal-Mart and its competitors have succeeded in lowering prices for Mexican consumers. "A basket of food and groceries typically costs about the same as in the United States," according to the *Dallas Morning News*. "By contrast, Mexicans typically pay more than Americans do for everything from telephone calls to banking services to computers."[57] While such anecdotal evidence abounds, it is harder to detect a retail modernization effect in overall price levels. Taking September 1997, the month Wal-Mart acquired Cifra, as a likely starting point for a "Wal-Mart effect," we find that food, drink, and tobacco prices grew at 99 percent the rate for overall price increases from 1997 to 2004. This compares to 96 percent during 1990–97, and 94 percent over the 1980s.[58]

The flip side of the impact on consumers is that giant retailers have replaced small businesses with large ones, shifting workers from the ranks of the self-employed, family members, and neighbors to employees of large organizations. Retail restructuring has triggered two waves of such employee-ization, one in retail itself and one among the industries that supply it. Simultaneously, Mexico and many other countries of the global South have removed trade protection for such supply industries, exposing them to global competition.

Without question, the resulting transition has been painful for small business owners. "All of the retailers in the downtown are in crisis," lamented a woman whose family has run a stand in the León municipal market selling clothing for two generations. "It's the result of so many businesses opening—Mexican businesses, foreign businesses, for example, Wal-Mart, Soriana, and Ley [a large regional chain]." As for suppliers, the large chains set quality and consistency standards that are difficult for small producers to meet. "They wanted consistent supply without ups and downs," the leader of a small Guatemalan vegetable cooperative said about a globally owned supermarket chain in his country. "We didn't have the capacity to do it." And for more durable goods, according to the executive of Mexico's Ropinta, the global chains searching for lower costs are "buying from China, and that's leading to the elimination of manufacturing in the rest of the world."

For Mexico, there are at this point no good estimates of how this shift has affected job *quality*. Though owners of small stores and businesses had "middle-class" status, it is not clear that overall the hourly pay of these workforces exceeded the pay currently available in larger stores and farms. In the case of production shifts from Mexico to China, on the other hand, lower pay rates motivated these overseas shifts in the first place. Moreover, the shrinking of a formerly widely dispersed middle class removes an important building block of stable communities.

In terms of job *quantity,* the rise of large retailers has clearly taken a toll. Within retail, the giant companies automated processes such as pricing and inventory management at the same time as they replaced across-the-counter service with self-service, slashing employment needs. Retailers shifted purchasing of goods to large, capital-intensive suppliers or out of the country altogether.

In the context of such sector-specific job losses, the difference between a difficult transition and long-term distress depends on the overall growth of the economy. Unfortunately, Mexican economic growth has not even kept pace with population growth. The result has been the explosion of the informal sector, officially estimated at 29 percent of the workforce, though many researchers argue that true figure is 50 percent or higher. Ironically, the informal sector is concentrated in retail, so that huge retail corporations have grown in step with tiny, one- and two-person operations, including street vendors and home-based selling. One expression of this irony is found in net sales per employed person, the standard measure of retail productivity. Net sales per person climbed from 47,000 in 1989 to 54,000 in 1994 (in 1999 pesos), reflecting efficiency increases. By 1999 (the most recent year for which data are available), however, net sales per person had fallen once more to 49,000, indicating a *decline* in overall efficiency, most likely due to the expansion of marginal businesses.[59]

Thus, the transformation of Mexican retail has contributed to the polarization of the Mexican economy, with retail-sector employment itself one important locus of this polarization. In turn, this polarization places limits on the expansion of Wal-Mart and other retailers, since the poorest cannot afford to shop in modern supermarkets. As the leader in Mexico's retail makeover, Wal-Mart makes a convenient target, but the serious problems in Mexico's retail sector and in the economy as a whole are much deeper and broader than any one company.

Working at Wal-Mart

Making the New Shop Floor: Wal-Mart, Labor Control, and the History of the Postwar Discount Retail Industry in America

Thomas Jessen Adams

In recent years, Wal-Mart has come to represent the vanguard of corporate power in America. As Nelson Lichtenstein and others have argued, Wal-Mart has become the paradigmatic representation of a new age in the history of capitalism.[1] Its workforce practices—a vociferous antiunionism, embedded gender discrimination, compulsive cost cutting, and near-comprehensive control over workers and the workplace—have drawn well-publicized ire from labor activists, community organizers, the mainstream media, and a large portion of the American public. Indeed, with its size, scope, influence, and ubiquity across both the physical and cultural landscape of America, it is no wonder that for many, Wal-Mart emblematizes the "template for twenty-first-century capitalism."

Yet, Wal-Mart does not exist in isolation from its broader historical context. When we look at the labor history of America's discount retailers, this picture of Wal-Mart as template becomes more complicated. In fact, Wal-Mart's labor practices are hardly new, but rather represent a perfection of a specific kind of workplace control that has been endemic to the discount retail industry in America since its flowering after World War II. While Wal-Mart is rightfully singled out as the exemplar of an era as antiunion as any

213

in recent memory, it is important to understand that Wal-Mart's difference from the discount retail industry—and quite probably, the low-wage service industry in general—is not a difference in kind, but in degree. When analyzing Wal-Mart's place in the new service economy, we must take care to understand the extent to which the company's labor practices are not the exception, but rather, the perfection of the rule.

In the aftermath of World War II, commentators across the political spectrum hailed the emergence of a supposedly classless society based on rising wages, attainable middle-class purchasing power, and unionized industries. Often identified with the 1950 collective bargaining agreement between General Motors and the United Auto Workers—the so-called Treaty of Detroit—this era of rising living standards and growing consumption was seen by many to be an indication of the triumph of Fordist capitalism.[2] But, there were always cracks in the facade of American Fordism. Despite much rhetoric about the end of class conflict, business began a massive assault on the power of organized labor.[3] Well-paid and heavily unionized jobs soon disappeared from the industrial East and Midwest, replaced by cheaper labor in rural areas, the American South and later, the global South.[4] And as American workers increasingly became employed in low-wage service industries rather than production, extraction, and agricultural work, new forms of labor control and exploitation developed. Such emergent practices were more attuned to an economy whose working-class did not make cars but sold clothing, did not cut steel but cared for the elderly, and did not grow food but rather stocked it in the aisles of places like Wal-Mart.

The discount retail industry has been at the vanguard of this process, creating conditions for the spread of these new forms of labor. In the late 1950s and early 1960s, the discount store was a new phenomenon, with four characteristics that in combination distinguished it from traditional retail and five-and-dime stores: lower price markups, higher merchandise turnover, almost total self-service, and large but nontraditional locations including "big box"–style warehouses and former mills.[5] By 1965, this new type of retailing had surpassed department stores in total sales volume, thereby leading to a vast increase in America's retail workforce.[6] In 1958, there was roughly one retail job in America for every three jobs in manufacturing.[7] By 2001 these two employment sectors had virtually equalized.[8]

Coincident with their expansion, discount stores led the charge to the lower wage rates and atomized bargaining that have been central to the post-Fordist era.[9] The period from the late 1950s to the present saw the average weekly earnings of a worker in manufacturing, construction, or mining (the three main categories of goods-producing industries) rise by between 16 and 39 percent in constant dollars.[10] Retail workers, on the other hand, saw their real wages decline by more than 12 percent, and they witnessed the differential between their wages and those of workers in manufacturing climb from roughly $60 a week to more than $250.[11] Even workers in America's other expansive service industries, like health care, security, tourism, and janitorial work, saw their real wages remain relatively constant over the same period of time.[12]

By the early 1960s, discount houses began to appear in every region of the country, particularly in fast-growth suburbs and outside of midsize towns.[13] The profit margins and rapid growth of these stores were unheard of in the retail industry. Between 1963 and 1970, Kmart, "retailing's *tour de force,*" saw its sales volume per store increase an astounding *eighteen* times over, nearly quadruple that of the most profitable old-line general-merchandise department store, JCPenney.[14]

Simply put, discount store chains turned such massive profits and were able to engage in voluminous expansion largely as the result of their labor costs, which were a staggeringly low 11 to 13 percent of total sales during the years from 1960 to 1977.[15] Kmart and its subsidiary Jupiter regularly saw wages as low as 7.7 percent of total sale volumes.[16] Classic downtown department stores were heavily unionized and often dependent upon highly skilled salespeople. These types of stores tended to pay out as much as 30 percent of their sales to labor.[17] Even when a store was not organized, salespeople were often able to create a work culture that gave them a large degree of control on the floor and a degree of insulation from managerial cost cutting.[18] Through the creation of a new shop floor whose purpose generally was to minimize labor costs and specifically to prevent unionization, discount stores like Wal-Mart and Kmart eviscerated much of the workplace camaraderie that had previously existed in the department store industry, atomized their workforce, and stretched their power over their employees into virtually every aspect of the workers' lives. In so doing, the discount stores' ability to institute this totalizing and flexible regime of labor control placed them at the vanguard of a "new economy" no longer based on production but on the cheap and controllable distribution of services.

From the 1950s through the 1970s and beyond, the discount retail industry simply engaged in the relentless drive toward lower labor costs and greater management control over production characteristic of capitalism since its inception. Historians have noted that it was specifically after World War II that the retail industry began to follow the model sketched out by the Marxist political economist Harry Braverman, whereby new forms of technology and management led to a quantum erosion in labor costs and worker power at the desk and counter.[19] Indeed, the Wal-Mart shop floor, like that of the Deptford shipyard, Pittsburgh steel mill, and the Detroit auto plant before it, has come to be recognized as the epitomous workplace of its respective epoch.[20]

Yet, the very organization of labor in these stores, while certainly part of a long history of managerial domination, nevertheless represents something new and highly innovative. By its nature, a discount store sells its products for far less than a traditional department store. Its greater profitability comes from one thing: stock turnover. This is the simple philosophy behind discount stores—lower markup yields more turnover and more customers who buy more items, which then leads to even more turnover and thus more profits. Sam Walton was famous for his obsession with keeping markup low to ensure "everyday low prices." As one of his early managers remembered,

> Sam wouldn't let us hedge on price at all. Say the list price was $1.98 (the manufacturer's suggested price), but we had only paid 50 cents. Initially I would say, "Well it's originally $1.98, so why don't we sell it for $1.25." And he'd say, "No, we paid 50 cents for it. Mark it up 30 percent and that's it."[21]

Such a philosophy made discounters like Wal-Mart particularly attractive for postwar consumers obsessively concerned with price and often squeezed by deindustrialization and inflation, but it also made the profits at such stores incredibly dependent on their labor costs. For instance, a department store and a discount store might both make an item vendible for a total cost of $30. That is, they buy the item, transport it to the store, do the necessary advertising, and pay for the labor that sells it, all for a total cost of $30. A discount store may then sell that item to a consumer for $35, while a more traditional department store might sell it for $50. The discount store is gambling that it will be able to sell more than four times as many items as the department store, thus accounting for its greater profitability. Now, holding everything else equal, what if the cost of labor for that item goes up $2? If both stores keep selling this item for $35 and $50 respectively, then the discount store now has to sell six times as many as the department store in order to make the same profit. This is a daunting prospect![22] Simply put, the lower the markup on a commodity, the more a given store's profits are determined by the costs of its labor.[23]

Thus, the discount store arose almost solely on the basis of its ability to control the unfixed and easily changeable cost of labor. This is a subtle, but important, distinction. In choosing outer suburban locations with lower rents, self-service layouts, and architecturally streamlined designs, discounters pushed down their fixed costs, ensuring that large profits and steady growth depended on a relentlessly increasing level of labor productivity.[24]

Even before the days of Frederick Winslow Taylor, managers sought to increase labor productivity either through the introduction of new technology or by the reorganization and intensification of work. Both strategies are dialectically complicit, of course. Nineteenth-century changes in the technology of steel production enabled Andrew Carnegie and Henry Frick to wrest control of their mills from the skilled workers who had reigned supreme for a generation, a development which enabled yet another generation of steel industry managers, including Frederick Taylor, to perfect the stringent time-management practices that came to characterize twentieth-century manufacturing.[25]

Discount stores are no exception to this developmental process. As James Hoopes points out in this volume, retail managers at Wal-Mart and elsewhere have been quick to deploy the latest technological and organizational innovations.[26] Yet, because the nature of these stores as *discount*, the thrust of the relationship between technological change and labor control has been overwhelmingly on the side of the latter. In describing the experience of immigrants in late nineteenth-century factories, the noted labor historian David Montgomery has argued that "the skill and knowledge required by manufacturing occupations . . . were embodied not in their training but in the technical organization of the factory itself."[27] In the case of the modern discount store this statement can be turned around—the organization and design of the discount shop floor itself embodied the managerial control of labor necessary to its functioning as a discount store.[28]

For the purposes of this analysis, we can identify four such managerial control strategies in discount retailing. The first is organizational. This includes both the financial and physical way the store was laid out and the location of different departments within a store. The second is what we can broadly call, after Harry Braverman, the degradation of work. This refers to the continual deskilling and automation of discount retail labor from its inception to the present. As Braverman put it, following the destruction of craft autonomy and traditional workplace knowledge, "what is left to workers is a reinterpreted and woefully inadequate concept of skill: a specific dexterity, a limited and repetitious operation, 'speed as skill,' etc."[29] Intense, continuous surveillance of employees is a third labor-control technique common to almost all discount operations, while outright opposition to trade unionism, often brutal and illegal, constitutes a final strategy designed to restrain labor costs.[30]

During its initial expansion across Arkansas and the Ozarks in the 1960s, Wal-Mart pioneered a novel technique to keep labor costs down and deter union organizing.[31] Instead of having a single corporation own all of its stores, at least the first three Wal-Marts were owned and run by different companies: Wal-Mart Inc., Wal-Mart of Springdale (Arkansas) Inc., and Wal-Mart of Harrison (Arkansas) Inc.[32] Majority ownership of each corporation was held by the partnership, Walton's 5 and 10 Cent Stores. This partnership itself had majority ownership in a trust administered by Helen Walton, while controlling ownership (40 percent) was in the hands of Sam Walton, Helen's husband. Sam Walton, the founder of Wal-Mart, was also chairman of the board of each of the three Wal-Mart corporations. Additionally, the stockholders of each corporation varied among Sam and Helen Walton's children, other relatives, and various friends from Bentonville, Arkansas.[33] If this division of ownership and control seems complicated, it is because it was meant to be. By establishing each of his stores as a separate corporation, Sam Walton achieved two cost-cutting and labor-control victories. An amendment to the Fair Labor Standards Act of 1938 held that retail establishments with less than $1 million a year in total sales volume were exempt from paying their employees a minimum wage. Not coincidentally, in 1964 and 1965 all three stores individually had less than $1 million in individual sales but more than $1 million combined sales.[34] Wal-Mart was thus exempt from paying its employees a minimum wage until a federal court ruled against it in 1967, arguing that it was "patently clear that Mr. Walton (Sam) is the primary driving force behind each of the corporations and that each of the stores is but a division of the Wal-Mart operation."[35] Wal-Mart lost this case, but the cost-control ingenuity, bordering on outright illegality, was never abandoned even after forty years. In this sense Sam Walton's legacy truly does march on.[36]

The strategy of dividing ownership also hindered union organization. As long as different Wal-Marts were considered separate corporations, any labor organizing would have to be limited to an individual store, thus nullifying companywide collective-bargaining potential. Kmart, which was then the most profitable and envied discount store in the country, took this strategy a step further. At many Kmart stores, different departments were licensed out to smaller companies, which leased space in the store to sell preapproved Kmart items. While the licensee was officially a separate employer, its managers, telephones, utilities, display cases, labor rules, janitorial services, cash registers, advertising, credit plan, and accounting practices were required to be those of Kmart.[37] The two things officially controlled by the licensee, hiring and product, were still subordinated to Kmart. Licensee workers wore name tags identifying them as Kmart employees and had to learn and follow all Kmart work policies.

This division of the shop floor served a dual purpose. On the one hand, it divided employees who might attempt to organize. For example, in 1965 the NLRB barred the Retail Clerks International Association (RCIA) from forming a storewide union in Jackson, Michigan, even though the majority of Kmart employees and licensee employees had voted for it.[38] Instead of establishing one union of all the workers under the same roof, organizers and employees had to form, in this case, eight unions, thus limiting the bargaining effectiveness of each unit.[39] On the other hand, dividing workers from each other served to disable cross-shop consciousness and solidarity. Even in the rare case that an entire store was organized, one worker could find herself a Teamster working for $1 an hour and no vacation time, while another worker doing virtually the same job and answering to the same work rules and storewide managers could find herself a member of the RCIA and earning 80¢ an hour with two weeks' paid vacation. In this way, Kmart created artificial divisions between workers that both limited the specific effectiveness of labor organizing and eviscerated a larger sense of cross-shop work consciousness and equality.

Such divisions could also manifest themselves spatially. Physically placing a licensee between two Kmart departments, combined with strict rules that prevented leaving one's department and "loud talking across the store," could prevent employees, though they might work less than fifty feet apart, from ever interacting during the day.[40] Indeed, in a model Kmart floor plan, management design experts put millinery, which was the most frequently licensed department, in the center of the store.[41] Millinery therefore had seven departmental borders, while only the checkout section also bordered more than five.[42] In this way, licensees could be used to balkanize Kmart employees and make collective identification across store and job title much more difficult.

Despite such division of workers by department and product, a craft consciousness was not generated in the modern discount store. The central union responsible for organizing retail workers, the Retail Clerks International Association, was a model of craft union consciousness and organization, as it generally focused its organizing efforts on skilled salespeople who saw themselves as having an important expertise in their product that aided both employers and consumers.[43] Even among unorganized saleswomen before World War II, their personal interaction with customers gave these women sole proprietorship of the knowledge of customer wants and desires, a knowledge that gave saleswomen a valuable skill, a commonality of experience, and a certain degree of control over the work process.[44] In the discount industry, however, divisions among employees proved so artificial, and the degradation of retail work so continual, that craft organizing among discount workers rarely succeeded.[45]

Speed has long been the most "desirable characteristic" of the modern checkout clerk.[46] Speed was facilitated by carefully designed rules that dictated the exact order in which everything was done. Failure to make sure one's register was completely stocked with tape, bags, change, pens, and stamps could result in dismissal, as could the breakage or spoilage of the merchandise.[47] When it came time for the customer to pay, the checker had first to tell the customer the total; then take the customer's money and repeat the amount in relation to the money given by the customer, as in "That's $14.21 out of $20"; then enter $20 into the amount-tendered button, tell the customer, "Your change is $5.79," count change from drawer into hand, then count change into the customer's hand, saying each bill and coin separately, thank the customer, close the drawer, and welcome the next customer.[48] Failure to follow the exact order of this procedure, like not having one's register ready, was grounds for reprimand and dismissal. Product expertise, once the key to the influence exerted by retail workers, like butchers and saleswomen, had given way to a workplace ethos where "speed as skill" reigned supreme.

The organizational structure of the discount store, designed long before any employees were hired, conspired to eliminate a shared sense of class solidarity. Many stores buttressed these control apparatuses with elaborate conduct policies that were mandatory for employees to sign before beginning work. These guidelines often allowed managers to reprimand or dismiss a worker for completely subjective reasons.[49] A Big Apple store's list of offenses warranting dismissal included such nondescript behavior as "horseplay," "loafing," "violation of sanitation rules," and "uncooperative attitude."[50] What constituted such behavior was up to the supervisor to decide, and thus management exercised an undefined and indeterminate degree of control over its employees. Most egregiously, a measure of control was extended to the store even when an employee was not working, as another typical rule stated that "conduct off the premises . . . which affect the employee's relationship to his job, his fellow employees, his supervisors, or the company products, property, reputation or goodwill in the community" was a dismissable offense.[51]

The flexibility management had to interpret these kinds of rules is illustrated by an Atlanta-area Retail Clerks grievance. At a Big Apple store in 1966, Herman McDaniel, a prounion employee, arrived at work wearing the slightly wrong color of shirt. A witness would later say that McDaniel's light gray shirt looked almost white, the regulation color, so it is not surprising that McDaniel complained to his manager when the latter told him to return home and change.[52] In response the manager told him that if he made an issue out of the matter he would be transferred or fired, but if he went home and changed, nothing would happen.[53] McDaniel changed his shirt. This was a minor incident, but it exemplifies the power inherent in management's ability to interpret and arbitrarily define unclear rules while meting out punishment for such transgressions. While such interchanges have been naturalized as an everyday part of the retail work life, they are nevertheless an extremely effective mechanism by which management both exercised control over the shop floor and enforced its will on employees who might protest.[54]

Both the strictest and most arbitrary of the everyday control policies that workers faced were the regulations that dictated how they dealt with customers. As the proper checkout procedure demonstrated, worker-customer interaction was meticulously regulated and detailed. At one store, employees followed the "Ten Commandments" of customer relations, including such rules as "Thou shalt not frown or scowl," "Thou shalt make yourself a storehouse for information for customers," and "Thou shalt keep your sunny side up even though weary after a day's labor."[55] Such policies, typical of discount department stores and large supermarkets, were nothing if not demeaning.[56] By infantilizing employees in this way, management not only strengthened its control over the work process, but degraded the intelligence and dignity of the workers.

Management authority often took a specifically gendered form, evident in the way stores divided labor tasks into male and female jobs. While Title VII of the Civil Rights Act of 1964 dictated that stores must offer equal pay for equal work, the use of manual tasks to foster division between men and women was present in the discount industry from its beginnings in the 1950s and 1960s and—as the depositions of the plaintiffs in the class-action lawsuit *Dukes v. Wal-Mart* make clear—continues to this day. Lifting requirements tended to be the most important way that employers produced a gendered division of labor. Such standards were not designed to reward those who might be able to lift more weight. Rather, these rules enabled management to pay women less, in the process closing the door on women's hiring and advancement to the better store positions. Effie Spain, a Greenbriar, Georgia, stocker for the discount supermarket chain Kroger, was often the sole worker on duty when the produce truck arrived each morning. Spain usually unloaded the entire truck, then stocked the store with items as heavy as a one-hundred-pound bag of fertilizer. Spain, though, was paid decidedly less than male stockers, who rarely lifted half the weight she did.[57] Marie Sewell, a fifteen-year employee at her store, was classified as a checker. Her close male friend was the head stocker, responsible for most of the heavy lifting in the store. Unfortunately, he had a bad back, so Sewell and her friend had effectively switched jobs for the previous two years.[58] In testimony by managers regarding these cases, all argued that they had never seen these women do the work they claimed to have done, much less required them to do it. (Such testimony was well refuted by evidence from employment records showing that Spain was the only person on the clock at the time the produce truck arrived each morning.) One district manager argued that women should not be placed in certain classifications not only because of their inability to lift, but because they "are absent more, more temperamental, cry more," and were much harder to manage.[59] To this manager, women were thus *naturally* a different class of employees, a class whose abilities and interests were inherently different from those of men.[60]

More than thirty years later, these same practices are echoed in the testimony of people like Paula Bird, an aspiring manager at Wal-Mart, who was not allowed to perform the prestigious duty of unloading trucks because she was a woman. Similarly, Christine Kwapnoski, another aspiring manager who shared heavy-lifting duties with men, still found her pay rate far less than these men's, despite her additional years of experience. Another Wal-Mart manager aspirant, Kathleen MacDonald, was told by her boss that "stocking cans was harder than stocking clothes," and thus, women should be paid less.[61] That the cases of women like Spain and Sewell occurred in the 1960s, years before women like Bird, Kwapnoski, and MacDonald helped bring to light similar instances at Wal-Mart, demonstrates the extent to which sex discrimination at Wal-Mart is not just endemic to the company, but has been part of the entire discount retail industry since its inception. While such discrimination helped create a shop floor that divided workers and let everyone know who was the boss, more egregious offenses committed by employees were met with a sophisticated surveillance apparatus that also generated an intrusive control of the retail shop floor.

In January of 1971, Connie Kreyling of Mexico, Missouri, was hired by Wal-Mart.[62] While the Mexico store was one of the first operated by Wal-Mart outside of Arkansas, Mexico, with a population of ten thousand, was similar in its rurality, population, low job growth, and isolation to the pioneer Wal-Mart stores of Rogers, Springdale, and Harrison. Kreyling's main job at Wal-Mart was head office cashier—thus, she spent the majority of her time counting the previous day's receipts, preparing deposits, and compiling generalized sales reports. She was a good worker. Over the course of a year's employment she received three raises, and after a late-January 1972 training trip to company headquarters in Bentonville, her manager, Robert Haines, remarked that "he was lucky to have found a cashier like her."[63] But two weeks later, on Monday, February 7, Kreyling was fired.

The previous Friday, Kreyling was angered by the way Haines had treated a clerk at the store. Over the weekend she had consulted her husband, signed a union card, and then called five fellow employees, all of whom enthusiastically agreed to sign the cards.[64] Upon arriving at work on Monday morning, Haines told Kreyling to gather her stuff, as she was being dismissed for poor work habits. Kreyling later sued Wal-Mart for wrongful dismissal, arguing that she was fired because of her union activities. The judge trying the case agreed, writing, "Haines learned on Sunday or early Monday morning that Connie Kreyling was thinking and talking about a union. . . . the real reason she was terminated was to rid the store of a union adherent."[65] While the judge admitted there was no direct evidence that Haines knew about Kreyling's prounion stance, he argued that given Haines's lie-filled testimony and the manufactured nature of his reasons for dismissal, he must have found out about Kreyling's union advocacy through a snitching fellow employee or a violation of her privacy.[66]

Wal-Mart's ability to engage in surveillance of its employees has become legendary. But that company is certainly not the first or only discount store to deploy such tactics. During an organizing drive at a Colonial store in Wilmington, North Carolina, R.J. Schnell, one of the AFL-CIO's main labor organizers in the South throughout the 1960s and 1970s, reported a novel strategy originated by Colonial. Antiunion high school teachers threatened students who were part-time Colonial workers with bad grades if they signed a union card. On the day of the election, Schnell reported, "anti-union teachers refused to let them out of school. I am positive that all these were our votes."[67]

Private investigators were also employed by discount stores for various surveillance operations. "Operative X," a private investigator hired by Richway, the discount branch of Rich's, the famous Atlanta department store, regularly meandered through the aisles, striking up conversations with workers about issues sensitive to management. In a typical exchange, Operative X remarked that he was from a small town nearby, and had seen in the local paper that a union was passing out cards at Richway; the conversation then continued:

> Mrs. Hill (employee): Yes, you know they've been trying to get in here for over a year.
> Operative X: No, I didn't know that—in fact, I just hadn't thought much about unions, particularly in department stores.
> (Mrs. Hill then remarks that she doesn't know about unions either and that while they're probably fine for big steel companies, she doesn't think they're needed in stores.)
> Operative X: Well I don't know much about unions, but I've always been of the opinion that if you had good management you didn't need things like that.
> Mrs Hill: Well, we have the best management we've ever had.[68]

After numerous exchanges like this, Operative X then reported to the company personnel department the union feelings of individual employees, as well as their friendships and the shop alliances of individual workers.[69] This kind of information was then used to transfer well-respected and outspokenly prounion workers to different departments, find reasons to fire them, and identify which employees defended management and could be valuable allies.

Throughout the 1960s and 1970s, Kmart had a security department whose sole job was to keep track of union activity across all of Kmart's hundreds of stores.[70] Its head, L.W. Zane, reported to the board of directors at virtually every meeting, informing them of employees' demands, the best strategies to counter union organizers in each store, and whether the manager of that store was putting enough effort into keeping out unions and organizers. A typical report praised the store manager at Wauwatosa, Wisconsin, for his rapid identification of the workers most in favor of the union, and it recommended a raise for the district manager in charge of the Bremerton, Washington, store who had thwarted a union effort to sign authorization cards and secure an NLRB election.[71] Another report noted that union enthusiasm at the Battle Creek, Michigan, store was largely the result of the manager, Mr. Daily, and his poor relationship with workers. The report argued that "Mr. Daily must improve his communications with the employees of the store" in order for it to remain union free.[72] Additional details about the investigative division of Kmart are hard to find, but it nevertheless seems significant that the corporation's board of directors thought it necessary to hear these surveillance reports at each meeting.

As early as the 1960s, private investigators were also hired by companies to administer lie detector tests to workers. Such tests often asked employees if they had stolen from the company, if they knew of anyone who had stolen, and whether they filled out their time cards correctly.[73] Workers were called off the floor and ordered by managers to go alone with the investigators into a back room where the tests were administered.[74] While the stated purpose of these tests was to make sure employees were not stealing from the store, they forced workers to snitch on each other and created a general work climate of fear and subservience to management.

Like lie detector tests, other forms of surveillance often turned workers against each other. Frequently, employees at stores were given extra money or offered promotions if they spot-checked workers at other stores. Lonnie Wells, a checker at Colonial in Atlanta, was fired after he supposedly cheated an employee of another store, Billy McDougal. The manager alleged that Wells was overcharging customers and pocketing the difference. Wells maintained, though, that the manager had it in for him based on previous disagreements and that in checking the difference between McDougal's bags and the receipt in private, the manager had removed some items from the bags.[75] Whoever was right, Wells was clearly frustrated by management's new tactic of using other employees to check on workers. As Wells put it, "I don't feel the person used in these checks should be someone we know."[76] This approach not only functioned to keep management abreast of events but also struck directly at shop floor solidarity, as it made employees both distrust and fear their friends and co-workers. Such tactics demonstrated that one of the quickest ways for advancement in a store was not merely hard work or product expertise but the placement of the company's interest over that of fellow workers and friends.[77]

Despite this Orwellian atmosphere, trade unions were sometimes successful in making a storewide breakthrough. The managerial response to this rare occurrence combined a seductive paternalism with a program of unrelenting institutional resistance. At an early Atlanta-area Richway, management rapidly found out that the RCIA was attempting to organize the store. Richard Rich quickly drafted a particularly paternalistic letter to his workers. He asked employees to personally bring to his attention any problems they may have had with Richway.[78] He noted that he was saddened to think that anyone might argue that his workers were " 'second class wage earners,' 'work too long hours,' under 'poor conditions,' " the charges that RCIA organizers leveled against Richway.[79] He asked any worker confused about the union and what it stood for to talk to his or her boss, as he "has all the answers."[80]

Such paternal treatment of workers could often be followed by harsher antiunion initiatives. The vagueness of employee guidelines and stores' insistence that virtually every offense was a dismissable one gave stores a built-in antiunion advantage and put the burden of proof on the worker or the union lawyers representing him or her. Prounion employees were fired for everything from talking to customers on their breaks to stocking sweaters in the wrong order.[81] Stores often gave workers the choice of voting for the union and losing their job or voting against the union and rewarding them with raises, promotions, and paid vacations.[82] Management offered employees raises and perks if they spoke against the union.[83] Although Wal-Mart has often threatened to close stores if its employees unionize, this tactic was given an early workout at the Atlantic Thrift

Company, one of the first discount department stores in the South.[84] Atlantic Thrift's strategy was so effective against the union that when Kmart was looking to take over an existing chain in the late 1960s, Atlantic Thrift was deemed a good option because of its lack of unionization.[85]

Organizers who entered stores universally reported extreme intimidation. George Seinfadden and Bobby Moses, two veteran RCIA organizers, were arrested for trespassing and disorderly conduct by an off-duty policeman working as a security guard. During their trial, the reasons for these charges were explained: they continued sitting in the store restaurant after finishing a cup of coffee and expressed disbelief that they were being arrested for trespassing, which led to the further charge of disorderly conduct.[86] While the judge threw out that charge, he upheld the trespassing violation and fined both unionists. Other stores hired lawyers to follow organizers around and call security if they broke any law or NLRB ruling.[87] A common tactic was to charge organizers with soliciting, which, while acceptable under NLRB rulings, often came into conflict with local laws. Once in court, stores often found sympathetic antiunion judges who would uphold the charges.[88] While the organizers and unions could often get the decisions reversed on appeal, the costs of paying a lawyer to do so tended to be significantly higher and more protracted than simply paying the fine or spending the night in jail.

When workers and organizers occasionally pulled off the feat of scheduling an NLRB election, they met intense and occasionally absurd efforts to divide the shop floor. At a Colonial store in Charleston, South Carolina, managers hired numerous new employees in the week preceding the election, all of whom spoke and voted against the union. Management at this same store also gave an ultimatum to prounion workers, telling them that they could either move to Charlotte and work at a new Colonial there or be laid off—a strategy reminiscent of Wal-Mart's relocation requirement for female managers.[89] In 1963 at a discount supermarket in North Carolina, management, rather than concede defeat and allow its workers to organize a shopwide union, forced separate elections for employees with different job descriptions. This generated a set of NLRB-certified bargaining units that contained as few as two members each.[90] The effect of this strategy was similar to what Kmart would achieve later in the decade with its licensees—a divided and competing shop floor.

While employers had long utilized many of these same antiunion techniques, they took on a special significance in the world of the discount workplace. By the late twentieth century, the shop floor of America's Wal-Marts, Kmarts, and Richways had become the largest in the country. Where U.S. Steel, General Motors, Ford, and RCA had once been the leading employers of the American working class, stores like Kmart and Wal-Mart and their numerous imitators replaced the old manufacturing sector as the single largest provider of jobs for the American workforce. In the early twenty-first century, Wal-Mart, Target, Home Depot, and Kroger employed more than 3 million Americans and represented four of America's ten largest employers.[91] The ability of these stores to control their labor costs was the indispensable and single most important factor in their astounding growth. This was not a passing concern of these stores, but as a Wal-Mart manager put it in the early 1990s, a "day in, day out" obsession.[92]

If this discount philosophy was to succeed it depended on high turnover and low wages. In this sense, the discount store was not the result of an evolution of the traditional department store, nor was it akin to the Taylorization of the American steel industry. Instead, discount hegemony is an entirely new phenomenon whose very *existence* has been predicated on one thing only—the control of its labor force and its labor costs. To achieve this end, discounters developed a new shop floor, designed not only to curtail labor organization specifically, but also to inhibit the preconditions for unionization: collective solidarity and a consciousness of class.

This was nothing less than shop floor totalitarianism. Some of the tactics used by management were new and innovative, and others had histories reaching back to the advent of wage labor and capitalism, yet what makes them important is not their individual uses or histories but their fusion in a new environment. Combined, they produced a workplace atmosphere of control and subservience. In order to comprehend the fate of the American working class in the last third of the twentieth century, it is not enough to study the internal politics of the AFL-CIO, the business assault on labor, the rise of free trade, and the global dispersion of capital. Scholars and citizens must understand how the success of America's most expansive workplaces has been predicated upon their ability to manage the labor of their workers with an iron fist. Furthermore, we must not focus on one corporation or employer—however large or powerful—but instead appreciate the extent to which the practices that Wal-Mart exemplifies represent not the exception to workplace control in the post-Fordist, service era of capital, but rather its unwavering rule. Long before the fiscal crises of Fordism in the 1970s and Wal-Mart's more recent expansion out of the South, the discount retail industry created an authoritarian shop floor environment that would become emblematic for American workers as the last decades of the twentieth century turned into the first years of the twenty-first.[93]

TEN

Patriarchy at the Checkout Counter: The *Dukes v. Wal-Mart Stores, Inc.,* Class-Action Suit

Brad Seligman

In June 2001, six women filed a class-action employment-discrimination lawsuit against Wal-Mart Stores Inc. in federal court in San Francisco. They charged that Wal-Mart discriminated against women in pay and promotions to management. Over the next several years, their lawyers were permitted unique access to Wal-Mart databases, documents, and witnesses as part of the formal investigation process known as "discovery." More than 1.3 million documents were produced by Wal-Mart, over two hundred witnesses had their deposition taken, and plaintiffs' experts were given access to Wal-Mart's payroll and personnel electronic databases going back to 1996. In addition, the lawyers interviewed hundreds of women across the country about their experiences at Wal-Mart.

At the close of this enormous effort, the plaintiffs filed a motion requesting that the case be certified as a class action, to include all women who have worked in Wal-Mart Stores in the United States at any time since December 26, 1998. Without class certification, the case would be limited to the claims of six women. If certified, however, the case to be tried would encompass the claims of the more than 1.6 million women who have worked at Wal-Mart since December 26, 1998. If plaintiffs win at trial, this means that the damages to be awarded (lost earnings and punitive damages), as well as the scope of any court-ordered injunction, would include all of these women, and all of Wal-Mart's operations in the United States. While the size of any jury award or settlement cannot be estimated at this time, a successful outcome would likely dwarf the largest civil rights recoveries to date (roughly $500 million).

The plaintiffs argued that class certification was warranted by the strong statistical pattern of unequal pay and promotions and the uniformity of Wal-Mart procedures, practices, and culture throughout its more than 3,600 stores. Wal-Mart claimed that each store was "different," that there were at best only a few "bad apples" among its managers, and that it had a right to individual trials against each of the more than 1.6 million class members.

On June 22, 2004, federal judge Martin Jenkins issued his eighty-four-page ruling certifying the class. The scope of the class is unprecedented—it is by many orders of magnitude the largest civil rights class action ever certified (no prior civil rights class action exceeded two hundred thousand class members). It is the first time Wal-Mart has ever faced a nationwide class action.[1] The judge acknowledged the "historic" nature of the motion, but rejected Wal-Mart's assertion that the sheer size of the class precluded a class action:

> Defendant emphasizes that the proposed class covers at least 1.5 million women who have been employed over the past five years at roughly 3,400 stores, thus dwarfing other employment discrimination cases that have come before. In its view, these numbers alone make this case impossible. . . . Title VII, however, contains no special exception for large employers. Enacted in 1964 during the height of the civil rights movement, this Act forbids gender- and race-based discrimination in the American workplace. . . . Insulating our nation's largest employers from allegations that they have engaged in a pattern and practice of gender or racial discrimination—simply because they are large—would seriously undermine these imperatives. Indeed, it is interesting to note, as a matter of historical perspective, that Plaintiffs' request for class certification is being ruled upon in a year that marks the 50th anniversary of the Supreme Court's decision in *Brown v. Board of Education*. . . . This anniversary serves as a reminder of the importance of the courts in addressing the denial of equal treatment under the law wherever and by whomever it occurs.

A Summary of Plaintiffs' Claims[2]

In support of their motion for class certification, plaintiffs' experts prepared detailed statistical, economic, and sociological studies. The statistical evidence of discrimination is of a consistency and strength rarely seen before in gender-discrimination litigation. The statistics show that these disparities, and the inference of discrimination that they create, consistently permeate the company, across job categories, geography, and time. The plaintiffs in this action, like women in every region of the United States, have been the victims of Wal-Mart's systemic discriminatory pay and promotion practices. Thus, for example, lead plaintiff Betty Dukes worked at Wal-Mart for nearly nine years yet was making less than $8.50 an hour. Yet, as late as 2003, a year and a half after the suit was filed, data produced by Wal-Mart showed that men hired in the last few years into the same job she held were being paid more than she. Plaintiff Chris Kwapnoski worked at a Sam's Club for years and sought a promotion to management. Despite her repeated requests, she was not even told what the process for promotion was. (Her first promotion occurred two weeks after the suit was filed.) Her requests for advancement were brushed off with sexist statements such as "You should brush the cobwebs off your makeup."

In addition to their stories, plaintiffs also submitted the declarations of over 110 current and former female employees whose stories explain this case in human terms that the numbers cannot. The declarations document the struggles of each of these women to receive equal pay or a chance to advance into management, often in the face of openly expressed gender bias. While these women have worked in stores from Anchorage, Alaska, to Ormond Beach, Florida, their stories are remarkably and painfully similar. Here are four.

Sandra Stevenson, who began work at the Gurnee, Illinois, Sam's Club at age forty-three, was employed there from November 1996 to June 2000. Throughout her employment, Ms. Stevenson requested promotion to management positions in the hopes that she could move up and, ultimately, retire with the company. Her dreams were shattered, however, after she was repeatedly denied the staff she needed to perform her responsibilities as an overnight supervisor while she watched as male managers supported and promoted less-experienced male employees. Eventually, Ms. Stevenson requested to be transferred to the day shift and accepted the position of team leader for produce and floral with the expectation that she would be promoted to produce manager. Again, she found that management would not support her with adequate staffing. At one point, Ms. Stevenson was forced to work in the produce department during a busy Easter weekend without any assistance because the store manager fired her only staff person and had failed to provide her with a substitute. This was particularly upsetting to her because she also was forced to miss the wake of a family member because of her huge workload. She also watched as male partners were groomed for management while she was left unsupported. Ms. Stevenson resigned from Sam's Club because she had had it with the repeated denials of support and promotion to management despite her qualifications and desire for promotion. She took a job with the U.S. Postal Service in 2001.

Kim McLamb worked for Wal-Mart from 1991 to 2001 as an assistant manager throughout several stores in Virginia. She was an excellent employee who continually received "exceeds expectations" ratings on her evaluations. From the beginning of her employment, Mrs. McLamb regularly expressed an interest in promotion to several store managers and district managers. At one point, she was required to commit, in writing, to working overnights for a full two years. Male assistant managers were only required to rotate through the overnight position on a six-month basis. Mrs. McLamb was also passed over for management positions in favor of less-experienced and less-qualified men. When she discovered that male employees made more than female employees working the same jobs, she complained to three different assistant managers. Each told her it was because the men "had families to support." At one point, in 2001, when Mrs. McLamb and a number of other female assistant managers were working around the clock to prepare for inventory, the male store manager and male assistant managers spent their time training for a triathlon. They would bring their bikes into the store and often left work early to train. Unlike the female assistant managers, the males would rarely work on weekends.

Ramona Scott worked for Wal-Mart in Florida from 1990 to 1998. While employed in Pinellas Park, Florida, Ms. Scott was a personnel manager with access to payroll records. She noticed that men generally made more than women who had as much or more seniority. When she asked the male store manager about the pay discrepancy, he told her, "Men are here to make a career and women aren't. Retail is for housewives who just need to earn extra money." When Ms. Scott later inquired about a raise that a male employee had received, she was told by a male assistant manager, "He has a family to support." When she pointed out that she was a single mother, the assistant manager ignored her and walked away. When Ms. Scott expressed an interest in promotion into the management training program, her district manager merely told her that there were no openings but did not give her guidance or information about how to get into the program. When a new male store manager took over her store, he laughed at Ms. Scott's pay rate and told her that the male personnel manager at his former store made "a lot more" than she did. This same store manager dismissed her renewed request to enter the management training program. He then told her that if she wanted to get along with him, she would have to behave like his wife and frequently asked her to get coffee for him and other male managers. At that point Ms. Scott gave up on the idea of further promotion.

Claudia Renati began working at a Sam's Club in Roseville, California, in 1993 as a marketing membership team leader. Early on, Ms. Renati became responsible for running the marketing programs in the region after the regional sales manager left. After two years of performing the tasks of both positions without the additional pay or the correct job title, she asked the director of operations to promote her into the position. He refused because she had not gone through the management training program. Over the next couple of years, the position of marketing manager was filled by several male next-door neighbors of the director of operations. None had gone through management training and none had experience in marketing. Ms. Renati was responsible for training these less-qualified and less-experienced men who were hired to be her supervisors. Over the next several years, she trained approximately twenty male managers, many of whom never went through the management training program and were not required to relocate. Ms. Renati continued to be passed over for promotions for positions that were consistently filled by males with no prior management experience and less seniority. At one point, the director of operations told her that before she could become a manager, she would be required to stack fifty-pound bags of dog food as a floor team leader. When Ms. Renati indicated that she could not repeatedly lift fifty pounds, he told her he could not help her advance. But Renati was aware of several male employees who never had to become floor team leader, nor were they required to stack fifty-pound bags of dog food in order to enter the Management Training Program. She left Sam's Club in August 2002.[3]

Together, this body of powerful evidence compels the conclusion that these claims deserve class treatment. Much of the statistical evidence was not disputed by Wal-Mart. The judge explained:

> Plaintiffs present largely uncontested descriptive statistics which show women working at Wal-Mart are paid less than men in every region, that pay disparities exist in most job categories, that the salary gap widens over time even for men and women hired into the same jobs at the same time, that women take longer to enter into management positions, and that the higher one looks in the organization, the lower the percentage of women.

Unequal Pay for Women

Since at least 1997, female employees of Wal-Mart Stores have been paid less than comparable male employees in every year and in every Wal-Mart region despite having, on average, higher performance ratings and more seniority. Instead of improving, this pay disparity has steadily widened over the last five years.

Pay decisions for both hourly and management employees are left to the manager, to whom company guidelines provide broad discretion to compensate store employees according to his particular subjective assessment. These compensation decisions disproportionately favor men in every major job category:

AVERAGE EARNINGS BY GENDER FOR 2001

Job	Men	Women	Difference
Regional vice president	$419,435	$279,772	$139,663
District manager	$239,519	$177,149	$62,370
Store manager	$105,682	$89,280	$16,402
Co-manager	$59,535	$56,317	$3,218

Assistant manager	$39,790	$37,322	$2,468
Management trainee	$23,175	$22,371	$804
Department head	$23,518	$21,709	$1,809
Sales associate	$16,526	$15,067	$1,459
Cashier	$14,525	$13,831	$694

Women are paid less then men at Wal-Mart even when objective factors such as seniority or performance are taken into account. Indeed, with greater average seniority and performance scores, one would expect that women, not men, would have higher average pay. Not in Wal-Mart's world.

The Promotion Hierarchy at Wal-Mart

Female employees at Wal-Mart Stores receive far fewer promotions to management than do male employees, and those who are promoted must wait longer than their male counterparts. Although the vast majority of Wal-Mart managers are drawn from the ranks of hourly employees, and women make up over *two-thirds* of those hourly ranks, women receive only *one-third* of all promotions to management positions. This pattern of underpromotion occurs in every region in which Wal-Mart operates.

But Wal-Mart's supervisory and management hierarchy is even more stratified than these numbers suggest. At its lowest level, women hold a disproportionate portion of hourly department heads (78 percent female) and supervisors of cashiers (CSM) (nearly 90 percent female). While one might assume this is the natural pool for promotion, the percentage of women at every step above these positions drops off at a startling rate, as the following summary chart (based on year-end 2001 data) shows:

PERCENTAGE OF WOMEN IN STORE MANAGEMENT
AND AS HOURLY SUPERVISORS, 2001

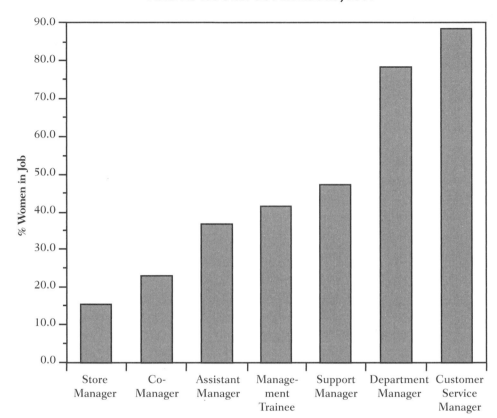

The pattern of gender hierarchy between management and hourly jobs is further reflected within the management and hourly supervisor positions. The support manager, department manager, and CSM (customer service manager, who supervises cashiers) are the main supervisory hourly jobs. Source: Impact Fund Web site.

Wal-Mart's track record is entirely anomalous in the retail industry, where women typically hold over 50 percent of management jobs. Indeed, Wal-Mart's own internal documents, including a memo from its highest-ranking human resources officer, recognize that "we are far behind the rest of the world." This officer, Executive Vice President

Coleman Peterson, also reported to Wal-Mart's board of directors that the percentage of women in management at Wal-Mart was "significantly behind several of the other retailers." He was not exaggerating. A study commissioned by the plaintiffs by economist Marc Bendick showed that Wal-Mart substantially lagged behind its twenty top competitors in the percentage of women in management. Indeed, he found that in 1999, the latest year data was available, the percentage of female managers at Wal-Mart was less than the average at its competitors in 1975!

Within Wal-Mart, the gateway from low-paying hourly jobs to the higher-paying management positions is the management training program. An employee must complete the management training program to become an assistant manager, the first rung on the management ladder. Until January 2003, on the eve of the discovery cutoff, Wal-Mart selected employees for the program entirely through a "tap on the shoulder" system. By design, there was no system by which an employee could apply for, or even express an interest in, the program. No written information was available to hourly employees about the program. Instead, district and regional managers applied their own subjective views about who would be appropriate for management. And in the majority of all cases, a man was selected for the training program rather than a woman, even though women were almost 80 percent of all hourly supervisors. This lopsided result is not surprising, as it is well understood that such highly arbitrary and subjective systems are particularly vulnerable to the influence of unconscious stereotypes.

Central Control and Culture

It is not surprising that Wal-Mart's discriminatory promotion and pay policies and practices have manifested themselves consistently throughout the company. Wal-Mart's corporate headquarters in Bentonville, Arkansas, monitors and controls—perhaps to an extent never before seen in corporate America—the minute details of operations at its far-flung stores, down to the temperature it sets for each store's heating and cooling system and the music played in each store. The company's success is due in large part to its ability to closely monitor activities in the field and maintain strict compliance with its internal policies and practices. Wal-Mart has a highly sophisticated information technology system that allows the Bentonville home office to monitor a wide range of each store's daily activities. Through dozens of daily reports and regular store visits, the home office ensures that all stores are on the company program. In addition, Wal-Mart has carefully constructed and aggressively maintains a distinct, consistent corporate culture throughout its operations. Every employee is educated daily on the culture, and employees are rewarded for following the "Wal-Mart Way." The strong culture encourages universal compliance with personnel policies and practices. As a result, store managers are frequently moved across districts and regions without any loss in consistency of company policies and practices.

The Wal-Mart culture has its dark side, notwithstanding the high degree of centralized control. There is strong evidence that negative gender stereotypes permeate Wal-Mart at all levels:

- At regular Monday executive-level Sam's Club meetings, senior management often referred to the female associates in the stores as "little Janie Qs" and "girls."
- Female managers have been required to go to Hooters restaurants and strip clubs in the course of business events.
- At an annual meeting in May 2001, Jim Haworth, executive vice president of operations and chief operating officer for Wal-Mart Stores, sat on a chair that looked like a leopard-skin stiletto-heel shoe.
- As early as 1992, a group of female Wal-Mart home office employees formed the Women in Leadership Group, which identified a number of concerns for women employees, some of which centered on the culture of Wal-Mart. Among their concerns: "[s]tereotypes limit the opportunities offered to women," [c]areer decisions are made for associates based on gender," "aggressive women intimidate men," "men are interviewed as the replacements, women are viewed as support," and "[m]en's informal network overlooks women."
- Coleman Peterson repeatedly and forcefully alerted the board and senior executives to the problem of diversity in management. In a remarkable effort to avoid the consequences of these early alerts to the board, Mr. Peterson disavowed one of these memos at his deposition, calling it "a lie" intended solely to get the attention of management.

Wal-Mart executives at the highest level have long been aware that women have been disproportionately excluded from management positions and underpaid compared to men. Wal-Mart management prides itself—and rightly so—on quickly and effectively addressing intractable problems when they adversely affect the company's bottom line. In sharp contrast, to address the identified obstacles to equal opportunity for its female workers, Wal-Mart has belatedly implemented a few half-hearted measures for which no one at any level of management has been held accountable. Although Wal-Mart talks a lot about the idea of diversity, it is singularly uninterested in why so few women are promoted or whether its pay practices disadvantage its female employees. As one former Sam's Club vice president put it, until Wal-Mart's diversity efforts are tied to manager pay, "it will continue to be lip service."

The Court's Findings

Judge Jenkins was careful to point out that he was not making any findings on the merits of the discrimination claims. Rather, he was called upon to determine whether the requirements for a class action had been satisfied. Perhaps the most important requirement is that there be common questions of law or fact—sufficient group characteristics to justify a class trial.

After surveying the record before him, the judge concluded that plaintiffs had established sufficient common issues by providing:

1. significant evidence of companywide corporate practices and policies, which include excessive subjectivity in personnel decisions, gender stereotyping, and maintenance of a strong corporate culture;
2. statistical evidence of gender disparities caused by discrimination; and
3. anecdotal evidence of gender bias.

Together, this evidence raises an inference that Wal-Mart engages in discriminatory practices in compensation and promotions that affect all plaintiffs in a common manner.

Wal-Mart's principal legal argument was that it had a right to contest the claims of each woman in the class, making any class-action trial endless, and thus unmanageable. The judge rejected Wal-Mart's theory, explaining that if classwide liability is established, the calculation of lost earnings can be performed on a classwide basis, utilizing a formula that takes into account electronic personnel data such as job, location, seniority, performance score, and other factors for each class member. The court explained that "this case presents the type of situation where a formula approach" should be utilized—defendant's lack of objective, documented procedures would lead any individual-by-individual approach into a "quagmire of hypothetical judgments."

Because a favorable outcome of this lawsuit might well have such a dramatic impact on Wal-Mart's entire managerial structure, the company seems likely to resist any settlement that reforms its discriminatory business culture and establishes a truly nondiscriminatory system of pay and promotion. So this litigation may continue for several years, in which case the class of women at Wal-Mart will continue to fight this important case for some time to come.

ELEVEN

How to Squeeze More out of a Penny

Ellen Israel Rosen

This chapter focuses on the structure of Wal-Mart's store operations in an effort to analyze how the firm's technology, culture, store policies, and covert and overt management practices shape the experience of Wal-Mart's workers. While men and women are employed at Wal-Mart, almost two-thirds of all employees are women (64 percent). Among hourly sales workers, even more (70.2 percent) are women.[1] Most hourly workers at Wal-Mart stack merchandise, help customers, and work as cashiers.[2]

Business analysts explain Wal-Mart's tremendous growth and productivity as a result of its sophisticated information technology (IT) and unique logistics systems.[3] Wal-Mart's efficiency, profitability, and size are seen as a function of the system's potential to gather information and for management to use it to rapidly distribute low-priced consumer goods to stores. Only infrequently do they look at the quality of work this produces for employees, the assumption being that the jobs require little education and are easy to learn. Yet, as I will argue, these new systems operate within the context of a management practice and a company culture which intensify work pressures on Wal-Mart's retail staff and lead to a form of "management by intimidation." Ultimately, these practices may contribute to illegal activities, particularly sex discrimination and wage abuse, issues that have publicly plagued Wal-Mart for several years.

Centralization

Wal-Mart's success is partly a result of its centralization. Even before the advent of computer technology, the firm had always sought to centralize operations and authority.

Executives at Wal-Mart headquarters at Bentonville, Arkansas, traditionally sent out managers to monitor each store through regular visits. Then field managers made weekly reports to company headquarters.[4] Today's computer technology allows Bentonville to collect vast quantities of information not previously available, which has greatly increased the firm's ability to centralize and standardize Wal-Mart's operation.

Wal-Mart is a traditional bureaucracy, autocratically run from the top down, from Bentonville, Arkansas, where the CEO and his closest associates make decisions for the company. All directives and policy changes decided at this level flow through the employment pyramid to all of Wal-Mart's stores and distribution centers, from the store managers to those at the very bottom of the pyramid, where "sales associates" unload merchandise and deal with customers, and cashiers check out merchandise. Managers of stores and distribution centers send data directly to the home office. The technology is specifically designed to allow corporate headquarters to be constantly abreast of information about its suppliers and its stores, so top management can respond to any event that affects Wal-Mart's stores.

Why pick on Wal-Mart? Other large retailers engage in many of the same practices, those both legal and illegal.[5] Yet Wal-Mart's rapid growth, size, and power have made it the leader—a change agent, or as Nelson Lichtenstein argues, "a template of the new global capitalism."[6] With a market power unequaled by any of its competitors, Wal-Mart has been the model on which America's, and a new kind of global, capitalism is now being built. Where Wal-Mart leads, others follow.

The Store Manager

The store manager provides the basic connection between the demands of corporate headquarters and the hierarchy of store management and hourly employees. He is also the face of Bentonville on the ground. The most important job of the store manager is to reduce the store's costs and increase the store's sales. Store managers may not always be able to control sales, but they can reduce the store's operating costs by the choices they make deploying personnel to manage the merchandise.

Bill Thomas[7] is a former manager of a Wal-Mart supercenter in Kentucky. One of the most important jobs he did was to figure out the "labor budget" for his store: how many employees he could schedule for the next three weeks, each at particular rates of pay, based on when they were available for work. After making this calculation, he forwarded the numbers to the district manager, the regional vice president, and the divisional vice president for approval.

"Every Monday morning," he said, "I would go in and evaluate my sales. I would do what's called 'forecasting.' For example, last year I did $1.2 million in sales. This year I think I can do $1.5 million. So I forecast a conservative percent increase or decrease, whatever my trend is, and then I key that into the computer. The computer spits out a daily payroll figure that is scaled and based on how much volume we did a day last year. It has last year's sales by hour and by department."

The purpose of this formula is to reduce labor costs as sales volumes increase. For example, if a store increased its sales by 7 percent last year compared to the previous year, the goal is to save 0.1 percent of that increase during the next year. The wage bill for the next year could not be budgeted to exceed 6.9 percent of sales. Should sales increase over 10 percent, the manager is required to budget 0.2 percent of sales for wage costs. Based on this estimate, each store manager must budget, on a monthly basis, how many hours to schedule workers.

Thomas's annual compensation, and his future at Wal-Mart, depend on this formula. Store managers get a basic salary. As Thomas put it, "What they do is give you a salary and then you make a bonus and where you make your money as a store manager is in your bonus. How you get your bonus is based strictly on your net profitability for your store. . . . Like the first million of profit you get 1.2 percent and then the next million you get like 0.8 percent and the next million you get 0.4 percent. In the last store I made $162,000 [with a yearly salary of $50,000]. That was at the supercenter," Thomas adds. "And I've known guys that have made a lot less, but lower-volume stores typically, like if you're in the $18 million to $25 million range, the person's going to net, but you have to cross a threshold of I think it's a million five to break even, to take a profit out of it."

According to Thomas, store managers are held accountable for sales growth even though sales are not entirely under their control. Their responsibility is to produce "good" sales figures every year and, at the same time, save costs. Wal-Mart provides store managers with a "preferred budget," which would allow them to staff adequately. But no store is actually allowed the preferred budget, which is in excess of the real labor costs that store managers are permitted to spend, i.e., the targeted budget. As a result, the stores are always chronically understaffed. Thomas says, "There is not a store out there that is allowed the run the kind of hours that are needed."

Wal-Mart's wage budget means that managers at every level—from store managers to assistant managers to department managers—have little control over the number of people they can have to run the store. Thomas said he always worked with a "skeleton crew," and constantly struggled to "put out fires." "Things get overbooked. . . . There are three trucks with merchandise that have to be put in the store. Freight and merchandise sometimes sit on the floors in aisles and boxes. The housekeeping is poor. You will find fire exits blocked, broken pallet jacks and ladders; there are things all over the floor. Floors are dirty and wet and shelves are stacked too high."

Salaried managers—store managers, co-managers, and assistant managers—work as many hours a week as they feel is necessary to get their work done, often sixty to eighty hours. Thomas believes that being a store manager or assistant manager is among the toughest jobs there is because it means taking ultimate responsibility for doing whatever needs to be done, with whatever personnel are allowed. To succeed, i.e., to get a store of their own, managers often work virtually all the time. Yet they also depend on the cooperation of subordinates—department managers, and full-time and even part-time salesclerks—to "get the job done."

Scheduling

In the past, department managers made up work schedules for the people in their departments. Today, Bentonville decides how workers will be scheduled. Recently the home office has introduced its own scheduling formula designed to be used with a computer program created in Bentonville. The technology is extremely agile. According to Mary Roland,[8] a department manager in the jewelry department, "The computer 'knows' " that the store is not very busy on Sunday morning between 9 and 11 a.m. So it will schedule eight people to run the cash registers. But the computer program cannot account for all variations in human behavior. Sometimes on one Sunday it will be very busy during those hours. If there is not enough staff on hand, customers will have to stand in long lines, which Bentonville doesn't like. Because too few cashiers are scheduled to work on Sunday, the store manager will have to call on other sales associates in the stores to run additional cash registers.

At Wal-Mart there are a wide variety of shifts, which makes scheduling even more difficult. Some employees are full-time, scheduled for forty hours. But a twenty-eight- or thirty-two-hour week is also considered full-time at Wal-Mart. Part-timers work twelve hours or more a week.

Employees often have to change their schedules, particularly part-time workers who have another job, or students whose academic schedules change frequently. Bill Thomas says that no one can be available 24/7 as Wal-Mart wants everyone to be. If people say they're available, they're lying. Besides, in addition to students, there are family emergencies, such as a sick child or an aging parent, which cause people to be absent from work.

Given these conditions, managers often find it difficult to accommodate employees, who, dissatisfied with untenable schedules, simply quit. This can contribute to additional holes in the store's staffing, putting more pressure on people who are already shorthanded.

Turnover is particularly high at Wal-Mart compared to the retail industry as a whole—35 to 45 percent a year among full-time workers, 56 percent among part-timers. Some claim turnover at Wal-Mart is even higher. According to Douglas Shuit at *Workforce Management,* "Every year 600,000 to 700,000 Wal-Mart associates can walk out the door and must be replaced by fresh faces willing to work for starting hourly wages of $7 to $8. An analysis by Staffing.org shows that the retail industry spends $2,379 for each new hire. At that price, the tab for hiring 600,000 workers would be $1.4 billion."[9]

High turnover, of course, means it becomes more likely that employees fail to learn their jobs properly. Further, regardless of their skill and experience, those working are shorthanded but still remain responsible for doing whatever needs doing, regardless of the time available to them. Managers struggle with skeleton crews, and sales clerks feel the company is insensitive to their needs.

Thomas says, "A lot of the assistant managers get fed up and they get like fire-breathing dragons" at the high rate of turnover. Mary Roland,[10] is also irritated by the overwhelming demands of her job. "At Wal-Mart," she says, "you are expected to do the work of three people."

Pressures at Work

The pressures of work at Wal-Mart are revealed by the daily activities workers report. When the goods arrive at the store, Wal-Mart associates remove them. Another worker scans the bar codes with a handheld computer called a "telxon gun."[11] Every stock-keeping unit (SKU), e.g., tube of toothpaste or bottle of shampoo, is followed as it is enters the store—whether it is shelved, or damaged and returned to the company, then again if and when it is marked down. It is entered when it is sold and again when reordered. Bill Thomas described the information that could be gathered by Wal-Mart's state-of-the-art computer systems when he said, "I could tell you last year on July 13 between the hours of 7 and 8 p.m. how much [in] sales a store did and how much of it was rung up by Sally Jo, the cashier with the operator number 342, [within] that hour."

The difficulties workers experience at Wal-Mart are illustrated by the demands imposed on them by managers, who themselves are pressured to "get the job done." Katie Mitchell[12] works from 10 p.m. to 6:30 a.m. She starts work after the unloading crew removes the merchandise from the trucks. Her job is to set the merchandise on pallets and bring it to the aisles, where it can be stacked. She has to "inventory" the merchandise after it is unloaded from trucks and remove the shrink-wrap from the packages. Using her telxon gun, Katie counts each item and enters it in the store computer. If she makes an error she has to check with the truck driver's invoice and make the correction. She says that when the truckers arrive they all want to rush to get into the bays and deliver their merchandise. If there is a miscount or an open box, everyone has to wait.

There is always too much work to be done and no one to help her. She often misses work breaks and once missed lunch entirely—that is, she worked off the clock—but she had to get the work done by the end of her shift or be "chewed out" by her supervisor. The biggest problem, though, was that after 10 p.m. the workers were locked in the stores. No one could leave even for an emergency like a sick child. Then, "after you kicked and screamed the supervisor might let you out the back door, which was far from the parking lot where the employee's cars were parked and was unlighted." Wal-Mart, under the pressure of bad publicity, has subsequently changed this policy and does not lock the door at night.

Kate Moroney,[13] employed in a Florida Wal-Mart, works at night, from 10 p.m. to 7 a.m., stocking the frozen foods in the deli department freezers. She also answers the phone and helps customers. After 4 p.m. the department managers leave, so sometimes she is the only one responsible for covering the other departments as well—food, greeting cards, small appliances, housewares, and household chemicals.

Other Wal-Mart employees have also told me that when the store is busy, they are often paged to the front of the store to run the cash register. Then they are required to complete their own work. Recently Kate was asked to train as a cashier, i.e., to study the computer-based learning (CBL) modules, which explain how to operate the store's cash registers, and learn the responsibilities of a cashier. Most training for jobs at the hourly-worker level is done this way. Having passed the test, Kate is now paged frequently to run the cash register. If she is unable to put out her stock for the next day, that job must be finished by the next day's crew, who then get behind on their own work. Billy Draper[14] was a college student who worked part-time at Wal-Mart. He told me that his job was "understaffed," that it was a revolving door and that many people quit. His supervisor often asked him to hurry up with the stocking so Zack could begin to stock the shelves of other departments—often three in one night. The supervisor kept rushing Zack to go faster.

Often about a half hour before closing, just when the staff was ready to clean up and go home, his supervisor would come up with new projects to do, for example, loading soda pop on the shelves on a display in the front of the store. When Billy said that one "couldn't do overtime" at Wal-Mart, his supervisor told him, "Don't clock in until midnight." But Billy said he refused to work off the clock in this way.

Patti Slater[15] works in Wal-Mart's office overseeing financial reports. She said she suffers most when management pulls her from the job she is hired to do, interrupting her work and asking her to "help out" elsewhere in the store. One time the store ran out of computer paper, so Patti was asked to go to a nearby Wal-Mart to get some. Another time a Wal-Mart vice president was scheduled to stop by the store and Patti was asked to go out and buy him some "hometown" souvenirs. Once during the holidays she was asked to clean up a messy Christmas shop. During the back-to-school fall rush, Patti was asked to help customers find copies of the school supply lists that Wal-Mart gives shoppers, a list of items Wal-Mart provides for every grade level in the community schools. When the checkout lines are too long, Patti is sometimes asked to do "line rushing"—to take the telxon gun and scan the customers' merchandise while it is still in their carts. This saves cashiers time, during which more merchandise can be sold. But these extra chores do not excuse Patti from having to finish her own work—and on time—despite what she describes as constant interruptions.

Information Technology

If understaffing generates constant complaints of insufficient time, the speed at which the IT systems allow Wal-Mart to purchase and deliver goods to its stores creates additional problems for Wal-Mart employees. The pressure is generated by both the information technology and the management. Trying to save labor costs, managers push employees to work to the speed of the new machines. Management depends on the large volume of information flows, and on workers who can move merchandise fast enough for the system's efficiency and precision.

All employees are expected to learn how to use the information technology effectively. Yet the proper use of IT itself is problematic. First, the technology is not easy to learn. Second, the high rate of turnover shortens the learning period of many employees. Finally, the detail and quantity of information that must be collected increases the workload and generates mistakes—which take more time to correct.

Patti Slater knows what this means. When I asked her to describe her job she said, "I come in at 6 a.m. I take the reports off the printer, separate them, and start checking them. All the cash received for every item is also input, summed and tallied by category, then printed out on a daily basis. There is a store manager's report, a payroll report, a cash office report . . . about fifty separate reports including ones for department managers." They are checked and tallied on a daily basis. The store manager must review the reports, sign off on them, and send them to the division manager. Then they go up the hierarchy to corporate headquarters, where Bentonville executives examine the payroll and merchandise data from all the stores, districts, and regions to make purchasing and merchandising decisions for all the stores.

When sales workers or department managers make mistakes, Patti must go out on the sales floor to review the problem with them and try to get the numbers to tally. "Sometimes," she says, "the figures can be as much as $1,000 off." The problem, as Patti sees it, is that management does not do a good job of training people to use the telxon guns properly or to manage the inventory. "The CBL modules are the only real training sales associates get in learning to do their jobs," Patti says, but "you can't learn what you need to do the job just by taking the CBLs." High turnover also contributes to this problem.

Patti Slater described her job as so complicated that even her store manager did not have a good understanding of all of Wal-Mart's systems. He often asks her to check out problems she believes were resolved weeks before. She then has to research them all over again in addition to doing the rest of her work. Computers do not make errors, but human beings do. Patti says, "Sometimes the computer says you have more than you can find. Then you have to find it. Was it stolen? Is it in the back room, damaged, lost?"

Sometimes it is necessary to hand-count the items on the shelves, or to look in the back room of the store, where unshelved merchandise is stored. Or damaged goods come into the store and have to be sent back to the vendor rather than be put on the shelves. Then there is employee and consumer theft, or "shrinkage" as it is called, that can also throw off the numbers.

Despite the goal of seeing just the right amount of merchandise in the right size, color, and model on the shelf, there is often too much merchandise. The job of Marty Spinner[16] is to "work the bins at night to find room to put the overstock, which comes into the store in large volumes because a lot is delivered all at once."

Jimmy Forester,[17] a store manager in St. Louis, says that sometimes the buyers get a good price on something, so they buy it, but then it doesn't sell as fast as it is supposed to—maybe thirty items in one week and only five the next. "The merchandise that doesn't fit on the shelves has to be put in the back room. When district and regional managers visit they don't like to see the stockrooms too full, so store managers have to find a way to sell it." They have few options for dealing with this. They can advertise the goods in the local paper or put it on a special display, but they only have the power to mark it down 3.5 percent.[18] The alternative is to store the goods in the back room in the hope of hiding them from the district manager. Jimmy told me that he once covered his overstock of tires with a sheet. Another time he made a display of all the tires to hide his overstocks from the division manager.

Promotions and Staffing

Patti Slater had worked at Wal-Mart for nine and a half years, doing almost every job in the store. When the store opened she was hired at $6 an hour to manage the pet department. Then the manager sent her to open another supercenter nearby to remodel the electronics department. After that she was made manager of the toy department, then the OTC (over-the-counter) drug department, the cosmetics department, and the stationery department. She was finally made a "zone manager," responsible for stationery, pets, paper goods, and furniture, a job which she did for several years. From her latest job, she was promoted to financial clerk.

Instead of being encouraged to pursue management training, a path to salaried management, Patti was put to work in the office. She was also among the highest-paid sales associates, earning $12.40 an hour. Soon after taking this job Patti began having anxiety attacks. She went to the doctor, who put her on medication. "I was taking Valium for breakfast and lunch and it made me sick." The pressure, she believes, "put her over the edge."

One might think that Patti, a competent person, would be offered a chance at the management track. But that was not to be. Wal-Mart promotes few women to salaried

A Wal-Mart in Wheeling, Illinois. Photograph by Tim Boyle.
GETTY IMAGES

managers.[19] Many believe the reason is sex discrimination. At Wal-Mart there are few formal criteria for promotion. Men are often moved up the management ranks through an offer of management training. Then they become assistant managers, store managers, district manager, and above. A full 85 percent of store managers at Wal-Mart are men, often men as young as their early thirties. According to Mary Roland, there don't seem to be any particular criteria for promotion, except being male and having a profitable department. This is confirmed in a study by a consultant to the plaintiffs in the Wal-Mart class-action sex-discrimination suit. Richard Drogin, a statistics professor, found that there were no formal criteria for promotion at Wal-Mart. People, mostly men, are simply "tapped on the shoulder" and moved up—often over the heads of the women who trained them.[20]

Not only does Wal-Mart understaff its stores; when business is slow, management also cuts hours. Anthony Sironno[21] works at a Wal-Mart as a customer service manager. Tony supervises twenty-three people at the "front end of the store," mostly cashiers. Unlike many people, Tony likes his job, appreciating the health insurance and the 401(k) plan. He also expects to be promoted.

He is entitled to a stockholder's bonus, which is dependent on the store's profit. He says his bonus can be anywhere from $0 to $1,700. This year he doesn't expect to get a bonus, because the store's sales have not improved 1.5 percents as was anticipated. He hopes he will next year, if the store's sales increase. Yet later in the interview he told me that the store he works in, on the West Coast, is in a community where there are four Wal-Marts in the area. The store's sales have not improved as projected, he believes, because the area is overstored.

Because of the slow sales, the store started cutting hours three weeks ago. Anthony's were cut from forty to thirty-five, a fact about which he is not happy. He has already started to cut the hours of the people he supervises. He sends one or two people home each week, and they lose two to four hours a person.

Cutting hours when sales fall is a regular practice at Wal-Mart. Sometimes management asks for volunteers to leave early. But others are sent home involuntarily and without warning. According to Katie Mitchell, this happens all the time, a practice confirmed by Jimmy Forester, the manager of the St. Louis Wal-Mart store. Jimmy says, "This is often done by asking someone during a quiet time in the store to simply clock out and go home." The employees are not paid for the lost time.

According to Jimmy, in April 1999 Wal-Mart vice president Tom Coughlin, got on the Wal-Mart satellite system and told all store managers that they all had to cut three hours a week of the work time of every employee. At an average cost of $7.50 an hour, that meant savings of about $20 million per week. Jimmy believes corporate management required this labor cut because it had to send out the first-quarter profit-and-loss statements, and needed these savings to bolster its next quarterly report. This would make the stock price rise, which, of course, favored the executives at the home office.

Store managers are responsible each month for filling out a profit-and-loss statement: sales, labor costs, and other expenses in which managers are expected to increase their sales and cut their wage costs. If they don't, Jimmy says, "the manager's head is put on the chopping block." There are no incentives, just responsibility. He calls it "management by intimidation."

Jed Stone,[22] who worked for Wal-Mart as a store manager from 1983 to 1991 (years that Sam Walton was still the CEO) said that Wal-Mart was unlike any other company he has worked for since. Bentonville's executives continually warned managers, "If you don't beat yesterday [i.e., increase sales, reduce costs], management could have your job at any moment." Bill Thomas had already told me of a "beat-yesterday book" that Sam Walton always used to carry around, which is now on display at the Wal-Mart Museum in Bentonville.

What Stone described was the practice of informally urging managers to break the rules that Wal-Mart formally upheld. To break the rules was a "terminable offense," but not to meet the goals—higher and higher sales, increasing cost reductions—was to lose credibility, to be "coached," demoted, and potentially fired. To "beat yesterday" Jed always had to "cut corners and break the rules." He said it was always a struggle to keep the shelves stacked and the floors shiny, and to get hourly workers to help customers. Inevitably he had to break the rules, mainly having employees work off the clock to avoid paying overtime. He surpassed the acceptable budget for markdowns and worked more than officially allowed, both official reasons for termination.

Senior management, he said, ignored all such offenses when sales were up and profits high. Yet, "as soon as my sales went down, there were audits. Everything I had signed my name to was investigated." Jed said that 10 to 15 percent of all store managers were demoted to assistant manager and moved to another store. Some would be promoted to store manager again. Jed finally left Wal-Mart to take another job. He says, "Store managers are just as much victims of the Wal-Mart system as hourly sales workers, cashiers, and floor cleaners."

A similar approach to the rules was found even at the lowest levels of Wal-Mart's employment structure. Billy Draper, the college student whose first job was to unload stock at night, asked for a day job when his class schedule changed. He was made a cashier. Then Wal-Mart management passed out a statement for cashiers to sign. It described cash scams customers sometimes use. As Billy put it, "The message is, I know and understand the scam. *If I get scammed I realize I will be fired.*"

The Wal-Mart Culture—Squeezing Pennies and Shaming Workers

Much of this behavior is a result of a policy designed to save pennies, because the saved pennies of more than 3,500 stores add up to millions of dollars. The people in the home office feel, to paraphrase Sam Walton, "if you can squeeze more out of a penny," then you should do it, a version of the Puritan ethic that resembles the model of Ebenezer Scrooge instead of Benjamin Franklin. Carolyn Thiebes was the personnel manager in one of Wal-Mart's Oregon stores. She was also a plaintiff in an Oregon wage-abuse case.[23] She told me that the store had no copying machine. The office staff had to go to the local Kinko's if something needed copying. Workers were told that if they needed a pen they should bring one from home. As workers quit or were fired, remaining sales associates were asked to take their dirty smocks home and wash them.

Employees are motivated by constant reminders that they are part of the "Wal-Mart family." Family and team members, of course, pitch in to do what has to be done for the good of the group. Because each employee is "responsible for the whole store," everyone needs to be "flexible." Such an analogy is flawed in two ways. First, Wal-Mart is not a family. Second, family members are not "coached" or "fired." Nor are they held responsible for things that are out of their control.

Carolyn Naster[24] told me that employees are told that at Wal-Mart, "everyone's responsible for everything. A department is everyone's department." Managers can make a person responsible for doing a job about which he or she knows little or nothing, and for which he or she has not been trained. This absolves the manager of responsibility for mistakes and puts the onus on subordinates. Managers delegate work arbitrarily. Should workers fail to complete all they have to do, as former manager Jed Stone described his own difficulties with Wal-Mart, they "take the fall." They can be blamed, even fired, when things go wrong. They discover that the rules Wal-Mart has repeatedly pressed on them are selectively enforced.

One of the rules is to be vehemently antiunion. Laverne Coates[25] had worked at a Wal-Mart in Ohio for several years. Based on her evaluations she believed she was a good worker, one management valued. When she began to show some interest in joining a union, her supervisors started finding fault with her performance. First she was "coached" for being out sick. The second coaching, a written and more serious one, was for falling on a wet floor on which she had accidentally spilled water while washing dishes in her job at the Radio Grill snack bar.

Her supervisor humiliated Laverne by screaming at her in front of all the other workers. Later, when she asked for some time off to take care of her dying sister in Washington, D.C. her supervisor allowed it after telling her that her "sister would die without her just as well." Then she was out sick again, a third violation, which precipitated a "D day," or "decision day." At a third coaching, employees are asked to write a letter explaining why they should not be fired. But even before these events, Laverne discovered that she had nine "pink slips" warning notices) in her file that she had never been informed about. That made it easy to fire her. Linda said that such pink slips are used without the knowledge of the employee. She said Wal-Mart often did this rather than laying off staff so that the firm avoids paying high unemployment insurance costs. Indeed, when Laverne tried to collect unemployment insurance, she discovered she was ineligible because she had been fired for cause.

People often get blamed for things over which they have little control. Carol Curtis,[26] a woman who likes her job at Wal-Mart, has noticed some new rules she finds offensive. She says if you have a car accident on your lunch break and are late, this counts as an "occurrence." If the school calls you to tell you your kids are sick and you leave to get them, this is also an occurrence. After four such occurrences you are coached, and given a pink slip.

Wal-Mart disciplines workers by shaming them. Alan Tripster,[27] like Laverne Coates, was treated to this type of punishment. He worked in domestics (bedding and curtains) in a Missouri Wal-Mart. As in other stores, after the Christmas rush management began to cut hours. Instead of laying employees off, however, the managers began to find reasons to fire them. As Alan described it, the managers were "writing up" everyone in his department. "People were getting fired left and right, so everyone tried to walk the straight and narrow." As he saw it, "They would fire people for cause. Then when they needed more help they wouldn't have to take back longtime workers who were making more money and could hire people at the starting wage." Alan remembers a manager saying, in front of a group of associates, "I can get rid of all these people and find others willing to work." The comment, he felt, was deeply humiliating, when spoken to people who needed their jobs so desperately.

Even if shaming doesn't lead to the loss of one's job, at Wal-Mart it is used to discipline workers. As workers are increasingly shamed, made to believe they did something seriously wrong, it becomes easier for managers to "order them around." Prior to being fired in the store where Alan worked, employees were called to the front office on the loudspeaker. Then they would have to walk all the way from the back of the store to the front. Allen called this "the walk of shame." When it happened to him, he said, "it was one of the most horrible experiences of my life." The managers "treat you like you were the worst thing to ever walk the face of the earth."

The same kind of shaming is also found at the top of the organization. Carolyn Thiebes, the personnel manager, had been to Bentonville and toured the corporate offices. She said that each Friday afternoon the management teams in Bentonville have a meeting in a "huge amphitheater" and watch a broadcast where Wal-Mart's CEO and other VPs talk directly to the audience. Executives discuss the week's successes and problems. A manager whose store has sent in a payroll with overtime, which is against company policy, is named and shamed in front of the entire audience.

Harry Borden,[28] another store manager, was also shamed. A man in his midforties, he was somewhat older than the other store managers, and had a heart condition. For the past two years his regional manager had publicly harassed him by making "jokes" about his weight. Harry had a heart condition, but was so "embarrassed and humiliated" by these "jokes" that, without telling his wife, he took diet pills to lose weight, even though the medication was contraindicated for heart disease.

Three months later Harry died from a heart attack. He was carrying a large television set out of the store at a busy time. There were no other associates around to help him. When his wife saw the diet pills in the medicine cabinet she instituted a wrongful-death suit against Wal-Mart, which she eventually won.

Conclusion

As business analysts argue, Wal-Mart saves operating costs and increases its productivity through the use of its innovative information technology and logistics systems. No doubt this is an important goal for all retailers. But how are the labor policies and practices Wal-Mart uses required for the new technologies to be so productive?

In industrial production, advances in technology are frequently followed by employee layoffs: the remaining staff must work faster because they must tend more machines or produce more per hour for the same rate of pay. This productivity increase is made possible not only by the efficiency of the new technology, but by a managerial "speedup."[29] The evidence suggests that Wal-Mart saves money in much the same way. Yet, unlike factory work, the operations of a retail store do not require an increasing number of repetitive tasks. Except for cashiers, the speedup of salesclerks results from Wal-Mart's understaffing, and management demands that all workers do more than what is in their job descriptions, and more work than is possible in the time allotted by their shifts.

Traditionally speedups have been designed to generate more work at the same pay, reducing the worker's real hourly compensation. Wal-Mart has been criticized for its low wages. But its wages may be even lower than they seem. Wal-Mart cuts its labor costs by requiring excessive amounts of work, then making employees work off the clock if they cannot finish in time. As of late 2004 there were thirty-eight lawsuits against Wal-Mart for wage abuse. Wal-Mart also cuts labor costs by cutting hours. High turnover also means constantly hiring new people at the starting wage.

Retail workers at Wal-Mart, unlike factory workers, never know exactly what work or how much work will be asked of them on any particular day. To secure their compliance, Wal-Mart culture is brought to bear. The culture is an effort to "educate" employees to be loyal to the company, to identify with authority, and to accept the demands of an authoritarian regime, a form of management by intimidation. Getting workers to accept this authority makes it possible to manipulate work rules, with employees expected to feel it is legitimate to do the extra work.

Today there are about 1.3 million Wal-Mart employees in the United States. Other retailers and other companies may be using these same methods to speed up their work-force. Despite these tactics, there are many people who believe in the Wal-Mart ethic and like their jobs. There are also many who start working at Wal-Mart with great expectations until they begin to experience the Wal-Mart *modus operandi*. Then a large number feel increasingly angry and betrayed.

TWELVE

A Wal-Mart Workers Association?
An Organizing Plan

Wade Rathke

Breakthrough in China?

A 2004 news alert flashes in from China. An understated release, carefully crafted by the company, indicates that Wal-Mart will conform to Chinese law and recognize unions in its stores in that country when "associates" request such action. The face-saving part of the release tries to assert an "if" after the "when," as if this were not a done deal. "Should associates request formation of a union, Wal-Mart China would respect their wishes."[1] After pressure by the All-China Federation of Trade Unions (ACFTU) and threats to sue Wal-Mart and other multinationals, Wal-Mart acknowledged the pressure and its change of course in China.

This is a victory for workers! Right?

Reaction in the U.S. is mixed, however. An article in the *New York Times* indicates a range of views, from the optimism of Rochester Institute of Technology marketing professor Eugene H. Fram, who called it a "watershed event" because it was the "first time they've given acceptance without saying 'let's go to a union vote,'" to the skepticism voiced by Greg Denier, speaking for the United Food and Commercial Workers in Washington, who said, "Wal-Mart always tries to deny workers a voice in the workplace, so let's see what happens."

New York Times reporter David Barboza speculated tellingly that "it was unclear whether Wal-Mart . . . intended to allow a *real union* to take shape here or whether a *strong union* could even be created, given the current status of labor organizations in China [emphasis added]."[2] Dear Mr. Barboza, please immediately send list of "real unions" which are also "strong unions" to 90 million unorganized workers in the United States.

The buzzwords then become whether the union is "government supported" or "independent." Without a shred of information we are supposed to make a lot of judgments here. The government supports unions in China—a bad thing! The government fights unions in the United States—a good thing?

A friend in the AFL-CIO International Affairs Department speculated that the deal with the government probably represented Wal-Mart's belated submission to the law and an agreement to recognize the ACFTU in exchange for the company's ability to enter the Shanghai market and build another twenty to thirty stores there. That's leverage! Isn't it? Earlier in the fall of 2004 Wal-Mart had announced that it had received governmental permission to open another thirty-odd stores, so perhaps this recent exchange of union-friendly press releases was but a footnote to the earlier agreement, delayed sufficiently so as not to reveal the club's mark on the body of the company. Sure enough, in January 2005 the company also announced a joint venture in China to open two hundred new stores in coming years.

Who knows? Maybe a dozen people, maybe a hundred in the world? I am not sure. But let's not be distracted from the main issue. For the sake of this discussion, let's assume that these Chinese unions are worker organizations in name only. From there we can move forward, because the question here is first about Wal-Mart, and then about the character of any union organization that might arise within that giant corporation.

The problem we face in developing an organizing strategy for Wal-Mart and its 1.3 million U.S. workers is exclusively a national, or perhaps a North American, rather than an international phenomenon. Ironically, and despite Wal-Mart's virulent antiunion reputation and the pains the company has taken to maintain this public posture, Wal-Mart workers are in fact working union in virtually every other country where Wal-Mart has stores. Certainly that is the case in much of the United Kingdom, where Wal-Mart purchased stores that were already unionized, and according to the union, the General Workers Union of Great Britain, it has kept them that way and has been reasonable as a collective-bargaining partner. In Mexico, Wal-Mart employees are under contract with the Confederación de Trabajadores en México—no matter what one might think of that federation. In Argentina Wal-Mart was required to be union, and in Germany the powerful trade unions there have fought the Arkansas-based company tooth and nail under that nation's industrywide bargaining regime. And now there will be some kind of union at Wal-Mart in China.

Another way of stating the point is that the institutional labor movement, such as it is, has actually been able to unionize Wal-Mart beyond North America, while this goal has eluded trade unionists living north of the Rio Grande. Why has the North American labor movement failed to accomplish the same goal?

Minority Unionism

Presumably, in the United States we have "real" and "strong" unions. Yet, the litany of our trials and tribulations is now repeated so frequently that they are almost rendered banal. To recite the lowlights, we have now fallen to less than 13 percent of the non-agricultural workforce, with about 13 million members; in the private sector our density is now hovering just over 8 percent and falling; we lack any organizing program or record of unionization in many new and growing occupations and industries, as well as among the burgeoning millions of contingent and part-time workers. No large new private-sector firm employing over twenty thousand workers has been completely organized during the last thirty years. Indeed, the labor movement's cost of acquisition of new members through either traditional or innovative strategies is an estimated $1,000 per new member, prohibitive for any kind of mass movement. Union certifications under the federal labor law are minuscule. Not unexpectedly, trade union membership is also falling in absolute numbers, which translates into a reduction of capacity and resources for organizing and political action. And, finally, the strike weapon seems bankrupt, which is one reason that so few large strikes have been called or won in recent years.[3] Add to this current witches' brew the fact that we are also fragmented as a movement and divided both internally and externally about strategies for either change or growth, and we have a labor movement in almost total disarray.

It is not simply a question of leadership, as many would wager. At the heart of the decline is a fundamental deficiency in the basic model of unionization in the United States. What has been done is not working. We have created an organizational system which is hugely successful in delivering real improvements in wages and benefits to workers in only a very small number of situations and sectors—largely, and importantly, where wages have been taken out of competition—but this system works only at a prohibitive cost in terms of the money, time, and sheer effort required even to maintain the status quo.

The organizing model is also totally unsustainable for most established labor organizations, which is part of the reason they are stagnating and shrinking. The sad case of the International Association of Machinists (IAM) is but one example. Thirty-five years ago, the IAM had 1 million members, but in 2005 it reported 380,000 active members, admitting that 100,000 of its members had been lost in the short period from 2000 to 2004.[4] Recapturing more than 600,000 members would require a war chest of $600 million—truly unimaginable—coupled with a will and a vision, neither of which may now exist.

Today, it is easier for the rich man to get into heaven than for a poor working stiff to get into the union under a collective-bargaining agreement and then stay employed under the contract for a decade or more.[5] Studies estimate that less than 50 percent of workers are able to win certification under the National Labor Relations Board, and less than 50 percent of that number ends up under a collective-bargaining agreement. And only half of them are still under contract ten years later.[6] This has become a situation where the abysmal state of federal labor law and its perverse and politicized enforcement have created a legal system that acts as a break upon workers' rights. Given Republican domination of the Congress, the chance of progressive labor law reform is negligible. And a Republican-dominated NLRB has also moved to outlaw many of the most promising union-organizing techniques, while most southern and Mountain states enforce an "open-shop" environment hostile to stable unionism. So even that lucky stiff formally covered by a collective-bargaining contract may not actually be a dues-paying union member. As a "business model," therefore, contemporary unionism in the United States is completely dysfunctional.[7]

Majority Unionism?

Workers still want unions! Or, at least, something much like them. Surveys indicate that a significant minority of unorganized workers would still vote for a union if they had the opportunity. Furthermore, a significant majority of workers—almost two-thirds—are clear that they want representation on the job by some kind of association or other organizational formation that looks, smells, and tastes like a union—though this may not be the same as the "real" or "strong" unions of our dreams. They are willing to fight, but they don't want a war. They want agreements, but the majority of the workers surveyed want to figure out a way to work *with* the company on some mutual program, rather than to be in a contentious relationship.[8]

This is all controversial. Are these sentiments to find fulfillment in an independent union; a collaborationist, management-supported institution; or some sort of hybrid institution? Labor advocates have begun to experiment with different kinds of organizations at various work sites around the country. In difficult-to-organize workplaces, such as nursing homes, day care centers, and farms, unionists have built organizations that emphasize institution building and membership above all, rather than establishment of a bargaining relationship to the employer. The emerging, half-million-strong job classification of "home day care worker," virtually created by Bill Clinton's "welfare-reform" initiative, is an excellent example. Organizing drives among these poorly paid women all started with grassroots efforts—mainly by ACORN (Association of Community Organizations for Reform Now)—to build voluntary, autonomous organizations of home day care workers, even in the absence of a legal framework that might have sustained collective bargaining with their employer, which was usually some level of state or municipal government. ACORN, followed by the Service Employees International Union (SEIU) and the American Federation of State, County, and Municipal Employees (AFSCME), undertook the painstaking work of signing up members, lobbying in legislatures for reimbursement increases, and fighting to get checks to providers on time. Starting in 1996, Chicago SEIU Local 880 pioneered this union-building project, creating the political and organizational context that made it possible for Governor Ron Blagovich to sign a 2005 executive order that enabled the SEIU to become the bargaining representative for forty-nine thousand home health care workers in the state.

Are such formations nothing more than "company unions" or "Chinese unions" with an inseparable relationship to the state or the corporation, and therefore worthy of little more than contempt? Do these terms still have the same meaning in modern U.S. organizing? Given the weakness of labor in sector after sector, market after market, firm after firm, one could make a credible argument that for many unions to survive they have by necessity entered into corporatist arrangements with the employer which allow management to set wage and benefit conditions in critical areas. This was the case at Saturn in Springhill, Tennessee, where the United Auto Workers allowed General Motors to rewrite an auto industry collective-bargaining contract that had been refined over more than half a century. Likewise, in the janitorial sector and in California nursing homes, success of the SEIU was predicated upon a set of preliminary contract concessions that enabled the union to get its foot in the door and, over time, build the kind of market density and organizational infrastructure that would pay off in the long run.

Today, there are very few industries remaining in which the unions can fight off a concerted managerial effort to eliminate them. At the airlines, once a model of high-wage, high-density collective bargaining, unions are holding on by their fingernails, negotiating huge, tragic, and unimaginable decreases in pay and benefits. Since the early 1990s, when United and American Airlines went into bankruptcy, airline unions have found themselves engaged in a protracted set of negotiations that have combined wage givebacks, corporate reorganizations, and big layoffs. It has not been a pretty sight, but perhaps necessary. By February 2005 unionized workers at USAir had agreed to take-aways that had some of the workers "making less than Wal-Mart cashiers."[9]

Does this make them company unions? Certainly not! Where there is no choice, how can it be a disgrace to survive? This is the essence of the famous Melian debate, which has long been a popular training exercise among community organizers. The ancient Melenians faced a conundrum when they found themselves at the mercy of a superior Athenian army. The Athenians argued that the Melians should surrender and survive, rather than fight, in which case they would be killed or enslaved.[10] Unlike the Melians, who did choose battle and death, the airline unions elected to surrender in hopes of fighting another day.

Indeed, many "company" unions, which were often established by management in the 1930s and 1940s as part of the corporate counteroffensive against the Congress of Industrial Organizations (CIO), have transformed themselves into "real" trade unions. The modern, militant Communications Workers of America (CWA) began more than fifty years ago as a company-organized union in the Bell system. Certainly it is not that today! And the story of the CWA is not unique. During the late Depression years the CIO took over the company-supported employee representation plans in the steel industry to create the powerful United Steelworkers of America; likewise at Chrysler, the celebrated militancy of the workers at Dodge Main and Jefferson Avenue had important roots in the dense system of shop steward representation first established by Chrysler management itself, which sought to forestall independent unionism. In more recent years this has often been the situation with public employee associations in state, local, and educational jurisdictions, which often have histories of management domination or political cronyism. Thus SEIU Local 660 emerged out of the transformation of the old Los Angeles County Employees Association, and in Ohio, AFSCME gained a robust and effective affiliate when the state employees association there voted to join nearly a million other state and municipal workers who were part of the house of labor.

Simply stated, how can workers build power in particular firms, across industries and sectors, and in the realm of politics if they do not adopt a majoritarian strategy? As a fundamental and permanent shift in strategy and objectives, the American labor movement seems to have no choice but to recast its basic organizing model, change, and embrace *majority unionism.*

As organizers, we need to take the dare and create an organizing plan that in fact gives workers what they want. Do we have a choice?

At the heart of this dilemma is the redefinition of the meaning of trade unionism and the character of its functions. Are "real" or "strong" unions only those that engage in arm's-length collective bargaining? I think not. Within the 13 million–strong AFL-CIO are a good number of workers, particularly in the public sector, who are union members but not covered under collective agreements; or they are covered by agreements where wages and benefits are statutorily excluded from bargaining; or they may be in unions that are allowed some economic bargaining yet are legally denied the right to strike. Certainly, this is the case in all federal sector unions, as well as in many other public employee unions, including many locals of ASCME, the SEIU, the American Federation of Teachers, and the National Education Association. Another telling example can be found in the bargaining dilemma created by the greatest organizing triumph of the 1990s, among home health care workers, where unions "invented" hundreds of thousands of hybrid employees and then bargained with a set of state and county authorities over a severely limited number of issues. There can be no "one size fits all" in the labor movement of the contemporary United States.

The Wal-Mart Organizing Problem

We need to think about new and alternative organizing models, and nowhere is this a more vital necessity than when we consider Wal-Mart, the retail phenomenon that is doing so much to reshape the social and economic life of the nation. In the United States there are more than 3,500 individual Wal-Mart stores employing 1.3 million workers. In Canada there are almost 300 stores. Wal-Mart is the largest private-sector employer in these countries, and in Mexico.

The United Food and Commercial Workers (UFCW) has been organizing Wal-Mart Canada on a store-by-store basis, taking advantage of the more union-friendly climate in some Canadian provinces. In Canada union density, even in the private sector, approaches 35 percent of the working population, which means that most Canadians see unionism as common within the workplace, a normalcy that is greatly helpful to organizers at antiunion firms like Wal-Mart. Even more important, in Quebec and Ontario the "cards do walk and talk" because workers can get their bargaining unit certified through "card check," in which a majority of all workers at a single work site have merely to sign authorization cards, rather than participate in an election, where experience demonstrates that employer coercion is almost always present. The UFCW program in Canada has therefore been serious, extensive, and aggressive, deploying scores of organizers in blitz operations and pulling in recruits from throughout the country.

An organizing breakthrough seemed on the horizon in 2004. The UFCW established itself in two Quebec Wal-Marts and became certified as the bargaining agent among workers in a unit the union carved out of a half dozen auto departments in the Wal-Marts of British Columbia. These breakthroughs followed fledgling efforts in another five stores across Canada where the UFCW has contended for representation rights and been embroiled in legal disputes with the company.[11] The UFCW has been proud of this program, asserting that Wal-Mart workers will organize if they are afforded legal protection from corporate retaliation and if the union on the scene is sufficiently aggressive.

But even in union-friendly Canada the UFCW strategy seems doomed. Early in 2005, five months after the union began bargaining with Wal-Mart at a store in Jonquière, 240 miles northeast of Montreal, the corporation abruptly announced that it would permanently shutter the entire store because of the UFCW's "unreasonable demands" over scheduling and staffing. This draconian level of hostility to unionism was reminiscent of Wal-Mart's response to the eleven butchers who voted to join the UFCW in a Jacksonville, Texas, Wal-Mart in 2000. That organizing foothold was obliterated when Wal-Mart declared that henceforth it would purchase only prewrapped meat, thereby eliminating the job of meat cutter in every one of its several hundred supercenters.[12]

The UFCW has gotten the message, certainly in the United States, where labor law is now stacked so heavily against trade unionism. Since his election in 2004, UFCW president Joe Hansen has largely pulled back from a store-by-store organizing strategy. Where the union once had field organizers targeting Las Vegas and other markets in a leafleting and outreach program to Wal-Mart workers, Hansen has reoriented the union toward a broader corporate campaign in the United States, even while he continues to support the Canadian organizing drive.

Indeed, there is no reason to believe that in the United States a store-by-store unionization strategy would have any possibility of success at Wal-Mart. Without a company declaration of genuine neutrality or the emergence of a real mass movement among the kind of people who are employed as Wal-Mart "associates," the obstacles are insurmountable. There are just too many workers spread among too many stores for one to believe that even a modestly successful drive could succeed within any reasonable time frame. If the UFCW organized thirty stores a year it would still take more than a hundred years to unionize the existing Wal-Mart system! This would not be an organizing plan but a death sentence.

The ruthlessness of the company also argues against a unit-by-unit strategy. Despite his folksy ways, Sam Walton was bitterly hostile to trade unionism, employing an early generation of antiunion consultants to break Teamster and Retail Clerks organizing efforts in Missouri and Arkansas.[13] Today, Wal-Mart maintains a staff of two hundred in its labor relations department, many available to fly to any store when the UPI—Union Prevention Index—hits a prescribed set of bells. This does not mean that workers in any given Wal-Mart are actually attempting to organize; rather, the UPI is keyed to diverse factors measuring morale, complaints, turnover, and other problems. Of course, when a real unionization effort is detected, Bentonville springs into action with all necessary resources. For example, in February 2005, when eighteen tire-and-lube-shop workers in a Loveland, Colorado, Wal-Mart prepared for an NLRB election, headquarters flew in a team of labor relations experts who hammered away at the luckless young workers for more than a week. "It wasn't a fair fight," complained Joshua Noble, the twenty-one-year-old union sparkplug. "Every day they had two or three antiunion people from Bentonville in the garage full time, showing antiunion videos and telling people that unions are bad." Not unexpectedly, the union lost, 17–1.[14]

Despite the UPI program, Wal-Mart has been unable, or unwilling, to train store managers to obey labor law. After surveying forty-one regions where Wal-Mart operated its stores, the UFCW found, over a five-year period, massive evidence of NLRB-certified unfair labor practices or illegal terminations. Wal-Mart does not like unions, the company is clear about it, and store managers are not afraid to show it.

We cannot expect to counter Wal-Mart's full-court press with the existing strength of our unions, no matter how militant. These two institutions, the union movement on the one side and Wal-Mart on the other, exist in parallel universes. For more than forty years Wal-Mart management concentrated stores and distribution centers in the South and the nation's midsection, with small towns and some of the newer exurbs as favored sites. The unions, on the other hand, have their strength in the big cities and the older suburbs. And in coastal America, these cities are Wal-Mart's last frontier. Only about 30 percent of the largest U.S. cities host one of the company's big boxes. Thus the high-profile "site fights" in Inglewood, South Chicago, Queens, and Contra Costa County have been defensive battles instigated by the UFCW and a shifting coalition of progressive community groups and the labor-liberal politicians who still retain some influence in local government. The UFCW is less interested in "organizing" Wal-Mart in these conflicts than it is in protecting the relatively high-wage contracts that unionized grocery workers enjoy in urban America. Given the life-and-death stakes, these site-fight battles are often waged with remarkably tenacity. In Philadelphia, for example, the president of UFCW Local 1776 reported that his local union had spent more than $7 million in a decade-long campaign to keep Wal-Mart and other nonunion discount firms from expanding into the retail market served by members of his big local.[15]

Thus it would be pure delusion to contend that a handful of isolated election successes in individual Wal-Mart stores would give workers significant power to bargain decent contracts with this giant, alien corporation. A strike threat would hardly be effective, and an actual strike would be job suicide for workers and an early exit from their misery for most local unions. Sitting at the bargaining table and having to live through the discussion of issues like dues checkoff, much less union shop, would be an exercise in futility.

If organizing Wal-Mart workers can be defined only in terms of the collective-bargaining paradigm, we will not be able to get these poor men and women into heaven. That is the plain and simple truth.

Organizing a Wal-Mart Workers Association

So, what is to be done? Unionizing Wal-Mart is the great organizing problem of our time, and it seems inescapable that to envision organizing hundreds of thousands of Wal-Mart workers means imagining something quite different for the labor movement. For an organizer evaluating this challenge, two innovations are essential. First, the union movement must give workers what we have had every reason to believe they want: an association where Wal-Mart "associates" can act in a concerted way with their co-workers to engage their employer around issues and concerns, or even just talk to each other, since at Wal-Mart management considers talking on the job "time-theft." And second, we condition membership in the association not on the permission and consent of the employer, which is at the heart of the current labor-relations scheme in the United States, but on the sole decision and individual action of the worker.

Within the range of these fundamental principles, I would argue for the creation of a Wal-Mart Workers Association. This association should be *rights based,* rather than benefits based.

Wal-Mart breaks the law. The relentless pressure exerted by Bentonville upon store managers ensures that labor law violations at hundreds of stores are unavoidable. The company has created a centralized command and control structure which gives local managers just enough discretion to ensure corporate deniability for any gross violations of labor, immigration, or civil rights laws. Such a structure easily produces the well-documented, increasingly litigated pattern of abuse: workers toiling off the clock, cleaning crews locked in at night, the abuse of immigrant workers in a host of situations, and sex discrimination in wages and promotions. Despite Wal-Mart's media-savvy public relations campaign, which emphasizes the good jobs and careers available at the corporation, working conditions are predatory, with a turnover rate that averaged 44 percent in 2003 and quite possibly 100 percent among new hires in particular locations.

Rather than upgrade the work and benefits to secure a stable workforce, the Wal-Mart employment strategy is to discard and recycle more than half a million workers each year.

A Wal-Mart workers' organization would make clear that rights exist, regardless of the strength of the employer, and that these rights must be asserted and protected rather than allowed to wither when these citizens and residents of the U.S. work for the largest private employer in the nation. Indeed, most U.S. employees believe that they have a set of rights on the job that cannot be taken away. "I've got my rights" is an Americanism that has survived even Wal-Mart's totalitarian embrace. The labor movement's task is to help workers realize that organizing actively around their rights has full—and active—support in their community and among many of those who shop at Wal-Mart. Such an understanding will shatter the atmosphere of fear, intimidation, and deference propagated by Wal-Mart and other labor-intensive retailers. Instead of operating "underground," union-oriented workers and their supporters need to revive the highly visible, direct-action tactics pioneered by the civil rights movement.

In New Orleans, for example, we found encouraging results with such a strategy in the hospitality industry, which dominates the labor market for low-wage work. In the late 1990s we developed the Hotel, Hospitality and Restaurant Organizing Committee (HOTROC)—a multiunion effort that was able to mobilize thousands in the street, pack governmental hearings, and picket recalcitrant employers, thus moving the local political structure to mandate an increase in wages and benefits at many of the city's high-profile hotels and restaurants. With the assistance of Mayor Marc Morial, later of the National Urban League, and much of the city council, HOTROC leveraged the city's political infrastructure to require minimum standards and a form of union recognition from any developer or investor who sought to build a new hotel or other hospitality enterprise. Such a strategy was successful in unionizing the first newly built hotel in fifty years, and it generated commitments for the development of several other projects, until all building plans were put on hold in the wake of the 9/11 attacks.

Governance of a Wal-Mart Workers Association could be a problem—and an opportunity. Would the Wal-Mart Workers Association be a legally defined labor organization under the terms of the Landrum-Griffin Act, or a freestanding, voluntary association, like the National Rifle Association, ACORN, or the Sierra Club? Does such an organization have a relationship to the AFL-CIO as a directly affiliated labor union, a DALU, which was a commonplace organizational vehicle in the early 1930s, when the American Federation of Labor chartered thousands of independent union locals? What relationship would the Wal-Mart Workers Association maintain with the UFCW or the SEIU, which might well have their own organizing projects on tap?

Dues would be nominal, but the certainty that Wal-Mart would refuse to deduct them from each worker's paycheck is actually the kind of obstacle that the association could turn to its advantage. In any organizing drive, including those of the CIO in the 1930s and the teachers and farm workers in the 1960s, the frequent conversations needed to convince a worker to part with his or her hard-earned cash prove invaluable to the creation of a deeply felt union consciousness and commitment to the organization. At Wal-Mart this kind of dues talk can be equally radical, transforming "associates" into union brothers and sisters.

If a relatively small proportion of all Wal-Mart workers joined such an association, they would nevertheless constitute a sizable organization. The new organization would enroll some 13,000 workers if just 1 percent joined. If such an organization could recruit 10 percent of all Wal-Mart employees then we are talking about an association of more than one hundred thousand members. This would make the new organization larger than most AFL-CIO affiliates. It could then begin to act and speak as an effective, independent voice for the entire Wal-Mart workforce. But let's not get carried away by mathematical speculation—every member will be hard-won and hard earned in any new association of workers within this corporation.

A rights-based association might well have a potent public-policy voice, pushing for increases in the minimum wage and for more generous family health coverage, and acting as an advocate for the hundreds of thousands of women and immigrants who suffer the most from Wal-Mart's employment policies. Although the Impact Fund lawyers who are suing Wal-Mart on behalf of Betty Dukes and other female employees have collected hundreds of employment narratives detailing gender discrimination at Wal-Mart, the public impact of this legal action would be magnified if an actual association of Wal-Mart workers were a party to the suit. Indeed, in the realm of union-side public relations, an organization of actual or retired Wal-Mart employees would have a huge impact. It is not preposterous to imagine that such an organization of workers and former workers might have an important voice in any possible resolution of the many legal actions that are now pending against the giant corporation. A Wal-Mart Workers Association should have a seat at any table in which lawyers and plaintiffs reach a settlement.

Most people don't realize that workers are almost always engaged in some kind of organizing within America's larger companies. In my experience as an organizer, I have found that in any campaign there is *always* a prehistory of worker action around some kind of grievance, whether it is an unjust firing, a missed promotion, or an inequitable wage adjustment. Unionism need not be on the agenda, but that does not mean that collective action of some sort is not under way. Many of these skirmishes turned into shop floor lore, and the individual heroes and heroines that arose—or more often fell— in these hidden battles inspired others to stick out their neck.

Thus, whenever I talk to "unorganized" workers I am always able to find and locate the history of something that passed for struggle and sometimes success: a firing prevented, overtime stopped, a lunch period extended, a pay mistake righted, a hastily drawn petition circulated about the office, a hand waved in the air and a voice raised at injustice. Norma Rae was something for the movies, but men and women in thousands of situations stand up and court job suicide. In the constant guerrilla warfare that characterizes the modern workplace, courageous workers are often fired or demoted, but sometimes they actually win a small victory, thus preparing the ground for yet another contest. We need to seed these struggles in stores all over the country.

This is what we call "majority" unionism. In these times of labor weakness we need to examine self-critically any strategy that does not engage and benefit the maximum number of people. For example, the SEIU invested at least $10 million in an organizing program for lower-wage nursing home workers that successfully unionized several thousand workers in Florida. But despite some NLRB election successes, the effort did not significantly boost union density in the state's nursing home industry. Many workers were unable to win collective-bargaining agreements at their work site, and those that did won but a modest wage increase, largely because the SEIU had failed to take wages out of competition.

On the other hand, ACORN's Florida campaign to increase the minimum wage in the state proved a stunning success in the 2004 elections, even as George Bush put Florida solidly in the red state camp. The $1-an-hour boost, with future increases indexed to inflation, will cost employers $250 million within the next year and deliver raises directly and indirectly to seven hundred thousand workers, most in the service sector, and not a few in the same nursing homes the SEIU tried so hard to organize. Neither project would have been possible without extensive organization and resources, nor were any but the most talented professional organizers involved in both campaigns. Yet one campaign proved a relative failure, the other a considerable success. This is the core of the debate between "minority" and "majority" unionism. Are we going to organize mass constituencies, or simply privilege small, tightly organized groups? As our strength decreases, progressives in and out of the union movement will have to choose.

Would such an approach "sentence" nonunion workers to substandard pay and benefits? The default answer is that the current implicit insistence on an organizing model that cannot prevail is already an on-the-job death sentence. The real answer, though, is that there is still real power in nonexclusive, noncertified, but active and aggressive on-the-job workers' organizations. The ability of such associations to maintain consistent activity, advance demands, and represent their members is the bedrock of any possible worker organization, including the classic union formation. When you have workers moving together and "organized" in the most fundamental fashion, their power trumps collective bargaining, which is simply the engineering of labor peace in exchange for a temporarily defined scale of wages and benefits.

Building an organization has always been the prelude, not the consequence, of collective bargaining. This was the situation before passage of the Wagner Act as well as in the dynamic union-building era right afterward. Then, union recognition for "members only" was commonplace, almost as routine as the "exclusive" representation of all workers by one union, which became the norm in the 1940s and the decades afterward. But today, with union density even lower than in the early 1930s, we should once again explore an organizational form put in place under Franklin Roosevelt's National Industrial Recovery Administration (NIRA), the idea of building workplace unions that vigorously represent their members but which do not claim to speak for or enroll a majority of all workers in any given work site. The legal basis for such an organization, then and now, is Section 7 of the NIRA, whose essential language was transposed to the Wagner Act and to every subsequent legislative reinterpretation of that law. Section 7 asserts that "employees shall have the right to self-organization, to form, to join, or assist labor organizations . . . and to engage in other concerted activities for the purposes of collective bargaining or other mutual aid or protection." In other words, labor law encourages collective bargaining, but it also protects "concerted activities" by workers seeking to advance their "mutual aid or protection." Section 7 does not mandate that a union have majority status, or even that there be an official union. It merely requires that workers seek to better their condition and make that aspiration known to their employer, in order to come under the protection of the labor law.[16]

Thus the first contract that John L. Lewis negotiated with U.S. Steel in March 1937 was a members-only agreement, as were 85 percent of all the early Steel Workers Organizing Committee agreements and 64 percent of those signed by local units of the United Automobile Workers. Indeed, in the late 1930s members-only contracts, signed by both AFL and CIO affiliates, were just as common as majority-exclusive agreements.[17] Today the experience of the 1930s is largely forgotten, and the courts have put some restrictions on the use of Section 7, but labor law's defense of "concerted activities" for "mutual aid and protection" has hardly been abolished. Indeed, I would argue that if employers are forced to confront such members-only organizations they will find themselves on the defensive because such employee organizations not only rely upon labor law for their legitimacy, but are also protected under the First Amendment rights of assembly, speech, and petition. And if such "unions" demonstrate sufficient strength within the workforce, employers will be forced to treat with them.

The experience of the Communications Workers of America at one General Electric plant is a case in point. Like Wal-Mart, GE is militantly antilabor. No union has organized a GE facility for more than twenty years, and today only about 10 percent of all GE workers are unionists. So the CWA adopted an organizing strategy called Working at GE, or WAGE. The perspective was long-term: building a sense of collective empowerment on the shop floor would be central to success, while preparing for an NLRB election would be far down on the CWA agenda. WAGE participants paid dues of $10 a month and they became voting members of the parent union.

CWA set up WAGE committees at a variety of GE plants, but the most successful initiative came at an Auburn, Maine, circuit-breaker factory. It was a "hot shop," ready to file for an election, but the spirited WAGE committee there sought to exercise power without going the union-recognition route.

They got their chance a year after 9/11 when Ken Townsend, a toolmaker, returned to the plant from Army Reserve duty only to find his employment slot downgraded to a production job at lower pay. GE was in technical compliance with the law protecting the jobs of servicemen called to temporary duty, but the Auburn workforce seethed at GE's patriotic hypocrisy. Instead of using the incident to get union-authorization cards signed, Auburn WAGE sought to use the specter of public criticism to shift management behavior. WAGE drafted a letter to Maine's U.S. senators and got 130 workers to sign it, a large majority of the plant workforce. Like a strike or other job action, the letter's greatest effectiveness was as a threat: if management did not back down, it might face public criticism on an issue tinged with patriotism and ethical conduct. The tactic produced results within a week, and Townsend soon got his old job back along with a check for back pay.

Victories of this sort were not uncommon at GE plants where WAGE committees were active. But the jump to full unionization was a parlous one. The WAGE committees participated effectively in CWA's 2003 GE contract campaign: surveying their members about bargaining issues, sending representatives to the New York City negotiating table, circulating contract language from unionized shops. But when the Auburn WAGE committee attempted to transform itself into a union organizing committee, GE knew just how to respond. Like Wal-Mart, the company had its seasoned staff of union-avoidance experts, who rushed to the factory, circulated hostile and divisive literature, and polarized the workforce. WAGE soon lost much of the goodwill it had earned, the shop divided along pro- and antiunion lines, and the nascent NLRB election drive fizzled.[18]

The Importance of Organizing Ex-Workers

Wal-Mart eats up its workers and spits them out. The current claim by the company is that its turnover rate is down to 40 percent per year. These are big numbers, though, when you have 1.3 million workers. Giving the devil his due on the turnover rate, that still means finding 520,000 new workers every year just to keep even. Hiring more workers each year than any other U.S. company employs is a huge undertaking, but the very size of the ex-employee labor pool also creates a huge source of unhappy workers who are potentially susceptible to a certain kind of "organizing."

To reform Wal-Mart, we have to organize this huge pool of ex-workers, who constitute a sizable part of the retail labor market. To grow, even to maintain an adequate workforce, Wal-Mart depends on their goodwill, as well as the desperation of those who

Protests by labor and community groups greeted Wal-Mart's efforts to build supercenters in Chicago. Photograph by Association of Community Organizations for Reform Now (ACORN).

return to work for the company again and again. Ex-employees are a "Wal-Mart–experienced" constituency that is no longer subject to the fear that exists within the four big-box walls. They have a direct interest in the various employment-related lawsuits that are working their way through the courts, and they have the most contacts with the people who are still working at Wal-Mart. Thus, an organization of these ex-workers would create a vital, potentially strategic link between the public, the community, and the main body of employed Wal-Mart workers.

But unions in the United States do not organize ex-workers. This may seem an immutable rule, even though it casts aside a huge reservoir of support that can be deployed

In November 2004 California labor-liberals were unsuccessful in their effort to make Wal-Mart and other big retailers pay more of their employees' health care costs. Poster by California Federation of Labor.

for political campaigns and community mobilizations. Ex-workers give weight and credibility to calls for change and heighten the urgency of the organizing project with their own stories of pain and peril. Union retirees have long been given status and recognition, but workers who simply quit or are fired, even after years working for the same firm, exist in a kind of limbo. This is because U.S. unions are defined not by the workers who are enrolled, but by the act of working. Thus, it requires an employer's consent for a worker to join an American trade union. Not only must a collective-bargaining agreement be in force, but the individual worker must stay on the payroll of a specific firm in a particular location. The unemployed, laid-off, retired, and injured—including many part-time, contingent, and casual workers—can no longer find a home within the house of labor. Their disenfranchisement must end.

Building a Community Alliance to Support Worker Organizing

Although U.S. unions will not be able to organize Wal-Mart in a traditional fashion, they do have allies, actual and potential, that can help them redefine the playing field so that it extends well beyond the four corners of any of the corporation's huge supercenters. Environmentalists and community activists are concerned about the impact of big-box sprawl on traffic, tax policy, land use, and residential concentration. Small businesspeople are worried about being squeezed out of the marketplace. Community organizations often focus upon long-term planning for their neighborhoods, preferential hiring programs, and guarantees against store abandonment. Women's organizations are rightly concerned about sex discrimination in hiring and promotions, while civil rights groups have noted that Wal-Mart's managerial culture retains a white, southern flavor. Antisweatshop activists have grown alarmed at Wal-Mart's squeeze on its overseas suppliers, while those involved in the national debate over health care financing protest that Wal-Mart's expensive and restrictive health benefit coverage pushes many employees to seek taxpayer-funded health assistance from thinly stretched state and municipal programs. And it is just possible that the Democrats have finally come to realize that their fate is tied to that of labor's revival in the red states. As Michael Tomasky, the executive editor of *American Prospect,* put it in a postmortem on the 2004 elections, "To me, the effort to organize Wal-Mart is what it's all about. That's a very hard fight that could take 20 years, but if the unions can organize the Wal-Mart stores that would be a titanic historical victory, like organizing the coal mines in the past."[19]

So Wal-Mart stands at the crossroads. It is the obstacle, the swampy low-wage terrain that stands athwart so many progressive initiatives in contemporary American politics and social life. The transformation of the Wal-Mart business model, let alone the organization of its employees, would have a transformative impact within the United States. And it is Wal-Mart's very size and visibility that have turned the company into such a focus of concern for so many who stand on the left, or even at the center, of our politics. The sheer size and multifaceted involvement of the company in so many issues of pressing social and economic concern give it a gravitational weight that pulls together a countervailing set of interests and social elements within the U.S. population.

The key to building a large community-labor alliance is coming to agreement on a common set of *rules of engagement* for the coalition and its work in convening all of these disparate formations. Such rules would include an agreement by all organizations not to settle on inferior terms until there is a more "global" settlement that includes protections and advancement for Wal-Mart workers. Such rules would need to address the kind of tactics deployed against the retail giant, holding in check the impulse of some liberals to attempt a boycott of Wal-Mart, which, as Barbara Ehrenreich has pointed out, might well divide one part of the progressive coalition from the Wal-Mart clerks and working-class consumers who have found the company an indispensable part of their daily routine. The point is to reform Wal-Mart, its business model, and its posture in our cities and suburbs.

This was the perspective taken by labor, ACORN, and minority politicians in Chicago when Wal-Mart sought to locate two stores within the inner city early in 2004. This labor-community coalition did not seek to deny the company entry to Chicago but sought to force it to operate on principles sustaining a set of "community benefits"[20] that included health care coverage, a high starting wage, and employment of local residents. This approach blunted the force of Wal-Mart's usual urban argument: it would bring hundreds of permanent jobs to desperate inter-city neighborhoods that were poorly served by existing retail outlets. Thus Wal-Mart had to bow out of the Chicago site fight. The company could not reposition itself as a good corporate citizen against the simple but persuasive argument that Wal-Mart was welcome, but had to meet community standards. This approach has actually been institutionalized in Los Angeles, where the city council passed a municipal ordinance in 2004, mandating that the largest big-box stores pay for an "economic impact assessment" before they win zoning approval. As in Chicago, this is just the sort of initiative that will make Wal-Mart's employment policies subject to political debate and potential reform.

Living-wage campaigns are themselves among the best tactical gambits because they define what constitutes fair and adequate employment, making Wal-Mart and its practices stand out in embarrassing relief. And such campaigns embolden Wal-Mart workers. If these campaigns are highly visible and well endorsed by clerics, environmentalists, and civic leaders, they can serve to focus and legitimize the heretofore inchoate aspirations of the Wal-Mart associates themselves.

Although a consumer boycott would be counterproductive at Wal-Mart, the growth of a boycott by potential workers is a real possibility. When companies get a bad reputation, the quality of the labor market from which it draws new recruits may well decline. And given Wal-Mart's huge turnover rate, and its outsized appetite for new hires, this very phenomenon seems to have begun to impact Wal-Mart's expansion plans. Executives of the company have declared, in depositions taken as part of the Impact Fund's gender-discrimination suit, that Wal-Mart would have the capacity to open more than three hundred stores a year *if* it could hire enough management and line workers to staff the new facilities. This is an Achilles' heel for the company and a critical place where our strategy of community, citizen, and worker engagement should focus.

Polarizing the marketplace is a brutal, hardball process, which often does not favor progressive forces, but certainly does not favor Wal-Mart either. Site fights in themselves, for example, have very little value in stopping the company or its expansion program. Wal-Mart will open hundreds of stores each year, even if they are not located in precisely those urban areas that resist the company with the greatest determination. But site fights do put the company, its practices, and its plans squarely in front of the entire public, and polarize public sentiment for and against Wal-Mart's labor practices.

Does the company understand this? Absolutely! Just walk into the entryway of any Wal-Mart store and observe the giant wall murals celebrating the local high school or other popular local institution. And more to the point, Wal-Mart now devotes the bulk of its radio and TV advertising budget to institutional spots that tout, not the firm's "always low prices," but the good careers and friendly people found at the giant company.

Indeed, when CEO H. Lee Scott told more than twenty thousand shareholders and workers attending the 2004 Wal-Mart annual meeting in Fayetteville, Arkansas, that the company would pay store mangers their bonuses based not just on store profits but on managerial adherence to labor law, top executives were making a concession to the public uproar over Wal-Mart's skirt-the-law business model.[21] But Scott has also made clear that he understands the ideological stakes at play in the Wal-Mart public relations counteroffensive. Speaking in Los Angeles, which may be the epicenter of resistance to Wal-Mart's invasion of coastal California, Scott declared in early 2005 that it was not just the UFCW that was "seeking to create public confusion" about company wages and benefits. Rather, "our critics seem to have a broader and, I believe, more troubling aim: to warp the vital debate the country needs in the years ahead about the proper role of business and government in assuring that capitalism creates a decent society."[22]

What Is to Be Done?

The American trade union movement recognizes that organizing Wal-Mart, or at least pressuring the company to substantially modify its low-wage, low-benefit employment strategy, is far too large a task to be left to any one union. This became absolutely clear in the wake of the devastating defeat suffered by the UFCW in 2003 and 2004 during a fifteen-week-long strike in Southern California designed to prevent wages and benefits in the unionized grocery markets there from falling to Wal-Mart levels. The AFL-CIO has singled out Wal-Mart as uniquely important and pernicious, and the unions have put millions of dollars on the line to start building a national coalition capable of reforming Wal-Mart's employment policies and inaugurating a long-term unionization project.

Perhaps this is all just posturing, more about tactics than strategy. But increasingly there seems to be real traction and commitment in the ranks of labor and its allies that goes back to the founding principle that "an injury to one is an injury to all." Wal-Mart is too big to be ignored. It is injuring everyone in the house of labor. To put these ideas and theories to field tests and trial runs—or any real organizing plan—will take a huge commitment of resources, both dollars and staff. These are not easy to find in George Bush's America, but this seems to be the time, and if it is not the right time, it still may be our last, best opportunity.

At the end of the day it still comes down to whether or not workers will move and engage the company. It is clear that Wal-Mart workers—and the vast majority of American workers—are voting with their feet right now, and moving nowhere. Workers organize and act when they believe that they have a chance not just to fight, but also to win. American labor is ready to assist them in building organizations that meet their needs in these difficult times. If we stumble on the right combination that meets the challenge of a Wal-Mart and those that would mimic its operations, then something very "real" and very "strong" indeed will once again be built by and for American workers.

The back of every blue associate vest in every Wal-Mart store says, "Can I help you?" If we can, something different and powerful will happen here!

Notes

Preface

1. "Remarks of William McDonough," Alliance for Justice, Washington, D.C., March 10, 2005.
2. Peter Drucker, *The Concept of the Corporation,* 2nd ed. (New York: John Day, 1972), 12.
3. Steven Greenhouse, "Wal-Mart: A Nation Unto Itself," *New York Times,* April 17, 2004, B7; Simon Head, "Inside the Leviathan," *New York Review of Books* 51, no. 20 (December 16, 2004).
4. "Wal-Mart and California: A Key Moment in Time for American Capitalism," an address by H. Lee Scott, president and CEO, Wal-Mart Stores, Inc., Town Hall Los Angeles, February 23, 2005, http://www.walmartfacts.com.
5. Richard Tomlinson, "Who's Afraid of Wal-Mart? Not Carrefour," *Fortune,* June 26, 2000, 186–90; Julio Moreno, "Wal-Mart and America's Retail Mission in Latin America," unpublished paper delivered at UC Santa Barbara conference, April 12, 2004.

ONE Wal-Mart: A Template for Twenty-First-Century Capitalism
Nelson Lichtenstein

1. Or as *Fortune*'s Jerry Useem put it on the eve of the Iraq war, "Wal-Mart in 2003 is, in short, a lot like America in 2003: a sole superpower with a down-home twang. As with Uncle Sam, everyone's position in the world will largely be defined in relation to Mr. Sam. Is your company a 'strategic competitor' like China or a 'partner' like Britain? Is it a client state like Israel or a supplier to the opposition like Yemen? Is it France, benefiting from the superpower's reach while complaining the whole time? Or is it . . . well, a Target? You can admire the superpower or resent it or—most likely—both. But you can't ignore it." Jerry Useem, "One Nation Under Wal-Mart," *Fortune,* March 3, 2003, 66.
2. Nicholas Stein, "America's Most Admired Companies," *Fortune,* March 3, 2003, 81.
3. Pankaj Ghemawat, Ken Mark, Stephen Bradley, "Wal-Mart Stores in 2003," Harvard Business School Case Study, revised January 30, 2004, 9-704-430.

4. Andy Serwer, "The Waltons: Inside America's Richest Family," *Fortune,* November 15, 2004, 86.

5. The Wal-Mart public relations offensive has not just targeted a mass of audience of potential consumers, but seeks to influence liberals and intellectuals as well. Thus the company has become a sponsor of National Public Radio, and in April 2005 it published an open letter to readers of the *New York Review of Books,* "Wal-Mart's Impact on Society: A Key Moment in Time for American Capitalism."

6. Both women quoted in Abigail Goldman and Nancy Cleeland, "The Wal-Mart Effect: An Empire Built on Bargains Remakes the Working World," *Los Angeles Times,* November 23, 2003, A1.

7. Abigail Goldman, "Sweat, Fear and Resignation Amid All the Toys," *Los Angeles Times,* November 26, 2004, A1.

8. "Wal-Mart Mgr. Wife," December 7, 2002, at http://www.walmartwatch.com.

9. Joseph A. Schumpeter, *Capitalism, Socialism, and Democracy* (New York: 1942), 127–55.

10. Sara Lin and Monte Morin, "Voters in Inglewood Turn Away Wal-Mart," *Los Angeles Times,* April 7, 2004, A1; Jessica Gamison, "Battles over Mega-Stores May Shift to New Studies; Law Requiring Economic Impact Reports Could Set the Stage for Skirmishes Across Los Angeles," *Los Angeles Times,* August 12, 2004, B1.

11. Michael Hiltzik, "Election 2004: Look at the Initiatives Money Can Buy," *Los Angeles Times,* November 4, 2004, C1.

12. Richard Appelbaum, "Fighting Sweatshops: The Changing Terrain of Global Apparel Production," in *Critical Globalization Studies.* ed. Richard Appelbaum and William Robinson (New York: Routledge, 2004), 120–40.

13. As quoted in Tom Frank, *One Market Under God: Extreme Capitalism, Market Populism, and the End of Economic Democracy* (New York: Anchor Books, 2000), 211.

14. Bob Evans, "Two Giants Toss Outsourcing Out," *Information Week,* September 20, 2004, 178.

15. Bob Ortega, *In Sam We Trust: The Untold Story of Sam Walton and How Wal-Mart Is Devouring America* (New York: Random House, 1998), 130, 131–33.

16. Richard Appelbaum, "The Emergence of Giant Transnational Contractors in Asia: A Fundamental Change in Global Supply Chains," unpublished grant proposal, Pacific Rim Research Program, University of California, January 2005.

17. Useem, "One Nation Under Wal-Mart," 64–70; and for a sad and humorous tale of one pickle company's demise, see Charles Fishman, "The Wal-Mart You Don't Know," *Fast Company* 77 (December 2003): 68–76.

18. "Wal-Mart, P&G Link Up for Efficiency," *St. Louis-Post Dispatch,* February 14, 1989, 12B; Constance Hays, "What's Behind the Procter Deal? Wal-Mart," *New York Times,* January 29, 2005, C1; Davidowitz quoted in Jeremy Grant and Dan Roberts, "P&G Looks to Gain Strength Through Unity," *Financial Times,* January 31, 2005, 25.

19. Brooks Blevins, *Hill Folks: A History of Arkansas Ozarkers and Their Image* (Chapel Hill: University of North Carolina Press, 2002), 147–78; Ben Johnson, *Arkansas in Modern America, 1930–1999* (Fayetteville: University of Arkansas Press, 2000), 200–202.

20. Ortega, *In Sam We Trust,* 86–90; and see also the favorable but revealing Sandra Vance and Roy Scott, *Wal-Mart: A History of Sam Walton's Retail Phenomenon* (New York: Twayne Publishers, 1994), 44–47.

21. Ortega, *In Sam We Trust,* 143–44.

22. Stanley Holmes and Wendy Zeller, "The Costco Way," *Business Week,* April 12, 2004, 76–77; Ann Zimmerman, "Costco's Dilemma: Be Kind to Its Workers, or Wall Street?" *Wall Street Journal,* March 26, 2004, B1; Michael Forsythe and Rachel Katz, "Retailers in Political Battle," *National Post* (Canada), July 21, 2004, 16.

23. Data taken from www.opensecrets.org, which provides names, employers, and political contribution amounts for any zip code. In 1992 the Waltons and other Wal-Mart executives contributed heavily to the presidential campaign of Bill Clinton. However, Wal-Mart's twenty-first-century affinity for the Republicans and their policies is detailed in Jeanne Cummings, "Wal-Mart Opens for Business in Tough Market: Washington," *Wall Street Journal,* March 24, 2004, A1.

24. Mary Jo Schneider, "The Wal-Mart Annual Meeting: From Small-Town America to a Global Corporate Culture," *Human Organization* 57, no. 3 (1998): 295.

25. Don Sonderquist, *The Wal-Mart Way* (Nashville: Thomas Nelson, Inc., 2005), 59–60.

26. Schneider, "The Wal-Mart Annual Meeting," 295.

27. Wal-Mart Stores, *2005 Annual Report,* 17.

28. Schneider, "The Wal-Mart Annual Meeting," 294.

29. Soderquist, *The Wal-Mart Way,* 45.

30. Sam Walton with John Huey, *Sam Walton: Made in America, My Story* (New York: Doubleday, 1992), 161–82.

31. David Chidester, *Authentic Fakes: Religion and American Popular Culture* (Berkeley: University of California Press, 2005); Kimon Sargeant, *Seeker Churches: Promoting Traditional Religion in a Nontraditional Way* (New Brunswick, NJ: Rutgers University Press, 2000); Christian Smith, *American Evangelicalism: Embattled and Thriving* (Chicago: University of Chicago Press, 1998); Zig Ziglar, *Secrets of Closing the Sale* (Grand Rapids, MI: Fleming H. Revell Company, 2003).

32. Wal-Mart Stores, *Sam's Associates Handbook,* 3, in Vertical File, Food and Service Trades Department, AFL-CIO.

33. Jack Kahl, *Leading from the Heart: Choosing to be a Servant Leader* (Austin: Greenleaf Book Group, 2004), 107–9. Kahl was for many years owner and CEO of Manco, which supplied duct tape to Wal-Mart.

34. Mike Troy, "Scott, Coughlin Set to Lead Wal-Mart," *Discount Store News* 38, no. 2, January 25, 1999, 48. And see also James A. Autry, *The Servant Leader: How to Build a Creative Team, Develop Great Morale, and Improve Bottom-Line Performance* (New York: Three Rivers Press, 2001). Robert K. Greenleaf, a secular management consultant, coined the phrase "servant leader" in 1970, but it has been heavily Christianized since then. See in particular Ken Blanchard, *The Servant Leader* (Nashville, TN: J. Countryman, 2003).

35. Thomas O. Graff and Dub Ashton, "Spatial Diffusion of Wal-Mart: Contagious and Reverse Hier-

archical Elements," *Professional Geographer* 46 (February 1994): 19–29; "About Wal-Mart: Senior Officers," found at http://www.walmartstores.com.

36. Brent Schlender, "Wal-Mart's $288 Billion Meeting," *Fortune,* April 18, 2005, 97.

37. Jon Lehman, telephone interview with author, June 7, 2005; and see Brad Seligman's essay in this volume.

38. Michael Bergdahl, *What I Learned from Sam Walton: How to Compete and Thrive in a Wal-Mart World* (Hoboken, NJ: John Wiley & Sons, 2004), 150–52; Carol Hymowitz, "Program Puts Students on the Leadership Path," *Wall Street Journal Online,* January 15, 2003. Unless otherwise noted, all information on SIFE is taken from its Web site, http://www.sife.org.

39. See the Wal-Mart Stores Web site at http://www.walmartstores.com. Among the top Wal-Mart executives who have served on the SIFE board are Jack Shewmaker and Tom Coughlin.

40. John Kerr, "Pass It On," *Inc. Magazine,* December 1995; Curtis DeBerg, telephone interview with author, June 1, 2005; information on SIFE expansion found at http://www.sife.org. Although Wal-Mart is careful to keep the relationship between its buyers and their vendor clients a highly formal one in Bentonville, SIFE provides a venue that is far less regulated. Indeed, the contributions so readily made by SIFE's Wal-Mart vendors purchase the kind of goodwill that might be quite remunerative.

41. Corporate Watch UK, "ASDA/Wal-Mart: A Corporate Profile" at http://www.corporatewatch.org.uk.

42. George Monbiot, "Economic Cleansing," *Guardian,* June 17, 1999.

43. Andreas Knorr and Andreas Arndt, "Why Did Wal-Mart Fail in Germany (So Far)?" Unpublished paper available from Institute of World Economic and International Management, University of Bremen.

44. "Wal-Mart's Impact on Society: A Key Moment in Time for American Capitalism: An Open Letter to Readers of the *New York Review of Books* from Lee Scott, President and CEO, Wal-Mart Stores," April 2005.

45. Women, children, and older citizens have composed a majority of the workforce in many employment sectors, including the garment trades, food processing, secondary-school teaching, and the old department stores, but these industries were not template enterprises at the core of the American political economy.

46. Statistics on company sales as a proportion of GNP taken from Useem, "One Nation Under Wal-Mart." By way of comparison, U.S. Steel sales were 2.8 percent of GNP in 1917; A & P held 1.5 percent in 1932; and Sears clocked in at but 1 percent in 1983.

47. Does a juxtaposition between Wal-Mart and General Motors compare apples and oranges, a retailer and a manufacturer? But these differences are less apparent than real. GM did manufacture lots of cars, but its franchised dealer system, which was always kept on a tight leash, sold them by the millions, and its wholly owned GMAC subsidiary financed them, and sometimes made as much profit as did the production side of the corporation. Wal-Mart started off as a retailer, but as this essay has tried to demonstrate, the increasingly intimate relationship between the discounter and its suppliers is transforming Wal-Mart into a de facto manufacturing company. At GM the manufacturing end of the enterprise squeezed the car dealers; at

Wal-Mart the retail sales operation wags the manufacturing tail, but in the end it may not matter all that much.

48. For the GM story see Nelson Lichtenstein, *Walter Reuther: The Most Dangerous Man in Detroit* (Urbana: University of Illinois Press, 1997), 228–47, 278–91; for a discussion of real wage growth, see Lichtenstein, *State of the Union: A Century of American Labor* (Princeton, NJ: Princeton University Press, 2002), 130–40.

49. E. Bruce Geelhoed, "Charles Erwin Wilson," in *The Automobile Industry, 1920–1980,* ed. George S. May (New York: Facts on File, 1989), 483.

50. "Wal-Mart and California: A Key Moment in Time for American Capitalism," an address by Lee Scott, president and CEO, Wal-Mart Stores, Inc., Town Hall Los Angeles, February 23, 2005 at http://www.walmartfacts.com; Bradford C. Johnson, "Retail: The Wal-Mart Effect," *McKinsey Quarterly* 1 (2002): 40–43.

51. Meg Jacobs, *Pocketbook Politics: Economic Citizenship in Twentieth-Century America* (Princeton, NJ: Princeton University Press, 2004), 1–11.

52. U.S. Department of Labor, *Handbook of Labor Statistics,* Bulletin 2217 (Washington, DC, 1984), 201–3.

53. Zimmerman, "Costco's Dilemma," B2.

54. Beth Shulman, *The Betrayal of Work: How Low-Wage Jobs Fail 30 Million Americans and Their Families* (New York: New Press, 2003); Eileen Appelbaum, Annette Benhardt, and Richard Murnane, eds., *Low-Wage American: How Employers Are Reshaping Opportunity in the Workplace* (New York: Russell Sage Foundation, 2003).

55. Data for Wal-Mart district managers taken from Ben Seligman, "Patriarchy at the Checkout Counter," in this volume; H. Lee Scott's total compensation of $28,963,872 (2003) is found in the Harvard Business School study by Pankaj Ghemawat and his associates. I estimated the pay of a Wal-Mart cashier in 2003 at $15,000, which is actually pretty generous. Charles Wilson earned about $500,000 in 1950, an autoworker about $3,500.

56. AFL-CIO, "Wal-Mart: An Example of Why Workers Remain Uninsured and Underinsured," October 2003, unpublished paper.

57. Arindrajit Dube and Ken Jacobs, "The Hidden Cost of Wal-Mart Jobs: Use of Safety Net Programs by Wal-Mart Workers in California," UC Berkeley Labor Center, Briefing Paper Series, August 2, 2004; Andy Miller, "Wal-Mart Stands Out on Rolls of PeachCare," *Atlanta Constitution,* February 27, 2004, 1B; Michele Jacklin, "Wal-Mart Passes Insurance Costs to Taxpayers," *Hartford Courant,* March 9, 2005, 1.

TWO Woolworth to Wal-Mart: Mass Merchandising and the Changing Culture of Consumption
Susan Strasser

1. John K. Winkler, *Five and Ten: The Fabulous Life of F. W. Woolworth* (New York: Robert M. McBride, 1940), 109–10.

2. Charles W. Hurd and M.M. Zimmerman, "How the Chains Are Taking Over the Retail Field, IV," *Printers' Ink,* October 8, 1914, 35.

3. Godfrey Lebhar, *Chain Stores in America: 1859–1959* (New York: Chain Store Publishing, 1959), 38.

4. Not all the new goods were, technically speaking, mass-produced. Philip Scranton has broadened historical understanding of the massive quantities of consumer goods produced during the decades after 1880 by explaining the importance of the many small firms that did "batch work," making consumer products like fashion apparel, jewelry, and furniture that came in many styles, sizes, and colors, and so were not amenable to the requirements and strictures of mass production. See Scranton, "Diversity in Diversity: Flexible Production and American Industrialization, 1880–1930," *Business History Review* 65 (Spring 1991): 27–90, and *Endless Novelty: Specialty Production and American Industrialization, 1865–1925* (Princeton, NJ: Princeton University Press, 1997).

5. This argument about branding is developed in my book *Satisfaction Guaranteed: The Making of the American Mass Market* (New York: Pantheon, 1989; Washington: Smithsonian, 2004).

6. For more on the two-way system of distribution, see Susan Strasser, *Waste and Want: A Social History of Trash* (New York: Metropolitan Books, 1999), 69–109. Harvard study: Harvard University Bureau of Business Research, *Management Problems in Retail Grocery Stores,* Bulletin No. 13 (Cambridge, MA: Harvard University Press, 1919), 47–48. On secret price marks, see Strasser, *Satisfaction Guaranteed,* 74.

7. Paul H. Nystrom, *The Economics of Retailing* (New York: Ronald Press, 1915), 192; Deborah S. Gardner, " 'A Paradise of Fashion': A.T. Stewart's Department Store, 1862–1875," in *A Needle, a Bobbin, a Strike: Women Needleworkers in America,* ed. Joan M. Jenson and Sue Davidson (Philadelphia: Temple University Press, 1985), 63; Stewart quoted in Harry E. Resseguie, "Alexander Turney Stewart and the Development of the Department Store, 1823–1876," *Business History Review* 39 (Autumn 1965): 314.

8. Gardner, "Paradise of Fashion," 64.

9. Neil Harris, "Museums, Merchandising, and Popular Taste: The Struggle for Influence," in *Material Culture and the Study of American Life,* ed. Ian M.G. Quinby (New York: W.W. Norton, 1978), 149; Rosalind H. Williams, *Dream Worlds: Mass Consumption in Late Nineteenth-Century France* (Berkeley: University of California Press, 1982); Susan Porter Benson, "Palace of Consumption and Machine for Selling: The American Department Store, 1880–1940," *Radical History Review* 21 (Fall 1979): 199–221; Alphonsus P. Haire, "The Telephone in Retail Business," *Printers' Ink,* November 27, 1907.

10. Meg Jacobs, *Pocketbook Politics: Economic Citizenship in Twentieth-Century America* (Princeton, NJ: Princeton University Press, 2005), 24; William Leach, *Land of Desire: Merchants, Power, and the Rise of*

a New American Culture (New York: Pantheon, 1993), 78; Susan Porter Benson, *Counter Cultures: Saleswomen, Managers, and Customers in American Department Stores, 1890–1940* (Urbana: University of Illinois Press, 1986), 46; Gardner, "Paradise of Fashion," 65.

11. Strasser, *Satisfaction Guaranteed,* 205–6.

12. Benson, "Palace of Consumption," 201; Ralph M. Hower, *History of Macy's of New York, 1858–1919: Chapters in the Evolution of the Department Store* (Cambridge, MA: Harvard University Press, 1943), 156; Alfred D. Chandler, *The Visible Hand: The Managerial Revolution in American Business* (Cambridge, MA: Belknap Press, 1977), 229.

13. Susan Porter Benson, "The Cinderella of Occupations: Managing the Work of Department Store Saleswomen, 1900–1940," *Business History Review* 55 (Spring 1981), 7; Benson, *Counter Cultures,* 22–24; Kathryn Kish Sklar, *Florence Kelley and the Nation's Work: The Rise of Women's Political Culture, 1830–1900* (New Haven, CT: Yale University Press, 1995), 146–47; Kathryn Kish Sklar, "The Consumers' White Label of the National Consumers' League, 1898–1918," in *Getting and Spending: American and European Consumption in the Twentieth Century,* ed. Susan Strasser, Charles McGovern, and Matthias Judt (New York: Cambridge University Press, 1998).

14. Benson, *Counter Cultures,* 135–65, quotation on 135; Benson, "Cinderella."

15. Rural population calculated from U.S. Bureau of the Census, *Historical Statistics of the United States, Colonial Times to 1970* (Washington, DC: Government Printing Office, 1975), 11–12. Boris Emmet and John E. Jeuck, *Catalogues and Counters: A History of Sears, Roebuck and Company* (Chicago: University of Chicago Press, 1950), 213; Fred L. Israel, ed., *1897 Sears Roebuck Catalogue* (New York: Chelsea House, 1968), 786.

16. Theodore H. Price, "Big Business Junior in America: The Mail Order Business," *The Outlook,* January 26, 1916, 227; Emmet and Jeuck, *Catalogues and Counters,* 74; Louis Asher and Edith Heal, *Send No Money* (Chicago: Argus Books, 1942).

17. Emmet and Jeuck, *Catalogues and Counters,* 67; Price, "Big Business Junior in America," 229.

18. Emmett and Jeuck, *Catalogues and Counters,* 118–19.

19. "A Great Mail-Order Plant," *Printers' Ink,* April 18, 1906, 20–23; Emmet and Jeuck, *Catalogues and Counters,* 132, 461–64; Price, "Big Business Junior," 165.

20. Emmet and Jeuck, *Catalogues and Counters,* 137ff (quote on 144).

21. "A Mail Order Bonfire," *Grocers' Magazine,* April 1912, 8. For other protests involving the destruction of catalogs, see Emmett and Jeuck, *Catalogues and Counters,* 151; "Some Live Wire Retailers," *Grocers' Magazine,* May 1912, 26.

22. See Emmett and Jeuck, *Catalogues and Counters,* 150; Daniel J. Boorstin, *The Americans: The Democratic Experience* (New York: Random House, 1973), 111.

23. Emmet and Jeuck, *Catalogues and Counters,* 160, Joseph J. Schroeder Jr., ed., *Sears, Roebuck & Co., 1908 Catalogue No. 117, The Great Price Maker* (Chicago: Follett, 1969), 8.

24. Lizabeth Cohen, *Making a New Deal: Industrial Workers in Chicago, 1919–1939* (Cambridge, UK: Cambridge University Press, 1990), 106–13, 116–20, 235–38.

25. Lebhar, *Chain Stores in America,* 120–32; Richard S. Tedlow, *New and Improved: The Story of Mass Marketing in America* (New York: Basic Books, 1990), 218.

26. See F.J. Harper, " 'A New Battle on Evolution': The Anti–Chain Store Trade-at-Home Agitation of 1929–1930," *Journal of American Studies* 16 (December 1982): 407–26; Carl G. Ryant, "The South and the Movement Against Chain Stores," *Journal of Southern History* 39 (May 1973); Emmett and Jeuck, *Catalogs and Counters,* 606–21; Lebhar, *Chain Stores in America,* 159–60; M.A. Adelman, *A & P: A Study in Price-Cost Behavior and Public Policy* (Cambridge, MA: Harvard University Press, 1966), 80; Richard S. Tedlow, *Keeping the Corporate Image: Public Relations and Business, 1900–1950* (Greenwich, CT: JAI Press, 1979), 91–96.

27. Lebhar, *Chain Stores in America,* 25, 29; GDP from http://www.census.gov/statab/hist/HS-32.pdf, accessed January 12, 2005.

28. Harper, " 'A New Battle on Evolution,' " 407; Federal Trade Commission, *Chain Stores: Final Report on the Chain-Store Investigation* (Washington, DC: Government Printing Office, 1935), 4–5; Roy J. Bullock, "The Early History of the Great Atlantic & Pacific Tea Company," *Harvard Business Review* 11 (April 1933): 298; Roy J. Bullock, "A History of the Great Atlantic & Pacific Tea Company Since 1878," *Harvard Business Review* 12 (October 1933): 59–69; Lebhar, *Chain Stores,* chap. 2, "The Birth of the System," 25, 35.

29. Charles W. Hurd and M.M. Zimmerman, "Chain Store Advantages in Organization and Financing, VII," *Printers' Ink,* October 29, 1914, 78.

30. Charles W. Hurd and M.M. Zimmerman, "How Big Retailers' Chains Outsell Independent Competitors, XI," *Printers' Ink,* November 26, 1914, 66–68; Charles W. Hurd and M.M. Zimmerman, "Chains Picking Up the Best Sites, IX," *Printers' Ink,* November 12, 1914, 58–62; Tedlow, *New and Improved,* 209.

31. Charles W. Hurd and M.M. Zimmerman, "Taking the Chains by Fields and Their Number in Each, V," *Printers' Ink,* October 15, 1914, 80.

32. Tedlow, *New and Improved,* 221.

33. Charles W. Hurd and M.M. Zimmerman, "Chains Outclass Individual Dealers in Buying Advantages, X," *Printers' Ink,* November 19, 1914, 64; Tedlow, *New and Improved,* 210–13.

34. Hurd and Zimmerman, "Taking the Chains . . . V," 72, 29; "How Big Retailers' Chains Outsell Independent Competitors, XI," *Printers' Ink,* November 26, 1914, 72. On substitution, see Strasser, *Satisfaction Guaranteed,* 83–87.

35. For a recent summary, see Stephen Martin, Industrial Economics Fall 2004 Course Materials, "Price Discrimination and Vertical Restraints," http://www.mgmt.purdue.edu/faculty/smartin/courses/461F04/VRPD.pdf, accessed December 29, 2004. See also Strasser, *Satisfaction Guaranteed,* 270–84.

36. Charles W. Hurd, "How Shall the Advertiser Regard the Newly Forming Chains?" *Printers' Ink,* December 28, 1916, 88–89; see also Bullock, "Great A & P Tea Company Since 1878," 62.

37. Tedlow, *New and Improved,* 191–93, 203–4.

38. Ibid., 231–35.

39. Sharon Zukin, *Point of Purchase: How Shopping Changed American Culture* (New York: Routledge, 2004), 79; Tedlow, *New and Improved,* 241.

40. Sandra S. Vance and Roy V. Scott, *Wal-Mart: A History of Sam Walton's Retail Phenomenon* (New York: Twayne Publishers, 1994), 24–28.

41. Ibid., 30–45.

42. I have not seen this quotation attributed to anybody else, but have not been able to find a source among Twain's writings, and it does not appear at http://www.twainquotes.com.

43. Peter J. Solomon, "A Lesson from Wal-Mart," *Washington Post,* March 28, 2004, B7; Simon Head, "Inside the Leviathan," *New York Review of Books,* December 16, 2004, 80.

44. Quoted in Liza Featherstone, "Down and Out in Discount America," *The Nation,* January 3, 2005, 13.

45. See Philip Mattera and Anna Purinton, *Shopping for Subsidies: How Wal-Mart Uses Taxpayer Money to Finance Its Never-Ending Growth* (Washington, DC: Good Jobs First, 2004).

46. See David W. Boyd, "From 'Mom and Pop' to Wal-Mart: The Impact of the Consumer Goods Pricing Act of 1975 on the Retail Sector in the United States," *Journal of Economic Issues* 31 (March 1997): 223–33; see also Charles Fishman, "The Wal-Mart You Don't Know," *Fast Company,* December 2003, http://www.fastcompany.com/magazine/77/walmart.html.

47. See Wal-Mart time line, http://www.walmartstores.com/wmstore/wmstores/Mainnews.jsp?pagetype=news&categoryOID=-8769&template=DisplayAllContents.jsp, accessed December 31, 2004; Bridget McCrea, "Tag You're It: Wal-Mart Is Forcing Its Suppliers to Adopt This Emerging Technology," *Logistics Management* 43 (February 2004): 44–48.

48. Both quoted in Featherstone, "Down and Out in Discount America," 11.

49. Solomon, "A Lesson from Wal-Mart."

THREE It Came from Bentonville: The Agrarian Origins of Wal-Mart Culture
Bethany E. Moreton

For their invaluable comments on earlier drafts of this essay, I am grateful to Glenda Gilmore, Michael Jo, Nelson Lichtenstein, Julia Ott Vermillion, and Pamela Voekel. Most particularly I thank all those in Northwest Arkansas who have so generously shared their recollections and insights, and made the Ozarks a second home for this Mississippian.

1. Thomas A. Stewart et al., "The Businessman of the Century." *Fortune* November 22, 1999.

2. Benjamin R. Barber, *Jihad vs. McWorld: How the Planet Is Both Falling Apart and Coming Together—and What This Means for Democracy* (New York: Times Books, 1995); Eric Schlosser, *Fast Food Nation: The Dark Side of the All-American Meal* (Boston: Houghton Mifflin, 2001); Lizabeth Cohen, *A Consumer's Republic: The Politics of Mass Consumption in Postwar America* (New York: Vintage Books, 2003); Thomas L. Friedman, *The Lexus and the Olive Tree* (New York: Farrar, Straus & Giroux, 1999); Francis Fukuyama, *The End of History and the Last Man* (New York: Free Press, 1992); Samuel P. Huntington, *The Clash of Civilizations and the Remaking of World Order* (New York: Simon & Schuster, 1996); Walter LaFeber, *Michael Jordan and the New Global Capitalism* (New York and London: W.W. Norton, 1999), 14.

3. Variations on this list abound; this one is drawn from Malcolm Waters, *Globalization,* 2nd ed. (London and New York: Routledge, 2001), 214–15. The original analysis appears in Antonio Gramsci, *Selections from the Prison Notebooks,* ed. and trans. Quintin Hoare and Geoffrey Nowell Smith (New York: International Publishers, 1971), 277–318.

4. Addressing critically a key component of the Fordist argument, Nelson Lichtenstein points out that "the legal straitjacket imposed by [the 1947 Taft-Hartley Act, which exempted most white-collar occupations from federal labor law and opened the door to state 'right-to-work' laws] ensured that the unions reborn in the New Deal would now be consigned to a roughly static geographic and demographic terrain, an archipelago that skipped from one blue-collar community to another in the Northeast, the Midwest, and on the Pacific Coast." Nelson Lichtenstein, *State of the Union: A Century of American Labor* (Princeton, NJ: Princeton University Press, 2002), 120. Thus Lichtenstein sees many of the currents of "post-Fordism" already well developed at midcentury—a conclusion with which a student of Wal-Mart can only agree wholeheartedly. Even those elaborating the analytical rubric of Fordism, however, concede that the conditions the term connotes only ever obtained in a minority of industries. Their point is rather that the entire web of socioeconomic relations was shaped by this core: however little it resembles a car factory, a rubber plantation in Indonesia is called into existence by the mass-consumed automobile, and a Levittown depends on both.

5. Please see Bethany E. Moreton, "Wal-Mart World," Ph.D. dissertation, Yale University, forthcoming in 2006. Research for that dissertation, and therefore for this essay, has been generously supported by the Coca-Cola World Fund at Yale, the Harvard Business School, the Louisville Institute, the Mellon Foundation, the Social Science Research Council, the Society for Historians of American Foreign Relations, the U.S. Department of Education, the Yale Center for International and Area Studies, the Yale Center for Religion in American Life, the Yale Department of History, the Yale Graduate School of Arts and Sciences; by the expertise of librarians, archivist, and private collectors at twenty-three institutions; and by the generosity of friends, family, and colleagues. As an inadequate token of my thanks, the proceeds from this article have been donated to a relevant nonprofit organization in Northwest Arkansas.

6. Useem, "One Nation Under Wal-Mart," *Fortune,* March 3, 2003, 64; Sarah Schafer, "A Welcome to Wal-Mart,' *Newsweek International,* December 20, 2004, 30; Bruce Upbin, "Wall-to-Wall Wal-Mart," *Forbes,* April 12, 2004, 76.

7. "Sam Walton Made Us a Promise," *Fortune,* March 18, 2002, 120–24, 128.

8. Ron Loveless, interview with the author, September 25, 2004. I thank Mr. Loveless for his kind help.

9. On prewar Christian radio, see Joel A. Carpenter, *Revive Us Again: The Reawakening of American Fundamentalism* (New York and Oxford, UK: Oxford University Press, 1997), 126–40; on Christian television broadcasting, see Razelle Frankl, "Transformation of Televangelism: Repackaging Christian Family Values," in *Media, Culture, and the Religious Right,* ed. Linda Kintz and Julia Lesage (Minneapolis: University of Minnesota Press, 1998), 163–89; on the Moral Majority's use of direct mail, see Sara Diamond, *Spiritual Warfare: The Politics of the Christian Right* (Boston: South End Press, 1989), 57–60.

10. Bruce J. Schulman, *The Seventies: The Great Shift in American Culture, Society, and Politics* (New York: Free Press, 2001), 109.

11. Rogers Historical Museum [Arkansas], *Cultural Diversity in Benton County* (Rogers, AR: Rogers Historical Museum, 2001).

12. A notable exception to this generalization is the Northwest Arkansas community of Tontitown, an Italian enclave dating to 1897.

13. Brooks Blevins, " 'In the Land of a Million Smiles': Twentieth-Century America Discovers the Arkansas Ozarks," *Arkansas Historical Quarterly* 61, no. 1 (Spring 2002): 1–36.

14. Jack Temple Kirby, *Rural Worlds Lost: The American South, 1920–1960* (Baton Rouge: Louisiana State University Press, 1987), 40.

15. Ibid., 119.

16. Milton D. Rafferty, *The Ozarks, Land and Life* (Fayetteville: University of Arkansas Press, 2001), 158–59.

17. On the use of this strategy in New England and the New South, respectively, see Thomas Dublin, *Women at Work: The Transformation of Work and Community in Lowell, Massachusetts, 1826–1860* (New York: Columbia University Press, 1979) and James C. Cobb, *The Selling of the South: The Southern Crusade for Industrial Development, 1936–1990* (Urbana: University of Illinois Press, 1993); for a brief guide to the literature on farm-subsidized capitalist expansion globally, see Saskia Sassen, *Globalization and Its Discontents: Essays on the New Mobility of People and Money* (New York: New Press, 1998), 83–84.

18. *The Nation*'s cover for January 3, 2005, is thus particularly apt: it features Dorothea Lange's iconic "Migrant Mother"—Florence Thompson—clad in a blue Wal-Mart vest. Thompson grew up outside Tahlequah, Oklahoma, home of Wal-Mart Number 10.

19. Louis Adamic, quoted in Mike Davis, *City of Quartz: Excavating the Future in Los Angeles* (New York: Vintage Books, 1992), 31; Carl O. Sauer, *The Geography of the Ozark Highland of Missouri,* Geographic Society of Chicago Bulletins (Chicago: University of Chicago Press, 1920), 186.

20. Thomas Hart Benton, "America's Yesterday," *Travel,* July 1934; quoted in Blevins, " 'In the Land of a Million Smiles.' "

21. David B. Danbom, *Born in the Country: A History of Rural America* (Baltimore: Johns Hopkins University Press, 1995), 234–40.

22. Rafferty, *The Ozarks,* 73–74, 217.

23. The Hispanic population of Benton and Washington counties—the Metropolitan Statistical Area of Fayetteville-Rogers-Springdale—stood at 2,885 in the 1990 census and 26,401 in the 2000 census, an annual growth rate of 24.8 percent. University of Arkansas scholars point out that these figures almost certainly undercount the real number of Hispanic immigrants, since many are undocumented. Gazi Shbikat and Steve Striffler, "Arkansas Migration and Population," *Arkansas Business and Economic Review* 33, no. 3 (Fall 2000): 2, 5.

24. Margaret Bolsterli, " 'Pretty Soon We Won't Even Be Us, Will We?' Prosperity, Urbanization and Cultural Change in Northwest Arkansas 1960–1997," unpublished paper presented at the Agrarian Studies Program, Yale University, April 17, 1998, 28. A book-length analysis of the Tyson phenomenon by sociologist Steve Striffler is forthcoming from Yale University Press in 2005; for an overview of the vertical integra-

tion of the region's poultry industry, see Ben F. Johnson, *Arkansas in Modern America, 1930–1999* (Fayetteville: University of Arkansas Press, 2000), 191–96.

25. Sedalia was the headquarters of the Knights of Labor District Assembly 101, representing the industrial union's members throughout Texas, Missouri, Arkansas, and Kansas. The strike that began on March 1, 1886, paralyzed all 4,500 miles of Jay Gould's railroad system in that region. Nell Irvin Painter, *Standing at Armageddon: The United States, 1877–1919* (New York and London: W.W. Norton, 1987), 41–42. Robert McMath points out, however, that though rural support for a similar 1885 strike was widespread and effective in securing the Sedalia-based Knights' demands, it waned somewhat by 1886 and may have contributed to that strike's ultimate failure. Robert C. McMath, *American Populism: A Social History, 1877–1898* (New York: Hill & Wang, 1993), 75–77.

26. Searcy and neighboring Prairie County, Arkansas, were centers for the Arkansas Agricultural Wheel, which moved through a series of alliances and dissolutions with various antimonopoly organizations throughout the 1880s and 1890s. Jeannie M. Whayne et al., *Arkansas: A Narrative History* (Fayetteville: University of Arkansas Press, 2002), 262–65. Members of the Farmers Alliance—the central precursor to the People's Party—gathered in 1886 in Cleburne, Texas, to produce the "Cleburne Demands," basis for Populist policy. "The demands sought 'such legislation as shall secure to our people freedom from the onerous and shameful abuses that the industrial classes are now suffering at the hands of arrogant capitalists and powerful corporations,' " including legal recognition of unions and cooperatives, punitive taxation on land speculation, and federally administered banking. Lawrence Goodwyn, *Democratic Promise: The Populist Moment in America* (New York: Oxford University Press, 1976), 79–80. The literature on the People's Party—capital "P" Populism—of course illuminates a much more complex movement than this context allows. One strain of the historical conversation over Populism, however, concerns the class position and resultant ideology of its participants: were Populists frustrated petit bourgeois kulaks, or did they entertain—even intermittently—a more inclusive social vision? As evidence from various points in the movement's chronological and geographical evolution can support both positions, the debate turns on differences in emphasis and on estimations of the movement's legacy. For important contributions to this debate, see Goodwyn, *Democratic Promise;* John Donald Hicks, *The Populist Revolt: A History of the Farmers' Alliance and the People's Party.* (Lincoln: University of Nebraska Press, 1961); Richard Hofstadter, *The Age of Reform from Bryan to F.D.R.* (New York: Knopf, 1985); Elizabeth Sanders, *Roots of Reform: Farmers, Workers, and the American State, 1877–1917* (Chicago: University of Chicago Press, 1999); C. Vann Woodward, *Tom Watson, Agrarian Rebel* (New York: Macmillan, 1938).

27. This protest echoed the "store wars" of the late nineteenth century, when department stores took on smaller urban retail outlets, and the small-town merchants' fight against mail-order companies at the turn of the century, when "trade-at-home" campaigns fought the convenience, economy, and privacy of catalog shopping with appeals to local loyalties. The antichain movement of the 1920s and 1930s, however, eclipsed both the struggle against mail-order business and its urban cousin, the anti–department store campaign, in its unprecedented legislative and judicial success. For accounts of these earlier distribution wars, see William Leach, *Land of Desire: Merchants, Power, and the Rise of a New American Culture* (New York:

Pantheon Books, 1993), 26–32; Susan Strasser, *Satisfaction Guaranteed: The Making of the American Mass Market* (New York: Pantheon, 1989), 215–21.

28. Martin J. Sklar, *The Corporate Reconstruction of American Capitalism, 1890–1916: The Market, the Law, and Politics* (Cambridge, UK, and New York: Cambridge University Press, 1988), 49–53.

29. In tracing the development of federal regulation in the early part of the twentieth century, Sanders emphasizes Congress's substitution of discretionary bureaucratic oversight of industries for the agrarians' preferred mechanism of specific statutory limits on corporations. Sanders, *Roots of Reform: Farmers, Workers, and the American State, 1877–1917*, 268–69, 387–89. This tendency, along with political concessions to powerful industries, produced antitrust legislation that could languish for decades. For an overview of antimonopolism, see Ellis Wayne Hawley, *The New Deal and the Problem of Monopoly: A Study in Economic Ambivalence* (New York: Fordham University Press, 1995), 4–9; Sklar, *The Corporate Reconstruction of American Capitalism, 1890–1916: The Market, the Law, and Politics*, 179–332.

30. The early Grange cooperatives, for example, explicitly sought to replace available retail outlets, and themselves suffered from the competition of mail-order companies. However, early Farmers' Alliance constitutions specified that a "country merchant" could be a member, provided he demonstrated belief in a supreme being and habits of personal industry. McMath, *American Populism: A Social History, 1877–1898*, 58–61, 70.

31. On the role of rural merchants in the crop lien system, see Thomas Dionysius Clark, *Pills, Petticoats, and Plows: The Southern Country Store* (Indianapolis and New York: Bobbs-Merrill, 1944), 78–79, 313–35; Goodwyn, *Democratic Promise: The Populist Moment in America*, 26–31; C. Vann Woodward, *Origins of the New South, 1877–1913* (Baton Rouge: Louisiana State University Press, 1999), 180–88. On the effect of the Wilson-era banking acts and their origin in agrarian demands for more liberal credit, see Sanders, *Roots of Reform: Farmers, Workers, and the American State, 1877–1917*, 244–61.

32. C. Wright Mills, *White Collar: The American Middle Classes* (Oxford, UK: Oxford University Press, 1951), 21. Mills, however, argues for the small retailer as a sanitized stand-in for the "captain of industry," whose unfortunate tendency to combine praiseworthy production with suspect finance made him unworthy of the status of folk hero. Since the merchants that Wal-Mart replaced were firmly rooted in an antiurban orientation, this lineage does not convince.

33. The connection between credit and chains merits more consideration than space allows here. Texas representative Wright Patman, Congress's most tireless antichain crusader, considered chain banking the ultimate threat to local sovereignty—a view he had many opportunities to express in his more than twelve years as chairman of the House Banking and Currency Committee. Lendol Calder establishes that a pioneering form of chain organization was an illegal system of loan offices that buffered the chronic instability of industrial wage work at the price of ruinous interest rates; Lendol Glen Calder, *Financing the American Dream: A Cultural History of Consumer Credit* (Princeton, NJ: Princeton University Press, 1999), 116–19. Nor was the connection between credit and chains lost on Sam Walton. While building up his original chain of Ben Franklin stores, Walton also bought a controlling stake in the Bank of Bentonville, which subsequently handled Wal-Mart payroll and benefits; the regional bank chain Arvest is an important part of Wal-

ton Enterprises, the Walton family partnership. Bob Ortega, *In Sam We Trust: The Untold Story of Sam Walton and How Wal-Mart Is Devouring America* (New York: Times Business, 1998), 51–53, 235. Most recently, Wal-Mart has riveted the attention of the banking industry with its introduction of financial services like a house Discover card, payroll check cashing, and money wiring. While current Federal law prevents its acquisition of full banking powers, some industry observers expect the company's recent attempts to buy banks may not be its last. Wendy Zellner, "Your New Banker?" *Business Week,* February 7, 2005, 28.

34. Alfred D. Chandler, *The Visible Hand: The Managerial Revolution in American Business* (Cambridge, MA: Belknap Press of Harvard University Press, 1977), 209–39; Leach, *Land of Desire: Merchants, Power, and the Rise of a New American Culture, 29–32;* Strasser, *Satisfaction Guaranteed: The Making of the American Mass Market, 219–21.*

35. T. Eugene Beattie, "Public Relations and the Chains," *Journal of Marketing* 7, no. 3 (January 1943): 247–48; Boyce F. Martin, "The Independent, et al., Versus the Chains," *Harvard Business Review* 9, no. 1 (October 1930): 47.

36. Theodore N. Beckman and Herman Christian Nolen, *The Chain Store Problem: A Critical Analysis* (New York: McGraw-Hill, 1938), 242; Harry W. Schacter, "War on the Chain Store," *The Nation,* May 7, 1930, 544.

37. The Federal Trade Commission investigation was instigated in 1928 by Senator Smith Brookhart of Iowa; its final report appeared six years later and was the basis for the two major congressional antichain victories. Wright Patman, congressman from Texarkana, and Senate majority leader Joe Robinson of Arkansas sponsored the 1936 Robinson-Patman Act, which prohibited price discrimination between chain and independent buyers from wholesale concerns. The confused qualifications to its major provision, however, rendered it difficult to enforce and left judgment in the hands of the Federal Trade Commission. The 1937 Miller-Tydings Act—sponsored by an Arkansan and a Marylander—sought to plug the holes in the prior bill, under the banner of "fair trade." Fair trade agitation dated back to the early years of the century, and had scored a number of successes at the state level. The limitations and legal confusion produced by this pair of bills, however, led Patman to introduce the "death sentence" bill on retail chains in 1938 that would have intentionally taxed them out of business. However, by that point the chains had launched a highly coordinated defensive PR campaign, and won over significant constituencies to their side; at the hearings in 1940, the opposition was able to produce testimony from organized labor, commercial farmers, and consumers' groups, and the Patman tax died in committee. See Hawley, *The New Deal and the Problem of Monopoly: A Study in Economic Ambivalence, 262–63;* Godfrey M. Lebhar, *Chain Stores in America: 1859–1950* (New York: Chain Store Publishing, 1952), 240–76; Carl G. Ryant, "The South and the Movement Against Chain Stores," *Journal of Southern History* 39, no. 2 (May 1973): 215–18; Richard S. Tedlow, *New and Improved: The Story of Mass Marketing in America* (New York: Basic Books, 1990), 214–26.

38. Hawley, *The New Deal and the Problem of Monopoly: A Study in Economic Ambivalence, 247.* Hawley, however, considers this appeal to market controls a purely self-interested and duplicitous economic ploy on the part of farmers and merchants both; he thus underestimates the emotional power of the antitrust critique for many in the old Populist heartland.

39. On the conflation of "consumer" and "citizen," see Cohen, *A Consumer's Republic.* The conflict of interest is not actually as fundamental as it seems: efficiencies in distribution that produce low prices are themselves supported through the public purse. Only the externalizing of these costs keeps the sticker prices low. For the case in point, see Philip Mattera and Anna Purinton, *Shopping for Subsidies: How Wal-Mart Uses Taxpayer Money to Finance Its Never-Ending Growth* (Washington, DC: Good Jobs First, 2004).

40. Schacter, "War on the Chain Store," 544.

41. Edward G. Ernst and Emil M. Hartl, "Chains Versus Independents: IV. The Fighting Independents," *The Nation,* December 3, 1930, 608.

42. Edward G. Ernst and Emil M. Hartl, "Chains Versus Independents: III. Chain Management and Labor," *The Nation,* November 26, 1930, 576.

43. Edward J. Larson, *Summer for the Gods: The Scopes Trial and America's Continuing Debate Over Science and Religion* (Cambridge, MA: Harvard University Press, 1997), 27.

44. Patrick E. Gorman, "Remarks of Mr. Patrick Gorman, President, Amalgamated Meat Cutters and Butcher Workmen of North America, A.F. of L., Before the Delegates of the American Federation of Labor in Convention, Cincinnati, Ohio, Tuesday, October 10, 1939, on the Matter of the Patman Bill, Which, If Enacted, Would Levy Additional Taxes upon Chain Stores," MSS 980, Patrick E. Gorman Papers (Madison: State Historical Society of Wisconsin, 1939), 3.

45. The classic elaboration of this thesis appears in Woodward, *Origins of the New South, 1877–1913,* 291–320.

46. Joe Bonner, letter, MS R563 18, Collected Papers of Senator Joseph T. Robinson, Series 9, Subseries 2 (Fayetteville: University of Arkansas Mullins Library Special Collections, 1936).

47. Representative Wright Patman (D-Texas, First Congressional District) speaking in the 75th Cong., 3d sess., A707, and in a letter to the *Dallas News,* February 25, 1938; both quoted in Nancy Beck Young, *Wright Patman: Populism, Liberalism, and the American Dream* (Dallas: Southern Methodist University Press, 2000), 89.

48. Nancy MacLean, *Behind the Mask of Chivalry: The Making of the Second Ku Klux Klan* (New York: Oxford University Press, 1994), 77–78.

49. Amy Johnson Frykholm, *Rapture Culture: Left Behind in Evangelical America* (Oxford, UK, and New York: Oxford University Press, 2004), 126.

50. George A. McArthur, letter, MS R563 18, Collected Papers of Senator Joseph T. Robinson, Series 9, Subseries 2 (Fayetteville: University of Arkansas Special Collections, 1935). Capitalization in original.

51. Montaville Flowers, *America Chained: A Discussion of 'What's Wrong with the Chain Store?'* (Pasadena, CA: Montaville Flowers Publicists, 1931), 280–81.

52. "Mr. Pro," "Shall We Curb the Chain Stores? Mr. Pro Attacks the Chains," *Reader's Digest,* December 1938, 29; reprinted in Daniel Bloomfield, *Chain Stores and Legislation* (New York: H.W. Wilson, 1939), 29.

53. MacLean, *Behind the Mask of Chivalry,* 77.

54. J.M. Egan, letter, MS R563 18, Collected Papers of Senator Joseph T. Robinson, Series 9, Subseries 2 (Fayetteville: University of Arkansas Special Collections, 1936).

55. Roland Marchand, *Creating the Corporate Soul: The Rise of Public Relations and Corporate Imagery in American Big Business* (Berkeley: University of California Press, 1998), 140–41, 185.

56. I am indebted to Julia Ott Vermillion for this point.

57. Ernest Dumas, "Government 'Partner' of Brothers," *Arkansas Gazette,* June 28, 1977, 1A, 5A.

58. Sam Walton and John Huey, *Sam Walton, Made in America: My Story* (New York: Doubleday, 1992), 6.

59. The earliest Walton discount stores bore this name.

60. Strictly speaking, Walton was not by birth an Ozarker at all, having been born in Kingfisher, Oklahoma; he is most often described as a midwesterner, albeit naturalized.

61. Ortega, *In Sam We Trust,* 16–19.

62. Austin Teutsch, *The Sam Walton Story* (New York: Berkley Books, 1991), 28.

63. Robert F. Hartley, *Marketing Mistakes* (New York: John Wiley & Sons, 1995), 264.

64. Robert Slater, *The Wal-Mart Decade: How a Generation of Leaders Turned Sam Walton's Legacy into the World's #1 Company* (New York: Portfolio, 2003), 24.

65. Teutsch, *The Sam Walton Story,* 13.

66. Mindy Fetterman, "USA's Richest Person; Media Mogul John Kluge Tops List at $5.2 Billion; New No. 1 Ushers In 'Grand' Style," *USA Today,* October 10, 1989, 1A.

67. http://www.walmartwatch.com.

68. Ellen Neuborne, "Book Promotions Hit Small Towns," *USA Today,* June 16, 1992, 5B.

69. Billie Letts, *Where the Heart Is* (New York: Warner Books, 1998).

70. Jacalyn Carfagno, "Walton Biography Thin on Drama," *USA Today,* November 21, 1990, 11B.

71. Fetterman, "USA's Richest Person," 1A.

72. James Kindall, "Searching for Uncle Sam," *Star* [Weekly Insert of *Kansas City Star*], December 16, 1984, 13.

73. Tonya McKiever, "Center Greeter Knows His Stuff," *[Benton County] Daily Record,* June 6, 1997, 8A.

74. Lebhar, *Chain Stores in America: 1859–1950,* 21, 26, 30.

75. Bloomfield, *Chain Stores and Legislation,* 206–14; Ernest Hugh Shideler, "The Chain Store: A Study of the Ecological Organization of a Modern City" (Ph.D. diss., University of Chicago, 1927), chap, 6, 16–19; "Shall We Affiliate with Profit Business?" *Cooperation* 15 (December 1929): 222.

76. Shideler, "The Chain Store," chap. 6, 7–8. For an overview of Butler Brothers and its relationship to Wal-Mart, see Sandra S. Vance and Roy V. Scott, "Butler Brothers and the Rise and Decline of the Ben Franklin Stores: A Study in Francise Retailing," *Essays in Economic and Business History: Selected Papers from the Economic and Business Historical Society* 11 (1993): 258–71. The authors deserve appreciation as well for two standard reference works on Wal-Mart, written before most other academic observers caught on: "Sam Walton and Wal-Mart Stores, Inc.: A Study in Modern Southern Entrepreneurship," *Journal of Southern History* 58, no. 2 (May 1992): 231–52; and *Wal-Mart: A History of Sam Walton's Retail Phenomenon* (New York: Twayne, 1994).

77. Strasser, *Satisfaction Guaranteed: The Making of the American Mass Market,* 235, 246.

78. Terry Webster Shroyer, "An Analysis of the Control Policies Used in a Voluntary Variety Store Chain Through the Study of Twenty-five Ben Franklin Stores in Eastern Colorado" (master's thesis, University of Colorado, 1957), 1.

79. Todd Mason and Marc Frons, "Sam Walton of Wal-Mart: Just Your Basic Homespun Millionaire," *Business Week,* October 14, 1985, 143; Howard Rudnitsky, "How Sam Walton Does It," *Forbes,* August 16, 1982, 42.

80. In addition to the Ben Franklins, the Waltons eventually experimented with various nonfranchised formats before settling on the Wal-Mart Discount City as the paradigmatic store. Ortega, *In Sam We Trust,* 49–56.

81. Hawley, *The New Deal and the Problem of Monopoly: A Study in Economic Ambivalence,* 248.

82. Nancy F. Cott, *Public Vows: A History of Marriage and the Nation* (Cambridge, MA: Harvard University Press, 2000), 168–69.

83. I make the assertions in this section based in part on many conversations, formal and informal, graciously granted me by early and long-term employees of Wal-Mart; for details see Moreton, *Wal-Mart World.* Such a nonscientific sample is of course self-selected to some extent: only those who were reasonably content with their work stayed for the long haul, and in the current climate of negative attention to the company, those who feel moved to defend it are likely to become more vocal. On a practical level, as many former Wal-Mart employees themselves point out, the company's explosive growth during the seventies and eighties meant that the stock-ownership and profit-sharing programs offered significant benefits that have no current parallel. And indeed the labor-liberal critique of the company has scored significant hits in recent years, with the class-action gender discrimination lawsuit (of which more below) and the revelations of public subsidy ranking as the most successful arguing points; see Liza Featherstone, *Selling Women Short: The Landmark Battle for Workers' Rights at Wal-Mart* (New York: Basic Books, 2004); Mattera and Purinton, *Shopping for Subsidies;* George Miller et al., "Everyday Low Wages: The Price We All Pay for Wal-Mart; a Report by the Democratic Staff of the Committee on Education and the Workforce, U.S. House of Representative, Representative George Miller (D-CA), Senior Democrat" (2002), http://edworkforce.house .gov/democrats/WALMARTREPORT.pdf. But Wal-Mart observers who ignore the testimony of loyalists risk an outrageous condescension to many of those they understand themselves to champion; as film director Oliver Stone said of the winning presidential candidate in the 2004 election, "He's worse than Nixon in his vulgarity. He looks like he shops at Wal-Mart. That's not what the president is supposed to be." Jeannette Walls, "Defending 'Alexander' " (2004), http://msnbc.msn.com/id/6234210/. Evidently many disagreed.

84. Nor is the simile unique: see Jacquelyn Dowd Hall et al., *Like a Family: The Making of a Southern Cotton Mill World* (Chapel Hill: University of North Carolina Press, 1987).

85. Caught by the U.S. Department of Labor paying sub-minimum wages in the 1950s, Walton unsuccessfully argued that each store should be considered an individual business, in itself too small to qualify for the regulations. Ortega, *In Sam We Trust,* 86–87. It is worth noting that the company is currently using the

same logic to dispute the validity of the class-action gender discrimination lawsuit *Dukes v. Wal-Mart Stores, Inc.* Aaron Bernstein, "Wal-Mart vs. Class Actions," *Business Week,* March 21, 2005, 73.

86. For an accessible critique of neoliberal economic assumptions, see Gordon Bigelow, "Let There Be Markets: The Evangelical Roots of Economics," *Harper's Magazine,* May 2005, 33–38.

87. This argument—again, treated in greater detail in Moreton, "Wal-Mart World"—draws heavily on the brilliant exegesis in Linda Kintz, *Between Jesus and the Market: The Emotions That Matter in Right-Wing America* (Durham, NC: Duke University Press, 1997). See also Susan Friend Harding, *The Book of Jerry Falwell: Fundamentalist Language and Politics* (Princeton, NJ: Princeton University Press, 2000); Michael Lienesch, *Redeeming America: Piety and Politics in the New Christian Right* (Chapel Hill: University of North Carolina Press, 1993); and Kristin Luker, *Abortion and the Politics of Motherhood* (Berkeley: University of California Press, 1984). This is emphatically *not* to imply that a conservative political orientation has been ubiquitous among Wal-Mart employees or Ozarkers generally; rather, attention is drawn to the prestige of women's emotional labor in a Christian cosmology whose gender arrangements frankly bewilder many secular observers.

88. Lee Scott, "Speech to Town Hall L.A." (Omni Hotel, Los Angeles, 2005).

89. Undoubtedly, the nation's weak labor laws and disgraceful under-enforcement of the few protections that do exist go far in explaining the decline of unionization in general and its complete failure at Wal-Mart in particular. Moreover, the company's own ferocious dissuasion of employee organization is notable even in the current anti-union climate. But these explanations do not entirely account for the marked inability of unions to appeal to Wal-Mart's original employee base, especially given that in the year that the first Wal-Mart opened, the retail union was the fastest-growing labor organization in the country; nor do they explain the many working women who historically have not been attracted to a liberal vision of workplace gender equity. For various perspectives on aspects of the postwar decline in American unions, see Elizabeth A. Fones-Wolf, *Selling Free Enterprise: The Business Assault on Labor and Liberalism, 1945–60* (Urbana: University of Illinois Press, 1994); Steve Fraser, "The 'Labor Question,' " in *The Rise and Fall of the New Deal Order, 1930–1980,* ed. Steve Fraser and Gary Gerstle (Princeton, NJ: Princeton University Press, 1989), 55–84; Lichtenstein, *State of the Union;* Kim Moody, *An Injury to All: The Decline of American Unionism* (New York: Verso, 1988); Bruce Nelson, *Divided We Stand: American Workers and the Struggle for Black Equality* (Princeton, NJ: Princeton University Press, 2001); for an attempt to address these conundra in the Wal-Mart context, see Moreton, *Wal-Mart World.*

90. This sex-based labor segmentation was hardly unique to the postwar service economy; indeed, it underwrote much of both management and labor ideology throughout American history. See, for example, Lawrence B. Glickman, *A Living Wage: American Workers and the Making of Consumer Society* (Ithaca, NY: Cornell University Press, 1997); Alice Kessler-Harris, *Out to Work: A History of Wage-Earning Women in the United States* (Oxford: Oxford University Press, 1982); Martha May, "Bread Before Roses: American Workingmen, Labor Unions, and the Family Wage," in *Women, Work, and Protest: A Century of U.S. Women's Labor History,* ed. Ruth Milkman (Boston: Routledge & Kegan Paul, 1985), 1–21; and Ruth Milkman, *Gender at Work.* However, it was only with the postwar entry of large numbers of married women into waged

work that the male-management, female-labor structure could grow to produce its own rival to Ford, GM, or ExxonMobil.

91. June Percival, "Store Happenings," *Wal-Mart World* LI, September 1975, 11.

92. Marc Bendick Jr., "The Representation of Women in Store Management at Wal-Mart Stores, Inc.," plaintiff's expert report, *Dukes v. Wal-Mart Stores, Inc.* (Washington, DC, January 2003), VIII:53–54, http://www.walmartclass.com/walmartclass_forthepress.html. Another report asserts, "Women employees at Wal-Mart are concentrated in the lower paying jobs, are paid less than men in the same job, and are less likely to advance to management positions than men. These gender patterns persist even though women have more seniority, have lower turnover rates, and have higher performance ratings in most jobs. The shortfalls in female earnings, pay rates, and promotion rates have a high degree of statistical significance." Richard Drogin, "Statistical Analysis of Gender Patterns in Wal-Mart Workforce," plaintiff's expert report, *Dukes v. Wal-Mart Stores, Inc.* (Berkeley, CA, February 2003), 46, http://www.walmartclass.com/walmart class_forthepress.html. Additional documents from the case are posted at www.walmartclass.com; an overview of *Dukes v. Wal-Mart, Inc.* is provided by Liza Featherstone, *Selling Women Short*.

93. "Wal-Mart Stores, Inc., the Nation's Largest Private Employer, Sued for Company-Wide Sex Discrimination," press release, http://www.walmartclass.com/walmartclass_forthepress.html.

94. Sassen, *Globalization and Its Discontents,* 91. Since the hidden half of the Wal-Mart service economy is the relocated production in low-wage countries, Sassen's wide-ranging analysis is actually much more fruitfully applied to "Wal-Martism" in the full context of its suppliers; however, space here does not permit elaboration. For a brief account of Wal-Mart use of sweatshop labor in the 1990s, see Ortega, *In Sam We Trust,* 318–45.

95. Stephanie McCurry, *Masters of Small Worlds: Yeoman Households, Gender Relations, and the Political Culture of the Antebellum South Carolina Low Country* (New York: Oxford University Press, 1995).

FOUR Growth Through Knowledge: Wal-Mart, High Technology, and the Ever Less Visible Hand of the Manager
James Hoopes

1. James Hoopes, *False Prophets: The Gurus Who Created Modern Management and Why Their Ideas Are Bad for Business Today* (Cambridge, MA: Perseus, 2003), chap. 5.

2. Ronald Coase, "The Nature of the Firm," *Readings in Price Theory,* selected by a Committee of the American Economic Association (Chicago: Richard D. Irwin, 1952), 333.

3. Alfred D. Chandler, *The Visible Hand: The Managerial Revolution in American Business* (Cambridge, MA: Harvard University Press, 1977), 490.

4. Michael Bergdahl, *What I Learned from Sam Walton: How to Compete and Thrive in a Wal-Mart World* (New York: John Wiley & Sons, 2004), 136.

5. Ibid., 135.

6. Virginia Postrel, "Economic Scene," *New York Times,* February 28, 2002.

7. Frances Cairncross, *The Company of the Future: Meeting the Management Challenges of the Communications Revolution* (Boston: Harvard Business School Press, 2002), 138.

8. Charles Fishman, "The Wal-Mart You Don't Know," *Fast Company,* December 2003, 168.

9. Christine Spivey Overby, "Wal-Mart Wins with Data Standards," *Forrester,* http://www.forrester.com, accessed June 17, 2004.

10. Michael Bergdahl, *What I Learned from Sam Walton,* 114–15.

11. Richard S. Tedlow, *Giants of Enterprise: Seven Business Innovators and the Empires They Built* (New York: Harper Business, 2001), 335.

12. Bergdahl, *What I Learned from Sam Walton,* 61.

13. Report by the Democratic Staff of the Committee on Education and the Workforce, U.S. House of Representatives, "Everyday Low Wages: The Hidden Price We All Pay for Wal-Mart," http://edworkforce.house.gov/democrats/WALMARTREPORT.pdf, accessed May 29, 2004.

14. Barbara Ehrenreich, *Nickel and Dimed: On (Not) Getting By in America* (New York: Metropolitan Books, 2001), 145.

15. Thomas W. Malone, *The Future of Work: How the New Order of Business Will Shape Your Organization, Your Management Style, and Your Life* (Boston: Harvard Business School Press, 2004), 55, 36.

16. Nelson Lichtenstein and Howell John Harris, eds., *Industrial Democracy in America: The Ambiguous Promise* (Cambridge, UK, and New York: Cambridge University Press, 1993).

17. Chuck Bartels, "Wal-Mart Plans Increase in Pay, Women Managers," Associated Press, Myrtle Beach *Sun News,* http://www.myrtlebeachonline.com, accessed June 17, 2004.

18. "A New Pay Scheme at Wal-Mart," *Business Week Online,* http://www.businessweek.com/bwdaily/dnflash/jun2004/nf2004063_3 893_db016.htm, accessed June 17, 2004.

19. Liza Featherstone, "Will Labor Take the Wal-Mart Challenge?" *The Nation,* http://thenation.com, accessed June 17, 2004.

FIVE Making Global Markets: Wal-Mart and Its Suppliers
Misha Petrovic and Gary G. Hamilton

We wish to acknowledge that the research on the retail industry reported in this chapter has been supported by the Committee for Industry Studies at the Sloan Foundation. We also wish to thank Elif Andac and Deenesh Sohoni for their comments on an earlier draft.

1. Most recent discussions of the Wal-Mart effect cite McKinsey & Company's 2001 study, *The U.S. Productivity Growth, 1995–2000,* http://www.mckinsey.com/mgi/reports/pdfs/productivity/usprod.pdf, which attributes 12 percent of the economy-wide productivity gains to Wal-Mart's drive for efficiency.

2. For a typical popular summary of such criticism see "Is Wal-Mart Too Powerful?" *Business Week,* October 6, 2003, 100.

3. Since we focus mostly on the making of supplier markets, we skip the discussion of the rise of "con-

sumer power" and the concomitant changes in consumer markets. We should note, however, that the increase in consumer power, as defined by the increased sensitivity of both retailers and manufacturers to consumer demand, was brought about mainly by the changes in industrial structure and the general increase in competition, as well as by the development of more efficient tools for assessing consumer preferences, and not by changes in consumer behavior or bargaining power. The so-called increase in consumer power, in other words, simply describes the increased efficiency of consumer goods markets.

4. For a good review of these arguments see Kusum L. Ailawadi, "The Retail Power-Performance Conundrum: What Have We Learned?" *Journal of Retailing* 77 (2001): 299–318.

5. Ibid.; see also Paul N. Bloom and Vanessa G. Perry, "Retailer Power and Supplier Welfare: The Case of Wal-Mart," *Journal of Retailing* 77 (2001): 379–96. Other indicators of retail power have been proposed, such as the increase in slotting allowances and similar forms of trade promotion, as well as the increase in the share of store brands, but in the absence of the profitability differential, it is not clear whether and how these indicators translate directly into market power.

6. Gary Gereffi's concept of buyer-driven supply chains was one of the first steps toward recognizing the global development impact of American retailers and brand-name merchandisers (see for example Gary Gereffi, "The Organization of Buyer-Driven Global Commodity Chains: How U.S. Retailers Shape Overseas Production Networks," in *Commodity Chains and Global Capitalism*, ed. Gary Gereffi and Miguel Korzeniewicz (Westport, CT: Praeger, 1994), 95–122. The linkages between the U.S. "retail revolution" and the Asian miracle are explored in more detail in Robert C. Feenstra and Gary G. Hamilton, *Emergent Economies, Divergent Paths: Economic Organization and International Trade in South Korea and Taiwan.* (New York: Cambridge University Press, 2005).

7. The first Woolco unit opened in June 1962 in Columbus, Ohio, an imposing one-hundred-thousand-square-foot store with a line of departments closely resembling the full-service department store and carrying mostly nationally advertised merchandise. Godfrey Lebhar, *Chain Stores in America, 1859–1962* (New York: Chain Store Publishing, 1963).

8. Barger's calculations show retail margins to be around 18 percent and declining for the supermarkets. See Harold Barger, *Distribution's Place in the American Economy Since 1869* (Princeton, NJ: Princeton University Press, 1955).

9. Ibid.; Kmart by itself accounted for 25 percent. All three retailers combined were still smaller than Sears. Only ten years later, Wal-Mart would pass Sears to become the biggest retailer in the world.

10. "1982 to 1992: Clubs and Category Killers Arrive on the Scene," *DSN Retailing Today,* August 2002.

11. Allied, Federated, Carter Hawley Hale, and Macy's all filed for bankruptcy in this period, as did many regional and specialty chains. At one point in the early 1990s more than one-quarter of the total department store retail space was under Chapter 11 proceedings. James R. Eckmann, "The Future of Retailing," in *The Retail Industry,* ed. Charles Ingene (Charlottesville, VA: AIMR, 1993), 32–34.

12. Hank Gilman, "The Most Underrated CEO Ever—an Interview with David Glass," *Fortune,* April 15, 2004, 242.

13. In general, the use of computers in manufacturing predated their use in retailing by almost two de-

cades. See James W. Cortada, *The Digital Hand: How Computers Changed the Work of American Manufacturing, Transportation, and Retail Industries* (New York: Oxford University Press, 2004). However, as we will see shortly, the initiatives to use computers for developing interorganizational links in the supply chain typically flowed from the retail industry to the suppliers. Moreover, the retail industry has, arguably, been transformed much more drastically by the implementation of IT than any other sector of the U.S. economy, with the possible exception of trucking.

14. Frederick H. Abernathy, John T. Dunlop, Janice H. Hammond, and David Weil, *A Stitch in Time: Lean Retailing and the Transformation of Manufacturing—Lessons from the Apparel and Textile Industries* (New York: Oxford University Press, 1999); Cortada, *Digital Hand*; in 1978, only 1 percent of grocery stores nationwide had bar code scanners installed, but these were the most progressive chain stores. By 1981, the proportion had climbed to 10 percent, representing the majority of big supermarket chains.

15. "Wanding: Slow, Steady Progress," *Chain Store Age Executive with Shopping Center Age,* June 1978, 33.

16. The concentration in the grocery sector stayed low throughout the period—the revenue share of the top twenty chains increased from 35 percent to only 37 percent between 1972 and 1987. Major merger and consolidation attempts were rare before the 1990s, as most chains relied on debt financing through leveraged buyouts and recapitalization as core growth strategies. In terms of direct competition, "peripheral markets were sacrificed and what commentators described as the 'geography of avoidance' or policies of competitive forbearance were practiced. . . . Overlapping geographic areas between the three major competitors were profoundly circumscribed. Only in 6 of 54 Grocery Manufacturers of America areas did the three major players (Kroger, Safeway, and American Stores) choose to compete with each other." Andrew Seth and Geoffrey Randall, *The Grocers: The Rise and Rise of the Supermarket Chains* (London: Kogan Page, 2001), 196.

17. Bob L. Martin, "From Vision to Reality," in *Twenty-five Years Behind Bars,* ed. Alan L. Haberman (Cambridge, MA: Harvard University Press), 39.

18. Ibid.

19. Abernathy et al., *A Stitch in Time.*

20. Philip B. Schary and Tage Skjott-Larsen, *Managing the Global Supply Chain* (Copenhagen: Handelshojskolens Forlag, 1998), 20–21.

21. Feenstra and Hamilton, *Emergent Economies.*

22. Cheng-shu Kao and Gary G. Hamilton, "Reflexive Manufacturing: Taiwan's Integration in the Global Economy," *International Studies Review* 3, no. 1 (June 2000): 1–19.

23. Kozo Yamamura and Walter Hatch, *Asia in Japan's Embrace: Building a Regional Production Alliance* (New York: Cambridge University Press, 1996).

24. This led to the emergence of U.S.-based computer firms, such as Dell (1984) and Gateway (1985), that from the beginning relied exclusively on Asian manufacturing.

25. The *Wall Street Journal* and *New York Times* ran several articles in the late 1980s, denouncing Wal-

Mart's impact on small towns. The referendum in Steamboat Springs, Colorado, in 1989 was perhaps the first organized *community* action against opening a Wal-Mart store. More frequently in those days, however, the press and local communities lamented the closing rather than the opening of Wal-Mart stores. Sandra S. Vance and Roy V. Scott, *Wal-Mart: A History of Sam Walton's Retail Phenomenon* (New York: Twayne, 1994), 153.

26. Wal-Mart Stores Inc., *Annual Report 1993.*

27. The expression was used by Stephen Kotvis, a retail consultant, in his research on Kmart and Wal-Mart location strategies in the early 1990s, quoted in Tibbett Speer, "Where Will Wal-Mart Strike Next?" *American Demographics,* August 1994, 11.

28. Wal-Mart was far from being a pioneer of direct buying from its foreign suppliers. As late as 1995, only 6 percent of its merchandise was bought directly from foreign suppliers, while likely more than 50 percent of merchandise on its shelves, and over 80 percent in apparel, toys, and similar categories, was not produced domestically. Even today, when the news of Wal-Mart buying $18 billion of merchandise in China frequently makes headlines, we should keep in mind that this amount, however large in absolute terms, still represents well under 10 percent of its total merchandise purchases.

29. Quoted by Sam Hornblower, "Wal-Mart and China: A Joint Venture," http://www.pbs.org/wgbh/pages/frontline/shows/walmart/secre ts/wmchina.html (accessed January 10, 2005).

30. In the U.S. this was partly a result of the segmentation of national mass media during the 1990s, which made building brand awareness through national advertising a much more costly proposition. Thus, a recent study by the Willard Bishop Consulting Agency "found that in 1995 it took three TV commercials to reach 80% of 18- to 49-year-old women. In 2000, just five years later, it took 97 ads to reach the same group" (quoted in Matthew Boyle, "Brand Killers," *Fortune,* August 11, 2003, 89). At the global level, of course, even fewer manufacturers can afford to maintain brand awareness through direct advertising.

31. For example, Wal-Mart recently warned major music labels that unless they drastically lowered the price of their CDs, it would cut back on the amount of music it sold. On the retailer's side, such a step would sacrifice less than 2 percent of its total revenues, but for the music industry it would mean losing nearly 20 percent of its sales. Warren Cohen, "Wal-Mart Wants $10 CDs: Biggest U.S. Record Retailer Battles Record Labels Over Prices," *Rolling Stone,* October 12, 2004.

32. These dimensions correspond to two main advantages of working with Wal-Mart that the retailer's existing vendors typically list in business surveys: the transparency of its business strategy in creating relationships with its suppliers, and the relentless pressure for logistic and operational efficiency (see, for example, Cannondale Associates' annual surveys of manufacturers, www.cannondaleassoc.com/press.asp).

33. Commenting on the dispute with the music industry referred to by Gary Severson, Wal-Mart's general merchandise manager in charge of the chain's entertainment section, specified: "The labels price things based on what they believe they can get—a pricing philosophy a lot of industries have. . . . But we like to price things as cheaply as we possibly can, rather than charge as much as we can get. It's a big difference in philosophy, and we try to help other people see that" (Cohen, "Wal-Mart Wants $10 CDs").

34. One element of contracting that is often emphasized by Wal-Mart in its dealings with large vendors of packaged consumer goods is the exclusivity clause, which requires that certain new products would be made exclusively for Wal-Mart either permanently or, more commonly, for a period of time, before they are sold to other retailers. Recently, however, a Wal-Mart spokesman announced that those deals will be reduced to fewer products and a maximum of a few months. Jack Neff, "Wal-Mart Weans Suppliers," *Advertising Age,* Midwest region edition, December 1, 2003, 1.

35. Charles Fishman, "The Wal-Mart You Don't Know," *Fast Company,* December 2003, 68.

36. Dawn Wilensky, "Ever-Shrinking Margins Unnerve Some Wal-Mart Vendors," *Discount Store News,* December 5, 1994, 103.

37. In a recent presentation, Linda Dillman, Wal-Mart's executive VP and CIO, specified that "inventory data is maintained on more than 693 million items, 335 million of which are reviewed every day to see if they need to be reordered." Dan Scheraga, "What Makes Wal-Mart Tick," *Chain Store Age,* March 2004, 49.

38. For example, product packaging is many times adapted to shelf dimensions rather than vice versa. Packaging may also be required to include similar graphic solution on multiple sides so that errors in positioning the product on the shelf are minimized. Apparel items may need to be outfitted with hangers. In general, having "floor-ready merchandise" relates most directly to minimizing the operational complexity and cost of moving the merchandise from the back room to the shelf.

39. An excellent discussion of these long-term historical trends can be found in Louis P. Bucklin, *Competition and Evolution in Distributive Trades* (Englewood Cliffs, NJ: Prentice-Hall, 1972).

40. When it moved full force into grocery retailing in the early 1990s, Wal-Mart also acquired a grocery wholesale business, McLane Company, which sold to convenience stores and independent grocers. There is no doubt that Wal-Mart's own grocery buyers benefited significantly from the interaction with this experienced grocery wholesaler. McLane was sold in 2003.

41. In terms of the proportion of store brands, Wal-Mart is behind Target (50 percent total, 80 percent in apparel) and Sears (55 percent, down from over 90 percent throughout most of the twentieth century) but ahead of major supermarket and drugstore chains.

42. "Vendor Partnerships Enhance Produce Quality and Pipeline Efficiency," *DSN Retailing Today,* June 2001, 14.

43. Ibid.

SIX The Wal-Mart Effect and the New Face of Capitalism: Labor Market
and Community Impacts of the Megaretailer
David Karjanen

309

NOTES TO PAGES 143–47

1. Le Corbusier, *The Radiant City* (New York: Viking Press, 1970), 70.

2. For an excellent discussion of much of the research on the effects of Wal-Mart on communities, see the 2004 Bay Area Economic Reform Report by Marlon Boarnet and Randall Crane, "Supercenters and the Transformation of the Bay Area Grocery Industry: Issues, Trends, and Impacts" (Oakland: Association of Bay Area Governments, 2004).

3. Herbert Gutman, "Work, Culture, and Society in Industrializing America, 1815–1919," *American Historical Review* 78 (1973): 531–88; see also Olivier Zunz, *The Changing Face of Inequality: Urbanization, Industrial Development and Immigrants in Detroit, 1880–1920* (Chicago: University of Chicago Press, 1983), and Thomas Segrue, "The Structures of Urban Poverty: The Reorganization of Space and Work in Three Periods of American History," in *The Underclass Debate: Views from History*, ed. Michael Katz (Princeton: Princeton University Press, 1993), 85–99.

4. William Cronon, *Nature's Metropolis: Chicago and the Great West* (New York: W.W. Norton, 1992).

5. June Nash, *From Tank Town to High Tech: The Clash of Community and Industrial Cycles* (Albany: State University of New York Press, 1989).

6. Patrick Reagan, *Designing a New America: the Origins of New Deal Planning, 1890–1943* (Boston: University of Massachusetts Press, 2000); Masahisa Fujita and Jacques-Francois Thisse, *Economics of Agglomeration: Cities, Industrial Location, and Regional Growth* (Cambridge, UK: Cambridge University Press, 2002).

7. For a discussion of flexible accumulation, see David Harvey, *The Condition of Postmodernity* (Baltimore: Johns Hopkins University Press, 1989); and for an excellent discussion of the effects of globalization on both labor markets and states, see Ankie Hoogvelt, *Globalization and the Postcolonial World* (Baltimore: Johns Hopkins University Press 1999). See also the essays by Thomas Jessen Adams and Bethany Moreton in this volume.

8. Joseph Perskey and Wim Wievel, *When Corporations Leave Town: The Costs and Benefits of Metropolitan Sprawl* (Detroit: Wayne State University Press, 2000). See also Neil Smith, *The New Urban Frontier: Gentrification and the Revanchist City* (New York: Routledge, 1996).

9. Manuel Castells, *The Informational City: Information Technology, Economic Restructuring and the Urban-Regional Process* (Oxford: Basil Blackwell, 1989). See also Owen D. Gutfreund, *Twentieth Century Sprawl: Highways and the Reshaping of the American Landscape* (Oxford, UK: Oxford University Press, 2003).

10. Eric Avila, *Popular Culture in the Age of White Flight: Fear and Fantasy in Suburban Los Angeles* (Berkeley: University of California Press, 2004).

11. William Julius Wilson, *When Work Disappears: The World of the New Urban Poor* (New York: Vintage Press, 1997); for a discussion of the urban poor, see also Douglas S. Massey and Nancy A. Denton,

American Apartheid: Segregation and the Making of the Underclass (Cambridge, MA: Harvard University Press, 1994), which describes the intersection between spatial inequalities and economic inequalities.

12. Saskia Sassen, *Global Cities* (New York: Columbia University Press, 1991).

13. See Alan Lipietz, "Rethinking Social Housing in the Hour-Glass Society," in *Social Exclusion in European Cities,* ed. Ali Madanipour, Goran Cars, and Judith Allen (London: Regional Studies Association, 1998), 177–88, and Erik Olin Wright and Rachel Dwyer, "The Patterns of Job Expansions in the United States, a Comparison of the 1960s and 1990s," unpublished manuscript, Department of Sociology, University of Wisconsin–Madison, 2003.

14. U.S. Bureau of Labor Statistics, Occupational and Employment Survey Data, Panel Years 1964–2003.

15. Ibid.

16. Annette Bernhardt, "The Future of Low-Wage Jobs: Case Studies in the Retail Industry," Institute on Education and the Economy Working Paper no. 10, Columbia University, March 1999.

17. See Alexander Vias, "Bigger Stores, More Stores, or No Stores: Paths of Retail Restructuring in Rural America," *Journal of Rural Studies* 20, no. 3 (2003): 303–18.

18. Kenneth Stone, "Impact of Wal-Mart Stores and Other Mass Merchandisers in Iowa, 1983–1993," *Economic Development Review,* Spring 1995.

19. Kenneth E. Stone, Georgeanne Artz, and Albert Myles, *The Economic Impact of Wal-Mart Supercenters on Existing Businesses in Mississippi* (Starkville, MS: Mississippi State Extension Office, 1999).

20. Institute for Local Self Reliance, "The Economic Impact of Locally Owned Businesses vs. Chains: A Case Study in Midcoast Maine," unpublished manuscript, 2003.

21. Angelou Economics, "The Economic Impact of Chain and Discount Stores on Local Businesses in Maine," unpublished manuscript, 2003.

22. Mark Fitzgerald, "Monster in a Box," *Editor & Publisher,* May 27, 2002, 8.

23. Matthew Grimm, "Wal-Mart's New Offensive," *Brandweek,* February 7, 2005, 23.

24. See the 2004 Bay Area Economic Forum Report, "Supercenters and the Transformation of the Bay Area Grocery Industry: Issues, Trends, and Impacts" (Oakland: Association of Bay Area Governments) for an excellent review of the research to date.

25. Jennifer Steinhauer, "Whatever Happened to Service?" New York Times, March 4, 1997, D1.

26. Edward Shils, "Measuring the Economic and Sociological Impact of the Mega-Retail Discount Chains on Small Enterprise in Urban, Suburban, and Rural Communities," unpublished manuscript, 1997; Thomas Muller and Elizabeth Humstone, *What Happened When Wal-Mart Came to Town? A Report on Three Iowa Communities with a Statistical Analysis of Seven Iowa Counties,* research report (National Trust for Historic Preservation, 1996). In September 2000, Wal-Mart was hit with three separate charges of predatory pricing. Government officials in Wisconsin and Germany accused the retailer of pricing goods below cost with an intent to drive competitors out of the market. In Oklahoma, Wal-Mart faces a private lawsuit alleging similar illegal pricing practices. See Associated Press, "Grocer Accuses Wal-Mart of Predatory Pricing," May 18, 2005.

27. See Julie Morris, "Store Shuts Doors on Texas Town: Economic Blow for Community," *USA Today,* October 11, 1990, 3A.

28. Emek Basker, "Job Creation or Destruction? Labor-Market Effects of Wal-Mart Expansion," unpublished manuscript, January 2004; see also Shils, Measuring the Economic and Sociological Impact of the Mega-Retail Discount Chains"; Kenneth E. Stone, "Impact of Wal-Mart Stores on Iowa Communities," *Economic Development Review,* Spring 1995, 60–69. G.M. Artz and J.C. McConnon Jr., "The Impact of Wal-Mart on Host Towns and Surrounding Communities in Maine," paper presented at the National Association of Real Estate Appraisers Meeting, Bar Harbor, ME, June 10–12, 2001.

29. Boarnet and Crane, "Supercenters and the Transformation of the Bay Area Grocery Industry."

30. In an excellent statewide study of Maine, Brian A. Ketchum and James W. Hughes, "Wal-Mart and Maine: The Effect on Employment and Wages, unpublished manuscript, 1997, the authors found that there was very little change in either wages or retail employment in counties that had Wal-Marts enter them.

31. Lee Scott, "Wal-Mart's Impact on Society: A Key Moment in Time for American Capitalism," *New York Review of Books,* April 7, 2005, 6–7. At the same time Wal-Mart admits that "only seven percent of our hourly associates are trying to support a family with children on their single Wal-Mart income."

32. Boarnet and Crane, "Supercenters and the Transformation of the Bay Area Grocery Industry," 39–40.

33. Arindrajit Dube and Ken Jacobs, "Hidden Cost of Wal-Mart Jobs: Use of Safety Net Programs by Wal-Mart Workers in California," UC Berkeley Labor Center, Briefing Paper, August 2, 2004.

34. Luis Rea and Richard Parker, "The Potential Economic and Fiscal Impact of Supercenters in San Diego; A Critical Analysis," Rea and Parker Research report, San Diego, 1998.

35. Boarnet and Crane, "Supercenters and the Transformation of the Bay Area Grocery Industry."

36. Dube and Jacobs, "Hidden Costs of Wal-Mart Jobs."

37. George Miller, "Everyday Low Wages: The Hidden Price We All Pay for Wal-Mart," report by the Democratic Staff of the Committee on Education and the Workforce, U.S. House of Representatives, February 16, 2004.

38. Good Jobs First, "Disclosures of Employers Whose Workers and Their Dependents Are Using State Health Insurance Programs," updated March 25, 2005, at http://goodjobsfirst.org/.

39. Data on sales per square foot for various retailers are available from Securities and Exchange Commission filings, or business information systems companies such as Hoover's or Dun and Bradstreet. For Wal-Mart, the figure of $325 per square foot is a typical estimate, and the figure was derived from http://www.Bizstats.com, accessed July 2003.

40. Boarnet and Crane, "Supercenters and the Transformation of the Bay Area Grocery Industry."

41. See Paul Lewis and Elisa Barbour, "Development Priorities in California Cities: Results from a PPIC Survey," Public Policy Institute of California, Oakland, 1998.

42. Al Norman provides a discussion of this apparent tactic in his book *Slam Dunking Wal-Mart: How You Can Stop Superstore Sprawl in Your Hometown* (Atlantic City, NJ: Raphael, 1997).

43. Boarnet and Crane, "Supercenters and the Transformation of the Bay Area Grocery Industry."

44. The United States as a retail market area already has an oversupply of retailing, and may in fact have reached market saturation of retailers in the late 1990s. See *National Retail Market Analysis* (Washington, DC: National Retailers Association, 2002).

45. Los Angeles Economic Development Corporation, "Wal-Mart and the Southern California Economy: What's in Store?" research report, Los Angeles, 2004.

46. See David Karjanen and Murtaza Baxamusa, "Subsidizing Wal-Mart," Center on Policy Initiatives, San Diego, 2003.

47. Theresa Burney, "High Court Hears Wal-Mart Tax Case," *St. Petersburg Times,* March 6, 2002.

48. Philip Mattera and Anna Purinton, "Shopping for Subsidies: How Wal-Mart Uses Taxpayer Money to Finance Its Never-Ending Growth," Good Jobs First, Washington, DC, 2004.

49. Ibid.

50. See Karjanen and Baxamusa, "Subsidizing Wal-Mart."

51. Ibid., 24, 37.

52. Wal-Mart, Annual Reports, 1998 and 1999, Wal-Mart Corporation, Bentonville, AR.

53. Boarnet and Crane, "Supercenters and the Transformation of the Bay Area Grocery Industry," 69.

54. Marcus and Millichap Retail Research Report, semiannual summary, 2005. This perspective was illustrated by Lee Scott, president and CEO of Wal-Mart, "Wal-Mart and California: A Key Moment in Time for American Capitalism," an address by Lee Scott, Town Hall Los Angeles, February 23, 2005.

55. Urban Land Institute, *Cost and Expenditure Patterns of Land Uses* (Washington, DC: ULI Press, 1999).

56. Boarnet and Crane, "Supercenters and the Transformation of the Bay Area Grocery Industry."

57. Bob Rodino "Report on Big Box Retailers for the City of Los Angeles," unpublished manuscript, 2003.

58. Boarnet and Crane, "Supercenters and the Transformation of the Bay Area Grocery Industry."

59. Eric D. Walker, "Site Plan Review #01-354 (Wal-Mart Stores, Inc.)," memorandum, Hood River County Planning Board, 2002.

60. James Howard Kunstler, *The Geography of Nowhere* (New York: Simon and Schuster, 1996); Jane Holtz-Kay, *Asphalt Nation* (New York: Crown Publishing, 1997).

61. James Madison, "Changing Patterns of Urban Retailing in the 1920s," in *Business and Economic History,* 2nd series, vol. 5, ed. Carol Uselding (Urbana: Bureau of Business and Economic Research, University of Illinois, 1976), 102–11.

62. Scott, "Wal-Mart's Impact on Society," 6.

SEVEN Wal-Mart and the Logistics Revolution
Edna Bonacich with Khaleelah Hardie

We want to thank the following people for their very helpful comments on earlier drafts of this chapter and a more general paper on the logistics revolution and its effects: Richard Appelbaum, Ralph Armbruster-

Sandoval, Carolina Bank-Munoz, John Cioffi, Jill Esbenshade, Peter V. Hall, Ted Levine, Peter Olney, Tom Reifer, Jake Wilson, and David Young. We also thank Nelson Lichtenstein for his very comprehensive editorial comments.

1. Peter Olney, "On the Waterfront: Analysis of ILWU Lockout," *New Labor Forum* (2003) 33–40.

2. World Trade Organization (WTO), *International Trade Statistics 2001* (Geneva: WTO, 2001), 21.

3. Ibid., 49. Minor discrepancies exist in these trade figures because of different ways of measuring international trade, but they do not negate the overall trends.

4. Lincoln Fairley, *Facing Mechanization: The West Coast Longshore Plan* (Los Angeles: Institute of Industrial Relations, 1979).

5. Jack Kyser, *International Trade Trends and Impacts: The Southern California Region; 2003 Results and 2004 Outlook* (Los Angeles: Los Angeles Economic Development Corporation, 2004), 5.

6. The Los Angeles Customs District includes the Ports of LA/LB, the Port of Hueneme, Los Angeles International Airport (LAX), and Ontario International Airport.

7. Kyser, *International Trade Trends,* 37.

8. N. Shashikumar and G. L. Schatz, "The Impact of U.S. Regulatory Changes on International Intermodal Movements," *Transportation Journal* (2000): 5–14; Gerhardt Müller, *Intermodal Freight Transportation,* 4th ed. (Washington, DC: Eno Transportation Foundation and Intermodal Association of North America, 1999), chap. 4.

9. Warehousing Education and Research Council (WERC), *The Mass Merchant Distribution Channel: Challenges and Opportunities* (Oak Brook, IL: WERC, 1994).

10. The push system is still common in some industries, but it is being replaced in most consumer goods industries.

11. Frederick H. Abernathy, John T. Dunlop, Janice H. Hammond, and David Weil, *A Stitch in Time: Lean Retailing and the Transformation of Manufacturing—Lessons from the Apparel and Textile Industries* (New York: Oxford University Press, 1999).

12. Stephen S. Cohen, "Economic Impact of a West Coast Shutdown," unpublished paper 2002.

13. Peter V. Hall, " 'We'd Have to Sink the Ships': Impact Studies and 2002 Port Lockout," unpublished paper, 2003; Olney, "On the Waterfront."

14. Jon DeCesare, interview with author, 2004.

15. Matthew Boyle, "Wal-Mart Keeps the Change: Suppliers Pay for New Technology, but Bentonville Really Benefits," *Fortune,* November 26, 2003.

16. For example, Jason Asaeda, "Standard and Poor's Industry Surveys: Retailing: General," (November 27, 2003), which defines the current retail environment as "living in a Wal-Mart world."

17. Peter M. Tirschwell, "Demanding. Exacting. Uncompromising," *Journal of Commerce,* January 19, 2004.

18. Robert Slater, *The Wal-Mart Decade: How a New Generation of Leaders Turned Sam Walton's Legacy into the World's #1 Company* (New York: Portfolio, 2003).

19. Hank Gilman, "The Most Underrated CEO Ever," *Fortune,* March 21, 2004.

20. Bob Ortega, *In Sam We Trust: The Untold Story of Sam Walton and How Wal-Mart Is Devouring America* (New York: Random House, 1998), chap. 8.

21. Michael Hugos, *Essentials of Supply Chain Management* (Hoboken, NJ: John Wiley, 2003), 38–39.

22. Ortega, *In Sam We Trust.*

23. Hugos, *Essentials of Supply Chain Management.* Almost every logistics textbook, and there are many of them, uses Wal-Mart as a prime example of cutting-edge logistics practices.

24. Ibid., 41, 94.

25. Nirmalya Kumar, "The Power of Trust in Manufacturer-Retailer Relationships," in *Harvard Business Review on Managing the Value Chain,* (Boston: Harvard Business School Press, 2000), 91–126.

26. Ibid., 121.

27. Ibid., 121–22.

28. Ibid., 122–23.

29. Tirschwell, "Demanding."

30. Ibid.; Philip Damas and Chris Gillis, "Retailers Seek Logistics Jackpot: Retailers Collaborate with Vendors, Logistics Providers to Ensure Quick Response to Sales Changes, Contingencies," *American Shipper,* (December 2003) 8–14; Dick Seifert, *Collaborative Planning, Forecasting, and Replenishment: How to Create a Supply Chain Advantage* (New York: AMACOM, 2003).

31. Boyle, "Wal-Mart Keeps the Change."

32. Tirschwell, "Demanding."

33. For example, Charles Fishman, "The Wal-Mart You Don't Know: Why Low Prices Have a High Cost," *Fast Company,* December 2003, 68–80, which reports a study by McKinsey and Company that found that about 12 percent of the economy's productivity gains in the second half of the 1990s could be attributed to Wal-Mart alone, thereby making a major dent in inflation.

34. Rosalyn Wilson, *Fifteenth Annual State of Logistics Report: Globalization* (Oak Park, IL: Council of Logistics Management, 2004).

35. For example, Bill Quinn, *How Wal-Mart Is Destroying America (and the World), and What You Can Do About It* (Berkeley, CA: Ten Speed Press, 2000); Al Norman, *Slam-Dunking Wal-Mart: How You Can Stop Superstore Sprawl in Your Hometown* (Atlantic City, NJ: Raphel, 1999). Critical Web sites also abound, for example, http://www.walmartwatch.com, run by the UFCW.

36. Barbara Ehrenreich, *Nickel and Dimed: On (Not) Getting By in America* (New York: Henry Holt, 2001), chap. 3 and 4, draws a devastating portrait of what it is like to work for Wal-Mart.

37. Fishman, "The Wal-Mart You Don't Know," 73.

38. Ibid., 71.

39. Ibid. The quote comes a former Vlasic executive, recalling the interview.

40. Ibid., 73.

41. Ibid., 78.

42. Abigail Goldman and Nancy Cleeland, "An Empire Built on Bargains Remakes the Working World," *Los Angeles Times,* November 23, 2003, A1.

43. Fishman, "The Wal-Mart You Don't Know," 70.

44. Jerry Useem, "Should We Admire Wal-Mart?" *Fortune,* February 23, 2004.

45. Goldman and Cleeland, "An Empire Built on Bargains," A30.

46. Pamela Varley, *The Sweatshop Quandary: Corporate Responsibility on the Global Frontier* (Washington, DC: Investor Responsibility Research Center, 1998), 95.

47. Quoted in ibid., 95–98.

48. Nancy Cleeland, Evelyn Iritani, and Tyler Marshall, "Scouring the Globe to Give Shoppers an $8.63 Polo Shirt," *Los Angeles Times,* November 24, 2003, A1.

49. Ibid., A19.

50. Donald F. Wood, Anthony P. Barone, Paul R. Murphy, and Daniel L. Wardlow, *International Logistics,* 2nd ed. (New York: AMACOM, 2002), 414.

51. Ibid., 413, describes the giant retailers as nine-hundred-pound gorillas, and since our first encounter with the epithet, numerous others have used a variant to describe Wal-Mart.

52. Ironically, in the industry, the term "shippers" does not refer to the companies that own ships but, rather, to the beneficial owners of the cargo—the importers and exporters. Transportation providers are called "carriers," and the ocean shipping companies are referred to as "ocean carriers."

53. Bill Mongelluzzo, "Clout Counts: Big Shippers Still Set the Benchmark for Most Rates in Ocean Transportation," *Journal of Commerce,* February 4, 2002, 12. See also Helen Atkinson, "King of the Jungle: Mass Retailers Dictate Terms for Suppliers and Transportation Providers, but Inventories Still Offer Huge Potentials for Savings," *Journal of Commerce,* February 4, 2002, 9–12.

54. This list is of shippers, i.e., the beneficial owners of the cargo. The *Journal of Commerce* used the PIERS data as a starting point, but some goods are not shipped under the company's name. Rather, they are shipped under the name of a non-vessel-operating common carrier (NVOCC), freight forwarder, or other third-party logistics company (3PL). It took extensive, multisource research, dealing with such problems as corporate privacy rules, mergers and acquisitions, and shipment under company division names, to achieve this list, which is the best available estimate.

55. Ehrenreich, *Nickel and Dimed;* Liza Featherstone, "Wal-Mart Values: Selling Women Short," *The Nation,* December 16, 2002, 11–14; see also Ellen Rosen, "How to Squeeze More out of a Penny," in this volume.

56. The organization has since changed its name to the Waterfront Coalition, extending its concerns to all of the nation's ports.

57. Olney, "On the Waterfront."

EIGHT Wal-Mart in Mexico: The Limits of Growth
Chris Tilly

I thank the Rockefeller Foundation, the Fulbright-García Robles Fellowship Program, and the University of Massachusetts Lowell for financial support. José Luis Álvarez, Patricia Jiménez de Greiff, and Beth O'Donnell provided outstanding research assistance, and Patricia particular help with this paper. Chris Cottier, Marisol Jiménez, and Maria and Valencia Kennedy did price checking. I would also like to thank Nelson Lichtenstein and David Turcotte for very helpful comments.

1. Wal-Mart de México Web site http://www.walmartmexico.com.mx (accessed May 2005), and Wal-Mart de México 2004, "Informe Anual 2003," http://www.walmartmexico.com.mex/informe2003.pdf (accessed July 2004).

2. Controladora Comercial Mexicana, "Informe Anual 2004," http://www.comerci.com.mx (accessed May 2005); Grupo Gigante "Informe Anual 2004," http://www.grupogigante.com.mx (accessed May 2005); Soriana "Informe Anual 2004," http://www.soriana.com.mx (accessed May 2005).

3. "Mexico's Retail Goliath," *Economist, Business Latin America.* March 2, 2002, 4.

4. "Wal-Mart Leviathan Squeezes Competition," *Miami Herald,* international edition, February 2, 2004.

5. Tim Weiner, "Wal-Mart Invades, and Mexico Gladly Surrenders," *New York Times,* December 6, 2003, A1, A9.

6. Geri Smith, "Mexico: War of the Superstores: Wal-Mart Is Trouncing the Locals, but They're Not Giving Up," *Business Week,* September 23, 2002, 60.

7. David Luhnow, "Crossover Success: How NAFTA Helped Wal-Mart Reshape the Mexican Market," *Wall Street Journal,* August 31, 2001, sec. 1.

8. Roberto González Amador, "Riesgo Para la Soberanía, el Poder de Wal-Mart en el Mercado Mexicano," *La Jornada,* July 8, 2004, 22.

9. Annette Bernhardt, "Business Strategies and Employment Practices of Wal-Mart and Other Mass Retailers," presentation at the annual meeting of the Industrial Relations Research Association, San Diego, CA, January 3–5, 2004; David Karjanen, "The Wal-Mart Effect and the New Face of Capitalism: Labor Market and Community Impacts of the Megaretailer," in this volume.

10. "Mexico: Economic Structure," *Economist,* April 19, 2001.

11. Jürgen Weller, *Procesos de Exclusión y Inclusión Laboral: La Expansión del Empleo en el Sector Terciario* (Santiago de Chile: CEPAL, 2001).

12. ISSSTE personnel, interviews with author, Mexico City, June 9–10, 2004.

13. DICONSA Web site, http://www.diconsa.gob.mx (accessed July 2004); Arturo Villanueva, API Consultores, interview with author, México City, June 29, 2004.

14. U.S. Department of Commerce, *County Business Patterns,* http://www.census.gov/epcd/cbp/view/cbpview.html (accessed July 2004).

15. INEGI, *Economic Census* Web page, http://www.inegi.gob.mx/difusion/espanol/fecono.html (accessed July 2004); U.S. Department of Commerce *County Business Patterns.*

16. "Changing Channels," *Progressive Grocer,* December 1999, 78.

17. Rogelio Rodríguez and Ian Reider, "Tendencias en México: Actitudes del Consumidor y el Supermercado," presentation at the Twenty-first Convención del Asociación Nacional de Tiendas de Autoservicio y Departamentales, Guadalajara, Mexico, March 12–15, 2004.

18. Rita Schwentesius and Manuel Ángel Gómez, "The Rise of Supermarkets in Mexico: Impacts on Horticulture Chains," *Development Policy Review* 20, no. 4 (2002): 487–502.

19. Ibid., 488.

20. Jorge Mendoza, Fernando Pozos Ponce, and David Spener, "Fragmented Markets, Elaborate Chains: The Retail Distribution of Imported Clothing in Mexico," in *Free Trade and Uneven Development: The North American Apparel Industry After NAFTA,* ed. Gary Gereffi, David Spener, and Jennifer Bair, 266–84 (Philadelphia: Temple University Press, 2002).

21. Jeff Wright, "Spending Spree: Mexican Retailers Reaping Rewards of Long-Lost Consumer Buying Power," *Business Mexico,* April 1, 1977.

22. U.S. Department of Commerce, *County Business Patterns.*

23. "Mexican Retailing: The Fiesta," *Economist,* June 18, 1994; "Mexico at Mid-Decade," *Market Latin America* 3, no. 2 (1995): 8; "Wal-Mart de México a Winner," *Mass Market Retailers* 18, no. 18 (2001): 128.

24. *Chain Store Age,* "Mexico: Peso Devaluation Forces Global Retailers to Stall Plans," December 1995, 32–34, 30–32; Luhnow, "Crossover Success."

25. Schwentesius and Gómez, "The Rise of Supermarkets in Mexico."

26. Manuel Chavez, "The Transformation of Mexican Retailing with NAFTA," *Development Policy Review* 20, no. 4 (2002): 371–88.

27. Luhnow, "Crossover Success"; Smith, "Mexico's War of the Superstores"; Weiner, "Wal-Mart Invades."

28. "Wal-Mart International: Resilience and Format Diversity Keep First International Entry *Excelente,*" *DSN Retailing Today,* June 1, 2001, 26; Luhnow, "Crossover Success."

29. "Wal-Mart International."

30. Luhnow, "Crossover Success"; Carlos Velasco, "Firma Wal-Mart Convenio con Campesinos," *El Universal* online, December 7, 2004, http://www.eluniversal.com.mx (accessed July 2004).

31. Luhnow, "Crossover Success."

32. This and a number of other quotations and observations are based on Mexican retail case studies consisting of 126 interviews at seventeen large chains, twelve local retail businesses, and four related businesses in Mexico, conducted in 2003–4. For more information on these interviews, see Chris Tilly, "Wal-Mart in Mexico: The Limits of Growth," paper presented at the Latin American Studies Association annual meeting, Las Vegas, NV, October 7–9, 2004. There is an important limitation on the information from these interviews. Except in a small number of cases where the research team contacted employees directly, we promised not to reveal the identity of the companies. As a result, I cannot reveal whether Wal-Mart partici-

pated in these interviews. Comments on Wal-Mart in the paper come from interviews with managers at other companies.

33. "Wal-Mart International," 26; Julio Moreno, "Wal-Mart y la Diplomacia Económica en América Latina," *Foreign Affairs en Español,* April–June 2004; Luhnow, "Crossover Success."

34. Luhnow, "Crossover Success."

35. A research assistant and I conducted thirty-eight short interviews with consumers about where they like to shop for food and clothing, supplemented by field observation of a variety of retail settings. The interviews were conducted in 2003–4 in seven Mexican states and the Federal District (the capital region that includes Mexico City).

36. "New Head Named for Wal-Mart in Mexico," *El Universal/Mexico News,* January 8, 2005.

37. Moreno, "Wal-Mart y la Diplomacia Económica."

38. Alexander Hanrath, "Mexican Stores Wilt in the Face of US Group's Onslaught," *Financial Times,* August 14, 2002, 21.

39. Valerie Seckler and Joanna Ramey, "Sears Unloading Bulk of Mexican Business, Said to Eye Eaton's," *Women's Wear Daily,* April 3, 1997, 1–2.

40. *Chain Store Age,* December 1999, 30–32.

41. Calculated by author from Wal-Mart de México 2004, INEGI 2004.

42. All prices were checked on Friday–Sunday, January 7–9, 2005, except for prices in Mexico City, which were checked on January 25, 2005. Mexican prices are the average of prices from a Wal-Mart in Tehuacán, Puebla, and a Wal-Mart in Mexico City. U.S. prices are based on price checks in Eugene, Oregon, and Niles, Illinois (in the Chicago area). Most prices were identical in the two U.S. stores. When they were different, I took the average of the two prices, unless one was a special sales price (in which case I took the higher price). To compare prices, I converted currencies using the January 7, 2005, exchange rate published in the *Boston Globe.* The Mexican minimum wage varies by geographic area; I obtained the Puebla and Mexico City minimum wages from the Comisión Nacional de los Salarios Minimos, "Salarios minimos vigentes a partir de lo de enero de 2005," http://www.consasami.gob.mx/estadisticas/docs/Desplegado%202005 .pdf (accessed January 2005). The Mexican minimum wage is a daily wage, so I divided by eight hours (a standard working day in Mexico) to come up with an estimated hourly minimum.

43. Theresa Braine, "Wal-Mart International: Good Things in Mexico Come in Small Formats," *DSN Retailing Today,* December 13, 2004; 43.

44. Schwentesius and Gómez, "The Rise of Supermarkets in Mexico."

45. Rodríguez and Reider, "Tendencias en México."

46. Wright, "Spending Spree."

47. Mendoza, Pozos, and Spencer, "Fragmented Markets."

48. Wright, "Spending Spree."

49. "Domestic Manufacturers Turning to Informal Economy to Sell Toys and Other Products During Holiday Season," *SourceMex News and Analysis on Mexico,* December 12, 2001.

50. Hanrath, "Mexican Stores Wilt."

51. These contracts are part of a larger sample of collective-bargaining contracts from Juntas Locales de Conciliación y Arbitraje (local labor-relations commissions) in the Distrito Federal (13 contracts), Guadalajara (Jalisco; 9 contracts) and León (Guanajuato; 12 contracts). There are a total of 34 contracts at 24 companies (some companies are represented at more than one locality, and/or have separate contracts for different sets of workers). For more information on these contracts, see Tilly, "Wal-Mart in Mexico: The Limits of Growth," 2004.

52. Secretaría del Trabajo y Previsión Social de México, "Salarios Minimos," 2004, http://www.stps.gob.mx/index2.htm (accessed July 2004).

53. ANTAD (Asociacion Nacional de Tiendas de Autoservicio y Departamentales), http://www.antad.org.mx (accessed January 2005).

54. "Wal-Mart Leviathan."

55. José Alfonso Bouzas and Mario Vega, "Condiciones de Trabajo y Relaciones Laborales en las Tiendas de Autoservicio del D.F.: El Caso de Gigante," in *Cambios en las Relaciones Laborales: Enfoque Sectoral y Regional,* vol. 21, ed. Enrique de la Garza and José Alfonso Bouzas, 453–484 (México, DF: Universidad Nacional Autónoma de México, Instituto de Investigaciones Económicas, 1999).

56. Thomas Reardon and Julio Berdegué, "The Rapid Rise of Supermarkets in Latin America: Challenges and Opportunities for Development," *Development Policy Review* 20, no. 4 (2002): 317–34.

57. Brendan Case, "Welcoming Wal-Mart to Mexico," *Dallas Morning News,* November 9, 2004.

58. Calculated by the author from Banco de México price data.

59. Calculated by the author based on data from the 1989, 1994, and 1999 Economic Censuses, accessed through INEGI 2004a and 2004b.

NINE Making the New Shop Floor: Wal-Mart, Labor Control, and the History of the Postwar Discount Retail Industry in America
Thomas Jessen Adams

For their astute criticisms of various drafts and incarnations of this project I would like to thank George Chauncey, Rachel Devlin, Bernard Dubbeld, Jenny Feldman, Alison Lefkovitz, Jon Levy, Mae Ngai, Gautham Rao, William Sewell, and Tim Stewart-Winter. Special gratitude is extended to Nelson Lichtenstein for his especially penetrating comments and for inviting me to contribute to this volume. Amy Dru Stanley deserves particular thanks for continually providing excellent guidance and comments on this paper far beyond her duty as a professor and mentor.

1. See other contributions to this volume, especially those of Nelson Lichtenstein, Susan Strasser, James Hoopes, and Misha Petrovic and Gary Hamilton.

2. See Nelson Lichtenstien, *Walter Reuther: The Most Dangerous Man in America* (Urbana: University of Illinois Press, 1995), esp. chap. 13, and Nelson Lichtenstein, *The State of the Union: A Century of American Labor* (Princeton, NJ: Princeton University Press, 2002).

3. Elizabeth Fones-Wolf, *Selling Free Enterprise: The Business Assault on Labor and Liberalism, 1945–1960* (Urbana: University of Illinois Press, 1994). The "end"-of-class-conflict argument is perhaps most famously elucidated in Daniel Bell, *The End of Ideology: On the Exhaustion of Political Ideas in the 1950s* (Glencoe, II: Free Press, 1960).

4. See especially Barry Bluestone and Bennett Harrison, *The Deindustrialization of America: Plant Closings, Community Abandonment, and the Dismantling of Basic Industry* (New York: Basic Books, 1982); Jefferson Cowie, *Capital Moves: RCA's Seventy-Year Quest for Cheap Labor* (Ithaca, NY: Cornell University Press, 1999); Thomas Sugrue, *The Origins of the Urban Crisis: Race and Inequality in Postwar Detroit* (Princeton, NJ: Princeton University Press, 1996); Bruce Schulman, *From Cotton Belt to Sunbelt: Federal Policy, Economic Development, and the Transformation of the South, 1938–1980* (New York: Oxford University Press, 1991); Thomas Jessen Adams, " 'Keep the CIO Away and the Workers Can Go to Town Everyday': The Defeat of Operation Dixie in the South Carolina Piedmont and the Rhetoric of Deindustrialization," paper presented at the 2004 North American Labor History Conference, Wayne State University, Detroit, Michigan, October 21, 2004.

5. Tom Mahoney and Leonard Sloane, *The Great Merchants: America's Foremost Retail Institutions and the People Who Made Them Great* (New York: Harper & Row, 1966), 347–48. Mahoney and Sloane's voluminous books are the most accessible resource for the taxonomies of different forms of retailing. The fact that many of the first stores were located in abandoned New England textile mills is a particularly telling example of the transition from an economy centered on production to one centered on services.

6. See Barry Bluestone, Patricia Hanna, Sarah Kuhn, and Laura Moore, *The Retail Revolution: Market Transformation, Investment, and Labor in the Modern Department Store* (Boston: Auburn House, 1981), 19–23.

7. "Employees on Nonfarm Payrolls by Major Industry and Select Component Groups, 1946–2001," in *Handbook of U.S. Labor Statistics: Employment, Earnings, Prices, Productivity and Other Labor Data*, ed. Eva Jacobs (Lanham, MD: Bernan Publications, 2003), 151–58.

8. In the aggregate, the retail industry averaged more than 383,000 job additions per year, while goods-producing industries averaged only 113,000 additions; see "Employees on Nonfarm Payrolls."

9. The centrality of practices like atomized bargaining, vociferous antiunionism, and lower wage rates to post-Fordism or "flexible accumulation" is delineated in David Harvey, *The Limits to Capital* (Oxford: Blackwell, 1982). His argument on flexible accumulation is simplified in *The Condition of Postmodernity: An Enquiry into the Origins of Cultural Change* (Oxford: Blackwell, 1990). See also the essays collected in Neil Brenner and Nik Theodore, eds., *Spaces of Neo-Liberalism: Urban Restructuring in North America and Western Europe* (Oxford: Blackwell, 2002).

10. "Average Weekly Earnings of Production or Nonsupervisory Workers on Nonfarm Payrolls by Industry in Current and Constant Dollars, 1947–2001," in *Handbook of U.S. Labor Statistics*, ed. Eva Jacobs, 174–75. Construction rose by 16 percent from 1958 to 2001, while manufacturing rose by 22 percent and mining by 39 percent in the same period.

11. Ibid.

12. Ibid., 175. Among the many questions yet to be addressed in our understanding of the history of the service economy is why many other service industries maintained their wage rates while retail's declined. My suspicion here is that the relative success of both the Service Employees International Union (SEIU) and the Hotel Employees and Restaurant Employees International Union (HERE) in organizing workers in these industries is largely constitutive of the difference.

13. Retail analysts and historians have generally noted that the first discount stores appeared in postwar New England in abandoned textile mills and cheap warehouses. By the early 1960s though, the expansion of Woolco, Kmart, Zayres, and later Target and Wal-Mart made this phenomenon distinctly national in scope. See Mahoney and Sloane, *The Great Merchants,* 347–49. A problem that I will not address here but that certainly deserves analysis is the relationship between suburbanization and the retail industry from the perspective of labor. That is, while many historians, the most prominent being Lizabeth Cohen in *A Consumer's Republic: The Politics of Consumption in Postwar America* (New York: Knopf, 2003), have addressed how consumption is related to suburbanization, few to none have addressed the historical effects of the spatial dispersal of American workplaces—of which the discount retail industry, along with other developments like the shopping mall are prime examples—far from affordable housing and community support. See also Thomas W. Hanchett, "U.S. Tax Policy and the Shopping-Center Boom of the 1950s and 1960s," *American Historical Review* 101, no. 4 (October 1996): 1082–110.

14. Quoted in Bluestone et al., *The Retail Revolution,* 19.

15. As early as 1962, traditional department stores recognized that discounters had vastly lower labor costs than they did. B.S. Klayf, "How a Discount Buying Office Operates," comments prepared for the January 10, 1962, meeting of the General Merchandise Managers Meeting, National Retail Management Association, Folder #4, Box #29, Richard Rich Papers (hereafter referred to as RRP), Special Collections, Robert W. Woodruff Library, Emory University, Atlanta, Georgia. On wages as a percentage of sales see "Statistical Comparison of Operations for K-Mart and the Average Discounter," Financial Statements, 1966–1970, Reel #6, Stanley S. Kresge Papers (hereafter referred to as SKP), Bentley Historical Library, University of Michigan, Ann Arbor, Michigan. Bluestone et al. *The Retail Revolution,* 20, 106–9, confirms these numbers.

16. "Controllable Expenses, March, 1966," Mailings, Reel #1, SKP.

17. Bluestone et al., *The Retail Revolution,* 106–7. The records of Rich's, Atlanta's most prominent downtown retail palace, bear out these numbers; "Gross Margin and Expense Comparisons," Folder #14, Box #31, RRP. On unionization and the skilled nature of employment in these types of stores see George Kirstein, *Stores and Unions: A Study of the Growth of Unionism in Dry Goods and Department Stores* (New York: Fairchild, 1950). Also see Michael Harrington, *The Retail Clerks* (New York: Wiley & Sons, 1962), 1–13, 75–90; Bruce Marion, Willard Mueller, Ronald Cotteril, Frederick Geithman, and John Schmelzer, *The Food Retailing Industry: Market Structure, Profits, and Prices* (New York: Praeger, 1979), 56–94.

18. On this point, see Susan Porter Benson, *Counter Cultures: Saleswomen, Managers, and Customers in American Department Stores, 1890–1940* (Urbana: University of Illinois Press, 1986).

19. Harry Braverman, *Labor and Monopoly Capital: The Degradation of Work in the Twentieth Century*

(New York: Monthly Review Press, 1974); Benson, *Counter Cultures,* 290–92. Stanford M. Jacoby briefly notes this process for postwar Sears; see Jacoby, *Modern Manors: Welfare Capitalism Since the New Deal* (Princeton, NJ: Princeton University Press, 1997), 95–142.

20. From the shipwrights of England in the middle of the eighteenth century to the weavers of Lancashire in the late eighteenth century to the steelworkers of Pennsylvania in the late nineteenth century to the jute-mill hands of Bengal in the twentieth century, such a process has been one of the enduring themes of the world histories of labor and capital. See especially Peter Linebaugh, *The London Hanged: Crime and Civil Society in the Eighteenth Century* (New York: Verso 2003), esp. 371–402; E.P. Thompson, *The Making of the English Working Class* (New York: Vintage, 1966); David Montgomery, *The Fall of the House of Labor: The Workplace, the State, and American Labor Activism, 1865–1925* (New York: Cambridge University Press, 1987), esp. 214–57; Dipesh Chakrabarty, *Rethinking Working-Class History: Bengal, 1890–1940* Princeton, NJ: Princeton University Press, 1989). On the changing nature of the workplace in postindustrial capitalism and service work's special place in it see Nelson Lichtenstein, *The State of the Union: A Century of American Labor* (Princeton, NJ: Princeton University Press, 2002). Discount labor's epitomization of labor exploitation in our current era is perhaps most famously elucidated in Barbara Ehrenreich's muckraking account of work at a Wal-Mart and in other low-wage service jobs: Ehrenreich, *Nickel and Dimed: On (Not) Getting By in America* (New York: Metropolitan Books, 2001).

21. Clarence Leis, quoted in Sandra Vance and Roy Scott, *Wal-Mart: A History of Sam Walton's Retailing Phenomenon* (New York: Twayne, 1994), 49.

22. While this is an oversimplification in respect to prices, formulaically, it holds true that no matter what the original prices of transportation, the original products, advertising, etc., a rising cost of labor will have a decidedly greater impact on profit the lower the markup.

23. On Wal-Mart's immense success at keeping other costs down, see James Hoopes's essay in this volume.

24. This could be better described in Marxian terms as profit resulting almost entirely from absolute surplus value. While Bluestone et al., *The Retail Revolution,* 10–29, does not make this argument in specifically Marxian language, the study is quick to point out how relative to other modes of retailing, discounting's profits are almost entirely determined by its control of labor costs. See also Marion et al., *The Food Retailing Industry,* 77.

25. Daniel Nelson, *Management and Workers: Origins of the New Factory System in the United States, 1880–1920* (Madison: University of Wisconsin Press, 1975), esp. 55–78; see Montgomery, *The Fall of the House of Labor,* 214–56. In addition, my understanding here comes directly out of Marx and his conceptions of absolute surplus value versus relative surplus value. See Karl Marx, *Capital,* vol. 1 (New York: Penguin, 1990), esp. 429–38, 960–63. Also, Karl Marx, *Grundrisse: Introduction to the Critique of Political Economy* (Middlesex, UK: Pelican, 1974), 549–741.

26. The literature here is appropriately massive. Some of the works that have influenced me most on this point include Linebaugh, *The London Hanged;* Thompson, *The Making of the English Working Class;* Montgomery, *The Fall of the House of Labor;* Sean Wilentz, *Chants Democratic: New York City and the Rise*

of the American Working Class (Urbana: University of Illinois Press, 1984); David Brody, *Steelworkers in America: The Nonunion Era* (Cambridge, MA Harvard University Press, 1960); Chakrabarty, *Rethinking Working-Class History;* Gunther Peck, *Reinventing Free Labor: Padrones and Immigrant Workers in the North American West* (New York: Cambridge University Press, 2000).

27. David Montgomery, *Workers Control in America: Studies in the History of Work, Technology, and Labor Struggles* (New York: Cambridge University Press, 1979), 34.

28. Bluestone et al., *The Retail Revolution,* 114–15.

29. Braverman, *Labor and Monopoly Capital,* 443–44; Benson, *Counter Cultures,* 2, briefly mentions the increasing automation that came to American retail in the post–World War II period and notes this process's seemingly perfect replication of Braverman's model.

30. See Robert M. Smith, *From Blackjacks to Briefcases: A History of Commercialized Strikebreaking and Union Busting in the United States* (Athens: Ohio University Press, 2003), esp. 75–96.

31. The vast majority of archival work for the following section comes from Kmart and Richway. Because Wal-Mart's archives are closed, and other stores, like Target and even Kmart remain incredibly secretive, especially regarding past personnel policies, I have also mined the more complete records of some supermarket chains and the unions that tried to organize them, especially Colonial and Kroger. While such stores have slightly different histories than Wal-Mart, etc. (particularly, a stronger history of unionization because of the militancy of the Butcher Workmen), their size, big-box style, and management imperative toward labor cost cutting and low markup make them ideal records to consult when the existing records of other stores prove scarce.

32. *W.W. West et al. v. Wal-Mart, Inc., et al.,* 264 F. Supp. 158 (U.S. Dist., 1967).

33. Ibid.

34. Ibid.

35. Ibid.

36. One of the always intriguing aspects of Wal-Mart's work culture is the extent to which its workers think of the company before and after Sam Walton's death in an almost jeremiac manner. As one worker said, "The day Sam died was the day Wal-Mart joined corporate America," quoted in Liza Featherstone, *Selling Women Short: The Landmark Battle for Workers' Rights at Wal-Mart* (New York: Basic Books, 2004), 86.

37. "K-Mart License Agreement," footnote #3, *Corollo v. S.S. Kresge Company,* 456 F.2d 306 (U.S. Circ., 1972).

38. *S.S. Kresge Company, K-Mart Division v. National Labor Relations Board et al.,* 416 F.2d 1225 (U.S. App., 1969). While these tactics were occasionally struck down, the nature of dividing a store like this has forced NLRB and court rulings to tend to apply only to the case at hand, thus making each decision applicable only to an individual store; see the above-cited case.

39. *S.S. Kresge Company v. National Labor Relations Board.*

40. "Rules and Regulations," footnote #7, *S.S. Kresge Company v. National Labor Relations Board.*

41. "The Evolution of a K-Mart," *Variety Store Merchandiser,* June 1965, in Reel #1, "Background,"

SKP. On the most common licensees, see "K-Mart Run Departments," in *Variety Store Merchandiser,* June 1965, SKP.

42. "The Evolution of a K-Mart."

43. On the RCIA and its structure and successes, see Harrington, *The Retail Clerks,* 1–13.

44. Benson, *Counter Cultures,* 227–82.

45. Harrington, *The Retail Clerks,* 87–90.

46. "Checkers Manual," Personnel Department, Big Apple Stores, Folder #507, Box #1058, John Jacobs Papers (hereafter referred to as JJP), Southern Labor Archives (hereafter referred to as SLA), Special Collections Department, Pullen Library, Georgia State University, Atlanta, Georgia.

47. Ibid.

48. Ibid.

49. As Liza Featherstone points out, the subjective enforcement of arbitrary rules is a major factor leading to the endemic sex discrimination at Wal-Mart. See Feathstone, *Selling Women Short,* 48–49.

50. "Rules and Disciplinary Action Covering Store Employees," Big Apple Stores, March 1968, Folder #511, Box #1058, JJP.

51. Ibid.

52. "Grievance Report," May 3, 1966, Folder #516, Box #1058, JJP.

53. "Brief of Union, RCIA Local 1063," Folder #516, Box #1058, JJP.

54. On the power of arbitrarily enforced rules, see Montgomery, *Workers Control in America,* 32–44.

55. "Ten Commandments for the Care and Feeding of Customers," n.d., Folder #511, Box #1058, JJP.

56. Kmart had a similar policy; "Customer Relations Memo," G.W. Morck, June 6, 1974, Customer Relations Folder, Reel #2, SKP.

57. Testimony of Effie Spain, "Arbitration of Female Clerks' Pay," Folder #514, Box #1059, JJP.

58. Testimony of Marie Sewell, "Arbitration of Female Clerks' Pay," JJP.

59. Testimony of Zone Manager Bazemore, "Arbitration of Female Clerks' Pay," JJP.

60. Leslie Salzinger's recent sociological study, *Genders in Production: Making Workers in Mexico's Global Factories* (Berkeley: University of California Press, 2003), argues that a gendered divide produced through work and production is especially key to the functionality of a global economy.

61. "Declaration of Paula Bird in Support of Plaintiffs' Motion for Class Certification," *Betty Dukes et al. v. Wal-Mart Stores,* Knob Noster, Missouri, 2003; "Declaration of Christine Kwapnoski in Support of Plaintiffs' Motion for Class Certification," *Betty Dukes et al. v. Wal-Mart Stores,* Concord, California, April 2003; "Declaration of Kathleen MacDonald in Support of Plaintiffs' Motion for Class Certification," *Betty Dukes et al. v. Wal-Mart Stores,* Aiken, South Carolina, April 2003. For more on Kwapnoski and MacDonald, see Featherstone, *Selling Women Short,* 93, 125–26.

62. *National Labor Relations Board v. Wal-Mart Stores, Inc.,* 488 F.2d 114 (U.S. Circ., 1973).

63. Ibid.

64. Ibid.

65. Ibid.

66. Ibid.

67. Organizing Report, R.J. Schnell, December 1965, Folder #5, Box #2766, AFL/CIO Region 5/8 Papers (hereafter referred to as AFL), SLA. An understudied aspect of the transition to a service economy is how, relative to previous industrial workers, employees in such jobs did not see such employment as their lifelong career, or often, even where they hoped to work the following year. Such a tendency could increase the effectiveness of a store's exercising power in locations like school and home where workers had a more vested interest, because such places were considered the gateways to better employment and lives.

68. Report of "Operative X," n.d., Folder #15, Box #34, RRP.

69. Reports of "Operative X," n.d. (6 total), RRP.

70. L.W. Zane to Board of Directors, "Meetings and Reports Folders," various, 1968–76, Reel #2, SKP.

71. 'Known Union Activity Throughout the Company Since Our Last Report of Jul 8, 1975," Meetings and Reports, 1975 Folder, Reel #2, SKP.

72. Known Union Activities Throughout the Company Since the Report of Last Month," January 10, 1968, Meetings and Reports, 1968 Folder, Reel #1, SKP.

73. Report of William Jenkins, RCIA Local #1063 Executive Council Minutes, January 14, 1964, Oversize Folder, L15R. The concern for time cards especially recalls Wal-Mart's infamous policy against "time-theft" that Barbara Ehrenreich exposes in her muckraking account, *Nickel and Dimed.*

74. Report of William Jenkins, L15R.

75. Grievance of Lonnie Wells, September 30, 1968, Folder #511, Box #1058, JJP.

76. Ibid.

77. If, as Michel Foucault argues in *Discipline and Punish: The Birth of the Prison* (New York: Vintage, 1995), eighteenth-century prisoners began to internalize the panopticon, then perhaps a fruitful line of historical research lies with pursuing the extent to which more modern service workers, through subjection to the *possibility* of their co-worker's gaze, internalize it to the effect that it becomes more successful in surveillance than more traditional means like labor spies and security cameras.

78. "Richard Rich to All Richway Employees," October 8, 1969, Folder #15, Box #33, RRP.

79. Ibid.

80. Ibid.

81. Affidavit of N.J. Quarton, October 25, 1968, Folder #21, Box #1431, JJP.

82. Joseph Jacobs to Walter C. Phillips, April 1, 1968, Folder #516, Box #1058, JJP.

83. Affidavit of Betty Ann Bryant, October 8, 1968, Folder #21, Box #1431, JJP.

84. "Charge Against Employer-Atlantic Thrift Company," U.S. N.L.R.B., 1962, Folder #506, Box #1058, JJP.

85. H.B. Cunningham to C.M. Booker, February 21, 1968, Meetings and Reports, 1968 Folder, Reel #1, SKP.

86. Proceedings, *Fulton County Bobby Moses and George Seidenfadden,* Folder #21, Box #1431, JJP.

87. Carey Haigler to John Livingston, November 18, 1963, Folder #11, Box #2774, AFL.

88. Proceedings and Testimony in the Matter of J.W. Kirvan and Audrey Hubbard, March 6, 1964, Folder #503, Box #1058, JJP.

89. Larry Larsen to Arnold Orman, November 1, 1963, Folder #63, Box 667, RWDSU Local 15-A Records, SLA.

90. Carey Haigler to John Livingston, November 12, 1963, Folder #11, Box #2774, AFL.

91. See, "Fortune 500," *Fortune*, April 2003. I have not taken up the question of whether retail and service work represents a metaphysical departure from manufacturing work but instead defer to Harry Braverman, who insists that a "worker who is employed in producing goods renders a service to the capitalist, and it is as a result of this service that a tangible, vendible object takes shape. . . . if the useful effects of labor are such that they cannot take shape in an object . . . the useful effects of labor *themselves* become the commodity." See Braverman, *Labor and Monopoly Capital,* 359–60. To paraphrase Marx on this point, it is only through fetishization that one would even conceive of the commodity existing a priori to its distribution.

92. Orson Mason, "Five Union Free Concepts," *Labor Relations at the Wal-Mart Distribution Center,* http://ufcw.org/issues_and_actions/walmart_workers_campaign_info/ index.cfm, September 1991.

93. On the end of Fordism and the profitability crises of the early 1970s, see Harvey, *The Limits to Capital;* Giovanni Arrighi, *The Long Twentieth Century: Money, Power, and the Origins of Our Times* (New York: Verso, 1994); Harvey, *The Condition of Postmodernity,* Brenner and Nik Theodore, eds., *Spaces of Neo-Liberalism.*

TEN Patriarchy at the Checkout Counter: The *Dukes v. Wal-Mart Stores, Inc.,* Class Action Suit
Brad Seligman

1. The class certification motion, the subsequent hearing, and the judge's order can be accessed at http://www.walmartclass.com along with other pleadings, expert reports, and declarations of over a hundred women. Liza Featherstone offers a larger study of gender discrimination at the company in *Selling Women Short: The Landmark Battle for Workers' Rights at Wal-Mart* (New York: Basic Books, 2004).

2. This section is in part taken from the class certification motion, the principal authors of which were Jocelyn Larkin of the Impact Fund and Christine Webber of Cohen, Milstein, Hausfeld and Toll.

3. These statements are taken from the "Declaration Summaries" page of the Impact Fund's Wal-Mart class-action Web site: http://www.walmartclass.com.

ELEVEN How to Squeeze More out of a Penny
Ellen Israel Rosen

1. Richard R. Drogin, "Statistical Analysis of Gender Patterns in Wal-Mart Workforce, 2003," http://www.impactfund.org.

2. The respondents in this study were current and former Wal-Mart workers—from hourly salesclerks

and cashiers to store managers. I was introduced to potential respondents by the United Food and Commercial Workers, who indicated my interest in interviewing Wal-Mart workers on their Web site. The Web message said that I was writing a book about Wal-Mart and would like to hear from people who worked in the stores. Those who responded by e-mail were contacted for their phone numbers. They were also asked to indicate convenient times for a telephone interview and assured anonymity and confidentiality. Over one hundred individuals were in touch with me about being interviewed. I was finally able to contact and interview more than fifty people. The interviews lasted one to two hours. I also asked William Wertz, then director of corporate communications at Wal-Mart, to help me find associates with whom to speak. However, he declined to participate in this research project. Therefore, the individuals I spoke with do not represent the entire spectrum of workers' job satisfaction at Wal-Mart, but probably over represent those individuals who are most unhappy or feel particularly abused. Their stories, however, tend to be internally consistent, revealing the nature of Wal-Mart's management practices. Department managers are also paid on an hourly basis, as are some office personnel. Salaried management begins at the assistant manager level.

3. McKinsey Global Institute, "U.S. Productivity Growth: 1995–2000," 2001, sec. 6, "Retail Trade."

4. Sam Walton and John Huey, *Made in America* (New York: Doubleday, 1993).

5. James Finberg, attorney engaged in litigation against Wal-Mart on wage abuse, conversation with author, May 22, 2002.

6. See Nelson Lichtenstein, "Wal-Mart: A Template for Twenty-First-Century Capitalism," in this volume.

7. "Bill Thomas" (not real name), former Wal-Mart store manager, telephone interview, April 7, 2003.

8. "Mary Roland" (not real name), former jewelry department manager, telephone interview, July 31, 2002.

9. Douglas P. Shuit, "People Problems on Every Aisle," *Workforce Management,* March 30, 2004.

10. Mary Roland, July 31, 2002.

11. A telxon gun is used to gather the information on bar codes, which describes the characteristics of the merchandise. Recording it on the telxon gun automatically sends the information to the store's main computer.

12. "Katie Mitchell" (not real name), telephone interview, June 11, 2003.

13. "Kate Moroney" (not real name), telephone interview, May 7, 2003.

14. "Billy Draper" (not real name), telephone interview, February 1, 2003.

15. "Patti Slater" (not real name), telephone interview, November 6, 2003.

16. "Marty Spinner" (not real name), telephone interview, January 18, 2003.

17. "Jimmy Forester" (not real name), former store manager, telephone interview, October 23, 2002.

18. "Jed Stone" (not real name), former Wal-Mart store manager in Tennessee, telephone interview, April 29, 2004. Stone told me he had a budget for markdowns.

19. See Lisa Featherstone, *Selling Women Short: The Landmark Battle for Women's Rights at Wal-Mart,* (New York: Basic Books, 2004).

20. See Drogin, "Statistical Analysis," 17.

21. "Anthony Sironno" (not real name), telephone interview, February 1, 2003.

22. Jed Stone, April 29, 2004.

23. Carolyn Thiebes, telephone interview, January 25, 2003.

24. "Carolyn Naster" (not real name), telephone interview, January 3, 2003.

25. "Laverne Coates" (not real name), telephone interview, April 10, 2002.

26. "Carol Curtis" (not real name), telephone interview, July 15, 2003.

27. "Alan Tripster" (not real name), telephone interview, February 2, 2003.

28. This story was recounted to me by "Harry's" wife, "Victoria" (not real names), in a telephone interview on July 31, 2002.

29. See Harry Braverman, *Labor and Monopoly Capital: The Degradation of Work in the Twentieth Century* (New York: Monthly Review Press, 1975); Simon Head, *The New Ruthless Economy: Work and Power in the Digital Age* (New York: Oxford University Press, 2003).

TWELVE A Wal-Mart Workers Association? An Organizing Plan
Wade Rathke

1. Wal-Mart press release, http://www.walmart.com, November 23, 2004.

2. David Barboza, "Wal-Mart Bows to Trade Unions at Stores in China," *New York Times,* November 25, 2004, C1.

3. Arguably the 1997 United Parcel Service–Teamsters strike was among the last national strikes that at least felt victorious.

4. Matt Bai, "The New Boss," *New York Times Magazine,* January 30, 2005, 40–47.

5. Steven Greenhouse, "How Do You Drive Out a Union? South Carolina Factory Provides a Textbook Case," *New York Times,* December 14, 2004, A30, reports the painful but true tale of the thwarted and expensive efforts of one group of workers to prevail in South Carolina.

6. Richard Freeman and Joel Rogers, *What Workers Want* (Ithaca, NY: Cornell University Press, 1999), 14–22.

7. For a longer treatment of the argument, see Wade Rathke, "Majority Unionism," *Social Policy* 35, no. 3 (Spring 2005), or an earlier piece done for the International Executive Board of the Service Employees International Union, Seattle, June 2003, available at http://www.chieforganizer.org/.

8. In one survey 44 percent of workers said they wanted an organization "strongly independent" of management, while another 43 percent wanted to be members of a "somewhat independent" group. Freeman and Rogers, *What Workers Want,* 147.

9. Micheline Maynard, "The Airline That Refused to Die; USAirways Defies the Nay Sayers, but Still Faces a Rough Ride," *New York Times,* February 5, 2005.

10. An account of the "Melian Debate" can be found in volume 2 of any edition of Thucydides' *History of the Peloponnesian War.* Scores of summaries and transcripts can be found on the Web.

11. Information received by the author in a personal interview with Mike Fraser, Canadian director, UFCW, Toronto, July 2004.

12. Adam Geller, "Canadian Wal-Mart Seeking Union to Close," AP Business Wire, February 9, 2005.

13. See particularly Bob Ortega, *In Sam We Trust: The Untold Story of Sam Walton and How Wal-Mart Is Devouring America* (New York: Random House, 1998), 87–90.

14. Steven Greenhouse, "At a Small Shop in Colorado, Wal-Mart Beats a Union Once More," *New York Times,* February 26, 2005, A7.

15. Peter Van Allen, "Push and Pull: Wal-Mart vs. Supermarket Union," *Philadelphia Business Journal,* January 2005.

16. Judy Atkins and David Cohen, "A Proposal for a 21st Century Trade Union Education League," *Working USA* (Winter 2004): 11–14.

17. Charles Morris, *The Blue Eagle at Work: Reclaiming Democratic Rights in the American Workplace* (Ithaca, NY: Cornell University Press, 2005), 5–6. Of course, most unions thought they could deploy more bargaining power if they were the exclusive representative of the workers, preferably under a union-shop contract.

18. Paul Bouchard, "In for the Long Haul: The Non-Majority Union Strategy," in *A Troublemaker's Handbook II,* ed. Jane Slaughter (Detroit: Labor Education and Research Project, 2005), 236–42.

19. "Left Behind: Can the Democrats Become a Majority Party Again? A Discussion," *New York Times Book Review,* March 6, 2005, 15.

20. A recent potential breakthrough in community-benefits agreements may be the landmark $500 million set of concessions to community and labor partners in Los Angeles around the expanded construction of the LAX airport facility.

21. Constance Hays, "Wal-Mart Plans Changes to Some Labor Practices," *New York Times,* June 4, 2004, C2.

22. "Wal-Mart and California: A Key Moment in Time for American Capitalism," an address by Lee Scott, president & CEO, Wal-Mart Stores, Town Hall Los Angeles, February 23, 2005, at http://www.walmartfacts.com.

Contributors

Thomas Jessen Adams is a Ph.D. student in the Department of History at the University of Chicago. His dissertation analyzes the political economy and social history of America's transition from an industrial to a service economy.
tadams@uchicago.edu

Edna Bonacich, Professor of Sociology and Ethnic Studies at the University of California, Riverside, focuses her work on class and race issues, with a special emphasis on labor. With Richard Appelbaum she is the author, most recently, of *Behind the Label: Inequality in the Los Angeles Apparel Industry* (2000). She is now studying the ports of Los Angeles and Long Beach as important nodes in the system of global production and distribution.
edna.bonacich@ucr.edu

Gary G. Hamilton is Professor of Sociology and International Studies at the University of Washington. He is the author, most recently, of *Commerce and Capitalism in Chinese Societies* (2006) and, with Robert Feenstra, *Emergent Economies, Divergent Paths: Economic Organization and International Trade in South Korea and Taiwan* (2005).
ggh@u.washington.edu

Khaleelah Hardie is a senior majoring in sociology at University of California, Riverside. She serves as a peer mentor for the campus Honors Program, where she first explored sociological research, including this project on Wal-Mart.
khaleelah.hardie@email.ucr.edu

James Hoopes is Visiting Frances Willson Professor of Leadership Studies at Kettering University and Murata Professor of Business Ethics at Babson College. His most recent book is *False Prophets: The Gurus Who Created Modern Management and Why Their Ideas Are Bad for Business Today* (2003).
jhoopes@kettering.edu / hoopes@babson.edu

David Karjanen is a visiting assistant professor in the Department of American Studies at the University of Minnesota. He publishes research on industrial restructuring and comparative political economy, and is currently working on a comparative study of regional socioeconomic inequalities in the United States and Eastern Europe.
dkarjane@weber.ucsd.edu

Nelson Lichtenstein is Professor of History at the University of California, Santa Barbara. He is the author, most recently, of *State of the Union: A Century of American Labor* (2002) and editor of *American Capitalism: Social Thought and Political Economy in the Twentieth Century* (2006).
nelson@history.ucsb.edu

Bethany Moreton is a fifth-generation Mississippian in her final year of a history Ph.D. at Yale. Her dissertation, "Wal-Mart World," is forthcoming in 2006.
bethany.moreton@yale.edu

Wade Rathke is the founder and chief organizer of ACORN—the Association of Community Organizations for Reform Now—and Local 100, Service Employees International Union (SEIU), AFL-CIO, headquartered in New Orleans. He works with the United Food and Commercial Workers, AFL-CIO, SEIU, and ACORN on organizing strategies for Wal-Mart workers in the United States and abroad.
chieforg@acorn.org

Ellen Israel Rosen is Resident Scholar at the Brandeis University Women's Studies Research Center, and author of *Making Sweatshops: The Globalization of the U.S. Apparel Industry* (2002) and *Bitter Choices: Blue Collar Women In and Out of Work* (1987).
eirosen@brandeis.edu

Brad Seligman is Executive Director of the nonprofit foundation the Impact Fund, which supports civil rights class actions. He has litigated more than forty-five such cases and is lead counsel in *Dukes v. Wal-Mart Stores, Inc.*
bs@impactfund.org

Susan Strasser is Professor of History at the University of Delaware. She is author of *Satisfaction Guaranteed: The Making of the American Mass Market* (1989), *Waste and Want: A Social History of Trash* (1999), and *Commodifying Everything: Relationships of the Market* (2003).
strasser@udel.edu

Misha Petrovic is a graduate student of sociology at the University of Washington. He is finishing a dissertation on the role of large retailers in the global economy.
misha1@u.washington.edu

Chris Tilly is University Professor of Regional Economic and Social Development at the University of Massachusetts Lowell. His books include *Half a Job: Bad and Good Part-Time Jobs in a Changing Labor Market* (1995) and *Stories Employers Tell: Race, Skill, and Hiring in America* (2001).
chris_tilly@uml.edu

Index